VICTIMS AND HEROES

victims

Racial Violence in the

AND HEROES

African American Novel

Jerry H. Bryant

UNIVERSITY OF MASSACHUSETTS PRESS
Amherst

Copyright © 1997 by
The University of Massachusetts Press
All rights reserved
Printed in the United States of America
LC 96-48656
ISBN 1-55849-094-9 (cloth); 095-7 (pbk.)
Designed by Milenda Nan Ok Lee
Set in Bembo
Printed and bound by Braun-Brumfield, Inc.
Library of Congress Cataloging-in-Publication Data
Bryant, Jerry H., 1928–
    Victims and heroes : racial violence in the African American novel /
Jerry H. Bryant.
        p.   cm.
    Includes bibliographical references (p.   ) and index.
    ISBN 1-55849-094-9 (alk. paper). — ISBN 1-55849-095-7 (pbk. :
alk. paper)
    1. American fiction—Afro-American authors—History and
criticism.   2. Afro-Americans in literature.   3. Race relations in
literature.   4. Violence in literature.   5. Racism in literature.   I. Title.
PS374.N4B74   1997
813'.009'355—dc21   96-48656
                                                                          CIP

British Library Cataloguing in Publication data are available.

For my son Craig, and my daughter Melaine

CONTENTS

Part III.   Images of Revolt: Black Violence against Whites

ACKNOWLEDGMENTS

I have lived and worked with this material for so many years that it's impossible to disentangle who owes what to whom. I do know that I am indebted to the many students in my classes and to those at California State University. Hayward, who were friends as well as students, Nancy Hardin and Herman Porter in particular. A small cohort of unremittingly generous colleagues and friends have, over the years, ploughed through parts and different versions of this book, giving advice, trying to save me from myself. I wish to acknowledge them here and now: George Cuomo, Michel Fabre, Jacob Fuchs, and Norman Grabo. I have always been grateful for their kindness and tact, and I hold them totally blameless for whatever weaknesses readers may find in this book. I also owe thanks to William L. Andrews, who read an outline of this project and made helpful suggestions; and to my daughter, Melaine Bryant, who, at a crucial time for me, shared some of the work she was then doing on the Homeric hero and helped me to create an important frame of reference for my own thesis.

Cal State, Hayward, provided a paid leave of absence from teaching for one quarter and a lightened course load for another. These injectons of free time at the right moment put new life in a dying battery.

VICTIMS AND HEROES

INTRODUCTION

In the last decade and a half the most widely publicized violence in America has been that of the black ghettos. Gang wars and drug killings; disputes over rank, territory, clothes; drive by shootings—all have made the inner cities killing fields for young black men. Murder, *Newsweek* tells us, repeating one of the most familiar statistics in the media, "is now the leading cause of death among African-American males between the ages of 15 and 24."[1] Yet, for all its catastrophic effects, this suicidal decimation of brother by brother is only a recent historical development. Moreover, while writers like John Edgar Wideman, in *Hiding Place* (1981), and Jess Mowry, in *Way Past Cool* (1992), have fictively explored the violent youth culture of the black ghetto, no substantial body of fiction has yet emerged from it. In fact, the most conspicuous development in black fiction in the last fifteen years has been the focus upon the personal problems of African Americans who make up the substantial middle-class black population whose lives are not determined by ghetto crime or violence, especially in the relationship between black men and women.[2]

The violence that has had the most widespread effect upon and has most concerned the black community in its 400-year presence in North America has been inter-not intraracial: whipping, lynching and its various tortures, race riots, the brutality of white police. That African Americans have suffered violence in a way unique even by American standards has become a truism. Herbert Shapiro's contention in *White Violence and Black Response* (1988), the most recent and thorough historical study of the topic, is that

subjection to violence in various forms has been a central ingredient of the Afro-American experience, that the lives of millions of black people have been and continue to be lived in the shadow of numberless episodes of racist brutality. Violence, the actuality or the threat of death or serious injury from assault, has constituted an ever-present reality in practically every black community and for practically every black person.[3]

My interest is in the "response" side of Shapiro's picture, and in its literary aspect rather than its historical: how the many black novelists who have treated the topic have reacted to the real-world violence committed by whites against them, and the debate over what they should do about it; what kinds of violence have drawn their attention, and what they found important to emphasize; what attitudes they have taken up; what literary methods and conventions they have used to express their perceptions; what literary form they have given to what was essentially a sociohistorical topic.

The topic involves tactics in the racial struggle; questions of political, social, and economic advancement; religious faith, self-esteem, and standards of morality. For black novelists who deal with it, whites are the source of the violence and therefore central antagonists in their stories, opponents to be overcome in the battle for dignity and a better life. Nor is the issue limited to fiction. It is, as Stephen Butterfield puts it, a "problem" that must be solved even for black autobiography:

how to confront human existence without the shadow of the white man—without relying on him, as *diabolus ex machina,* to condition, by negative example, the meaning of a life well lived. Although some [autobiographies] turn aside from overt politics, the presence of the white man is the single most pervasive influence in every book. It might be that this problem can only be taken up after the historical questions have been resolved—for any attempt to define the meaning of black life in apolitical terms must appear as a failure to deal with white power, as long as that power's control over history remains intact.[4]

The "presence of the white man" is also the defining condition for the African American novel of racial violence. The main aim of that novel is to consider, in what Richard Wright might call the laboratory of the imaginative world, the most effective way to break the hold whites have maintained over black lives through violence. The violent act itself is starkly simple: the slaveowner whips a slave; Nat Turner's rebels kill fifty whites. The difficulty comes in deciding the moral attitude to take up toward the act and those engaged in it, and whether counterviolence is desirable. In the imaginary world of the novel, racial violence occasions a claim of grievance by one side against the other. In the most morally simplified cases, white violence against blacks produces a victim, black violence against whites a hero. The figure of the victim—the whipped slave, the lynched freedman, the beaten ghetto resident, the assassinated civil rights leader—assumes the villainy of the victimizer. The figure of the hero who kills whites in retaliation assumes the validity of his counterviolence. In the black world of fictive violence, though, morality is usually no more one-dimensional than in the real world. Victims and heroes tend to be constantly shifting and changing shapes. The black victim may gain sympathy for the black community but not the respect or self-esteem that the novelist searches for. On the other hand, the victim may change at the moment of his victimization into a figure of courage, dying as a martyr and stimulating heroic revolt in a formerly quiescent people. The hero, who, as James M. Redfield says of the great soldier of the Homeric epic, inflicts "harm . . . in behalf of [his] philoi, those to whose honor and welfare he is unreservedly committed," may use his force "in the service of . . . justice." But this same hero, says Redfield, "is also latently the savage beast,"[5] a threat to the very civilized order his violence had been employed to prop up.

This is the ambiguity that most haunts the African American novelist of racial violence, the uncontrollability of violence, its inherent potential for destruction. Two reasons lie at the center of the novelists' disquiet. First, they are alert to the moral relativity of violent acts and the "hero" who might commit them. What John W. Roberts says of the hero of black folklore may also apply to the concerns of the African American novelist on violence:

We often use the term "hero" as if it denoted a universally recognized character type, and the concept of "heroism" as if it referred to a generally accepted behavioral category. In reality, figures (both real and mythic) and actions dubbed heroic in one context or by one group of people may be viewed as ordinary or even criminal in another context or by other groups, or even by the same ones at different times.[6]

The other reason that black novelists worry about the violent hero and his latent savagery is the double standard by which whites and blacks are judged in America. Since blacks and whites arrived in the New World, for most American whites, to speak of a black "hero" is a contradiction in terms. Blacks simply do not occupy the same moral world as whites. Any claim made by a black person upon the values of heroic behavior universally honored by whites has been discounted on the same ground argued by Roger B. Taney in his majority decision in the Dred Scott case in 1857:

Blacks inherently have no right to be judged by the same standards as whites. Frederick Douglass faces up to this reality in *The Heroic Slave* (1853), his story about Madison Washington, the black man who led a mutiny of slaves against the white crew of the brig *Creole*. Washington justifies the violence the slaves used in the uprising by invoking the principles of the Declaration of Independence. Speaking to Tom Grant, the white mate, Washington says, "We have done that which you applaud your fathers for doing, and if we are murderers, *so were they.*" Grant is sympathetic, but he cannot accept the argument. "It was not that his principles were wrong in the abstract," says Grant, the narrator of this part of the tale, "for they were the principles of 1776. But I could not bring myself to recognize their application to one whom I deemed my inferior."[7] The violence whites celebrate as virtuous in one venue they condemn as criminal in another. They claim a moral right to the use of violence in the service of their good which they deny to blacks. In a most cogent article on the subject, Richard Yarborough concludes:

Simply put, blacks were not granted the same freedom of action as whites, and yet they were condemned for not meeting popularly held norms of behavior. Black men were viewed as unmanly and otherwise inferior because they were enslaved; at the same time, they were often viewed as beasts and otherwise inferior if they rebelled violently. Moreover, black writers like Douglass must have realized at some level that to make their heroic figures too independent, too aggressive, might permit white readers to evade acknowledging that they themselves must intervene in order to end the horrors of slavery. Many African American authors saw no easy way to make their black male characters deserving of sympathy and at the same time to celebrate their manhood.[8]

These are the conditions that produce the ambivalence in the African American community toward the use of counterviolence as a response to violent whites. The same ambivalence in the black novelists interferes with their creation of a consistent heroic image grounded in the use of force. The novelists swing between the poles of unequivocal advocacy to unambiguous rejection of counterviolence all through their 150-year history of treatment of the subject. In their imaginative representation and interpretation of American racial violence, therefore, they create a multifarious, even contradictory, picture. They hate and praise it, abhor but reluctantly condone it. They see it as the mark of a man's passage from childhood to adulthood, celebrate it as both heroic and diabolical, regard it as the source of all their trouble or the solution to all their problems. They present it in images of great beauty and emphasize its ugliness. It is a constant real threat, an injustice unfairly visited upon innocent victims; it is a heroic way to dignity and independence; it is a desperate resort to self-knowledge. It is the ultimate obstacle to autonomy and the shame of the white nation they live in. In this book, I try to make sense out of these conflicting views.

[1]

BEFORE THE WAR

[1]

VIOLENCE, VICTIMS, AND HEROES
IN THE ANTEBELLUM
SLAVE NARRATIVE

IMAGES OF VIOLENCE

The first images of violence important to the African American novel are those created by the authors of the antebellum slave narrative, especially those written between 1830 and 1860. Slavery was, after all, a culture held together by violence. "The relation of master and slave," as abolitionist Theodore Parker says, "begins in violence; it must be sustained by violence —the systematic violence of general laws, or the irregular violence of individual caprice. There is no other mode of conquering and subjugating a man."[1] If the slave was slack in his or her work, or ran away, or damaged property, or sassed a white man, the slaveowner exercised all the offices of a public judicial system, and physical punishment was inevitable. The range of abuse recorded by the slave narrator is staggering. The slave is bound— to a tree, or to four stakes, or over a log, sometimes spread-eagled on the ground, sometimes hanging painfully by the wrists from a hook designed for the purpose—then whipped or paddled or both, or just left there. He or she is "cat-hauled," pinched, punched, knocked. Ears can be nailed to the wall, flesh seared, bodies mutilated. "I have often seen slaves tortured in every conceivable manner," writes William Craft. "I have seen them hunted down and torn by bloodhounds. I have seen them shamefully beaten, and branded with hot irons. I have seen them hunted, and even burned alive at the stake."[2] The slave narrators identify every devilishly ingenious device for punishment and torture, and they do so with a chilling thoroughness and objectivity. John Brown depicts the "cobbing" paddle, for instance, as "a piece of wood from eighteen inches to two feet long, having a handle about eight inches in length. It is made of oak, one end being broad and flat, and between five and six inches in width, with eight holes drilled through it. Before being used, it is wetted and rubbed in sand." [3] Then there is "cat-hauling," which Charles Ball describes in *Slavery in the United States* (1836):

The cat, which was a large grey tom-cat, was then taken by the well dressed gentleman, and placed upon the bare back of the prostrate black man, near the shoulders, and forcibly dragged by the tail down the back, and along the bare thighs of the sufferer. The cat sunk his nails into the flesh, and tore off pieces of the skin with his teeth. The man roared with the pain of this punishment, and would have rolled along the ground, had he not been held in his place by the force of four other slaves. . . . After the termination of this punishment [the sufferer] was washed with salt water, by a black woman, and . . . dismissed. [4]

Mistresses have their own devices and are no less heartless than the masters in the pain they inflict upon the slave. Mary Prince, a West Indian slave, tells of a mistress whose boisterous punishments seem to be her daily entertainment. "I was," says Mary, "licked, flogged, and pinched by her pitiless fingers in the neck and arms." Mattie J. Jackson's mistress "was constantly pulling our ears, snapping us with her thimble, rapping us on the head and sides of it." [5] Some mistresses do considerably more than rap their bondservants on the head. Marion Wilson Starling recounts the story of Robert, whose New Orleans mistress makes "a hole with hot tongs in one of Robert's cheeks." And at a dinner party, when he slightly touches her elbow causing some tea to be spilled, she cuts his neck with a carving knife, "so that the blood run a stream." [6] In the most extreme cases, such as accused rape or murder, a slave might, as William Craft said, be burned at the stake with the full approval of the most respected southern persons and institutions. Kenneth Stampp reports that one Alabama editor "justified the burning of a slave at the stake by 'the law of self-protection, which abrogates all other laws.' " [7] This gave no comfort to the African slave, for self-protection was a right reserved only for whites.

But the most universal instrument of slave punishment was, as Frederick Douglass put it, the "bloody paraphernalia" of the whip, which was "indispensably necessary to the relation of master and slave." [8] Men and women, owner and overseer, professional whipper, sheriff, patrollers, or even other slaves all turned to the whip. So frequently and so universally did whipping occur that a veritable typology grew up to identify its forms. "Bucking" called for a stake to be placed under the slave's knees. The chin was forced to the knees by tying the hands to the ankles. This placed the victim in a position that tautened the curved back and made it impossible for him or her to move. The "picket," as John Brown described it, called for the slave to be hung by his wrists, his right foot tied to his left knee so that he whirls when flogged and suffers both pain and nausea. When he tries to stop his whirling by putting his free foot on a knife-sharp stake in the ground beneath him, a helper gives him another turn so that the sharp picket point "perforates the heel or the sole of the foot, as the case may be, quite to the bone."[9] The two most frequent methods for administering formal punishment to a slave by whipping required (1) tying the victim spread-eagled and face down to four stakes on the ground, and (2) tying him or her by the wrists to a joist, then placing one end of a heavy piece of timber between the bound ankles with the other end on the ground. The weight stretched the body painfully and increased the vulnerability of the body's flesh to laceration.

The repetitiveness of the details of whipping supports James Olney's conclusion about the "overwhelming *sameness*" of the slave narrative of the antebellum period. The composers of the narratives avoid individual uniqueness, he says, for a purpose. To press their idiosyncratic memory would be fictionalizing, or "lying." Consensus establishes an empirical truth, and the truth about slavery is the main weapon of their argument against the institution. Olney finds that this consensus produces accounts of slave experience that are "fitted to a pre-formed mold" and that share strict "conventions of content, theme, form, and style." The ubiquitous accounts of flogging establish a convention in which we get a formulaic "description of a cruel master, mistress, or overseer, [and] details of [the narrator's] first observed whipping and numerous subsequent whippings, with women very frequently the victims."[10] Implied in Olney's analysis is the suggestion that these repeated images coalesce into what is in effect a synecdoche—whipping as a condensation of all that is painful, arbitrary, and dehumanizing in slavery, its trademark a picture of a black figure hanging by his or her hands receiving the lashes of a whip wielded by a grim master. The ubiquity with which the details of this image appear in the slave narrative gives the reader the feeling he is dealing with a single story, a story so common that it detaches itself from its temporal historicity and enters, as so many commentators have suggested, the heightened reality of myth or legend.

In his narrative, John Thompson compresses the conventions of the whipping image into a few phrases of a single sentence. When Thompson's sister refused to submit to the sexual advances of her master, the white man became so enraged that he "ordered two of his men to take her to the barn, where he generally whipped his slaves; there to strip off her clothes and whip her, which was done, until the blood stood in puddles under feet." [11] Moses Grandy himself feels the lash when his master "flogged me naked with a severe whip, made of very tough sapling; this lapped round me at each stroke; the point of it at last entered my belly and broke off leaving an inch and a half outside. I was not aware of it until, on going to work again, it hurt my inside very much, when, on looking down, I saw it sticking out of my body. I pulled it out, and the blood spouted after it." [12] Solomon Northup describes a beating that commences with a paddle in which "Blow after blow was inflicted upon my naked body." When the paddle breaks, his master turns to the whip, still plying "the lash without stint upon my poor body, until it seemed that the lacerated flesh was stripped from my bones at every stroke." [13] John Brown, in his account of the cobbing paddle, tells of a similar sequence from the paddle to the whip, in which his master first brought blisters to a slave's back with the paddle, then "took a raw cowhide and flogged him across the blisters till they burst, the blood flying out all over him, and round about the bench on to the ground. When he had flogged him till the poor fellow's back and loins were like jelly, they rubbed the parts with red pepper and salt and water, and sent him to quarters." [14] Moses Roper's famous Mr. Gooch took Roper "to a log-house, stripped me quite naked, fastened a rail up very high, tied my hands to the rail, fastened my feet together, put a rail between my feet, and stood on one end to hold me down; the two sons then gave me fifty lashes each, the son-in-law another fifty, and Mr. Gooch himself fifty more." [15]

Women did not escape flogging whether they were pregnant or not. Pregnant women were often laid over a hole in the ground to accommodate their large abdomens and whipped in that position. Other times they were tied in the conventional manner, but their condition leads to some of the most painful effects of the form. In Mary Prince's narrative, a master orders Hetty "to be stripped quite naked, notwithstanding her pregnancy, and to be tied up to a tree in the yard. He then flogged her as hard as he could lick, both with the whip and cow-skin, till she was all over streaming with blood. He rested, and then beat her again and again. Her shrieks were terrible." Of course she loses her child. And she herself dies "ere long." Moses Grandy writes of the agony of the slave husband who is "obliged to stand by and see [his wife] taken home at night, stripped naked, and whipped before all the men. On the estate I am speaking of, those women who had sucking children suffered much from their breasts becoming full of milk. . . . I have seen the overseer beat them with raw hide, so that blood and milk flew mingled from their breasts." [16]

VICTIMS AND THE SENTIMENTAL

At center stage in these descriptions is the victim, whose role it is to project not a dominant warrior avenger to induce pride in a putative black reader but an example of the deep injustice of slavery to evoke indignation and sympathy in the minds of the slave narratives' many white readers. The victim's suffering takes place within that Victorian redoubt of virtue and goodness, the family, for most of the sufferers of whipping are identified by their place in a family—a father or mother, son or daughter, aunt or uncle, brother or sister. These relationships are smashed by the brutally strong with the lash. However agonizing in the reality, the telling of this experience falls into the field of sentiment, and as recent commentators have pointed out, the slave narrators do appeal to a reader already conditioned by the sentimental novel, that form of victim literature that was approaching its zenith in the decades before the Civil War.[17] Many readers of the slave narrative would surely have recognized the figure of the suffering slave—Innocence, helpless before unjust Cruelty—and would be ready to respond compassionately. The function of the sentimental was to draw from the reader compassion for the weak and the helpless—the orphaned child, the seduced and abandoned young woman, the pathetically insane, the tragically imprisoned. The politically correct reaction for the bourgeois reader was tears, deep feeling, pity, a "species feeling," as Philip Fisher calls it, giving "full human reality" to types from whom such humanity had "been previously withheld."[18] Northern abolitionists in particular, according to Ronald G. Walters, were sensitive to relationships of "domination and possession" in both gender and racial issues, especially when they involved a potential for the unleashing of disorderly sexual passion and threatened, as slavery did, that "centre of earthly bliss," the Victorian family. William Goodell, editor of both the *Female Advocate* and the *Emancipator*, claimed that both journals spoke for "the helpless and uncomplaining."[19] This sensibility had been a century or more in developing and was coming to a climax in America in the years of the abolition movement, in England in the years that Parliament began passing laws controlling the employment of women and children in the new factories. The sentimental feeling, says J. M. S. Tompkins, grew out of "modern security, leisure and education." The economic progress of Western Europe produced a class with time to refine itself, to advance "the idea of progress of the human race" and develop "a delicacy of sensation, a refinement of virtue. . . . The human sympathies which a rougher age had repressed, expanded widely, especially towards the weak and unfortunate, and the social conscience began to occupy itself with prisoners, children, animals and slaves."[20] Historically, the sentimental attitude and the broader movement of human rights in the Enlightenment produced a "pervasive shift" in attitude that took place in America about the time of the Revolution and brought slavery into question for the first time. "Especially significant," writes Peter Kolchin, "were changing notions of what constituted legitimate treatment of those who were poor, weak, or different."[21]

The literary expression of these ideas lies in the scores of sentimental novels published between Richardson's *Pamela* (1740) and *Uncle Tom's Cabin* (1852). Courtney Melmoth captures the essence of the sentimental in a passage from *Emma Corbett,* in which the humanitarian impulse at the heart of the sentimental is tied to the pleasure experienced by the feeling observer:

The feeblenesses to which the tender frame of woman is subject, are, perhaps, more seducing than her bloom. The *healthy* flower looks superior to protection, and expands itself to the sun in a kind of *independent* state; but in nursing that which *droops* (sweetly dejected) and is ready to fall upon its bed, our care becomes more dear, as it becomes more *necessary.*[22]

Though Melmoth was not even distantly thinking of slavery when he articulated the sentimental so succinctly, the passage has everything to do with slavery and the way the sympathizers with those in bondage perceived slavery. For example, referring to attitudes of the reading public toward Frederick Douglass's first two autobiographies, William S. McFeely remarks that many "white observers, opposed to slavery, preferred to think of the slaves as helpless victims, whom only white Northern benevolence could carry toward a happier existence."[23] These feelings had long been injected into American fiction. In what is usually called the first American novel, *The Power of Sympathy* (1789), William Hill Brown presents the world of slavery in the terms of the Melmothian sentimentalist. The young Harrington, whose letters make up most of this epistolary novel, encounters a slave woman in his travels through "Southcarolina." When he questions her about a mark on her shoulder, she reports, "It is the mark of the whip," which she received when she took a beating to protect her ten-year-old son. And when she thanks "the best of beings that I was allowed to suffer for [my]" child, Harrington is propelled into the raptures promised by the "sympathy" of the novel's title. His feeling for the slave woman is a "tide of affection and SYMPATHY," and it flows from the "Author of Nature . . . whose tender care extendeth to the least of thy creation—and whose eye is not inattentive even though a sparrow fall to the ground." In addition to being sanctified by God's own intent, these feelings have a sociopolitical dimension, for Harrington anticipates "the happy time when the sighs of the slave shall no longer expire in the air of freedom."[24] This episode constitutes only a few pages of a novel whose main focus is upon its epistolary moral effusions, sermons on virtue, and exclamations on the pleasures of the virtuous life, besides a couple of slight narratives involving Harrington's nick-of-time rescue from marrying his half sister and the seduction and ruin of Ophelia Shepherd by her brother-in-law. But it exploits a group of images and stimuli that grow out of the natural relationship between the sentimental and the white abolitionist's perception of slavery: the punishment by whip that enforces the evil of dominance-possession, the tender love of a mother for her child, a humble but sacred religious piety, and a compassionate witness to the mother's suffering. This fusion of slavery and the sentimental receives its most popular and influential form in *Uncle Tom's Cabin* more than half a century later, and it is defined by the sympathy felt for the suffering.

WHIPPING, SENTIMENT, SEX, AND SADE-ISM: DOUGLASS'S *NARRATIVE*

There is also in the whipping synecdoche a highly charged sexual element. Besides the blood and the pain and the victim as family member, in virtually every account of the whipping ritual the narrators remark on the disrobing of the slaves, male and female, for their punishment. A sign of its universality is the offhand way in which the authors make the reference. It is true that by removing the victims' clothes the punisher strips them not only of that modicum of literal protection against the direct lash but also of the social respectability which requires certain body parts to be covered. Nakedness renders the slave as vulnerable as possible. But a more central role for the whipped slave's nakedness is sexual. Inflicting pain on a powerless and submissive subject seems to be a universal way of augmenting the erotic. The narrators, while not directly and explicitly probing the psychology of the white men and women who disrobe their slaves to whip them, suggest the deep prurient interest whites take in their black bondspeople. The southern woman, that paragon of modesty and virtue, commands the male slave to be stripped and, unembarrassed, looks on with satisfaction as the whip lays open his naked flesh. The male slaveowner often undertakes the whipping of a female slave specifically out of anger over frustrated sexual aims, and the punishment becomes highly symbolic. For example, the language in which Moses Grandy recounts the generic slave husband being forced to watch his wife "taken home at night, stripped naked, and whipped before all the men" can hardly be read in any other way than as a suggestion of public rape. In the most supercharged and the most complex imagery, the prurient and the sentimental converge. In the depiction of those nursing slave women whose swollen breasts spew milk *and* blood when they are whipped, the symbol of motherhood and nurture combines with the symbol of rape and brutality. And when we consider the possibility that the whipper might be father of the child in the pregnant woman's womb, sentimental compassion and moral disgust reach a zenith. These techniques for highlighting slave victimization and the effects they evoke are often highly complex, even self-contradictory, containing an impulse toward social criticism as well as a play upon the reader's own hidden erotic appetite.

There is some disagreement about narrator intent among scholars of the form. Robin Winks suggests that "one might call" the slave narratives "the pious pornography of their day . . . fit for Nice Nellies to read precisely because they dealt with black, not white, men." [25] William Andrews argues to the contrary that "the overwhelming majority of male slave narrators drew a veil between their readers and the details of interracial sexual relations on the plantations." [26] But Winks says that the veil the narrators drew was transparent enough to make unmistakable what was going on behind it, and what was going on was indeed "sexual relations." The "horrific tales of whippings, sexual assaults, and explicit brutality" are surrogate sexual images, acceptable to polite northern readers because they deal with black slaves rather than free whites. Moreover, he claims that the white abolitionist editors are behind the sexual content of the slave narrative and urge its use as a way of preserving "the sense of outrage against slavery without actually leading anyone to invite a black man to dinner." [27] Whatever label we give to the descriptions of naked slave bodies, the beating of pregnant women, the oaths of masters frustrated in their lust, they make up a collective report of the connection between the slave victim of violence and the widespread sexual relations between masters and their slave women. The slave narrators, working within the limits of Victorian prudery and the common code of silence enforced by politically and economically powerful slavemasters, refuse to be muzzled. They employ the Victorian's own devices of the sentimental mode to disclose the hidden, the shocking, the forbidden, while at the same time outlining the injustice suffered by the slave victim.

The sentimental, with its preoccupation with women's chastity and men's constant assault upon it, had always contained a strain of the popular eighteenth-century (and earlier) genre, the pornographic or the "philosophical" novel, "philosophical" because discussions of morality and ontology go hand in hand with masturbation and intercourse, the freedom of unbridled sex as a sign of a free mind as well as a free body. According to historian Robert Darnton, such French narratives as *Histoire de Dom B . . .* (1740), *Thérèse philosophe*(1748), and *Histoire de Marguerite* (1784), by revealing the wild sexual habits of the elite, expose the ruling class's hypocrisy and gain a liberation for their characters which only libertinism can grant them. These stories are, says Darnton, "a vehicle for social criticism" and provide "a general indictment of the Old Regime, its courtiers, manor lords, financiers, tax collectors, and judges, as well as its priests." [28] As good practicing Victorians, the slave narrators, of course, stay clear of hard-core sex. The disclosure of sexual activity in the violent punishments of slaves is not a means to any sexual liberation. But it does indict the Christian clergy that approves of slavery, and the professed Christians who hypocritically practice the atrocities their religion forbids and then justify that practice through their religion. A more illuminating link between the pornographic novel, the sentimental novel, and the slave narrative is the convention of the voyeur. I have already cited the pivotal role of the observer of the oppressed in the sentimental novel—often a character in the narrative itself, as well as the reader. Darnton says that the device of the voyeur in the "philosophical" narratives of the eighteenth century establishes the framework in which the action takes place, for "the reader is made to look over the shoulder of someone looking through a keyhole at a couple copulating in front of a mirror or under pictures of copulating couples on the wall." [29] Similarly, few whippings take place in the slave narrative without an observer. Almost always, though, the slave narrator turns this device to ironic use. For the *philosophe* of pornography, observing others in the sexual act is a liberating experience. For the viewer of the pain of a helpless woman or child, the experience can be a form of pleasure. The observer of the slave whipping is either the master, whose reaction is normally sadistic pleasure, or another slave, for whom the spectacle is intended, in a way ironically different from what it is for the budding libertine, to be "educational."

Frederick Douglass is by far the best illustrator of the way these attitudes, conventions, and devices can be artistically exploited and manipulated. The example of this is his account, in *Narrative of the Life of Frederick Douglass* (1845), of the whipping of his Aunt Hester by Captain Anthony. In it he packs all the hidden sexual implications and a number of the less hidden ones. In his two later autobiographies, *My Bondage and My Freedom* (1855) and *The Life and Times of Frederick Douglass* (1881), he not only changes her name to Esther but makes his aunt's punishment an example of the cruelty of slaveowners toward the young women who especially need their protection from brutal overseers. Although the later accounts imply Captain

Anthony's lust for Aunt Hester as a motive in the beating he gives her, the context simply makes it one more example of the "rage and cruelty" of the slavemaster. Douglass adds it after he has already recounted the sad tale of a cousin of his who had unsuccessfully pleaded with Captain Anthony to protect her from the coarse and brutal overseer Mr. Plummer. Both of these episodes occur in chapter 5 of the 1855 and 1881 autobiographies, the first entitled "Gradual Initiation into the Mysteries of Slavery," the second "A Slaveholder's Character."[30] In the *Narrative* the whipping of Aunt Hester is one of the most important episodes in the book. It climaxes the scene-setting first chapter and marks "the blood-stained gate, the entrance to the hell of slavery," through which Douglass passes when he witnesses it.[31]

Douglass places his account of Aunt Hester's whipping in the darkly tangled miscegenational world of the plantation. A good Victorian, Douglass can only hint at the appetites that drive the slaveholder and create secret blood relationships in which children are ignorant of their fathers. He speaks, though, of the question of his birth and the whispers that his father was Captain Anthony himself. He alludes to the ubiquitous sign of the master's sexual relations with his black slave women: the mulatto. And he laments the degradation of the black family, for the Victorian mind the most sacred of all institutions. What should be a warm system of loving relationships, in which parents nurture and protect, is turned into a confusion of mystery and denial. Out of this relationship grows a perverted violence that lies at the heart of slavery—fathers flogging their own children, brothers whipping their own brothers, male masters beating the women they lust after. And all of this suppressed, kept hidden beneath a veil of Christian respectability, in a world that remains hypocritically silent on its most volatile and explosive relationships.[32]

The causes that bring about the whipping are both implicitly and explicitly sexual. Hester breaks Captain Anthony's order not to see her sweetheart, Ned Roberts. His ostensible reason for disciplining her is to protect her virtue. The real reason is to save her for himself. Douglass expresses neither of these motives in explicit language. That would violate Victorian propriety as well as the slavery code of silence about such things. The most compelling part of the scene seems to be total invention, for in *My Bondage,* Douglass says that "I saw but few of the shocking preliminaries, for the cruel work had begun before I awoke."[33] One would never know it from the vivid and meaningful details he gives us in the *Narrative:*

Before he commenced whipping Aunt Hester, he took her into the kitchen, and stripped her from neck to waist, leaving her neck, shoulders, and back, entirely naked. He then told her to cross her hands, calling her at the same time a d——d b——h. After crossing her hands, he tied them with a strong rope, and led her to a stool under a large hook in the joist, put in for the purpose. He made her get upon the stool, and tied her hands to the hook. She now stood fair for his infernal purpose. Her arms were stretched up at their full length, so that she stood upon the ends of her toes. He then said to her, "Now, you d——d b——h, I'll learn you how to disobey my orders!" and after rolling up his sleeves, he commenced to lay on the heavy cowskin, and soon the warm, red blood (amid heart-rending shrieks from her, and horrid oaths from him) came dripping to the floor. (52)

This episode contains all the parts of the whipping synecdoche—the tying up, the nakedness of the victim, the flow of blood, and, a feature that is only slightly less frequent in other slave narratives, the horrible oaths of the enraged, whip-wielding master. But Douglass's diction, phrasing, and allusiveness put the passage into quite a different category from that of other slave narratives. The kitchen in which Anthony violates Hester is a nightmare world in which the usual protective moral values are reversed. The hook in the joist from which Anthony hangs Hester, for example, not present in the later narratives, has in the *Narrative* been "put in for the purpose." It is typical of Douglass's self-conscious art in the *Narrative*. The normally secure and protected kitchen is deliberately equipped for crucifying those domestic workers who attend to the warmest and most life-giving and intimate phases of hearth and home, the preparation of food and the ceremony of the table. This system does not just tolerate the existence of such a monster as Captain Anthony. It enthrones him as an all-powerful monarch. It endows him with the approval of the putatively virtuous and the support of the allegedly good, and validates him with Christianity's most sacred texts. Here, Douglass shows "the widest possible difference" between the "Christianity of this land" and the true "Christianity of Christ" (153). The religion that supports the abomination of slavery is anti-Christian. In this way he discredits, in Andrews's words, "the false oppositions and hierarchies of value that have arisen as a consequence of slavery's perversions of the true oppositions between good and evil, the natural and the unnatural."[34] Douglass represents the nightmare world of perverted religious values with an inversion of the Garden scene in the Book of Genesis. "I'll learn you how to disobey my orders!" Captain Anthony shouts at Hester. In an act that is part farce and part blasphemy, Anthony assumes God's role. But he has the corrupting effect of Satan, preserving Hester from the slave she had gone out to meet for his own concupiscence, not for the good of her soul.

The implied sexual violence here serves Douglass's abolitionist purpose. His technique, as I have already pointed out, refers back to the novel of sentiment and pornography. It is appropriate to mention here the method of what David S. Reynolds calls the "immoral reformers." This method picks up my discussion of the sexual content of the slave narrative's whipping synecdoche and contains at the same time parallels to the narratives of the Marquis de Sade. In *Beneath the American Renaissance,* Reynolds points out that authors like Mason Lock Weems in *Onania* (mid-1790s) and *McDowell's Journal* (1833–34), Maria Monk in *Awful Disclosures* (1836), and George Lippard in *The Quaker City: or, The Monks of Monk Hall* (1845), under the guise of pious reform, employed a sensationalism verging on the pornographic, appealing to the popular avidity for reading about the very vices the literature purported to eradicate: violent murder, drunkenness, incest and other illicit sex. The very terms "virtue" and "vice," says Reynolds, echoing William Andrews in another context, became "unfastened . . . from clear referents." [35] Douglass himself had a teacher who practiced the rhetoric of the "dark" reformers. As Reynolds points out, William Lloyd Garrison turned to "subversive" sensationalism to attack the immorality of slavery, entitling some of the first articles in *The Liberator* "Burning Alive," "Horrible Butchery," "Barbarity." [36]

I do not suggest that Douglass consciously and deliberately employed the methods of the "immoral reformers," but these methods seem almost implicit in his topic; when a brilliantly perceptive commentator like Douglass determines to pull the veil aside from the southern master's treatment of the female slave, the "reformers' " vocabulary of images seems inescapable. Certainly Douglass goes beyond the conventional treatment of women in slave narratives as "victims of sexual abuse." [37] The whole Aunt Hester passage resounds with the sense of seduction-rape. Douglass meticulously notes each stage of the process, like a scene from de Sade. [38] Captain Anthony carefully guides the object of his lust to the designated spot and prepares her for the outrage, with the insinuation that much of the prurient pleasure derives from such fore-activity. "Before he commenced whipping Aunt Hester, he took her into the kitchen, and stripped her from neck to waist, leaving her neck, shoulders, and back, entirely naked." In this series of sentences, "he" is the acting subject: "He then told her . . . he tied them . . . and led her. . . . He made her get upon the stool." There is a sacrificial quality to these phrases as well as a salacious one, and they end with a sudden shift to a feeling of the passive and a change of the subject to "she" —Hester: "She now stood fair for his infernal purpose." It is impossible to do adequate justice to this sentence and its placement. Not only is it in itself a poetic line, cast in the rhythm of blank verse and emphasized with the subtle alliteration on the s's and f's, it also evokes the sentimental melodrama of nineteenth-century didactic and moral writing. Douglass deploys these literary methods to condense into this single artful sentence a full rendering of the sexual vulnerability of the slave woman. Here is the Victorian sexual drama, the double entendre on "fair," the theatrical but effective opposition between virtue and sin, good and evil, beauty and ugliness, the pure victim and corrupt victimizer. It is de Sade moralized by the new Victorian constraint reshaped by Douglass to depict the moral atrocity of American slavery. What John Weightman says about de Sade, moreover, applies perfectly to Captain Anthony and evokes the whole abolitionist disgust with slavery's dominance-possession powers. The marquis, says Weightman, makes a "basic pathological assumption that *le droit du seigneur* is paramount. . . . *Les Cent vingt journées de Sodome* and *La Philosophe dans le boudoir* are dreams of absolute power, manifesting itself through rape, mutilation, and murder, and exercised by groups of seigneurs over their helpless victims." [39] In his own artfully wrought description, Douglass uses a vocabulary that suggests the whole corrupt scheme of slavery, coming to rest upon its two foundations: violence and sex. Douglass represents in Captain Anthony the mix of Victorian puritanism, an appetite for the salacious, and its companion pleasure of inflicting pain. The ameliorating superego that might curb the worst of these impulses is nowhere to be found, except in Anthony's hypocritical and self-serving "purpose" of teaching Hester to avoid sin.

The capstone of the resemblances between Douglass, de Sade, the immoral reformers, and the sentimental novelist is the voyeur. We view Dr. Rodin's scandalous acts through the eyes of an innocent observer, Justine herself (though de Sade looks cynically at Justine's attempts to preserve her virtue), who has taken a position "near a partition" and looks into the torture room "through cracks between its ill-joined boards." [40] Douglass's voyeur, of course, is himself, a combination of the Sadean observer of a sex act and a sentimental viewer of the abuse of a helpless woman. As in his use of the other conventions of the immoral reformers and the pornographic writers, Douglass converts them here to the Victorian sentimental and a version of the Christian. In the story he tells, Hester's whipping has a more important effect upon Douglass the child than upon Hester herself, for it transforms Douglass's Edenic children's world. Like the biblical Satan, Anthony forces upon the young Douglass knowledge of the world, the "depravity of man," as Andrews puts it, linking it with Calvinism. The spectacle profoundly affects the youngster, striking him unforgettably, "with awful force." It is his initiation into "the hell of slavery" (51). Having witnessed this whipping, Douglass is ejected from his grandmother's world of prelapsarian innocence, where he had played with the other children, ignorant of "the bloody scenes that often occurred on the plantation" (52). Unlike Adam and Eve, he is faultless, the quintessential victim violated by the one man who should have protected him, his father. He is forced through "the blood-stained gate," and until he finds redemption he is locked into the underworld of slavery's hell. Like the voyeurs in the pornographic novels, Douglass gets an education and loses his innocence. But it is a tragic imprisoning experience, not a liberating one. And contrary to the sentimental observer, Douglass cannot get up and walk away, his compassion a badge of his virtue as a human being. That he is a helpless child plays into the sentimental, all right, but that he is consigned to the hell of slavery turns the romantic convention into sharp realism. Nevertheless, Douglass has brilliantly employed the abused-woman and orphaned-child imagery of sentimental literature, reinforcing them with the themes and conventions of Sadean sexuality and the immoral reformers, with a reformer's intent to evoke sympathy from a reading public that could promote abolition.[41]

But sentimentalized sympathy for the victim is a decidedly double-edged affair. It may encourage social reform and stimulate abolitionist sentiment. But it also reinforces the inequality between the slave-object of sympathy, who has no power, and his or her white bourgeois sympathizers, who have, collectively, a great deal. In fact, if we listen to Edmund Burke's reflections on the sublime, high feeling for the weak and unfortunate contains an element of the exploitational. We feel delight in the misfortunes of others, says Burke, in the form of "pity . . . a passion accompanied with pleasure, because it arises from love and social affection," and it is the pleasure we feel in pitying that makes benevolence possible.[42] Control, agency, and effectiveness in the sentimental, moreover, are highly elusive. Its essence lies in the inability of the observer to do anything to relieve the suffering that provokes so delicious a compassion. The victim always remains an object of sympathy, dependent on help from others, not an autonomous subject capable of choice and action.

Because the slave narrators must always keep in mind this feature of the victims of violence, their narratives always contain conflicting impulses: one toward the powerless sufferer, to arouse indignation in the "sympathetic" reader; the other toward the autonomous self, to assert one's own identity and self-esteem. Eric J. Sundquist points out that the first impulse expresses itself in "the language of sentiment," the second in "the language of revolutionary liberation." In Frederick Douglass's *My Bondage and My Freedom,* Sundquist sees a constant reminder that the two languages "are virtually synonymous, not just in the best antislavery writing but in the

whole era's grappling with the problem of bondage."[43] Sundquist emphasizes the closeness between polar opposites and demonstrates how those
opposites operate toward a common goal—liberation and autonomy. I
would emphasize the polarity. In the representation of violence in African
American narrative (the slave narrative as well as the novel), and of the
figures that grow out of the violence, that polarity is unresolvable. The
language of sentiment excludes revolution. It is passive. It relies upon pity,
feebleness, defenselessness. It begs for attention as a gift for the helpless.
Revolution is active. It demands respect, forces recognition from those
who would withhold it. The ethic of benevolence and the theory of
compassion, the two philosophical underpinnings of the sentimental reform position, assume an almost total focus upon the feeling reader, whose
delicate sensibilities respond deliciously to the plight of the unfortunate.
They do not encourage the kind of autonomy required for true freedom.
Autonomy comes from the force of the self. And, as Douglass himself
writes in *My Bondage and My Freedom,* the same narrative in which Sundquist finds a synonymy between the languages of sentiment and liberation,
"A man, without force, is without the essential dignity of humanity.
Human nature is so constituted, that it cannot *honor* a helpless man, although it can *pity* him; and even this it cannot do long, if the signs of
power do not arise."[44] Pity is what sentimental reform confers upon the
suffering object. Honor is what an autonomous man gains through his own
independent action. This in turn endows him with authentic manhood, in
the sense both of forceful manliness and of his identity as a full human
being who stands apart from the brute. These attributes cannot come
merely from pity for slavery's victims. They must also be based upon
slavery's heroic resistors.[45] This, though, does not detract from the artistry
of Douglass's dramatization of the whipping of Aunt Hester. In it, we are
drawn the pure victim of the slave system.

DOUGLASS'S *NARRATIVE:* AUTONOMY AND THE HERO

By and large, neither the slave narrator nor the slaves themselves had any
historical models of either a quasi-historical hero like Daniel Boone or a
national figure like George Washington. Even their best rebels—Vesey,
Gabriel, Turner—either end up ignominiously hiding in the swamps after
their uprising or have their revolt aborted in the first hours. The narratives
therefore generally lack a hero whose resolute courage and strength give
him a victory over white power. Within the slave world, hero images were
sparse. To judge from the spiritual and the folktale, says Lawrence W.
Levine, the slaves reacted to their victimization either by projecting the

dream of a "sacred universe" that would come in another reality to the pious and the faithful or by coping with the present reality of oppression and violence through trickery and deceit. The sacred universe takes shape in the spirituals, calling for stoical suffering and passivity in the face of treatment the slaves can do nothing about. The slave tales celebrate the sly animal or the shrewd slave, who saves himself by outwitting the strong and by practicing caution to survive: "A smart man ain't gwin to buck 'gin a mud-hole; he walks 'round it ev'ry time," says one of the many proverbs from the slave repertory.[46] The important thing about these images for my discussion is that they are nonviolent. They substitute subversion and evasion for heroic violence. As Stephen Butterfield says, "The most common method of dealing with force is by means of guile."[47] Examples of such a response are also recounted in many slave narratives, in which escape and survival depend upon shrewd deceits, lies, disguises. Frederick Douglass dresses as a seaman. Nearly white Ellen Craft impersonates a white slave-owner, while her husband, William, pretends to be her slave. Henry Box has himself "mailed" north in a box. Josiah Henson carries a bridle in his hand as if he were looking for his master's horse. Many slaves regretted the need for deception and lies but mitigated their "immorality" by pointing out the nature of the system. Harriet A. Jacobs apologizes for the untruths she had to tell whites when she gets to the North on the ground that "It was the system of violence and wrong which now left me no alternative but to enact a falsehood."[48]

This does not mean that the slaves, as depicted in the narratives or elsewhere, cowered like whipped beasts. According to Eugene D. Genovese, the whole thrust of the slaves' existence was to preserve their human sense of self and to refuse being made "an extension of the master's will." One of the ways they resisted was by creating a hidden communal life "in the interstices of the system." The most common slave experience, in Genovese's view, was made up of thousands of small, unspectacular resistances: pretending to be sick, lying about the master's benevolence, stealing, sneaking off to meeting against orders, even running away for short periods of time. It was by this latter method that "a surprising number of slaves" refused to be whipped.[49]

Genovese's point is corroborated by the slave narratives and the scholars who study them. Gilbert Osofsky, for example, refers to the ease with which many slaves ran away, at least temporarily, and hid in the woods and swamps. "The frequency of such stories in slave autobiographies makes clear that running away was a common means of black protest and rebellion against slavery [and] a means of protest against unusually brutal and unjustified physical punishment."[50] The slaves even practiced accommodation, says Genovese, which in some forms "contributed to the cohesion and strength of a social class threatened by disintegration and demoralization." Much of the time they avoided direct physical confrontations. But there was also violent resistance. The best-known examples are the slave revolts, especially of Gabriel Prosser, Denmark Vesey, and Nat Turner. In what Genovese calls "isolated but not necessarily infrequent incidents," individual slaves were known to kill their masters or overseers. These incidents, he says, "represent the high point of slave assertion within the system, for although they concerned individuals and only occasionally a group, they did not threaten the interests of the collective [slave community] and reminded all that the Man's power could effectively be challenged."[51]

The hero material is clearly there, and in the slave narratives, accounts of such physical resistance are widespread. William L. Andrews writes that as the facts came out about the barbarity of the treatment of slaves, "black autobiographers became less hesitant to recommend violence as a tool of resistance to tyranny." He cites Samuel Ringgold Ward, Frederick Douglass, Martin Delany, and James Roberts among those taking a more aggressive stand. They were seeking, says Andrews, a justification of violence and force that would rationalize action over the quietistic humility and suffering of Uncle Tom, the forgiving Christian figure. Andrews emphasizes the inconsistency in their using the morality of the very white culture they are trying to escape, and thereby undercutting the legitimacy of their revolutionary rhetoric. The important point for my purposes, though, is that, except for Douglass, the slave narrator seldom produces a true hero figure, noble, dignified, effective.

Those who challenged slavery in the way Genovese mentions had little effect on the system. Sometimes, the violent reaction verges on the pathological, as when Pomp, a Massachusetts slave, in 1795 axes his master after having convulsions and hearing voices urging him to "kill him now! now or never!"[52] Marian Wilson Starling recounts a story she puts together from several *Liberator* articles in 1838 about a slave woman who, desperate, enraged, and "unhinged" over the beating and the sale of her own children, kills the children of her master after vowing that no child of his "should live to horsewhip a child of hers."[53] And Solomon Northup tells of the slave so maddened by the pain and injustice of being whipped by his overseer for an offense of which he was not guilty that he seized an axe and "literally chopped the overseer in pieces." Northup finds heroism in the act, but in his account the man seems less noble and heroic than frenziedly deranged.[54] One of Northup's own personal experiences makes the connection between violent resistance and mental aberration even more explicit. Northup revolts against his owner, Tibeats, by throwing him down and whipping the man with the whip intended for himself. "My blood was up," writes Northup. "It seemed to course through my veins like fire. In the frenzy of my madness I snatched the whip from his hand. . . . I cannot tell how many times I struck him. Blow after blow fell fast and heavy upon his wriggling form. . . . The stiff stock of the whip warped round his cringing body until my right arm ached." Nor does Northup feel released or proud of his reaction. When Tibeats goes off to get help to punish him, Northup feels he has committed an enormous error, and "feelings of unutterable agony overwhelmed me . . . the most painful sensations of regret. . . . I could only bow my head and weep."[55] Northup, in other words, does not fight Tibeats with the calm resolve of a man determined to save his honor no matter what the price. He reacts with a kind of temporary insanity and then, like a child who realizes he has gone beyond his limits, deeply regrets his loss of control.

And if much of the retaliatory slave violence in the narratives seems to result when slaves lose their reason, so even their rational violent resistance nearly always ends in either terrible punishment or death, with the slaveholder sneering and triumphant. Northup's hatchet killer is horribly killed along with two acquaintances. When the slave Randall in William Wells Brown's *Narrative* (1847) determines "not to be whipped by any man living," his master calls together several friends who finally subdue him, give him a hundred lashes, wash him with salt water, and leave him tied up all day.[56] Josiah Henson's father "sprang upon [his overseer] like a tiger" for beating his wife, but he in turn is beaten so badly that he is changed from a "good-humored and light-hearted man" to a "sullen, morose, and dogged" man brooding "over his wrongs."[57]

The appetite for heroism, however, is voracious. Guile and piety offered survival but not honor. Slaves and free persons, blacks on both sides of the Mason-Dixon line, craved the kind of action that would substitute pride and dignity for the shame of bondage. Those advocating the heroic response of retaliatory or self-defensive violence believed that the very condition of slavery should automatically activate any response necessary for breaking free of it. "The instant a person is claimed as a slave," says a character in Martin Delany's *Blake,* "that moment he should strike down the claimant."[58] What God gave, he expected his children to fight for, even if it meant violence. One of abolition's most potent black orators, Henry Highland Garnet, insisted that it was "sinful in the extreme" to submit voluntarily to the "degradation" of slavery. ". . . it is your solemn and imperative duty to use every means both moral, intellectual, and physical, that promises you success."[59]

This is the heroism that Frederick Douglass brings to the genre, particularly with the *Narrative*. Not only does he present a liberating physical resistance to whipping, he imbues the imagery of the hero, as he did that of the victim, with a metaphorical force that other slave narratives achieve only in collective repetition of detail and the sameness of the language in which whipping is depicted. For this reason critical opinion is virtually unanimous that it is Frederick Douglass who, among all the slave narrators, most effectively carries us out of the conventional and the literal to, in the best sense, the literary and symbolic.[60] And this is most true of the *Narrative*. It is less history than art, and less autobiography than legend. Eric Auerbach provides a distinction here that is useful. History, he says, runs erratically, "variously, contradictorily, and confusedly," qualities that might apply to the more historical *My Bondage*. "Legend arranges its material in a simple and straightforward way; it detaches it from its contemporary historical context, so that the latter will not confuse it; it knows only clearly outlined men who act from few and simple motives and the continuity of whose feelings and actions remains uninterrupted."[61] This is why looking closely at the *Narrative* gives us our best window onto the later African American novel of violence.

After Aunt Hester has been whipped and Douglass the child has been imprisoned in the hell of slavery in chapter 1, a hero is needed to redeem the victims. According to legend, he must be tested in order to be found worthy for his project. In the next ten chapters, Douglass traces the series of tests to which he is subjected in his hellish world. First he reports more violent punishments: Mr. Severe whipping "a woman, causing the blood to run half an hour at the time" (55); Mr. Lloyd making old Barney "kneel down upon the cold, damp ground, and receive upon his naked and toil-worn shoulders more than thirty lashes at the time" (61); Mr. Gore shooting Demby and leaving only the slave's "blood and brains" to mark "the water where he had stood" (67). Though Douglass is too young to feel the whip himself, evidence of the lash is everywhere, confirming the example of Aunt Hester's beating and suggesting the future that lies in wait for him when he matures. Then there is an interlude of hope, when he is sent to Baltimore and feels that a personal Providence is working in his favor. The Baltimore experience, in which he serves the Hugh Auld family in more freedom and autonomy than he has ever felt before and in which he learns to read and write, is indispensable for the shaping of his character for the final test. By whetting his appetite for total freedom, it creates the conditions that result in his battle with the slave-breaker, Edward Covey. But before that final turning point, the legend calls for one more condition to be fulfilled. Douglass must be brought low personally. Slavery must verge on victory. Thus, when he returns to Talbot County, his half-freed mind collides with the brutal country rules. He is impertinent to his master, Thomas Auld. "A number of severe whippings" (100) do no good, and Auld sends him to Covey, under whom Douglass suffers the kind of violence to which he had been only a witness as a youngster. At the hands of Covey, Douglass hits bottom, striking that state of mind which, as the narrative abundantly illustrates, it is the goal of slavery to induce in the bondsperson: "I was broken in body, soul, and spirit. My natural elasticity was crushed, my intellect languished, the disposition to read departed, the cheerful spark that lingered about my eye died; the dark night of slavery closed in upon me; and behold a man transformed into a brute" (105).

This "dark night of slavery" is also a "dark night of the soul," [62] that lowest point when, in the mystical ascent, the climber seems farthest from godhead and is engulfed in despair. In the hero story, the knight has come, exhausted and depleted, to the Chapel Perilous that looks out on a wasteland of drought and famine. For the slave, it is that point when slavery has extinguished all that is human in the self, leaving only the animal. Despairing, Douglass turns to a higher power, his master Thomas Auld. If the legend is to be true to conditions that obtain, however, the slave system can provide no support. Thomas Auld dismisses the battered Douglass, and the young man returns to the theater of his despair.

This is the point, however, toward which Douglass has been building. Only when the culture hero stands totally alone before that vast power which the system reposes in Covey does he find the resources for self-renewal. The energy that drives him finally to resist the whipping that Covey is bent on giving him comes like a miracle, from some untapped reservoir of self-respect and determination. To this point, we have seen Douglass attribute to his attendant Providence his generally hopeful character (75), and listened to his "prayer" to the free-flying sailboats on Chesapeake Bay that concludes with the optimistic "There is a better day coming" (107), and heard the anticipatory statement of his transformation from slavery to manhood (107). Yet, when the moment comes, he has no explanation for his sudden resolution "to fight" (112). The heroic fire eludes accounting for. It cannot be defined in so many words but, like the mystical experience itself, remains a mystery. And so in the barnyard of the Covey farm, when Covey tries to seize him, he fights back. For "nearly two hours" Douglass holds off the puffing slave-tamer, successfully driving away Covey's cousin in the bargain and profiting from the refusal of another slave to help the white man. The result of this resistance is a sense of freedom so exhilarating that it is a virtual equivalent of the mystical union with God. It is an expression of courageous manhood, and a rite of strengthening that fits him for his later difficult labors. It produces in him something near mystical ecstacy. He describes it with a jubilance, an exaltation that is downright Whitmanesque:

This battle with Mr. Covey was the turning-point in my career as a slave. It rekindled the few expiring embers of freedom, and revived within me a sense of my own manhood. It recalled the departed self-confidence, and inspired me again with a determination to be free. The gratification afforded by the triumph was a full compensation for whatever else might follow, even death itself. He only can understand the deep satisfaction which I experienced, who has himself repelled by force the bloody arm of slavery. I felt as I never felt before. It was a glorious resurrection, from the tomb of slavery, to the heaven of freedom. My long-crushed spirit rose, cowardice departed, bold defiance took its place; and I now resolved that, however long I might remain a slave in form, the day had passed forever when I could be a slave in fact. (113)

This is a supreme symbolic moment, both as one of the critical instances that determine the course of Douglass's life as it moves "upward" toward the great and ultimate reward of freedom and as a model of slave courage and success. In legend, the dramatic moment is everything, a single act or event that is fraught with meaning and representativeness. Douglass's victory over Covey is just such a moment. It projects the image of the hero who metaphorically acts for the entire slave community, who shows courage, endurance, hardihood in employing a physical force that, as Douglass says later in *My Bondage,* gives him "the essential dignity of humanity." [63] The dark night of the soul is transformed into the dawn of resurrection. The desolate wasteland turns fertile. The brute becomes the prince. The hero redeems the victim. If the violence of whipping can make a man a slave, heroic physical resistance can make a slave a man. His fight with Covey is the climactic event that seldom occurs in life but stands as the essence of any narrative organized for dramatic effect. Douglass's rendering of the event extracts from reality its symbolic, representative center. All the contradictory and ambiguous extraneous details of actual life are swept aside. Only the heart of the cause and effect is left as a lucid epitome of blurred reality. And with the biblical language as a vehicle, this epitome is a culture-general representation of a mythic group rather than a realistic expression of an individually unique moment. By putting his experience in the terms of one of the basic stories of Western civilization, Douglass universalizes it. It is not only his resurrection from "the hell of slavery," in which Aunt Hester's whipping had entombed him and the further atrocities of the institution had secured him. It is a reenactment of the triumph of the Christian spirit over death, of the slave over the brutifying system, of the human state over the animal state. Douglass liberates himself from both the literal tyrant and the internalized oppressor in his own mind. In this case, physical force is both redemptive and regenerative. In violence Douglass is reborn. And in violence he observes the larger national morality, the principle of the defense of one's own freedom against tyranny that is enshrined in the Declaration of Independence.[64] At no other moment in African American narrative does a purer, more autonomous hero arise.

[2]

PROTOTYPES IN THE
ANTEBELLUM NOVEL

The literary importance of Frederick Douglass's fight with the slave-tamer Covey lies in its metaphorical force, not its real-world effectiveness. The physical power that Douglass uses to transform himself from a brute slave into a man is a low-level self-defensive violence that does permanent harm to no one. Covey walks away from it with no more than his ego damaged. This is not to diminish the potency of the Covey fight as a symbol of early black courage and its significance to Douglass's legend. At the same time, it is easy for Douglass's white, abolitionist, northern audience to approve of such an act, for it reinforces rather than challenges their racial sentiments. Douglass does not ask uncomfortable questions or require his readers to contemplate the kind of serious resistance that would involve blacks killing whites to liberate themselves from slavery, or simply to protect their own. This, though, is precisely the issue that the first three African American male novelists take up in the decade before the Civil War: William Wells Brown in *Clotel; or, The President's Daughter* (1853), Martin R. Delany in *Blake; or, The Huts of America* (1859–62), and Frank J. Webb in *The Garies and Their Friends* (1857). In addressing the question, they appreciably broaden the consideration of violence in African American letters. The prototypes they imagine and put into play in their stories lay the foundation for all future treatments of the topic in the African American novel.[1]

CLOTEL; OR, THE PRESIDENT'S DAUGHTER

Of these prototypes, that of the victim remains the most constant. Indeed, in the first African American novels the prototypical victim looks much like that of the slave narrative. Weak and helpless women and children are whipped, thumped, and pinched; strong men are brutally beaten or killed; all are subjected to the morbid whim or sadistic appetite of white men, women, and children in a system that turns humans into brutes on both sides of the color line. In *Clotel,* Brown presents a victim who is treated with a more grotesque cruelty than even those of the conventional slave narrative. Quoting from the Natchez, Mississippi, *Free Trader,* Brown describes a scene that anticipates what becomes a convention in novels fifty years later, the burning alive of a black man, this one a runaway slave:

The torches were lighted, and placed in the pile, which soon ignited. [The victim] watched—unmoved—the curling flame that grew, until it began to entwine itself around and feed upon his body; then he sent forth cries of agony painful to the ear, begging some one to blow his brains out; at the same time surging with almost superhuman strength, until the staple with which the chain was fastened to the tree (not being well secured) drew out, and he leaped from the burning pile. At that moment the sharp ringing of several rifles was heard: the body of the Negro fell a corpse on the ground. He was picked up by some two or three, and again thrown into the fire, and consumed, not a vestige remaining to show such a being ever existed.[2]

Delany, in *Blake,* describes a number of instances of brutality by whites of all ages upon slaves of all ages. In Cuba, where Blake goes in search of his wife, the violence is as bad as in the American South. One slave woman tells Blake of how her white wards "pull my hair, scratch my face, and bite me." Then they complain to their mother, and "she falls upon me and beats me to please them." Another white mistress sinks her "thumb nail deep into [a slave woman's] ear, nearly cutting it through." The same mistress whips the little black playmate of her white son, then forces the boy's mother to whip him, too. A slavemaster sends his impertinent slave, his old childhood friend, to a "professional whipper" who "completely reduced him, taking out the last remnant of his manhood, so that he's as spiritless as a kitten!" And in a more protracted scene in part I a slaveowner, for the entertainment of two gentlemen visitors, plies a long whip upon the back of a particularly lively and fetching eleven-year-old boy in order to make him "whistle, sing songs, hymns, pray, swear like a trooper, laugh, and cry, all under the same state of feelings." The white man goes into action on the bare flesh; the boy starts desperately to whistle, then pleads for the white man to stop. But the white man, in high spirits, continues, and "at every cut the flesh turn[ed] open in gashes streaming down with gore." Only when the northern guest can bear it no longer is the whipping stopped.[3]

In neither novel do these scenes play a direct role in the development of the action of the main characters. Their function is to establish the nature of the system which leads to extreme responses by implicated blacks. In *Clotel,* for example, such long scenes of violence as the auto-da-fé, as well as briefer allusions to other kinds of brutality, provide the background for the main action involving Clotel (who is the daughter of Thomas Jefferson), her mulatto siblings and mother, her daughter Mary, and their tribulations in slavery as light-skinned bondspeople. Clotel herself commits suicide rather than continue a slave, but Mary successfully flees to Paris where she marries another slave runaway. These characters suffer little direct violence themselves. But they are subject to sale and separation, and they witness the ubiquitous physical cruelty of their masters and mistresses. It is the victimization of blacks in all these senses that provokes the violence of the hero figure that these novels inaugurate.

The heroes in *Clotel* and *Blake* are of a different species from those of their contemporaries in the slave narrative. The principal differentiating feature is the nature of the hero's revolt. A Frederick Douglass, a Henry Bibb, a Solomon Northup act out their defiance as individuals or in small groups against their particular individual owner or driver. The hero prototype created by Brown and Delany revolts against the slavery *system.* They emphasize his qualities as a leader and teacher who has personal courage and fortitude, a powerful concern for the people, and above all, a readiness to wage violent war in their service. He contains a faint hint of that messianism defined by Wilson Jeremiah Moses which involves leading his people on a divine mission to redeem the world.[4] He is the original figure frequently imagined by subsequent fiction writers and popular leaders, the kind of person Bigger Thomas dimly perceives, with perhaps too much totalitarian zest, when "He felt that some day there would be a black man who would whip the black people into a tight band and together they would act and end fear and shame."[5]

In a very brief passage, Brown, as our first African American novelist, does two things at once. He sketches in the features of the first fictional hero, and he makes one of the earliest contributions to the creation of the legend of Nat Turner. He devotes only a couple of pages to the Southampton insurrection and gives Turner no role in the lives of Clotel or her family. He draws Nat in only the faintest outline as "a preacher amongst the Negroes, and distinguished for his eloquence, respected by the whites, and loved and venerated by the Negroes" (191). We do not see him, as the whites did, as a half-mad fanatic and get no dispassionate inventory of the whites killed in his revolt that Thomas Gray reports in the *Confessions*

(1881). But in alluding to the bloodiest of all slave uprisings, Brown makes Turner larger than history.

Brown brings the slave rebel in at a critical moment in the fortunes of the protagonist. Clotel, having previously escaped to the North, returns to Richmond looking for her daughter just at the point when Nat leads his Virginia slaves in revolt. Unable to find her daughter and pursued by slave traders intent on capturing her, Clotel leaps from the Long Bridge over the Potomac, into "the deep and foamy waters" below. It is a leap of protest, carried out "within plain sight of the President's house," where as Jefferson's daughter she might be said to have been conceived. With this gesture, she demonstrates "the unconquerable love of liberty the heart may inherit; as well as a fresh admonition to the slave dealer, of the cruelty and enormity of his crimes" (196). Brown frames his brief account of Nat Turner's rebellion between Clotel's arrival in the city and her suicide, making it a comment upon the heroic tragedy of these two dramas, whose protagonists are morally related but never meet. The causal connection between these events is that Turner's bloody insurrection leads to the capture and imprisonment of Clotel, for the authorities are more watchful than usual and catch the disguised woman in the net they cast for Turner and his accomplices. Thus her death roughly coincides with that of the great rebel, and the image of her personal revolt is superimposed upon Nat's general one.

These two characters resist dehumanization in ways Brown explicitly links. Light-skinned slaves like Clotel—and, for that matter, Brown—feel a special grievance as children of their own masters. They "tolerate, if they do not encourage in themselves, low and vindictive passions." Recognizing these passions and their own unacknowledged guilt, the slaveowners of the South are in constant fear of "an outbreak among the slaves" (190). Nat Turner's is one of those outbreaks. Nat is moved by quite different motives from those of the mulatto. First, he is a "full-blooded Negro." Second, whatever "vindictive passions" he feels, they are general rather than personal. They arise from his observation of the whole panoply of slave atrocities which we have seen Clotel, her family, and her friends suffer. Turner, says Brown, "had heard the twang of the driver's whip, and saw the warm blood streaming from the Negro's body; he had witnessed the separation of parents and children, and was made aware, by too many proofs, that the slave could expect no justice at the hand of the slave owner" (190–91). Thus Nat does not *personally* feel bitter vindictiveness; he is above such low emotions.

Those "vindictive passions" that the mulatto feels, however, are deeply fixed in a fictional character Brown calls Picquilo, perhaps his most original prototype. Picquilo acts as a foil to the more dignified Nat Turner. He is

purely Brown's invention, a slave runaway who joins Nat's band of insur-
gents when, in Brown's version of the story; they retire to the swamps to
avoid attack. Like Nat, Picquilo is a "full-blooded Negro," and he receives
a full page of attention. Brown does not endow him with a resolution to
relieve the anguish of the slave. He dwells instead upon his Rousseauesque
nobility, the purity of his African blood, the authority of his bearing, his
almost supernatural skill as a fighter. He is not a man we take to as a friend
but one of whom we stand in uneasy awe. Like a sinister prince from a
Jacobean revenge tragedy, he has "a bold, turbulent spirit" (192).[6] He arms
himself with only one weapon, but it is a memorably forbidding one—"a
sword, made from the blade of a scythe, which he had stolen from a
neighbouring plantation" (191). With this intimidating instrument, Picquilo "from revenge imbrued his hands in the blood of all the whites he
could meet" (192). His "sanguinary" look establishes him as the first
"avenger" in African American fiction. Picquilo is the satanic side of the
hero, for whom the larger enterprise of liberation is merely the vehicle for
fulfilling his revenge. Brown suggests something just a bit off-center about
him. Despite his role as a kind of wish-fulfillment fantasy for Brown, we
sense a slight madness in him, perhaps from the humiliations slavery has
forced upon an African aristocrat. When he appears on the scene, the
shading darkens and the tone becomes more ominous.

Brown does not express unqualified admiration for Nat Turner and
Picquilo. Though he cannot but applaud their courage and take satisfaction
with their facing up to the white tyrants of the South, neither can he fully
approve a slaughter that brings no material good for anyone. As Brown tells
it, Nat Turner's rebellion only caused blood to flow for both black and
white and illustrates the awful consequences of slavery and the violence it
encourages. These conditions produce the "vindictive passions" that lead
to revolt, and revolt leads to ever more rounds of bloodshed:

Without scruple and without pity, the whites massacred all blacks found beyond their owners' plantations: the Negroes, in return, set fire to houses, and
put those to death who attempted to escape from the flames. Thus carnage
was added to carnage, and the blood of the whites flowed to avenge the blood
of the blacks. These were the ravages of slavery. (193)

Brown's account, of course, does not square with the historical events.
The bloody retaliation against blacks that whites in Southampton County
carried out did not really take hold until the end of the forty-eight-hour
uprising, when the rebels had been dispersed, most of them captured, and
Nat had hidden out by himself in the woods in the vicinity of the Travis

plantation where he was a slave. It is not Brown's historical accuracy, though, that is important here but the attitudes he expresses in the figures of Nat and Picquilo. The ambivalence toward violence in the passage quoted above reflects the main problem in the construction of the hero in the African American novel. The tendency of African American novelists, over the 150 years of their literary history, is to admire the hero's willingness to wage war against the white oppressor but to be uneasy with the results of the behavior they admire. They feel deep anger toward the violence whites visit upon black Americans, a justifiable sense of grievance and a resolve to retaliate, to act the man; but they express a similarly deep disquiet about that retaliatory violence, afraid that it brings no end to itself, only havoc to both sides, that in its core and according to the highest law it is wrong. Nat Turner and Picquilo may be two degrees of a potential hero, but it is a hero whose propensity for violence contains troubling flaws.

This same ambivalence marks the public debate concerning the means by which slavery should be fought, particularly in the years between 1830 and 1860. In his *Appeal* (1829), David Walker takes the extreme militant stand. The slaves should rise up against their masters and overthrow the detested institution by force: "kill or be killed."[7] Henry Highland Garnet advocated similar armed insurrection in his 1843 "Address to the Slaves of the United States of America" that I mentioned in chapter 1. "Brethren, arise, arise!" cries Garnet with the vehement rhetoric of the *Communist Manifesto:* "Strike for your lives and liberties. Now is the day and the hour. Let every slave throughout the land do this, and the days of slavery are numbered. You cannot be more oppressed than you have been—you cannot suffer greater cruelties than you have already. *Rather die freemen than live to be slaves.*"[8] William Whipper, on the other hand, was known not only for his work on the Underground Railroad but also for his consistent stand against violence. Frederick Douglass, more than any of the three men I've mentioned, illustrates the difficulty that black writers had with the question of aggressive resistance. He became a man in his fight with Covey. Then, in the North, he took the side of his patron William Lloyd Garrison, who argued against an armed slave uprising. But by the late 1840s Douglass had become "less hopeful of [slavery's] peaceful abolition," and his public position "became more and more tinged" with John Brown's "strong impressions" about an armed slave revolt.[9]

The position toward violence William Wells Brown takes in *Clotel* is no clearer than that of later novelists. When he introduces George Green after the Turner uprising and Clotel's suicide, we hear an argument familiar in this antebellum period. George had joined Nat's forces, and when, after he is captured, he is given a chance to argue why he should not be executed for a criminal act, he insists that he was behaving in no way different from the founding fathers in the American Revolution. Indeed, the grievances of the revolutionaries were "trifling in comparison with the wrongs and sufferings of those who were engaged in the late revolt." [10] On this basis, we would have to see George's enlistment as justified and Nat's leadership as heroic. Instead, the whites treat them like beasts and criminals, sentencing them all, including George, to death. This is only to be expected, though, George suggests with resignation. It is the victors, he says, who get to decide upon the morality of the act by which they triumph. Your forefathers, says George to the judge, "were revolters, but their success made them patriots—we were revolters, and our failure makes us rebels. Had we succeeded, we would have been patriots too" (203). Green is angrily cynical—not because the criterion whites use for judgment is race but because it is success. It may be true that it is the victors who write history. But, for Brown's purposes, such a general truism does not serve his need to establish the slave's grievance.

He gets that grievance mixed up with his own genuine concern that violent revolt, authentically heroic though it may be, can result in nothing but a Pyrrhic victory, if there is any victory at all, and that violence, when judged by some higher standard we intuit, is wrong. The better way is deceit and disguise, like the old slave tales and many of the slave narratives had it. That is how George Green escapes from prison and his death sentence. With the shrewd and courageous assistance of his slave sweetheart, Mary, Clotel's daughter, he escapes his jail cell by impersonating her, flees to Canada, then makes his way to Europe, where he eventually reunites with Mary, and awaits the time when he and his bride can return to America. It is true that, unlike Nat Turner and Picquilo, George is "somewhat ashamed of his African descent" (209). He is no hero in the sense that Nat is. But he is an admirable young man, capable of learning languages and acquiring education's panache. He lacks the dramatic glory of the great rebel, but he has his own kind of strength and courage. And his escape and eventual reunion with Mary follow the dark chapter in which both Nat and Clotel die violently. Their deaths do not free the slave through resurrection, as Douglass's fight with Covey did him. They represent a night that has to be passed through in order that Clotel's children might see the day, not as harbingers of that day but as horrors characteristic of slavery. George and Mary will show up in later novels much more frequently than Nat and Picquilo. And in later incarnations they will take on the trappings of heroism.

BLAKE; OR, THE HUTS OF AMERICA

Martin Delany develops the prototypes of the violent warrior-hero and the avenger in much greater detail than Brown does and treats them with much less ambivalence. Whereas Brown devotes just two pages to the idea of a slave uprising, Delany devotes the whole of his novel to it. And whereas Brown questions the moral validity of violence by implication rather than by direct argument, Delany has his hero, Henry Blake, attack the issue head on. Blake suggests that there is a correspondence between the way masters treat their slaves and the degree of the slaves' anger. That anger, in turn, measures their willingness to use violence in retaliation or escape. The "curse" of the slave, says Blake, is not "cruel and inhuman" treatment but the "confounded 'good treatment' and expectation of getting freed by their oppressors" (127). Good treatment thus is said to work against the liberation struggle.

This doesn't jibe with the statistics compiled by Marion D. de B. Kilson, who finds that "Slave revolts tended to cluster in less oppressive slave areas and the catalyst for a revolt was an individual who had opportunities to play multiple roles."[11] Nor does it reflect what seems the more valid insight that Frederick Douglass expresses in *My Bondage and My Freedom:* Treat a slave badly and he will follow his master with doglike devotion; treat him well and he dreams of freedom.[12] Delany's passage might be a bungled attempt at satirical irony. If Floyd Miller is correct in his introduction to his edition of the novel, Delany writes *Blake* at least in part in reaction to Stowe's *Uncle Tom's Cabin*. In chapter 1, Stowe has her narrator say that "the mildest form of the system of slavery" occurs in Kentucky, and here "the good-humored indulgence of some masters and mistresses" produces "the affectionate loyalty of some slaves."[13] Delany's Blake reports, in perhaps tongue-in-cheek frustration, that he was successful in enlisting slaves to his planned revolt everywhere but in Kentucky. There the masters give "good treatment" to their slaves, and so the slaves are satisfied. It is hard to take Blake's complaint seriously, especially since Stowe herself goes on to say that the mild treatment in Kentucky simply cultivates a "poetic legend," beneath which lies the hard reality of "law" that blacks are "things" which belong to an owner. But Blake reasons with apparent seriousness that kind masters soften the slaves' proclivity to revolt. Physical punishment hardens it. Thus, even Blake, who when this discussion takes place is attempting to organize a general slave uprising throughout the South, "could not have the heart to injure Mrs. Franks," his considerate mistress (128). Similarly, although Mr. Franks breaks his word by selling Blake's wife, Blake rejects violent retaliation. He decides instead to translate his own personal need for vengeance and liberation into "avenging the general wrongs of our people" (128).

This capacity for a selfless transcendence of the personal distinguishes him as the highest type of hero. Like Brown's Nat Turner, Delany's Henry Blake identifies himself with his people's wrong, not with his own. But Delany intentionally makes a more forceful symbol of Blake, presenting him as the heart and soul of his nation, not a man working narrowly for himself, though he has plenty of reason to. For his lofty purposes, violence is justified, and so in part 1 of the novel Blake has set about planning "for a general insurrection of the slaves in every state, and the successful over-throw of slavery" (39), and "inducing the slave, in his might to scatter red ruin throughout the region of the South." Violence to correct the wrong of slavery is authorized by a moral code that transcends the evil statutes of master and mistress. The "mighty lesson" Blake teaches the American slave in his journey throughout the South to put his plan into execution is the same as David Walker's: "strike for Liberty. 'Rather to die as freemen, than live as slaves' " (128). The explicit function of the hero is to sow "the seeds of future devastation and ruin to the master and redemption to the slave" (89). When Blake himself does kill, he kills symbolically, attacking the most hateful emblems of white oppression—the pack of fine bloodhounds trained to run down blacks, the black driver who does the work of his master in whipping the field girls, the white cracker who tries to take Blake into custody as a runaway.

Blake's plan for revolution really develops only when he gets to Cuba in part 2. This is where he was born, where he pursues his wife, and where he is eventually reunited with his parents. On this Caribbean island, slave revolts were more frequent than in the United States, so he finds the rudiments of a revolutionary movement already formed. He completes its formation, calls for war, and preaches to his rebel angels about their man-hood and the divinity of their purpose. The final chapters in which the revolt would be expected to take place have never been found, if they actually exist, so the book ends with the uprising about to begin.

Cuba is also where the pure spirit of militancy, shorn of its nationalistic morality, emerges in the character of Gofer Gondolier. Gofer is an ex-panded version of Brown's Picquilo, an "avenger" whose animosity toward whites has narrowed into an all-consuming obsession. Like Picquilo, Gofer has a distinctive weapon. As The Cuban captain general's "caterer of the police cuisine," Gofer invented a special knife, ostensibly for harmless use in his work but in actuality so that it could pass into the slave population without being thought of as a weapon. Thus distributed, "on a general rising the blacks in every house might have good weapons without suspicion" (254). He calls his knife the "Cuban carver" and "Gondolier's carving knife." Delany invests Gofer with a certain nobility. Indeed, one of the illustrious guests at a gathering of high-placed blacks organizing for the revolt calls him a "Noble fellow" (255). And in soliloquy, as he observes a group of whites "in the full enjoyment of an evening's pleasure," he speaks in lofty terms of black equality and manhood, and of the principle of justifiable force used against unjust oppression. "The authority of the slave-holder ceases the moment that the impulse of the slave demands his freedom, and by virtue of this divine attribute, every black is as free as the whites in Cuba, and I will resist this night, and henceforth every attempt at the infringement on my inherent privileges" (273).

The thoughts are Gofer's; the language is that of Delany's narrator, for Gofer in direct dialogue speaks in less elevated English. He may be a "Noble fellow," and like Picquilo he may have his small band of followers, but he lacks the breeding of the true hero type. If he is "noble," it is as a savage is noble. As Picquilo is for Nat Turner, Gofer Gondolier is a foil for the real hero. Henry is "the master spirit" of the revolution. Gofer Gondolier is the vindictiveness that has its place in the rainbow of insurrectionary feeling. Henry never allows his emotions to dominate his behavior or motives. He speaks in exalted language of the divinity of the Cuban slaves' cause and God's grace. He stands at the top of a natural aristocracy, which is made up of poets, of large landholders, of light-skinned backers of action. Gofer says of the Cuban population of American whites, who have launched a campaign of humiliation against Cuban blacks, "Curse them! I hate 'em! Let me into the streets and give me but half a chance and I'll unjoint them faster than ever I did a roast pig for the palace dinner table" (312). It is this outburst that ends the unfinished novel, and Gofer's are the last words we hear: "Woe be unto those devils of whites, I say" (313). But like Picquilo, Gofer (whose name was corrupted from "Godfrey" by a process Delany does not explain) can never be the commander-in-chief. His rancor taints his reason and limits him to secondary positions. Yet, it would be hard to think of the revolution existing without his energy. If Henry is the revolution's heroic ego, Gofer is its id. Freed, Gofer is pure destruction. But given direction by Henry, Gofer becomes an indispensable force.

The victims whom Blake's revolutions will redeem abound in both part 1 and part 2. But not all of them wish to be saved if it means violence and disobedience to the master. These are the "forgiving Christians," and in the characters of Mammy Judy and Daddy Joe, Delany writes into the African American novel the figure's first prototype. They counterpoint Blake's intrepid militancy. Well-meaning and humble, they have bought the white man's version of Christianity, which teaches them never to disobey their master or to contemplate violence in any form, under benevolence or cruelty. Against their general travail, the universal application of the whip, and the selling away of their own daughter, Daddy Joe urges his suffering fellows to "look to de Laud! as he am suffishen fah all tings" (12). Eventually, Blake leads them and others to escape to Canada. But in the beginning they refuse to be unfair to or steal from their master, and they are aghast when Henry tells them of his plans for insurrection, rebuking him for abandoning his religion and for planning to hurt anyone, even those whites who have hurt blacks. Delany does not ridicule these people so much as demonstrate their pathetic wrongheadedness. They are the folk, who take their enslavement as part of God's system and agree to put off their hopes for freedom until they get to heaven. Through them Delany attacks the figure of Stowe's Uncle Tom. In showing them as uneducated and childlike, Delany brings them close to the minstrel figure. When, for instance, Henry speaks to Mammy Judy about a "round metallic box" during an explanation, she responds impatiently: "Wat dat you 'talic, Henry? Sho, boy! yeh head so full ob gramma an' sich like dat yeh don' know how to talk" (132).

We go to Delany, however, not for the roundness of his characters or even the coherence of his action but for his unique vision of the slave system and his clear view of the types that it produces. The humble forgiving Christian that he throws up as a contrast to Henry Blake becomes a mainstay in the postbellum African American novel that deals with the question of violence and its uses. This goes against what more recent scholars say about religion during slave times. Vincent Harding in particular demonstrates that much of the resistance and outright rebellion came from preachers who believed that God gave aid to his revolting black children just as he had to the Israelites who overthrew their Egyptian masters and fled across the Red Sea.[14] The three best-known slave uprisings were led by religious men who believed in a "divinely aided deliverance" from slavery and were willing to shed blood to achieve God's wishes. The Uncle Tom advocacy for peace at any price shows how the simple can be taken in by white hypocrisy. But in *Blake* these submissive Christians are, like Stowe's Uncle Tom, neither evil nor cowardly. They show unswerving loyalty to Henry. They offer him money to support him in his fugitive travels, even though they disapprove of his mission. And they steadfastly refuse to inform on him when pressed by their master. Their weakness is, as Delany explains elsewhere, that they carry a good thing "too far. Their hope is largely developed, and consequently, they usually stand still—hope in God, and really expect Him to do that for them, which it is necessary they should do themselves." [15] Until Henry finally spirits them off to Canada, virtually every sentence they speak to him urges him to trust in the Lord and submit to his situation.

We know the hero by his immunity to these misguided pleas and his clear understanding of the slavemaster's hypocritical religious practice. When Mammy Judy urges Blake to put his faith in the Lord when he finds his wife sold, he angrily counters: "Don't tell me about religion! What's religion to me? My wife is sold away from me by a man who is one of the leading members of the very church to which both she and I belong. . . . I and my wife have been both robbed of our liberty, and you want me to be satisfied with a hope of heaven. I won't do any such thing; I have waited long enough on heavenly promises; I'll wait no longer" (16). Henry is himself no atheist. He simply rejects the slaveowner's self-serving Christianity that would justify bondage. When he embarks on his journey through the South to lay the foundations of the general insurrection, he initiates a quasi–mystical conversion experience by determining "to renew his faith and dependence upon Divine aid." In one of many prayers he raises in both part 1 and part 2, he cries, "Arm of the Lord, awake! Renew my faith, confirm my hope, perfect me in love. Give strength, give courage, guide and protect my pathway, and direct me in my course!" This experience renews him, and he stands up "a new man" (69). This is not the vocabulary of conventional Christianity. But it is not pagan, either. It illustrates the devoutness of a leader who submits only to the divine, who is "bold, determined, and courageous, but always mild, gentle and courteous, though impulsive when occasion demanded his opposition" (17).

Henry is thus no godless heathen and is not driven by brutish bloodthirstiness. Rail though he might at the religion of the slaveowner, he himself cannot do without the civilizing order of belief. At the same time, he will not accept the mistaken principle of quietism. The hero brings to the waiting black nation a militant piety. Such militancy permeates the prayers Henry raises as the "General-in-Chief of the army of emancipation of the oppressed men and women of Cuba" (249), first at the "Grand Council" meeting, then at the "Grand Official Council of the seclusion" (256). These are long statements about having God's help and doing God's will. At other times, the third-person narrator even refers to Blake in the language of the New Testament. His journey through the South in part 1 takes on the character of Christ's teaching of the multitudes. By some mysterious elixir, the slaves along his way know of his presence and await his "advent," like a savior (116).

It is the concept of these prototypes that draws our attention to Delany rather than his execution. *Blake* is, as Addison Gayle, Jr., says, "a sprawling, cumbersome book," whose "implausible plot sequences" and "over-all episodic quality" might derive from the fact that it is a "fragment." It is not only its fragmentary quality, however, or its "inept characterization and stilted dialogue" that mar this novel.[16] It is the fact that there is no true conflict between the characters; and it is in the opacity and clumsiness of Delany's prose, his occasionally incomprehensible sentences, the omission of transitional details that would allow us to follow the twists of the story. As an orator and a straightforward polemicist, Delany is a perfectly adequate writer. His late quasi-anthropological discourse, *Principia of Ethnology* (1879), while we may greet its contentions about the development of Ethiopia from Ham with skepticism, nevertheless reads clearly and coherently, as does his better-known *Condition, Elevation, and Destiny of the Colored People of the United States* (1852). *Blake* simply shows that Delany is a much better discursive writer than novelist. Its importance lies in Delany's cutting through to the basic parts of one of the major issues of his day. The heroic rebel, the avenger, and the forgiving Christian, which he draws so clearly, are not picked up in the African American novel until the end of the century. But when Sutton Griggs and Charles Chesnutt do explore them in new forms, the ghost of Martin Delany hovers about.

The militancy that motivates Henry Blake, however, had apparently been abandoned by Delany himself when he started publishing the novel serially in 1859 in the *Anglo-African Magazine*. He was an inveterate organizer of northern free blacks and spent his life leading efforts to achieve the vote, free the slaves, develop plans for emigration, and even investigate the possibility of the kind of armed slave revolt advocated by John Brown. But he wavers on the issue of organized violence. In 1839, for example, as a member of a free black group in Pittsburgh, Delany as spokesperson for his "Philanthropic Society" warns the authorities that the city's blacks would arm and protect themselves if whites carry out their threat to start a race riot. In the same year, he joins with the same blacks in writing a letter to the editors of the Pittsburgh *Gazette* in which they "deeply reprobate a resort to violence under any circumstances . . . as being alike disgraceful to ourselves and our country, and feel ourselves bound on all occasions to maintain the peaceful administration of justice and the supremacy of the laws." On the more private question of defending one's house, Delany speaks out with great vitality. If any white tries to enter his house under the authority of the Fugitive Slave Act (1850), Delany tells an audience gathered to discuss the new law, "and I do not lay him a lifeless corpse at my feet, I hope the grave may refuse my body a resting place, and righteous Heaven my spirit a home." Yet by the end of the 1850s, discouraged by the effects of the Fugitive Slave Act, he has concluded that the slaves never would revolt, and he turns to the solution of emigration rather than rebellion.[17] Thus the novel that appears between 1859 and 1862 in the *Anglo-African Magazine* and the *Weekly Anglo-African Magazine* is a fantasy of what might have been rather than a contemplation of the possible, an expedition into options Delany no longer entertains. As fiction, it expresses a collective dream, but it contains the central prototypes of the debate over violence.

THE GARIES AND THEIR FRIENDS

In the third antebellum African American novel, *The Garies and Their Friends* (1857), Frank J. Webb makes a somewhat different fictional statement about violence from those of Brown and Delany. Much more of a novel than either *Clotel* or *Blake,* Webb's narrative has a definite plot line (as well as several busy subsidiary plots) and true dramatic conflict between characters. Consequently, it deals less with heroic prototypes and more with real people and personal motives. Webb minimizes the institutionalized violence of slavery by bringing blacks and some whites together on the same side against prejudice and unfairness, and by setting the action mainly in Philadelphia. The character who gives his name to the title, Clarence Garie, is a white man who falls in love with the light-skinned slave woman he buys at an auction and, after two children are born, takes her north as Mrs. Garie. They all become close to the Ellises, a successful free black family, and Mr. Walters, a black man whose genius and energy have made him a millionaire in spite of the obstacles to such achievement posed by his color.

Addison Gayle's critical-scholarly perspective barely conceals the rancor he feels toward Webb's middle-class strivers. For Gayle, Webb commits the ultimate crime by explicating the program of Booker T. Washington "more articulately than [Washington] did himself" thirty-seven years later.[18] But this, it seems to me, is very much the wrong connection for Webb. It is true that *The Garies and Their Friends* is not an abolitionist novel, that Webb does not write it in order to show solidarity with the suffering slave or to insist upon nationalist segregation or emigration, themes Gayle so admires in *Blake.* It is about that unique society, as Harriet Beecher Stowe calls it in her preface to the novel, of free Negroes that developed in Philadelphia on the "frontier" between the North and South, the problems that arise because of their color, and how they solve them. But its central characters are hardly the worker-artisans idealized by Washington who humbly accept disfranchisement and secondary social status. In making his characters struggle against the bias they face in everyday life, Webb creates a model of self-confident as well as ambitious seekers after the American dream. The

Garies, the Ellises, Mr. Walters, and Kinch de Younge all recognize the impediments to the free play of their talents raised by color. They abhor those impediments, but the best and the brightest of them refuse to renounce their color *or* their ambitions. And if Webb essentially ignores slavery, he does not ignore the prejudice that continues to make life difficult in the North for those blacks who have escaped the southern institution. It may be that there was, in 1857, more pressing business for the African American than making the white economic system work for them. But Webb looks beyond that business to the "free" black for whom racial prejudice is persistent and pervasive. His novel speaks to the future rather than the present. In a sense, Webb was ahead of his time, for *The Garies and Their Friends* reads more like the novels of the turn of the century and the Harlem Renaissance than like the other two published within short years of his own. In fact, in his treatment of the problems of the mulatto, he more closely resembles James Weldon Johnson in *The Autobiography of an Ex-Colored Man* (1912) than he does William Wells Brown or Martin Delany. As Arthur P. Davis says in his introduction to the modern edition of the work, Webb's approach "characterized Negro novels until the 1940's." [19]

In the race riot on which the novel turns, Webb compresses the essence of the challenges that he sees confronting the free African American. The motives that drive the whites to riot against the Philadelphia blacks could not exist in the South during slavery, for they arise from the fact that the Philadelphia Negro is free and competitive. Webb anticipates one of the principal themes of African American novelists from after the Civil War to the present era—that much violence arises from whites' envy and anger over the commercial success of blacks. The basis of their anger is twofold: They do not like blacks getting ahead, and they resent black competition. Thus Webb's "pettifogging" white lawyer, George Stevens, a vehement and aggressive racist, is put out that the free blacks are developing property in their own section of the city, even though they rent much of it from white landlords. He hatches a plot to exploit antiblack sentiment by arousing a mob, causing instability, then getting the landlords to sell on the assumption they will lose their money unless they depart before the values go down. This will give Stevens the opportunity to buy up valuable property at a bargain-basement price (175–76).

Stevens conceals his economic motivation beneath his inflammatory racial rhetoric. He plants articles in the friendly white newspaper that decry the "insolence" of the city's free blacks and their excessive abolitionist "agitation." This shows Webb going beneath the appearances to the root cause of white violence. In her preface, Stowe writes of Webb's riot as an example of the kind of "excitement, which existed in the city of Philadelphia years ago, when the first agitation of the slavery question developed an intense form of opposition to the free coloured people" (vi). Webb says that the riot in his novel does indeed contain a heavy tincture of antiabolitionist animosity. But he makes clear that the real motive is white greed, the determination to keep blacks out of the economic system. In his end-of-the-century study, *The Philadelphia Negro* (1899), W. E. B. Du Bois demonstrates the complexity of the real context within which Webb is working. From 1820 to 1860, says Du Bois, the fortunes of Philadelphia blacks had their ups and downs, affected by the immigration of southern blacks who came without skills or education and contributed to the incidence of crime and thievery in the city, the arrival of European immigrants who got most of the new jobs emerging from the growing manufacturing industry, and the agitation against slavery, which many lower-class whites resented. Out of this turmoil grew several decades of riots, some periods worse than others, when whites burned down blacks' houses and churches and themselves suffered substantial casualties in street fighting. Millionaires like Walters and businessmen like Ellis were few and far between. Robert Bogle and Peter Augustin became wealthy as caterers, Stephen Smith through lumber, William Still in coal. But the overwhelming majority of blacks worked as domestics.[20] Webb thus writes about a tiny minority of this community of some 20,000.

What is important for my purposes is the way Webb has this minority respond to the riot. Many of the blacks who live in the area and are threatened by the attacking whites "fled from their homes . . . and sought an asylum in the houses of such kindly-disposed whites as would give them shelter" (203).[21] But Walters and the Ellis family fortify themselves in the millionaire's mansion and arm themselves with everything from guns and bullets to stones and boiling water. They thwart the mob, but when Ellis goes out to warn the Garies that the mob is coming after them, he is cornered by the whites, beaten, and mutilated. However, a sympathetic white family shelters him and nurses him back to health. The mob, in the meantime, feeds itself on the murder of white Clarence Garie and the trashing of his house.[22]

The violence of the riot is not the violence of the master over the slave but that of a white immigrant underclass (mostly composed of tavern-tough down-at-the-heels Irish) exploited by unprincipled middle-class whites out of cupidity and racial bias. Neither does Webb present a pathetic victim of superior white power, nor is there a mythic avenger like Picquilo or Gofer Gondolier. The blacks who fight back against the white rioters are equal to the task and, in their restraint and understanding, stand above the white lower-class street fighters who make up the mob. The attitude toward violence Webb's characters express is the same as Frederick Douglass's in the *Narrative*. Their resistance, Walters insists, must be "strictly defensive," though they must leave no means available unused. They are gentlemen warriors. The black women possess the same fierce sense of independence and pride, helping their men to fend off the mob in a variety of ways. It is the men, of course, who stand on the brunt of the defense and use the rifles and pistols that are stacked at strategic places. We admire them, but Webb makes no attempt to show them as generalized captains of a black uprising or to express a general comment on the use of violence in the North. It is melodrama pure and simple, with idealized but realistic black characters behaving like true men and women, with dignity and spirit.

None of these fighters are heroes in the legendary sense that Nat Turner and Henry Blake are heroes. They are, instead, credible models for a new world in which free blacks must be willing to turn the whites' firepower back upon them. Their resistance is plausible but limited in its literary symbolism. It does not embrace the entire black community, seek to end all slave cruelty or terminate slavery as an institution. It is a defense of what is theirs conducted on a sensible scale, in a somewhat more tractable world than that of the southern slave. No questions about the legitimacy of violence are asked, and so none is answered. The right to use defensive violence is assumed, not argued. Beneath this assumption lies a yet more basic one—that blacks are equal to whites in all particulars. These assumptions set the tone of the novel and its theme. It is not about how cruel whites keep black victims down but about how black men and women look when they feel no need to *argue* about their right to protect themselves. These are free Negroes who carry the dignity of their freedom easily and firmly. Nor is the entire white world arrayed against them. The despicable minority even arouses the resentment of respectable whites who are appalled "that such a thing [as the riot and the treatment of Ellis] can be permitted in a Christian city" (219).

In the end, Stevens falls victim to his own conscience by committing suicide out of an inescapable sense of guilt. But the focus of the novel after the riot is upon the next generation. The children of the Ellis and Garie families are confronted with no violent challenges and so need make no decisions concerning violence. But the order of the action suggests that it is their fathers' fortitude and determination that provide them with a model for their own choices. Charlie Ellis, for example, takes pride in his color, marries another black girl, and carries the struggle to the whites by competing with them on the labor market and in commerce. When his color makes it difficult for him to find the kind of work he seeks, he expresses his determination in the language of combat: "I don't intend to be conquered," he says. "I'll fight it out to the last—this won't discourage me" (293). He lives happily and prosperously, generously helping other blacks and contributing to the independent spirit of the black community. But young Clarence Garie rejects figurative combat by evading his color. He tries to pass and marry a white girl, renouncing his family and his past. This is the act not of a proud man but of a coward, and he is punished for it. He dies in sorrow and dissatisfaction, failing to imitate metaphorically the example of Ellis and Walters who fought physically for their position in life.

The Garies and Their Friends imitates the popular novel of its time, the sort Dickens had written two decades earlier in *Oliver Twist* and *Nicholas Nickleby*—full of melodramatic action and suspense and sentimentalized love interests. It also contains an impressively insightful relationship between a wicked father (Stevens) and his plain daughter (Lizzie), who genuinely loves him and suffers profoundly when he dies, and enough serious social commentary to make the book more than a mere evaporation. Its contribution is to the realistic current of the African American novel, anticipating, in its treatment of violence, works like Pauline Hopkins's *Contending Forces* (1900), Herman Dreer's *The Immediate Jewel of His Soul* (1919), and even Waters Edward Turpin's *These Low Grounds* (1937). Like its descendants, *The Garies and Their Friends* is "romantic" but not a "romance." The latter genre is better applied to *Clotel* and *Blake,* whose worlds, while not symbolic like those of, say, the Leatherstocking tales, are nevertheless generalized and action-oriented and seem set apart from the ordinary details of everyday life. I do not see Brown or Delany intentionally employing the romance genre. The closeness comes more from a failure of literary control than from deliberate choice. Thus, while they attempt to project the reality of slavery, it seems in their narratives to occupy that wavering "borderland" that Richard Chase speaks of, a neutral territory "where the institutions and manners of society" do "not obtain."[23]

Whatever their stylistic and generic differences, these novels lay out the principal character types that act out African American novelists' perception of and reaction to the violence in the black experience: the helpless victim who is beaten or killed, the forgiving Christian, the avenger, and the activist hero. The last figure is most subject to variations. He can be the figure of myth or romance, larger than life, a symbol of the black community, equal to any exigency, and acting on the basis of race pride and the rescue of the victim. He can also be a more realistic character, less grand and noble than his mythic parallel but courageous and hardy. Later times produce different novelists, who give different form to these characters. The antebellum novel reacts to the conditions of the time—the unspeakable injustice and brutality of slavery and the suffocating animosities of the North. It will be several generations before the violence produced by these conditions ceases to be an immediate concern for African American novelists. That day will come, but before then the question of how to react to white violence remains an issue they examine through different forms of the original prototypes.

[2]

AFTER THE WAR:
LYNCHING AND OTHER
RECREATIONS

[3]

SEARCHING
FOR THE HERO,
1865–1900: BLACK WARRIOR,
FORGIVING CHRIST

THE WARRIOR

Eric Foner says that after the war, in "large parts" of the South, there occurred "a wave of violence that raged almost unchecked." Most of this violence was directed against blacks and "reflected the whites' determination to define in their own way the meaning of freedom and their determined resistance to blacks' efforts to establish their autonomy, whether in matters of family, church, labor, or personal demeanor."[1] The violence whites inflicted upon blacks in the postbellum period seemed to carry a particular malevolence and vindictiveness. As a congressional report puts it, "Dead bodies of murdered Negroes were found on and near the highways and by-paths. Gruesome reports came from the hospitals—reports of colored men and women whose ears had been cut off, whose skulls had been broken by blows, whose bodies had been slashed by knives or lacerated by scourges."[2] This may stand as a "summary," as Herbert Shapiro calls it, of the African Americans' problem in the first days of their freedom. In her novel *Iola Leroy; or, Shadows Uplifted* (1892), Frances E. W. Harper also alludes to the general surge of violence against blacks after the Civil War, to "how our folks hab been murdered sence de war," as old Aunt Linda says, and how dangerous it is for an educated Negro to stay in the South because he may "get into trouble and be murdered, as many others have been."[3] Writing in 1905, William A. Sinclair depicts a South that has fallen under the rule of the white mob:

mobs torture human beings and roast them alive without trial and in defiance of law and order; mobs shoot down women and children who have never been charged with crime, and against whom there is no suspicion,—it is enough that they are negroes. Mobs take possession of the streets of great cities and assault and shoot down innocent colored people, driving them from their homes and burning their property. . . . Mobs intercept and hold up the regularly constituted officers of the law, take prisoners from their possession and shoot them to death. Mobs break into jails and take out prisoners and hang them, sometimes in the jail yard, and riddle their bodies with bullets. Mobs even invade the sacred precincts of the court-room, and during the actual process of the trial, take prisoners from the custody of the lawful authorities and shoot them in the very temple of justice, or hang them in the court-yard in the presence of judge, jury, and court officers, amid the shouts and cheers of hundreds, and, at times, thousands of people.[4]

In the thirty years or so that elapse between the publication of the last known chapter of Martin Delany's *Blake* and the appearance of Harper's *Iola Leroy,* the novel that opens the first main period of the African American novel, the search among black writers for a figure responsive to all this white violence resolved itself into two basic images: the forgiving Christ figure that follows the sense of the spirituals, and the violent warrior that embodies the anger of Frederick Douglass and Delany's Henry Blake. That search does not take place in the African American novel, for in those thirty years only a handful of novels appear.[5] And among those, except for an allusion to the murder of blacks in California, no representation of violence or Reconstruction life in general is made. Instead we get a religio-historical allegory, a couple of odd little domestic tales, some sentimental moral exempla about white people, and a fictional slave narrative.[6] The debate over the appropriate hero image goes on instead in pamphlets, oratory, history books and biographies, newspaper and magazine editorials and articles. This is the bedrock upon which the novels I deal with in chapter 4 are based. The labels of the forgiving Christian and the warrior oversimplify the variegated and often contradictory picture. But they lie at the two poles of the spectrum of the African American response to white violence that emerges in the nineteenth century. Both figures reflect admired values that give life worth. The violence of the warrior was retaliatory or self-defensive, and it meant manhood and self-respect. The nonviolence of the forgiving Christ meant a moral superiority that proved blacks worthy to enter the Christian civilization as full partners. Each image implied the desire for the respect and protection of the laws enjoyed by whites, freedom from white oppression and violence, safety and satisfaction. And often one figure imagined by black spokespersons contains elements of both images.

The importance of such symbolic figures is suggested by Richard Slot-kin, writing in another context. The early colonists, he says, "required an image, a symbolic heroic figure, whose character and experience would express their own sense of history, of their relationship to the American land, of their growing away from Europe." [7] In Slotkin's analysis, Daniel Boone became that figure, blending the violent hunter, who first subdues the wilderness, with the social man who helps create peace-giving order. This fusion of the nonviolent with the violent resolves the dichotomy of the traditional hero whose strength as a warrior serves the social group in battle but also embodies, as I suggested in the Introduction, a dangerous savagery. The African American who, unlike the white colonist, came to the New World under duress is perhaps in even greater need of such a hero. The animal trickster or the deceitful slave might have been practical reactions to an intractable situation, but they did not command much respect in the general American hall of fame. Postbellum black writers, therefore, sought a figure analogous to the Daniel Boones and the Davy Crocketts, and they were quick to celebrate such models when they found them. Slave rebels like Gabriel Prosser, Denmark Vesey, and Nat Turner were held up by black writers as examples of courage, intelligence, and manliness. William Wells Brown, writing in 1867, says that Vesey's plan for a slave insurrection showed "considerable generalship," and his use of vio-lence "to strike the chains of slavery from the limbs of their enslaved race will live in history." [8] William J. Simmons, in his biographical *Men of Mark* (1887), calls Nat Turner "a modern Regulus," "one of the greatest emanci-pators of the nineteenth century," whose men in the "real battle . . . fought hand to hand with whites." [9] Black writers praise black soldiers, too: Cris-pus Attucks, who fell at the head of the small band of Bostonians in the Boston Massacre; Peter Salem, who allegedly saved the day at Bunker Hill; Sergeant Plancionois, color sergeant of the black First Louisiana Regiment, who died heroically in the Civil War battle of Port Hudson.

Having emerged from a condition in which they were sometimes ranked with animals or treated like retarded children, the freedpersons, no less than the slaves, needed to think of themselves as full human beings who believed in their own manliness. The warrior image provided that model. The warrior's violence asserted one's masculinity as well as one's humanity. It is in this spirit that *New York Globe* editor T. Thomas Fortune issued his famous policy of "stand and shoot" rather than "stand and be shot." "If white men," wrote Fortune, "are determined upon shooting whenever they have a difference with a colored man, let the colored man be prepared to shoot also. . . . If it is necessary for the colored men to turn themselves into outlaws to assert their manhood and their citizenship, let them do it." [10] Even respected ministers of the Gospel like African Methodist Episcopal bishop Henry McNeal Turner sometimes advise the black man to keep guns in his house. "We advise him," says Turner, "to keep them loaded and prepared for immediate use, and when his domicile is invaded by bloody lynchers or any mob day or night, Sabbath or work day, turn loose your missiles of death and blow the fiendish wretches into a thousand giblets." [11] The audience addressed in such statements seems to be white as much as black, as if manhood and self-respect can come only when blacks wrench recognition from whites. And the belief in some quarters was that violence can force recognition. A character in Sutton E. Griggs's novel *Imperium in Imperio* (1899) makes the point directly: "We should let the [Anglo-Saxon] know that patience has a limit, that strength brings confidence; that faith in God will demand the exercise of your own right arm; that hope and despair are each equipped with swords, the latter more dreadful than the former." [12]

But whether they fight or not in the years after Reconstruction, too often it all seems to come to the same thing. As in slavery, the African American loses. With the collapse of the radical Republican coalition in 1876 that had pushed southern reform in the decade after the war, and Rutherford B. Hayes's compromise that resulted in the removal of the rest of the Union troops from the South, the old landholders who had been defeated and the new merchants who profited from the postwar confusion returned to full control. In a complicated picture, blacks were returned to a de facto slavery and held under control by a pattern of forces, not the least of which was violence. There were, of course, the Thirteenth, Fourteenth, and Fifteenth Amendments, proclaiming their freedom, their citizenship, their constitutional right to due process, equal protection, and the vote. There simply was no federal provision for enforcement. So whites stole blacks' land and blacks' labor, burned their houses, barred them from even minimal education and the courts, and, over the last years of the century, increasingly disfranchised, segregated, beat, shot, and lynched them. Powerless, they admired power, and folkloric figures they created, like Stackolee (sometimes Stackalee, Stackerlee, or Stagolee) and John Henry, whose exploits are embodied in song and story, possessed pure power. Tough, ruthless, courageous, and angry, Stackolee [13] is honored not for leading the attack against whites or working to change society and force recognition for blacks but for his amoral willingness to use his power against the weak as well as the strong in an almost totally black world, made up mainly of seedy neighborhoods, barrooms, and gambling joints. He even takes on the Devil himself:

Take dat pitchfork, Tom Debbil,
An lay it on da shef;
I'm dat bad man, Stackerlee,
An I'm gonna rule Hell by myself.[14]

John Henry, too, uses his strength not as a social weapon against whites but to sustain his honor against the steam drilling machine that the whites have brought around to bore through the mountain for the railroad tunnel. The steam drill wins, John Henry dies. Yet, he is an object of pride for his anonymous folk creators because of that strength and because of his refusal to bend. It is the spirit this oral tradition celebrates, apart from consequence or social cause.

THE MARTYR

This spirit is certainly important to the larger picture being composed by black writers. It contributes, in fact, to some of the blurring of the hero figure. More familiar with the victim than with a dominating hero like Daniel Boone, these late-nineteenth-century writers seem to miss the subtle shift they make from the hero as a man who successfully asserts his manhood through force to the hero as victim-martyr. In his story of Sergeant Plancionois, William J. Simmons expresses his admiration for the color sergeant's vow to bring back the Union colors or die in the battle at Port Hudson. "Noble words these, and brave!" writes Simmons, "and no more fitting epitaph could mark the resting-place of a hero who has laid down his life in defence of human liberty!" Nominally, Plancionois and his fellows do die in the struggle against slavery. But in reality nearly the entire regiment goes to a futile and needless death against an impregnable artillery position simply to prove their mettle to the whites. For just a few days before the battle the white commanders dismissed the outfit's black officers, and white soldiers jeered and taunted the blacks. The heroic element for Simmons in the battle is not the ability of the black soldiers to use violence against whites but the extent of the punishment they are able to absorb. As their cause seems more futile, the more worthy to Simmons seems their refusal to give it up—even when charge after charge results in a field littered with black corpses and "slippery with gore and crimson with blood."[15]

The spectators Simmons plays to are white, and there is deep pathos in that. Charging against an enemy that cannot be dislodged, flinging themselves toward their own deaths, these black soldiers make a statement, as

Simmons sees it, to the white race: We do not lack the courage and fortitude to stay the course, even in the face of certain death. The victory of the First Louisiana Regiment is the fact that it "convinced the white soldiers on both sides that they were willing and able to help fight the battles of the Union." Thus George H. Boker's celebratory poem: "Never, in field or tent, / Scorn the black regiment." [16] William Wells Brown, summing up the same battle, addresses the same question: "had [the First Louisiana] accomplished anything more than the loss of many of their brave men?" He answers like Simmons: "Yes: they had. The self-forgetfulness, the undaunted heroism, and the great endurance of the negro, as exhibited that day, created a new chapter in American history for the colored man." [17] There is an eerie parallel between Sergeant Plancionois and his men dying on the bloody field of battle and the great John Henry dying with his hammer in his hand. Giving their lives for black honor in an encounter whose agenda is set by whites, they are both as much victim-martyrs as they are heroes.

In the figures of the soldiers at Port Hudson, then, the warrior image is modified to include the loyal martyr, for whom violence is not a weapon to be used but a force to be endured, with the hope—always futile—that whites will eventually acknowledge blacks as patriots worthy of being accepted into the larger American family. The image of the loyal martyr is in turn just a step or two away from the Christ image and the belief in total nonviolence, humility, forgiveness, love. All three of these images exist side by side in the last half of the nineteenth century, and sometimes all three reside at once in a single perception of the black hero.

THE MYTHOLOGY OF WHITE MANHOOD: MEN AND BRUTES

The forgiving Christ figure contended that the Christian spirit, not the use of force, would achieve for blacks the equality and self-esteem of which white violence and other instruments of oppression deprived them. Frances Harper, for example, set out to write *Iola Leroy* in order to "awaken in the hearts of our countrymen a stronger sense of justice and a more Christlike humanity." [18] Like many of her writer contemporaries, Harper mistakenly believed that, by creating fictional images of African American cultural worthiness and patient forbearance, she could change the attitudes of those whites who called themselves Christians by appealing to the principles of their faith. That neither she nor anyone else succeeded in doing so did not discourage the convinced forgiving Christian. Stoical endurance of a reality they could not control had, since slavery, been a survival technique. In freedom, many blacks tried to make it a means for modifying their world

—changing white attitudes by associating black people with an ideal that most whites professed to respect. The image of the forbearing but forgiving sufferer embodied separate but complementary qualities that recall the sentimentalized victim of the antebellum slave narrative—social inferiority on the one hand, which undermined their self-respect, and moral superiority on the other, in which by turning the other cheek they linked themselves with Christ. As S. P. Fullinwider has suggested, the nonviolent Christian response helped in blacks' physical and psychological survival, for it taught the moral worth of behavior that was least likely to stimulate white violence. Humility acted like natural selection, granting greater longevity to those who chose not to fight back.[19]

The logic that black people deserved better because they were authentic Christians failed to influence whites, not because whites resented the claim but because they could not believe that blacks lived under the same laws as they did. This becomes a factor in the making of a supportive symbol for blacks to live by. My reference in the Introduction to Frederick Douglass's story of the "heroic slave," Madison Washington, is relevant here. Douglass points out that Washington invokes the morality of the American colonist when he leads the mutiny on the brig *Creole*. Tyranny justifies violent revolt. The white first mate of the *Creole* agrees with the principle but cannot admit that black mem have the right of appeal to sacred a law.[20] No claim, however reasonable, could dislodge that prejudice from the minds of most nineteenth-century whites.

The picture whites had of themselves, as well as of blacks, contributed heavily to the picture that blacks sought to project of themselves. The forgiving Christ figure was an attempt to disconnect blacks from the white stereotype of blacks, to tap into the self-justification for which whites employed Christianity. To whites, Christianity disclosed that they, not black people, had been divinely selected to receive God's benefits and live his life here on earth. The white, not the black, person had been manifestly destined to subdue the continent and enjoy its fruits. The only arguments that were rational according to white standards supported this position, especially the version of evolutionary theory that played to their advantage. Whites allegedly occupied a higher place in the scale of evolution than the colored peoples of the world. The white race, says racial extremist William Patrick Calhoun, has always been "noted for principle, civilization and high-tone . . . has always been talented, ambitious, moral and religious."[21] Favored of God and the gene pool, whites used their alleged racial superiority to justify their violence against putative inferiors. The enemy to "civilization" was the barbarity of the lower savage races, like blacks and Indians and the "little brown brothers" who stumbled awkwardly in other areas of the world. As Theodore Roosevelt put the position, "In the long run, civilized man finds he can keep peace only by subduing his barbarian neighbors." Indeed, says Roosevelt, "every expansion of civilized power means a victory for law, order, and righteousness." [22] The image of the superior being as a white man included the moral right—in fact, the necessity—to use violence to protect the superior world deeded to him by God.

This picture defined a manhood to which only whites had access. The idea of manliness, implying grace, virtue, and strength, enlisted a large following of romantics and a popular audience for whom not all democratic values were a virtue. Roosevelt and newspaperman Richard Harding Davis cultivated a taste for a kind of democratic aristocracy. Gentlemen for whom honor came before most other values, they would knock down the boor who insulted a lady or the vulgarian who overstepped the bounds of civility. They invoked the chivalric values of the Old World and sought out danger just to face it. The figure they helped popularize emerges in the heroes of romantic best sellers by white authors like Maurice Thompson, Winston Churchill, F. Marion Crawford. Their heroes distinguish themselves not only by winning the girl but by possessing the "birth and breeding," as Churchill puts it in *Richard Carvel* (1899), to know when to run the villain through and when graciously to spare an honorable opponent. In them are mixed the rugged democratic individualist whose personal strength guarantees his independence and the aristocrat who treasures the tradition that courage arises from winning swordplay and successful fighting. Only the Anglo-Saxon, however, enjoys a character of such tempered steel. The inferior races have not quite reached the level of human being. In Thompson's *Alice of Old Vincennes* (1900), the Indian Long-Hair can never hope to achieve civilized status, for he is a savage. When he saves the life of the hero in a quid pro quo, we must think of his behavior as animalistic and instinctive rather than rational and moral, for he is a "hideous atrocity of nature." Blacks are less pugnacious, but they reside at more or less the same place in the scale of existence. When Thompson's hero and heroine return to Virginia, they live happily "in a stately white mansion on a hill over-looking a vast tobacco plantation, where hundreds of negro slaves worked and sang by day and frolicked by night." [23] No plantation novel by Thomas Nelson Page or Harry Edwards could have put more simplistically the belief at the base of the southern myth.

That blacks were allowed no place in this scenario of manhood suggests one of the reasons for the attractiveness and the practicality of the model of the forgiving Christ figure. It was not merely that humility might momentarily palliate the oppressor's anger. To identify with Christ was to stake a claim on being human, a status denied blacks in freedom as well as slavery. Henry Highland Garnet was only one of many who warned the slaves that whites were "endeavoring to make you as much like brutes as possible." [24] In the course of the century, as the ideas of evolution became more wide-spread, the awareness of those who failed to come up to the highest evolutionary standards became more intense and the use of the word "brute" became more frequent. It worked as a shorthand term for the whole set of values that created an aristocracy in a democratic land. For the romantic novelist, the word expressed not only the characteristics of a lower species, like Long-Hair or the blacks in the plantation novels, but the qualities of white gentlemen when they surrender to their baser appetites. Getting drunk always makes a "brute" out of what otherwise is a perfectly good aristocrat. The word also applied to those of unacceptable political persuasion. Thomas Bailey Aldrich describes an anarchists' meeting he attended: "The brutes are the spawn and natural result of the French Revolution; they don't want any government at all, they 'want the earth' . . . and chaos." [25] The upper classes claimed order as their own monopoly. The lower types loved chaos. The better people could expect, however, from their place atop the evolutionary ladder, to watch the humanoids beneath them gradually wither away, brutish traits and all. "The ape and tiger in human nature," says John Fiske, "will become extinct." That will be a great day for true humans, since man's original sin, as Fiske sees it, "is neither more nor less than the brute-inheritance which every man carries with him, and the process of evolution is an advance toward true salvation." [26]

The distrust of the "brute-inheritance" plays into the same kind of ambivalence toward manly heroism as James Redfield's description of the Homeric warrior's latent savagery. [27] In the last two decades, scholars have explored the nineteenth-century understanding of manhood, manliness, and heroism and found that brute-inheritance plays an important role in that understanding. The compleat male contained aggressive, even animalistic, impulses that supported the self-reliance and individualism of the "self-made" man. Physical and mental dominance, competitiveness, personal power—all contributed to the manliness of the total man. The truly manly pursuit was business, not the ministry or book learning. The phenomenal success, the unbridled greed and profit taking of the Carnegies, the Morgans, the Rockefellers testified to the image of manhood widely admired in the period. Honored though these characteristics were, however, they embodied dangerous antisocial tendencies. Their antidote was the woman, who nurtured the civilized in the domestic realm by means of her innate feminine qualities like spirituality, virtue, gentleness, understanding of human feelings. On the aggressive, competitive male side, though, stood the vital energy that moved the world. And, ultimately, the white male was confident that woman was the recessive element in the pattern, too weak to protect herself and her family against threats from a world ruled by a nature red in tooth and claw.[28]

Since the brute was alleged to comprise more of the black nature than of the white, any adequate black image under construction had to include an answer to the case against African Americans. They would have to prove they were "men" in a different sense than a manly use of violence would permit them to do. Thus the highest accolade the black biographer can confer upon his subject is the label "man." "He was a man," says William J. Simmons of Frederick Douglass. "He was not going to remain bound while his legs could carry him off." [29] George Washington Williams says that Nat Turner "was a Christian and a *man*. He was conscious that he was a man and not a 'thing.' " [30] But what being a man entailed was not, as I have suggested, always clear. For the black warrior, manhood meant fighting back, asserting oneself through force. The whites' value system robustly reinforced this perception of what it meant to be a man in the construction of their own heroic image. But that same value system supported the Christian concept of nonviolence, too. Teddy Roosevelt and Richard Harding Davis may have caught the enthusiasm of the nation with their fisticuffs, big-game hunting, and celebration of war. And Daniel Boone may have embodied the myth of the hunter who killed splendidly. But the transcendent American hero was Lincoln, who, though he took the country into battle, did so reluctantly and sadly and seemed to suffer profoundly from the slaughter. What made him a real hero to the American imagination, as Dixon Wecter observes, was his capacity to forgive, his magnanimity, his Christ-like humility. Thus, even in the white mythology, a true man need not court danger to prove himself or show his worth by retaliating against an insult. "It is a vulgar error," wrote Ralph Waldo Emerson, "to suppose a gentleman must be ready to fight. The utmost that can be demanded of him is that he be incapable of a lie. . . . You may spit upon him; nothing could induce him to spit upon you,—no praises, and no possessions, no compulsion of public opinion. You may kick him;—he will think it the kick of a brute: but he is not a brute, and he will not kick you in return." Even a great soldier like Robert E. Lee was admired for his mature self-control, his refusal to swagger, his gentlemanliness in the Emersonian sense. He expressed no bitterness toward his victorious opponents after the Civil War and made himself conspicuous by refusing to lead an unrepentant South in a continued war of resistance against Reconstruction. He found the heart of manliness to be honesty, and like Lincoln he held no malice toward his enemies.[31]

OVERCOMING THE BRUTE-INHERITANCE

Both the black warrior hero and the humble Christ figure owe much to the popular morality of white America. But the forgiving Christ figure seems the most characteristically black and held the most powerful sway over the African American writers of the late nineteenth century. For a people with every right to feel vindictive and to crave divine retribution for their enemies, African Americans showed amazingly little rancor. This is not to say none ever expressed anger or called for retaliatory violence. It is simply that, given the magnitude of their grievance, they reacted in these years with considerable restraint. Whatever lay behind their moderation, one thought must have been that the most effective weapon for proving that the black man was not a brute impelled by animal violence was the projection of the values of order and nonviolence. Thus nearly every account praising a black man for his courageous use of violence also contains a celebration of his gentleness and charity, qualities that contribute to the strengthening of a society threatened on the one hand by the ideal of self-interested individualism and on the other by the brutal and illegal use of violence to suppress an entire race. This fusion of the opposites of violence and social order illustrates the same yoking together of contradictions that Slotkin found in the formation of the historicoliterary character of Daniel Boone.

William Wells Brown admires the power of Nat Turner and Madison Washington, but he also praises their humanity. Nat sets out not to gain vengeance, says Brown, but to erect a Christian state. Madison Washington does not allow a massacre of whites on board the *Creole* when the slaves mutiny. He prevents his men from killing two whites who had wanted to kill him. "They have proved themselves unworthy of life which we granted them," Brown quotes Washington; "still let us be magnanimous." This is a telling gesture for Brown, "an act of humanity [that] raised the uncouth son of Africa far above his Anglo-Saxon oppressors."[32] Washington's Christian act seems to be in harmony with his African nature. What Brown implies—that blacks by nature are capable of contributing to civilized peace and order—becomes an explicit argument as the postbellum period develops. The words "intelligent," "cultivated," "civilized" are used frequently as terms of high praise. William T. Alexander admires Frederick Douglass for "rearing an intelligent and cultivated family and . . . placing himself in the front rank among intelligent and cultivated men."[33] Frances Harper's Iola Leroy is "refined and lady-like," and one of Sutton E. Griggs's characters says that "There are Negroes that can meet every test of civilization."[34]

To be civilized was to be worthy of full American citizenship, to be a man, not a brute. If the African American could prove himself a civilized Christian, he could not only reassure himself of his own worth but also claim the full protection of the Constitution, invoke the power of the state to guard him against white violence, and even renounce retaliatory violence as a weapon in his struggle for respect. The proof came in a complicated argument drawn perhaps more from myth than genetics. Different writers employed different parts of the argument at different times, but George Washington Williams develops the entire syllogism in the first volume of *The History of the Negro in America* (1883). Like so many of his contemporaries, Williams does not question the values that guide American life. For him, Christian civilization is the expression of the highest form of humanity, and America is its model. He defines civilization in terms of the Protestant ethic, combining Christian piety with thrift, industry, and social order. God intended his children to give their lives to him and to commerce, to live moral lives as the stimulants of "peace and plenty." Williams does not condemn whites for regarding blacks as naturally inferior pagans incapable of absorbing the arts of civilization, nor does he attack the exploitative system that was unfolding out of the principles of profit taking and Manifest Destiny or advocate the overthrow of the standing social and economic order. Instead, he requests the privilege of joining it, adopting the entire value system by setting out to prove to the whites' satisfaction that blacks not only are capable of civilization but are the founders of it.

It started with Simon the Cyrenian, who carried Christ's cross to Calvary. Convinced that Jesus was indeed the Son of God, Simon returned home to Libya after the crucifixion taking Christ's doctrine with him. In this way, Africa became, Williams says, "one of the first countries to receive Christianity."[35] No one had to force the Africans to accept Christianity. They were ready for the light, because, as one of the most ancient of peoples, they had pioneered all the civilized arts. Not in Libya, though. The great African fountainhead of all Western culture was the Ethiopian city of Meroe, on the banks of the Nile. It was the model of all the European cities that had since been held up as examples of the white West's cultural achievement. Williams singles out its burgeoning commerce as its most admirable feature: "Through its open gates long ceaseless caravans, laden with gold, silver, ivory, frankincense, and palm-oil, poured the riches of Africa into the conscious lap of the city." This was the "eastern" beginning of the march of human culture.

The learning of this people, embalmed in the immortal hieroglyphic, flowed adown the Nile, and, like spray, spread over the delta of that time-honored stream, on by the beautiful and venerable city of Thebes,—the city of a hundred gates, another monument to Negro genius and civilization, and more ancient than the cities of the Delta—until Greece and Rome stood transfixed before the ancient glory of Ethiopia. Homeric mythology borrowed its very essence from Negro hieroglyphics; Egypt borrowed her light from the venerable Negroes up the Nile. Greece went to school to the Egyptians, and Rome turned to Greece for law and the science of warfare. England dug down into Rome twenty centuries to learn to build and plant, to establish a government, and maintain it. Thus the flow of civilization has been from the East—the place of light—to the West; from the Oriental to the Occidental.[36]

Nineteenth-century black writers widely accepted this interpretation of the African origins of modern civilization and of their own race in America, "Ethiopianism," or in the modern term, Afrocentrism.[37] Some of them made the relationship between the ancient culture builders and the contemporary freedperson even more explicit. William T. Alexander writes:

The builders of the Pyramids and Obelisks, sat at the feet of the Ethiopians to learn Architecture, Philosophy, Letters and Religion. From the Colored Race, Egypt obtained its civilization, and a visit to the twenty-two Universities and Colleges in our own land that are educating young colored men and women for the highest walks of life, will convince the most skeptical that in an educational sense there are no impossibilities in the way of their receiving the highest education, of which they are truly susceptible.[38]

The need for authorized status comes out powerfully in these protests of black worth and equality—even superiority. More important, the appeal makes no threats of force or violence to wrench equality from an unwilling majority but insists that blacks are capable of being judged by the highest standards of any Christian culture.

But if the black race did pioneer the world's highest culture, how did it come to its present state in America? The answer is central to this interpretation of the African American's experience in America. As the northern Africans, whose newly acquired Christianity gave added energy to their ancient civilization, spread southward, they broke into many groups. With that fragmentation, as Williams says, their faith began to weaken and they began to turn to "idolatry." When that process was complete, having lost their Christianity, they "lost their civilization" as well,[39] since civilization and Christianity go together. A different kind of Negro came out of this double loss, no longer a true African but an ignorant, degraded, immoral, physically unattractive offshoot of the original high strain. This type, trapped in Africa's low swampy places, provided the slavers with their merchandise.

Slavery was the "nadir," to use the word Rayford Logan applies to the last part of the century, of the descent of the ancient African civilization, and the direct result of the Africans turning away from Christianity to idolatry, the worship of "snakes, the sun, moon, and stars, trees, and water courses." Since the black man "early turned from God," writes Williams, "he has found the cold face of hate and the hurtful hand of the caucasian against him." [40] Slavery, like the Indian captivity for the early Christian pilgrim,[41] was the trial for the "fallen" or "inferior" Negro. It was both a punishment for the sin of idolatry, since, according to this version, it was principally the idol worshipers who were captured for the middle passage, and the vehicle of redemption.[42] Thus Williams writes that slavery was "a severe ordeal through which to pass to citizenship and civilization." It was a blessing in disguise, for it drew the Negro back from godlessness and degradation, from primitive savagery into the heaven of Anglo-American Christian society. Slavery "had the effect of calling into life many a slumbering and dying attribute in the Negro nature. The cruel institution drove him from extreme idolatry to an extreme religious exercise of his faith in worship." [43] The call of order is thus a call to black nature. The African American slave has passed through a redeeming trial that has left him a better creature, more qualified to take his place beside other Christians and move closer to God.

Paradoxically, the white man became not only the blacks' enslaver and oppressor but their redeemer, for he gave them back their lost religion. Slavery thus illustrates the benevolent presence of God's concern for black people. Booker T. Washington saw the divine hand in the blacks' bondage, too: "when we rid ourselves of prejudice, or racial feeling," he wrote in *Up from Slavery* (1901), "we must acknowledge that, notwithstanding the cruelty and moral wrong of slavery," those blacks who "went through the school of American slavery, are in a stronger and more hopeful condition, materially, intellectually, morally, and religiously, than is true of an equal number of black people in any other portion of the globe." This is not to justify slavery in principle, Washington assures us, "but to call attention to a fact, and to show how Providence so often uses men and institutions to accomplish a purpose." [44] Slavery is not a disruption or break in black history, according to this reasoning, nor is it a barrier to black growth. It is the last phase but one of a long historical process, an organic part of a unified evolutionary experience, designed by God and discovered now to give hope to a powerless people. These black writers were not so much trying, in their minds, to deny their past by assimilating into the white culture as seeking to complete the historical process begun when their ancestors fell away from the faith. Just as Daniel Boone embodied a historical process in which settlers became more intimate with the wilderness of the land they were destined to civilize,[45] so the Christian freedperson symbolizes the penultimate stage of a long journey from the ancient city of Meroe to the Christian democracy of America. Blacks may now thank "Providence" and look forward to greater "plenty" and better "commerce," the moral goods of the Protestant utopia and the foundation of the American dream.

Anna Julia Cooper uses this same historical process to celebrate the peace-loving attributes of the African American. The white race, she says, admires the Napoleon figure and values force and aggression, finding it "immensely noble" to see every other race as an enemy to be subjected to their strength and authority. "But somehow it seems to me that those nations and races who choose the Nazarene for their plumed knight would find some little jarring and variance between such notions and His ideals." Her ancestor is not the bloody-armed warrior of Gallic or Anglo-Saxon descent but Simon the Cyrenian, who, used to carrying burdens, helped Christ carry his, without any intention of gaining historical fame. Significantly, Simon had come from the very country that had given Moses succor when he had been threatened with bloody murder by his masters, reinforcing the virtues of fostering and sheltering rather than killing and subduing, of *"loving service* to mankind" as the highest good. "With such antecedents then the black race in America should not be upbraided for having no taste for blood and carnage. It is the fault of their constitution that they prefer the judicial awards of peace and have an eternal patience to abide the bloodless triumph of right." Thus it is not cowardice that makes them prefer nurture and forgiveness over violence and revenge but their nature, their history. In this sense, it is no surprise that they watched over the white families of the South when the men were gone from the plantations, without burning a building or insulting a white woman.[46]

The final stage of the historical process implied by Cooper and outlined by Williams was yet to come, however, and in it we see the Christ figure fuse with the black warrior in a triumph of Christian manliness. The Reverend Henry McNeal Turner, a bishop of the African Methodist Episcopal church, who wrote the introduction to Simmons's *Men of Mark,* hedges no bets about that triumph. As surely as oaks from small acorns grow, at the end of their evolutionary climb, African Americans, guided by reason, will inevitably force "the white man of the South" to yield, and then the race "shall gather wealth, learning and manhood, and occupy the land." Turner was a solid citizen of his century. Biology and geology had stimulated Hegelianism, Darwinism, Marxism. In their popular form, most of these views assumed an evolution, governed by a set of ineluctable laws, toward some utopia. Turner remarks that Simmons himself wrote his graduation oration on the "Darwinian theory, a subject then very popular in literary circles." As many did, Turner put the theory into a Christian context. It was a law, he said, that races weaken and die out. In America, the Indian had died out. He represented the past. The white man represented the present, but he was undergoing the same weakening as the Indian had already passed through. The future belonged to the blacks. "When the white race reaches decrepitude, the Negro will have reached his prime, and being in possession of all he has and will acquire from the whites, and his genius and industry to manufacture more and lift him to a higher civilization, he will stand the wonder of the ages." [47]

As Bishop Turner saw it, the evolutionary process that would produce this new form of African American served God's plan. This figure, a combination of the humble Christ and the heroic warrior, was inherently nonviolent and characteristic of black nature. Consequently, the African American would not only win self-respect and a place in the scheme of things. He would win the world. And he would do so without "a bloody conflict," without violating his God-given nature. This figure expresses the vision of utopia upon which the collective African American writing establishment worked during the nineteenth century, a world in which loving kindness held sway rather than hateful violence. This is the finest quality of the African American hero figure. And, says Turner, anticipating Cooper, it is a quality already there in the black personality during slavery, when blacks never descended "to the level of the brutes." Kind, loving, faithful, they "patiently waited till God broke their chains." Indeed, the sublimest moment in black history, Turner proclaims, occurred during the Civil War, when "the slaves waited, humbly feeding the wives and children of those who went to battle to rivet their chains." [48] At this moment, the worst of their ordeal was over, and they could take comfort in the fact that the future was theirs. Their gentleness was prologue to the future and a promise of what the new world would be like.

This was a rags-to-riches story on a grander scale than any Horatio Alger novel. It was the nearest thing to a completed myth the nineteenth-century African American had: audacious, grandiose, and gratifying. But since it was a myth of the future rather than of the present, and since its discrepancy from what was actually happening in the black world was so great, it lacked the compelling force to settle the running dispute over how to save those blacks who suffered from the very unmythlike treatment of everyday white violence. A few black writers could not will the two poles into an organic whole, and the models of the Christ figure and the black warrior continued to offer separate and conflicting means for dealing with white violence. Anna Julia Cooper expressed the core concern when, even while she praised black nonviolence, she worried that "the principles of patience and forbearance, of meekness and charity, have become so ingrained in the Negro character that there is hardly enough self-assertion left to ask as our right" what unrequited black labor has earned.[49] Both models of the black hero had their drawbacks and advantages. The warrior could become an outcast and produce an anarchy inimical to the black future. The nonviolent black risked accepting humiliation as a norm of life. Circumstances could make each model attractive at some point. Violence appeared tantalizingly manly when a mob of jeering whites set upon a lone black man, but it might in another case seem simply brutish. Nonviolence might have a moral and Christian appeal, but it could also appear the reaction of a coward. The nineteenth century produced no black consensus on violence. The divisions and debates that resulted from this absence of consensus emerge in the narratives that make up the first major period of the African American novel.

[4]

THE TRUTH
ABOUT LYNCHING, 1892–1922:
HARPER, HOPKINS, GRIGGS, AND
THEIR CONTEMPORARIES

THE HISTORICAL CONTEXT

Frances E. W. Harper's *Iola Leroy; or, Shadows Uplifted* (1892) is a romantic story of slavery, family separation, and postwar reunion. Its noteworthiness lies in its being the first African American novel that attempts to interpret the postslavery years from a black point of view and that refers to the increasing practice of whites lynching blacks. When Iola is chided for brooding too much "over the condition of our people," she answers that perhaps this is so, but "they never burn a man in the South that they do not kindle a fire around my soul."[1] It is no coincidence that Harper pays special attention to lynching, for 1892 is the year in which more blacks were lynched in the United States than ever before or since. The number of black lynching victims had been increasing since the end of Reconstruction in 1876. In 1886, for the first time in American history, more blacks were lynched than whites. By 1892 black lynching victims outnumbered white ones by nearly two and a half to one, in 1900 by over four to one, and in 1922 by eight and a half to one. Most of these lynchings took place in the South, lynching's "special scene," as Joel Williamson calls it.[2] I am using the word "lynching" here to mean the killing of a black man or woman by a conspiracy of two or more white persons without due process of law by hanging, burning, shooting, beating, dragging, stabbing, or other violence, because of an alleged violation of the morality of the community. To qualify as a violation, an act by a black person could be virtually anything a white man decided it to be, from an insolent look to being caught in bed with a white woman to killing a white man—for whatever reason. An African American killed in a race riot is not "lynched" because there is no conspiracy and no alleged crime or charge. A black person killed by one man or woman is "murdered," not "lynched."

Although the number of blacks lynched in a single year never again reached the 161 who died in 1892, for the next four or five decades African Americans perceived lynching to be the single most troublesome issue with which they had to deal, even as the practice itself declined.[3] In 1893 Bishop Henry McNeal Turner of the African Methodist Episcopal church established his Equal Rights Council in order to fight lynching and mob violence. "Until we are free from menace by lynchers," he said, "we are destined to be a dwarfed people."[4] When three of her prosperous and respectable friends were lynched in Memphis in 1892, Ida B. Wells undertook a vigorous one-woman antilynching campaign. She became the best-known agitator in the United States, publishing accounts of atrocities and tirelessly lecturing around the country.[5] One of the reasons for founding the National Association for the Advancement of Colored People (NAACP) was to end "this reign of lawlessness and terror."[6] Over the 1890s and the first decade and a half of the new century, other organizations were formed to fight lynching, such as T. Thomas Fortune's Afro-American League, the National Association of Colored Women (for which lynching was high on its agenda), the Georgia Equal Rights Movement, and southern white groups like Albion Tourgée's National Citizens Rights Association, the Constitution League, and the Commission for Interracial Cooperation, a southern group which opposed lynching but not the caste system that encouraged it.[7]

The period I deal with in this chapter thus opens in 1892, with the publication of *Iola Leroy* and the cresting of black lynching. It ends in 1922 with the passage of the Dyer antilynching bill by the House of Representatives[8] and the permanent decline in the annual number of lynching victims to below fifty. The year 1922 also marks the end of the early literary era, for the next year sees the publication of Jean Toomer's *Cane,* a work which ushers in the Harlem Renaissance and introduces a new vein in African American fiction, in which the artistic treatment of lynching advances appreciably. The novels written during this period do reflect awareness of the wide range of violence I cited in chapter 4, and I will refer to it over the course of my discussion. Historically, major and minor race riots proliferate in these years. There were bloody upheavals in Brownsville, Texas, and Atlanta, Georgia, in 1906, and the Springfield, Illinois, riot in 1908, which was one of the main causes of the formation of the NAACP. But of the novelists of this period, only Charles Chesnutt takes the race riot as a topic. His *Marrow of Tradition* (1901), which I take up in the next chapter, deals with the Wilmington, North Carolina, riot of 1898. Those novelists who treat racial violence focus their attention on lynching. Of the sixty or so novels published between 1892 and 1922 listed by Edward Margolies and David Bakish in *Afro-American Fiction, 1853–1976* (1979), some twenty-four contain references to lynching.[9] All of what most literary historians today would consider the major novelists of the era, except Paul Laurence Dunbar, wrote at least one novel in which lynching is an issue. Charles W. Chesnutt and James Weldon Johnson, the best writers of the group, though in widely different ways, wrote three such novels between them. Sutton E. Griggs, who published and marketed his own works from his ministerial base in Nashville, wrote five. Pauline E. Hopkins, the influential editor of the *Colored American Magazine,* wrote two, and Frances Harper and W. E .B. Du Bois one each.[10] Thus the writers to whom we continue to pay most attention regarded white violence, especially lynching, to be a feature of black life that demanded attention. They account for half of the twenty-four novels of racial violence written in this period.[11]

Chesnutt and Johnson have rightly received the most attention from literary critics over the years, and I will treat them in a chapter by themselves. But Benjamin Brawley, writing in 1916, had little but contempt for most other African American fiction written since the Civil War, saying it was made up of nothing but "traditional tales, political tracts, and lurid melodramas."[12] He seems to have included in this number Harper, Griggs, and Hopkins, and indeed they—and the rest of the novelists in the group I am talking about in this chapter—fall considerably below Chesnutt and Johnson in literary quality. But both literary and historical interest in them has increased over the years. Such early historians of the African American novel as Sterling Brown, Hugh M. Gloster, and Robert A. Bone noticed them with varying degrees of fastidiousness, Gloster, for one, emphasizing biography and summary, Bone focusing on social and literary background and assigning them places on a ladder of merit.[13] Later historians of the novel, like Addison Gayle, Jr., and Bernard W. Bell, give Griggs fairly prominent billing but have little to say about Harper and nothing about Hopkins or the other novelists except Chesnutt and Johnson. Gayle, for example, whose combative *Way of the New World: The Black Novel in America* is one of the more readable and persuasive examples of Black Aesthetic criticism, spends his four sentences on Harper complaining that *Iola Leroy* follows what he would call the accommodationist views of antebellum novelists William Wells Brown and Frank J. Webb rather than the more militant ones of Martin Delany.[14] With the burgeoning of black feminist criticism in the last fifteen years both Frances Harper and Pauline Hopkins have come in for more extended treatment. Barbara Christian places *Iola Leroy* at the center of her wide-ranging discussion of the effects of slavery, Reconstruction, and the patriarchal moral code upon the black woman, and Harper's attempt to construct "an image of the black woman that would elicit sympathy and appreciation for her and therefore for black people as a whole."[15] Elsewhere, she fits Harper's novel into the context of the sentimental romance, which she points out is a literary form tradition-ally employed for propaganda in the service of worthy social causes.[16] Hazel Carby broadens the perspective considerably in *Reconstructing Womanhood* (1987) by devoting full chapters to both Harper and Hopkins, providing helpful biographical information and imaginative close readings of their novels.[17] In the late seventies, Arlene A. Elder produced an astute treatment of both the male and female novelists of this period, with useful analyses not only of *Iola Leroy* and *Contending Forces* and Sutton Griggs's five novels but of more minor works such as J. McHenry Jones's *Hearts of Gold* (1896), Walter H. Stowers and William H. Anderson's *Appointed: An American Novel* (1894), and G. Langhorne Pryor's *Neither Bond nor Free: A Plea* (1902). A decade later, Dickson D. Bruce, Jr., included some of these same novelists in his discussion of the whole range of black writing during what Rayford Logan called the "nadir," seeing them as reflections particularly of the evolution from the affectation of genteel assimilationism to the develop-ment of the folk and the lower class as a source of cultural value and appropriate literary subjects.[18] All of this attention has conferred upon many of these novels a literary legitimacy they did not possess in the twenties and thirties and makes them mandatory objects of attention as embodiments of the period's literary treatment of racial violence.

The importance these novelists attributed to lynching in this period perhaps outweighed the absolute numbers involved. In terms of the deaths from other causes—disease, malnutrition, natural disasters, intrablack vio-lence—African Americans who died from lynching made up a very small part of the total mortality figures: 161 out of a population of 7,500,000 in 1892, or about 1 out of 100,000, as compared with a total death rate of 30.2 per 100,000.[19] Moreover, in the general tumult of intraracial violence, both white and black, the absolute number of lynchings was small. Most violent encounters in the South, as well as the North, occurred between members of the same race and class. Edward L. Ayers reports that in Savannah, Georgia, between 1889 and 1892, of sixty-nine assaults listed in the local newspaper, three-quarters involved members of the same race. Only 8 percent had a black victim and a white assailant; 15 percent, on the other hand, involved a white victim and a black assailant.[20]

But by 1892 lynching had acquired a symbolic power far greater than the numbers involved. It demonstrated the total political, social, and economic powerlessness of the African American, representing the most vindictive of all the forms of violence whites invented for terrorizing blacks, restoring white supremacy, and identifying blacks as sinister, subhuman threats to the racial purity of the southern Anglo-Saxon. By the end of the nineteenth century, when the post-Reconstruction white supremacist campaign had become most intense and most successful, lynching, though hardly the only form of violence in black life, had become the most conspicuous and dramatic. Thus, though they also deal with rape, beatings, and riots, lynching is the principal symbol of white violence the African American novelists treat in the first decades of the novel's development. Harper, for example, though very much aware of the general atmosphere of violence, is most assertive on lynching. A sympathetic northern white man, Dr. Gresham, worries that "The problem of the nation is not what men will do with the negro, but what will they do with the reckless, lawless white men who murder, lynch, and burn their fellow-citizens. To me these lynchings and burnings are perfectly alarming" (405). Harper identifies lynching as the central image of white violence at the historical point when lynching had become one of the most prominent objects of the African American community's attention.

THE IMAGERY OF LYNCHING AND THE LYNCH MOB

Harper treats lynching by reference and allusion, naming the atrocity rather than showing it. So does Charles H. Fowler in his *Historical Romance of the American Negro* (1902). The one "blot" he finds on the record of the freed slaves' advancement is lynching, which comes from laxity in Washington (213). In *The Colonel's Dream* (1905), Charles W. Chesnutt's Colonel French alludes to the lynching of "uppity" Bud Johnson with great bitterness but also with poetic restraint: "A rope, a tree—a puff of smoke, a flash of flame —or a barbaric orgy of fire and blood—what matter which? At the end there was a lump of clay, and a hundred murderers where there had been one before" (277). Grace Ennery, in Sarah Lee Brown Fleming's *Hope's Highway* (1918), hears "the sizzling and crackling of the fire," smells the burning of "human flesh," and discerns that the faces of the mob seem to have lost their "humanity" (39–40) in the lynching she witnesses with horror from her hotel room. J. A. Rogers's protagonist in *From Superman to Man* (1917), who finally brings the mind of a white supremacist to a greater understanding of blacks, inveighs generally against lynching, complaining about the American Christians who can weep over Christ dying 2,000 years ago but tolerate or even applaud a black man today hanging from a tree (112). In something under half of these novels, lynching is reported or commented upon rather than depicted, most of the reports generalizing upon the barbaric aspects of the practice.

Many novelists, though, show that barbarism in explicit and harrowing detail. Blacks are hanged, riddled with bullets beyond recognition, burned alive, mutilated, dragged and stabbed by men and boys along the way, skinned, and decapitated. Whites gouge their eyes out, drive corkscrews into their flesh, break their limbs, and carry off body parts for "mementos." We see their eyes roll back into their heads with terror and pain, their flesh quiver, the humanity of their faces obliterated, their bodies turned into battered cinders. If the slave hanging by his or her tied hands feeling the lash of the whip is the synecdochal image of slavery as composed in the slave narrative, the charred and beaten body of a black man hanging by his neck from a tree limb is the synecdochal image of the post-Reconstruction condition of the freedperson. Historically, not all lynchings were equally vicious. Many were straightforward executions through "mere" hanging or shooting. But when the burnings, beatings, dismemberings occurred, they drew more attention than the less spectacular vigilante actions. Accounts of all kinds of lynchings were disseminated by the white southern press and picked up by northern newspapers, both black and white, and by the organizations seeking to end lynch law. Lynching stories were part of the public discussion.[21] The novelists, searching for maximum shock value and sources of the highest indignation, tend to use the reports of the most horrendous lynchings to put the worst face possible on the hated practice, sometimes importing newspaper articles verbatim into their narratives.

One of the more frequently cited lynching accounts in the novels of this period appears in Sutton Griggs's *Hindered Hand; or, The Reign of the Repressionist* (1905). This particularly grisly atrocity is a double execution of a man and his wife. Bud and Foresta Harper, in their attempt to protect their land against a jealous redneck who has come after them with a rifle and started shooting first, kill the white man in self-defense. Infuriated that these two black people would claim a right reserved only for white men, the lynch mob goes to work.

Bud was tied to one tree and Foresta to the other. . . . Wood was brought and piled around them and oil was poured on very profusely. . . . One by one [Foresta's] fingers were cut off and tossed into the crowd to be scrambled for. A man with a corkscrew came forward, ripped Foresta's clothing to her waist, and bored into her breast with the corkscrew and pulled forth the live quivering flesh. . . . [Bud's] fingers were cut off one by one and the corkscrew was bored into his legs and arms. A man with a club struck him over the head, crushing his skull and forcing an eyeball to hang down from the socket by a thread. A rush was made toward Bud and a man who was a little ahead of his competitors snatched the eyeball as a souvenir. (133–34)

After the torture and mutilation, the mob burns the bodies.

In *Exorcising Blackness* (1984), which is still the standard work on the topic of lynching in African American literature, Trudier Harris refers to Griggs's passage as a model of the "lynching and burning ritual," which she finds in both contemporary historical and literary accounts. She also surmises that Griggs probably took his description from a story in the Vicksburg, Mississippi, *Evening Post*. The ritual lynching, as Harris rightly points out, involves a sequence of capture; collecting the means for killing the victim such as ropes, railroad ties, gasoline or kerosene, and wood; torture; killing; and finally the seizing of appliances used in the process and the collecting of "mementos" from the victim's body parts.[22] Harris does tend to overplay the commonness and the regularity of the pattern she describes in the historical and literary representations of lynching. The full elaborate ritual of her scenario infrequently appears in either the newspaper accounts or the novels. Even so, we are indebted to her for establishing the fact that lynching does have a ritualistic quality to it, and I gratefully employ her term for shorthand convenience to refer especially to the practice of burning victims alive, riddling them with bullets, mutilating their bodies (emasculation is virtually never mentioned in the novels of this period), and carrying off such mementos as finger joints, pieces of flesh, and gouged-out eyeballs. Other kinds of lynching appear in African American novels between 1892 and 1922 and will call for our attention, but it is the ritual lynching, because of its potent symbolism, that usually takes center stage.

The accounts of this rite by African American novelists form a composite picture composed of the standard features, and these features fall into two parts. First, there is the emphasis upon the terrible battering inflicted upon the victim's body. Pauline Hopkins quotes from a newspaper article in *Contending Forces* (1900): The victim "was bound to a tree, pieces of his flesh were stripped from his body, his eyes were gouged out, his ears cut off, his nose split open, and his legs broken at the knees" (223). In Stowers and Anderson's *Appointed* (1894), the victim is drawn through the streets while onlookers "gratified their desire of torture and their hatred of the Afro-American by kicking and beating him all the way, others by thrusting their knives into his quivering flesh" (347). Ultimately, as others try to save him from hanging, a mob leader "emptied part of the contents of a revolver into Saunders' body" (348). J. McHenry Jones's Harvey Meeks is also dragged through the streets to his death, while "little boys wantonly stuck their knives into his quivering flesh" (225). And he, too, is dispatched finally by gunfire, "a hundred revolvers" filling his "swaying body full of holes, putting the struggling soul beyond the reach of misery" (226). G. Langhorne Pryor's victim, in *Neither Bond nor Free* (1902), is subjected to the same kind of torture as Bud and Foresta Harper: "while the wretch was alive parts of the muscles of his arms and legs were chipped off. The flesh was cut from around his ribs, and the points of the knives were run into the loose folds of his flesh" (193). Like the details of whipping in the slave narrative, these descriptions are intended to demonstrate the un-Christian barbarity with which blacks are generally treated and the unbelievable inhumanity of the widespread practice.

The second part into which the standard features of the lynching picture fall has to do with the mob itself—not its psychological motives but the impact of its behavior upon the senses and emotions of the reader, represented by the novelists as something like the sound effects of a movie. In fact, one of the more effective devices used by several of the authors is the "voice" of the lynch mob to convey its peculiar awfulness: "with fiendish glee, the crowd shouted" (*Appointed,* 347); "A wild yell, like the roar of a horde of hungry, ferocious brutes, greets this information"; "The bystanders hurled vile epithets at him as he passed" (*Hearts of Gold,* 225, 226); Abe Overley's sister, who is whipped to death in Robert L. Waring's *As We See It* (1910), suffers the "curses" and "vile remarks and jeers of these merciless wretches" (107). Like the slaveowner or the overseer in the slave narratives, the lynch mob has a "voice." Its unearthly cries are analogous to the furious oaths of those who applied the lash to the erring slave and have something of the same function: to demonstrate the contrast between the animalistic irrationality of the white man and the suffering humanity of the innocent black victim.

A distinction must be made here between what African American novelists in this period saw to be significant in the lynch mob and what more recent commentators have come to emphasize. For Trudier Harris, whose useful work on the topic pretty much sums up perhaps thirty years of psychological analysis of the lynch mob, the most important thing about this mob is what its actions say about the southern white man. His proclivity for lynching grows largely out of his psychosexual problems, his adherence to "the myth of the black man's unusual ability in sexual intercourse,"[23] and his fear and jealousy of and irresistible fascination with that ability. In her paradigm, ritual lynching is a sexual drama in which the white man, driven by these repressed sexual emotions, symbolically rapes the black man, experiencing ecstasy over both the achievement of superiority and the sexual release that comes with it. The "shout" or "yell" of the mob marks the highest point of tension in the ritual, rising to its highest pitch when the victim finally dies. At this point, the yell gives "way to the silence of complete (sexual) purgation, the ultimate release from all tension."[24] This pattern, it seems to me, conforms more accurately with Freudian theory than with the evidence of the novels. The references to the noise of the mob I quoted above locate its yells not at the point when the victim dies but at the moment he is found, or freed from jail, or when he is being dragged along the streets *before* reaching the designated lynching spot and before the flames reach him—if there are flames at all. But even if the shout does occur at the height of the flames or when the victim seems at last to have succumbed, the novelists show no interest in using it as a metaphor for the sexual release of the repressed mob. For them the terror of the mob's voice comes in its threateningness, not its sexual pathology. One of the problems is that Harris extrapolates from far too few sources to get an accurate picture of these works. Of the twenty-one pieces, both novels and shorter works, she surveys over the course of her discussion, which contain explicit depictions of lynching, just four novels and a short story were written in the period 1892–1922. And of those, Chesnutt's *Marrow of Tradition* contains only a near lynching and hence no lynching scene, and *The Colonel's Dream* contains a lynching that is referred to only indirectly. Certainly the majority of these lynching novels do contain various phases of Harris's "ritual" lynching. A mob seizes and then tortures and kills a black victim.[25] But their aim is not to understand "the white man's need to suppress the black man" sexually[26] or to dramatize how lynching is a white man's device for "exorcising blackness" from his own twisted psyche.

This is easily seen in Pauline Hopkins's account of the mob's voice in *Winona: A Tale of Negro Life in the South and Southwest* (1902). In this novel, which first appeared as a serial in the *Colored American Magazine,* she has virtually an entire small town engulf its intended lynching victim, "like a dark river, with cries whose horror was indescribable. It was not the voices of human beings, but more like the cries of wild animals, the screaming of enraged hyenas, the snarling of tigers, the angry, inarticulate cries of thousands of wild beasts in infuriated pursuit of their prey, yet with a something in it more sinister and blood curdling, for they were men, and added a human ferocity." As the flames rise around the bound black man, "A thousand voiced cry of brutal triumph arose—not to the skies, so vile a thing could never find the heavenly blue. . . . They who speak or think lightly of a mob have never heard its voice or seen its horrible work" (367).[27] Hopkins's allusions are not to the repressed sexual jealousy of white males or the dark and subtle turnings of the unconscious. They are direct statements about the mob's terrifying animality. Nor could any contemporary living in that time of Social Darwinism and discussions of race miss the point: Whites place blacks near the animal bottom of the ladder of evolution, while they themselves behave like animals. This is what John Fiske claimed the higher species were losing, that "brute-inheritance" which was the human original sin.[28] Darwin, not Freud, is in Hopkins's mind, and in that of her contemporaries. Justice and outrage, not psycho-analysis, drive the novelists' depiction of lynching. Their concern, further-more, is for their own responses and their own outraged manhood, rather than the psychic workings of the white mind.

If the animality of the mob is expressed in its fearful yells, it also appears in the use of the lynching as an entertainment and the good humor with which the crowds observe the agony of the victim and the macabre scram-ble for the man or woman's flesh or other body parts as souvenirs of the event. In *Neither Bond nor Free,* "The pieces of flesh were then distributed among two or three hundred men in the mob who wrapped the bits in paper" and carried them off (193). Edward Austin Johnson, in *Light Ahead for the Negro* (1904), tells how a mob in Springfield, Ohio, takes a black man who shot a policeman out of jail, knocks him to the ground, shoots him, hangs him to a pole and crosstie, and riddles him with bullets. "Throughout it all perfect order was maintained and everyone seemed in the best of humor, joking with his nearest neighbor while reloading his revolver" (39). Negroes, he says, were hanged or burned "sometimes in the presence of thousands of people, who came in on excursion trains to see the sight, and, possibly, carry off a trophy consisting of a finger joint, a tooth or a portion of the victim's heart" (42). Charles Henry Holmes uses very much the same language in *Ethiopia* (1917) for recounting the lynching of his hero, Allan Dune, falsely accused of rape by a young white woman. The event draws spectators from the surrounding countryside. Ice cream is sold and children wait excitedly. The accusing girl lights the fire, and the brave black man dies without a "groan." "Only when the fire was so burnt out that the witnesses could denude the place of every scrap that might serve as a memento,—even to the very ashes,—did the mob slowly dis-perse" (128). Perhaps the most macabre "memento" is that taken from Harvey Meeks, when two members of the mob decapitate him, take his head into a tavern, and ask for a drink "for old Harvey" (*Hearts of Gold,* 227).

The children Holmes refers to in *Ethiopia* are frequently identified as members of these mobs, being trained up in the same kind of insensitive brutality as their fathers. In one of my previous references, "little boys wantonly stuck their knives into" Harvey Meeks as he was being dragged to his death. Sutton Griggs frames his account of the lynching of Bud and

Foresta Harper with the experience of nine-year-old Melville Brant, who feels that his status among his friends depends upon his seeing a lynching. The callousness he absorbs from the grown-ups' behavior comes through when he finds "a piece of the charred flesh in the ashes and bore it home," triumphant now that he has something to show his friends (133). Clearly, our novelists were banking on the expectation that a Victorian audience who believed that children's innocence needed protection from a wicked world would be appalled at the training of children to such violence. For most of our authors, the force behind this frightful education is the lower classes of uneducated whites. The lynch mobs are all but universally composed of white trash (see *Hearts of Gold,* 225) or "poor whites" (*Neither Bond nor Free,* 238) rather than the "best citizens." Cracker "blood asserts itself, no matter where you find it," says a white planter sympathetic to blacks in Waring's *As We See It.* Sounding the theme of several of these novelists, Waring's white planter contends that "anywhere this 'cracker' blood predominates, there you find a bloodthirsty sentiment towards the Negro" (179). Waring's strong imagery evokes the Darwinian point in favor of the African American. The crackers "are intractable, unteachable and incapable of cultivation. They simply multiply like the germs of a contagion, fighting ever at the vitals of the body politic" (180). This does not perhaps reach apocalyptic proportions, but it does turn the tables on the race-hatred books of the period that sail under the banner of science and contend that the Negro poses one of the great threats to the purity of the superior white race. It is, for most of these authors, the redneck who resides at the bottom of the evolutionary ladder and who represents the obstacle to a world of racial harmony. These forerunners of William Faulkner's Snopes clan are so endemic in these novels that there is no avoiding the detestation in which African Americans held them in this period.

THE VIOLENT HERO: A MINORITY REPORT

The lynch mob was a useful metaphor. It could be used to single out those elements of the white race which were most pernicious, allowing the novelists to excuse what they saw as a majority of whites who wished them well but were impeded in their good intentions by bad people. The white lynch mob broke its own laws, invading jails and seizing black prisoners awaiting due process. It carried out its nefarious acts with all but total impunity. Its members were seldom arrested or tried, much less punished for their crimes.[29] Such protection for the element that stood so frighteningly in the way of its advancement left the black community cut off from judicial protection or redress and saddled it with the responsibility for discovering ways to deal with the white peril. This turns us from the literary imagery evoked by racial violence back to the question of how to respond, what model of behavior best serves the besieged community. Frederick Douglass and T. Thomas Fortune had, in the early stages of the lynching phenomenon, created the "militant wing" of the black reaction. As Donald L. Grant says, this sentiment flourished during the 1890s and the early twentieth century "in the literary, cultural, and historical socie-ties." [30] It was founded on the policy of the well-known phrasing of Thomas Fortune I referred to in the last chapter, "stand and shoot" rather than "stand and be shot."

The "conservative wing," on the other hand, says Grant, was "repre-sented by the fundamentalist clergy and the Southern educators, financed by white philanthropy and relying upon divine Providence and the devel-opment of liberal capitalist democracy to overcome the vestiges of slavery and to eliminate lynching." [31] It was a war of rhetoric, though, rather than action, in which pride and honor vied with realism and practicality. It is true that in the decades after the Civil War freedpersons organized among themselves and used firearms and group action to prevent lynchings. Her-bert Shapiro, Edward Ayers, and Eric Foner, three of the most recent commentators on the subject, identify isolated instances of blacks banding together and rescuing men or women threatened with lynching or pro-tecting threatened persons or property. But on the whole, they turn up no evidence of any widespread use of violence in the black community as a defense or retaliation against white violence. In general, most of Shapiro's details are of black victimization; Ayers contends that "Black violence against whites was not a common occurrence"; and Foner is "surprised" at "how few instances" there were in the years after the Civil War in which "blacks attacked whites." The Freedmen's Bureau records frequent attacks of blacks against blacks, but "violence or even threats against individual whites were all but unknown." [32] In *The Anti-Lynching Movement,* Grant concludes that "The Black consensus [on responding to lynching] fell between the extremes of retaliatory violence and quiet acceptance. In the 1890s there was general agreement that individual Blacks would sometimes find themselves in situations where militant self-defense was called for, and such martyrs were to be admired, but the race as a whole should avoid major confrontations." [33]

These oppositions express the models of the violent warrior-hero and the nonviolent forgiving Christian advanced in the post-Civil War years that I reviewed in the previous chapter. The public discourse on violence between 1892 and 1922 was no more uniform or consistent than in the previous period. As before, our novelists, participating in that discourse, set out to create images to promote self-esteem and project models of pride and manliness, culture heroes and heroines. They sought to articulate in character, action, and imagery community attitudes toward lynching and other violence, which played such havoc with their sense of self-respect and their climb out of poverty and ignorance. As in the previous period, the nonviolent model predominates, but with qualifications and modifiers. Let me cite first the two of the twenty-four novelists I cover in this period who produce an unequivocal warrior-hero in the line of Martin Delany's Henry Blake. They are Robert L. Waring in *As We See It* (1910) and Herman Dreer in *The Immediate Jewel of His Soul* (1919). Though both authors take a clear stand in favor of retaliatory violence, their heroes are quite different from each other. Waring's youthful Abe Overley follows a very private, even secretive, line of action. Dreer's Will Smith is very much a public man, a leader, an organizer. Together the two characters represent a wide range of belief—from the conviction that black men must act on their own to the advocacy of social action and politics based on a strong, courageous leader.

Waring's originating act of violence is not a lynching in the conventional sense. It is the murder of two respectable black women. Waring does call it a lynching, and he does have conventional lynch mob types carry it out— a gang of five crude rednecks who are envious of the men to whose family the women belong. But they are not typical. They make up what W. Fitzhugh Brundage calls a "private mob," small groups who "devoted more attention to secrecy than to ceremony. Elaborate ritual served little purpose for [such mobs]," because they were "consumed by personal griev- ances and the lust for revenge."[34] This precisely applies to the men who kill the Overley women, for Buck Lashum, an unregenerate "cracker" for whom education can do nothing, despises the intelligent and well-liked young Abe Overley for embarrassing him at the northern college they both attend. We can see Waring, though clumsily, working to use literary techniques to produce literary effects.[35] That is, he seeks to give his story a classical quality, in which the action is based on private vengeance, like a Greek or Shakespearean tragedy. The same effort accounts for another atypical feature that Waring writes into his atrocity: the method of violence. Lashum and his brutal cronies employ whipping carried out like the old slave punishment. Waring's account of the atrocity, in fact, seems a deliber- ate imitation of similar passages in the slave narratives, right down to the outrage against feminine virtue of disrobing the victims. The old and the young women are bound to trees and whipped in the slave fashion "with a leather horse-trace," both "stripped bare to the waist by these 'Alabama gentlemen.' " The girl, by the end of the last phase of the ordeal, is "perfectly nude" (106–7). Waring is the only author who suggests a substantial quotient of prurience in the lynching process, and in this case that is because he brings back in the slave experience. Waring is also one of the few of these authors to make the lynching central to the hero's experience. He creates a crime that strikes at the heart of black manly self-respect, for it suggests that black men are so weak they cannot protect their women. This is the same code, of course, that ostensibly drives the lynching myth, the powerful symbolism of women for the patriarchal world. It implies that the culture's demonic enemies attack the male through their weak and helpless women. Basic to the male's manliness is his obligation (and ability) to protect his most valuable cultural possession. Waring, like Dreer, adopts the same code as Thomas Dixon, Winston Churchill, Maurice Thompson.

Waring presents the two extreme responses to the outrage against the Overley women. He does not scorn forgiving old Abe Overley's attempts to dissuade his lifelong friend and former master, Malcolm Overley, and his other white friends from seeking their own justice for the bereaved ex-slave: "Ef yo' does 'venge yo'se'f on dese people," says the old man, "an' take dey life, yo' souls will be los' . . . I dun forgin dese people. Why yo' gemmen not do de same?" (131–32). Abe's capacity to forgive, doubtless modeled after Stowe's Uncle Tom, is made all the more pious by the white minister's readiness to bend the commandment about not killing: "Still, when one considers the wanton brutality attending the crime," the "good minister" says, "there may be some excuse, should the passions and desire for revenge, common to all human beings, get beyond control" (110). But Waring is far too ambivalent about Abe to make him a pure Uncle Tom. "I tink," says old Abe, "dat a 'nigger' oughter fight ebry po' white man dat don't treat him or he kinfolks right" (27). And in a declaration that essentially endorses his son's later quest for vengeance, he claims he would have killed the white trash drunk who tried to attack his daughter, Sally Jane, "on de road dat night," if Malcolm had not hidden his gun (29).

Young Abe is an advanced version of his father. Educated, never knowing the humiliation of slavery, he is a blend of the avenger and the warrior. He, not the white men led by Malcolm Overley, undertakes to avenge the violation of his mother and sister. Moreover, he sets his determination in the context of a higher and larger justice. A college student with a strong sense of justice and his own rights, young Abe embodies the generation of the new Negro who rejects the Christian humility of Uncle Tom. He is cultured, articulate, and well spoken. But it is just these qualities that charge Abe with the dynamic tensions with which Waring wants to elevate the action to potentially tragic levels. Like Macbeth, like Ahab, he invokes the "avenging demon" to help him kill the five white murderers of his sister and mother:

If there be a demon; if there be a devil; if there be an imp of hell; if there be a force that will turn blood to gall, love to hate, good to bad—come to me that I may feel thy full force; come to me that I may forget that I am human, until I have avenged this wrong, perpetrated upon my mother and sister! . . . By the God that made me, and with aid of the demons of hell, whose help I implore, I will be revenged! (121)

These melodramatized Shakespearean cadences are loaded with the contradictions of the various debates over the use of violence, the choice of the model hero, the question of black humanity, and the discussion of evolution. If, as James M. Redfield says, the great Homeric hero "is also latently the beast,"[36] Waring is tapping into that tradition as his protagonist eagerly casts off a humanity that was transcendently precious to blacks in other contexts. Indeed, Abe springs upon one of his enemies "with a cry that resembled [that of] a wild beast" (194). His heroism lies precisely in his courage to violate the normal laws of civilization, for they don't, of course, work for him. "Though I face death at the fiery stake in this world, though I am sure to be engulfed in the fires of hell in the next world, my mother shall be avenged" (171). Waring's implication seems to be that it requires barbarity to do away with barbarity. "[W]hen the State was not strong enough, as in this case, to right such wrongs," says young Abe, the aggrieved must act on his own. "The time is now come when Negroes should kill the man or men who on the slightest provocation lynch or take the lives of their kinsmen. When they learn to do that, we will have fewer murderers of this character to mar our civilization" (161). As Leslie Fiedler might say, Waring gives young Abe Overley the courage to damn himself in order to achieve a higher goal than his own salvation.

In what seems to be a deliberate paradox, Waring suggests that Abe's vengeful savagery is ultimately the sign of the highest civilized attainment. It is only to be expected, says Oberlin College's Dean Sternly to a group of white professors who object to Abe's plans for revenge, that Abe, educated "along your lines," would act the man in the same way "any other human being [would] that has taken on your education and civilization" (130). To control one's rage in the face of such provocation is, suggests Waring, not civilized behavior but a renunciation of one's humanity. To give way to the animal in one is more "natural" and manly than self-control. To deny this, says Dean Sternly, is to use one "code of ethics" for whites and another for blacks (129). "You educate him, then ostracize him, apparently for taking on your teachings" (131). He finds justification for his retaliatory violence in Oberlin College president Dr. Finley's soberly judicious concluding words: "in the absence of courts and juries," blacks have to take upon themselves the duty of revenge (131–32). There is no other source of justice, for the grand jury exonerates the five white killers, to the smug sneers of the Lashums.

So Abe, whose honor is as sacred as that of any white man, aristocrat or redneck, slays the white murderers that his father forgives. One by one he tracks them down, a relentless nemesis, killing each one separately with the same trace with which they killed his mother and sister, glorying in their terror when he catches them, and scorning their cowardly pleas for mercy. This is an act of heroic manliness that should make other blacks proud and show whites that blacks will not let murder go unpunished. In fact, he returns to the North and school, and he is assisted by two wealthy and powerful white men into a prosperous career as owner of the very land his old father lived on as a slave. He has killed not in order to become white but to live his black life with self-respect and the material rewards his intelligence, breeding, and education deserve. Appropriately, therefore, he marries the beautiful mulatto heroine who has shown herself worthy by supporting Abe in his heroic enterprise. These are the compensations of "those Negro men who dare defend the womanhood of their race," as Waring says in his "Forward" (5). The races can live together more peacefully when both deserve and receive the respect of the other.

This is not, however, the opening skirmish in a racial war against all whites. The true enemy is the ignorant, Negro-hating cracker. Waring even finds a black analogy to the Lashums, sinister and devious Black Sue, a kind of harpy who loves evil and hates good. It is she who encourages Buck Lashum to kill the Overley women, out of her own bottomless spite. But she is repaid when one of her own sons is killed for informing on Abe: "This drunken, worthless scion, the most worthless of all her illegitimate brood, was her favorite" (155). The "better whites" are friends of the African American. If old Abe is ready to defend himself and other blacks against the coarse and hateful incursions of the Lashums, even while in the end he balks at actual killing, he does feel that blacks cannot claim equal footing with the "better whites" and therefore should not have the effrontery to dispute with them on anything. They are the true America for which, in the end, young Abe expresses his undying love. In a deliberate mirroring of the conventional romantic white novel, Waring leaves Abe "on his plantation in the full enjoyment of home life, surrounded by his father and growing family, his wealth and usefulness increasing as the years speed by, increasing as the wealth and usefulness of many Negroes before him, and as the wealth and usefulness of many Negroes who come after him will increase," the grateful beneficiary of what finally is a benevolent system in which good whites, controlling the ultimate power, collaborate with the good blacks to produce a prosperous and happy world (232). It is hard to say to what degree this is purely a crude wish-fulfillment fantasy or a defiant appropriation of white romance. In either case, *As We See It* is one of the more unusual novels of this period.

Dreer, nearly a decade later, is less flamboyant than Waring in his portrayal of the resistance to lynching, but his focus is the same. Old Uncle Abbot, his forgiving Christian, of whom Dreer is considerably less forgiving than Waring of old Abe Overley, reacts to a particularly vicious and unjustifiable lynching with a pusillanimous quietude. His solution to the terror, like Uncle Tom's, is to "Just wait on the Lord" (25).[37] Dreer makes his argument against this retreat a generational one, reflecting the influence of the World War I period when dramatic changes were sweeping through the black community. He explicitly gives his characters the label of "old" and "new" Negro (243). His hero has none of the avenger in his makeup. William Smith is a warrior-hero of the purest type. Whereas young Abe Overley is driven by his sense of honor and the rage to "kill! kill! kill!" (122), Dreer's Smith has a vision of a "new South" in which the manly type he represents will take his rightful place in a reformed democracy. This can be brought about only by courageous resistance against the lynch mob. When a rabble of disgruntled crackers mobilize to attack Smith's agricultural cooperative and lynch the far-seeing young agronomist and minister, he arms his farmers and turns the cowards away. Like Delany's Henry Blake, Smith turns to violence not for personal satisfaction but rather to bring into existence a more expansive South and a larger social good. An unmixed warrior-hero, he puts whites on notice that blacks will use violence to protect their rights. If we all did this, says Smith, "the problem [of lynching] would be solved overnight" (243). In Dreer's fantasy, Smith's firm stand is the first step toward the creation of a "New South" (243). Indeed, Smith marries a "new woman" at the end of the novel, one over whom "Outworn creeds and customs have no power" and who is at Smith's side when he turns away the lynch mob.

TRYING FOR CONCILIATION

Robert Waring and Herman Dreer present strictly minority opinions in the case of the black response to lynching. The other novelists reflect the community's deep ambivalence about violent self-defense and retaliation, forgiveness, right and wrong, and the practical and ideal means by which blacks can best achieve a free, safe, and competitive place in American society. On the whole, after much pawing of the dirt and waving of the horns, they reject counterviolence as an effective solution to the problem of lynching and the general racial oppression it stands for. But, in doing so, they show the dynamics of the broad debate transpiring in the black community and their frustration that they cannot demonstrate their manhood through physical force against injustice and at the same time keep to the standard of Christian nonviolence and protect their dependents from jeopardy. We find them often blending conciliation with aggressiveness, reassurance with threats. The attempt to go in opposite directions at the same time is not surprising when their aims are contradictory. While they want to show their black readers models of courageous men and women in whom all can find self-esteem, they also want to calm the uneasiness of whites by demonstrating they have nothing to fear from blacks. Their stated purpose is to bring concord between the races, not provoke war. Frances Harper hopes, as I pointed out in the last chapter, that *Iola Leroy* will "awaken in the hearts of our countrymen a stronger sense of justice and a more Christlike humanity" (462). Pauline Hopkins's aim in writing *Contending Forces* is "to raise the stigma of degradation from my race" and cement "the bond of brotherhood among all classes and all complexions" (13). And Charles Henry Holmes addresses *Ethiopia: The Land of Promise* to "the enlightened members of each of the races" in order to persuade them to "do their best to ameliorate [the conditions he describes in the book] by diffusing more freely the light of education and culture" and help the African American to acquire "the fullest and most complete title to the enjoyment of life, liberty; and unalloyed happiness." [38]

The figures in these novels, however, vary greatly in carrying out this mission. The handful of "avengers" that appear are hardly instruments of reconciliation. They fall into the tradition of Brown's Picquilo and Delany's Gofer Gondolier. Charles W. Chesnutt's Josh Green and Sutton Griggs's Gus Martin both smile, even as they die, after killing their own personal white enemies. Griggs even satirizes the type with his character "A. Hostility," who defines himself as "the incarnation of hostility" to the Anglo-Saxon race.[39] Pauline Hopkins's Judah, in her magazine novel *Winona: A Tale of Negro Life in the South and Southwest* (1902), passionately hates former slave trader Bill Thomson, saying, "I am the Lord's instrument to kill this man." But unlike the other avengers, Judah loses his fierceness. Under the moral urging of his foster sister Winona, at the point when he could dispatch his enemy, he feels himself mastered by "the sheer human repulsion from such butchery" (394, 423). The "forgiving Christian," like Delany's Mammy Judy and Daddy Joe, is often not much more helpful than the avenger. This personage reappears in these novels in garb as ambiguous and various as that of the antebellum novel. On the one hand, there is the sympathetic, but wrong, old Abe Overley in Waring's *As We See It.* On the other, there is the fawning and servile turncoat in W. E. B. Du Bois's *Quest of the Silver Fleece,* a "white folks' nigger" who informs on his own people for attention from whites.[40] To complicate matters, the "avenger" some-times mutates into a warrior-hero, and the "forgiving Christian" into a nonviolent activist hero or heroine.

It is the latter figure that dominates in these novels and that seeks to carry out the peaceful enterprise outlined by Charles Henry Holmes. This character comprises a definition of "hero" that excludes the use of violence. As Frances Harper is the first to lay lynching at the center of the condition most in need of redress, so she is the first to create in the post–Civil War period this new type of hero. It is not that she is unaware of the militant approach or refuses it due respect. Like the other novelists of the period, she associates the call to violence with the younger generation, in whom Iola's older aunts and uncles perceive a new hardiness, a refusal to accept passively the blows of the white man. They are ready, as old Salters's grandson says to him, to "pull a trigger as well as a white man." This does not arouse suspicions among Harper's oldsters. It hardens their resolve. Salters makes up his mind "dat my boy should neber call me a coward" (367). But Harper gives no more than minor billing to the warrior stance. Perhaps it is her roots in the nonviolent prewar abolitionist movement, but the valid position among the activist young is that of Iola and the man with whom she falls in love, Dr. Frank Latimer. Representing her "ideal of a high, heroic manhood" (446, 453), Latimer operates not through revolu-tion or retaliation but with civility, goodwill, and the Christian virtues. His position dovetails with that of the older generation. As the elder Dr. Car-micle puts it, with the hearty approval of Iola, "For the evils of society there are no solvents as potent as love and justice [and] a religion replete with life and glowing with love" (442).

Lynching does not drive the plot in *Iola Leroy.* The novel is about the separation of the Leroy family under slavery, the tenacious efforts of the children to reunite it, and the upheavals of the Civil War that both help and hinder those efforts. It takes us from the South to the North and back again, and it tracks Iola's late-in-the-book love affair and the emergence of a cultivated and activist postwar African American community devoted to eradicating lynching and unfair discrimination. For all its tangentiality, though, lynching, for Harper, is the symbol of a South that makes reunion difficult and continues to endanger members of the family who wish to stay in the region to work. Reunion and the struggle against violence, and its offshoots of politicoeconomic oppression, stimulate the need for Iola to marry her hero. She and Frank Latimer embody all that is finest in the freed Negro, members of a revitalized segment of African Americans which W. E. B. Du Bois later calls the "talented tenth." They lead the struggle by action and example. Both Iola and Frank could pass, but they pointedly refuse to do so. Something in their blood seems to give them a natural superiority. Instead of turning to the violence meretriciously glorified by the Ku Klux Klan, Harper's ideal African Americans assume the role of the progressive humanitarian, becoming "friend[s] of the poor and ignorant" rather than "men who mask their faces and ride the country on lawless raids" (407). Harper spotlights the refusal of Iola and Frank to live as members of the "favored race," having them prefer to spend their "future among the colored people of the South" (420). Their mixed blood contains a kind of consecration, exalted by "grand and noble purposes." They are the harbingers of a new age, a "new commonwealth of freedom," and it is a "blessed privilege" for them to stand on its "threshold" (453). Their role is not only to reunite the immediate Leroy family and the larger extended family from the old plantation but nonviolently to redeem the violated, restore social cohesion, and set in motion the machinery for a better world. Such is the state of affairs as the novel closes: "The shadows have been lifted from all their lives; and peace, like bright dew, has descended upon their paths. Blessed themselves, their lives are a blessing to others" (461).

THE NONVIOLENT HERO

Like *Iola Leroy,* most of the other novels of violence in this period demonstrate the belief in the use of fiction for purveying political and social propaganda and the continued influence of a popular taste that is both pious and sentimental. It is easy to see the unsentimental anger in many of these novels, but it is overlaid by a tone of earnest optimism mixed with ambivalence and caution and the tenacious hope that gentility of style and character will, as Barbara Christian puts it, "affect the historical moment."[41] Their dominant vision is that of reasonable, civilized Christians attempting to nurture a struggling culture against the unprovoked excesses of social passion and political brutishness, though the image of the gun-toting, militant upholder of racial honor never completely disappears from their horizon. They claim that whites are more likely to respond to peaceful, unthreatening action than to violence. As William Wells Brown had suggested in his first version of *Clotel* (1853), violence only brings more violence and so negates the result desired. Yet, there is almost always a character who argues for the gun.

After Chesnutt and James Weldon Johnson, Sutton Griggs is the most important of these early novelists, partly for his output—five novels between 1899 and 1908—and partly for his skill in embodying the intractability of the issue of violence. He recognizes its allure for black manhood and its commensurate danger; the anger and frustration that make it appealing to otherwise orderly people and its threat to comity. Griggs is a bit hamhanded with symbols, but he has a real sense of how to project the opposing sides of the argument to emphasize their irreconcilability, often casting a radical character against a conservative one—Earl Bluefield against Ensal Ellwood in *The Hindered Hand,* for instance. He does this most effectively in *Imperium in Imperio: A Study of the Negro Race Problem* (1899). Peace-inclining Belton Piedmont is unable to accept the proposal for armed revolt his old friend Bernard Belgrave presents to the Imperium, a secret national organization convened to plan for dealing with the African American's deep problems. When the group ratifies the plan, Belton resigns rather than support the organization against his principles. This is a choice for death, however, because only death can remove a member (254). With tears in his eyes for his old companion, Bernard, as president, orders Belton executed. Though Griggs lacks the artistry to convey the feeling of tragedy here, he clearly intends this situation to be tragic. As narrator he takes no sides. It is the conflict that interests him. In the last chapter, however, he gives the reader some guidelines for judging by shifting back to the point of view of Berl Trout, whose "papers," as Griggs has explained in the prefatory "To the Public," are the novel we have just read and who is himself one of the members of the firing squad that executes Belmont. In a kind of fusion of the John of Revelation and the John Bunyan of *Pilgrim's Progress,* Griggs creates a visionary world in which Bernard Belgrave is revealed as an anguished but fanatical avenger, whose violent plans could ignite an apocalypse which Berl "sees" in his mind's eye.

I felt [writes Berl] that beneath the South a mine had been dug and filled with dynamite, and that lighted fuses were lying around in careless profusion, where any irresponsible hand might reach them and ignite the dynamite. I fancied that I saw a man do this very thing in a sudden fit of uncontrollable rage. There was a dull roar as of distant rumbling thunder. Suddenly there was a terrific explosion and houses, fences, trees, pavement stones, and all things on earth were hurled high into the air to come back a mass of ruins such as man never before had seen. The only sound to be heard was a universal groan; those who had not been killed were too badly wounded to cry out. (264)

This is a powerful image for catching the volatility of the southern racial situation during this period. It epitomizes the whole difficult question of how to respond to white atrocities, embracing the irreconcilable concerns of needing to play the man with violence and worrying about cataclysm. It warns of the dangers of continued white violence that could ignite a holocaust in the dried tinder of black rage. With such a vision tormenting him, Berl determines to expose the Imperium as the current gravest danger, believing it will cost him his life, as it cost Belmont Piedmont his. But "I die for mankind," says Berl, "for humanity, for civilization" (264). He pleads in his final moments for "all mankind" to "help my poor down-trodden people," for while they will for the time being await their liberty peacefully, they will not wait much longer: "Love of liberty is such an inventive genius, that if you destroy one device it at once constructs another more powerful" (265). Griggs as author avoids making a choice for either approach. He leaves that for his characters to argue out. The result is that figures in his novels who embrace opposing philosophies might both be called heroes. This may produce unsettling ambiguity, but it does give us the broad picture of which in other novelists we may see only a part.[42]

Most of the other novelists of the period take the same attitude toward the hero that Griggs takes. They transform the warrior and his avenger cohort into nonviolent activists. Indeed, if a culture hero emerges in this fiction, this is it. He is manly without killing, reasonable without coward-ice, moderate without passivity. He is no servile lickspittle; he may forgive, but he never surrenders his manhood. He is educated and mannerly, as much at home in the laboratory or the academy as in the drawing room. Above all, he seeks change through nonviolent action, with the threat of violence as the very last resort of desperation. The first of the type is Iola Leroy's sweetheart, Frank Latimer, but he is by no means the last. The sympathetic protagonist of J. McHenry Jones's *Hearts of Gold* (1896) ap-proaches lynching through the kind of intelligent and informed sensitivity that Frances Harper put into her hero: "just so long as the conscience of a people is so callous that it finds entertainment in seeing human beings roasted alive with all the eclat of a political barbecue, such people need missionaries rather than cold lead."[43] Will Smith, Pauline Hopkins's version of Frank Latimer in *Contending Forces* (1900), maintains that "Brute force will not accomplish anything. We must *agitate*," just as the abolitionists did before Emancipation, and "appeal for the justice of our cause to every civilized nation under the heavens" (272). The novelists who hold this position suggest, like Frances Harper's Dr. Gresham, that lynching will yield to reason, agitation, evidence of black worthiness, and that to answer violence with violence is neither logically nor morally consistent.[44] Griggs makes the point relative to John Wysong in *Overshadowed* (1901). Wysong's "error" in killing a white man was his appropriation "to his own use the very principle from the effects of which he believed himself to be suffering" (171).

S. P. Fullinwider suggests that the Christian ideal, during slave times a practical means of survival, later became a "source of self-esteem because it allowed the Negro to compare favorably the Christ-like Negro with the inhuman white man," who talked Christianity but practiced barbarity. If the Christian position could lead to death at the hands of the white lynch mob, the martyr deliberately allows himself to be used as a "weapon" in what Fullinwider calls "a mission to make reforms in this world."[45] But these novels, full of victims, contain few of the sorts of martyrs like Sergeant Plancionois and the members of the First Louisiana Regiment that we met with in the last chapter. Except for two or three occasions,[46] the lynching victim is not the protagonist-activist but either a secondary character, whom we sometimes like and sometimes do not, or one whose only role is to be subjected to the atrocities of the practice. The hero and his sweetheart survive and help to recast America morally.

IT ISN'T RAPE: THE WAR OF THE COUNTERSTEREOTYPES

These young activists pose no material threat to whites, and that is one of the functions of their nonviolence. This is how these novelists reassure nervous whites that they have nothing to fear from the people whose friends and relatives are being lynched. As Griggs's Ensal Ellwood writes in his appeal after the lynching of Bud and Foresta Harper in *The Hindered Hand*, "We love your institutions, and if your flag could speak, it would tell you that it has no fear of the dust when entrusted to our sable hands" (159). This is an answer to the black stereotype southern whites invent and then use to prove the black man's danger to the white men and their women.

In *Southern Horrors*, Ida B. Wells says that the white press defends lynching on the ground that it protects "weak and defenseless women" from "the horrible and beastly propensities of the Negro race." Wells quotes from an editorial in the Memphis *Daily Commercial*, whose argument suffers from the logical fallacy of begging the question, proving an increase of rapes by the increase in lynching. Whites cannot feel safe, says the editorial, in their own houses with such creatures prowling around, especially in the rural sections. Nor can "laws or lynchings . . . subdue his lusts." The problem is that the Negro has lost his "traditional and wholesome awe of the white race which [during slavery] kept the Negroes in subject[ion], even when their masters were in the army, and their families left unprotected except by the slaves themselves. There is no longer a restraint upon the brute passion of the Negro." Wells's purpose is to counteract these absurd stereotypes and self-serving exaggerations and distortions, and to "give the world a true, unvarnished account of the causes of lynch law in the South," through "an array of facts . . . which it is hoped will stimulate this great American Republic to demand that justice be done though the heavens fall." "The Afro-American is not a bestial race," she asserts in her preface. "If this work can contribute in any way toward proving this, and at the same time arouse the conscience of the American people to a demand for justice to every citizen, and punishment by law for the lawless, I shall feel I have done my race a service." [47]

The abundant commentary on lynching and rape makes it necessary only to recall the topic's main outline: that from the beginning white men claimed that rape was the main reason blacks were lynched, that historically blacks sought to disprove the charge, and that nearly every study done on lynching has found the claim to be exaggerated at the least and false at the most. [48] The stereotype hinges on the nineteenth-century image of first the slave and then the freedman as a brute, an animal capable of speech, perhaps, but forever immune to the restraints of civilized society and devoting every waking effort to couple with the white female. From this axiom, other assumptions followed: that racial purity was under constant threat, that proximity of black men and white women inevitably led to rape, and that lynching was the only effective response to this danger. The insatiable appetite of slavering black brutes for virginal white women posed a unique and extreme threat that had to be met with unique and extreme methods by this besieged superior civilization. In *The Crucible of Race,* Joel Williamson makes a case for this stereotype being a product of the early 1890s, when a "crisis of sex and race" occurred. Black rapists sprang up all over the South, and rapes increased wonderfully. The white supremacists claimed that this crisis produced the sudden increase in lynching. [49] Williamson does not explore the causes of the emergence of the stereotype of the black brute and the abrupt increase in the white man's concern for protecting his women from blacks. But it was widely alluded to, with some scorn, by Negro observers, who pointed out that such a fear had not prevented the southern soldier from leaving his family in the care of black slaves while he went off to war. White supremacists replied that slavery had kept the black man's carnal appetites in check. Freedom removed that check. Winfield H. Collins sums up the argument in *The Truth about Lynching* (1918). When blacks were freed and given power they were incapable of handling by self-serving northern carpetbaggers, they began using their new authority to rape white women. This was more than the honorable white southern male could bear, so he responded with the most effective weapon he could muster: lynching. "[It] is seen," writes Collins, that by 1873–75 "rape was practically the only cause for the lynching of Negroes in the South." Indeed, "rape continued to be, if not the whole cause for the lynching of Negroes in the South, anyhow almost that, with other crimes as merely incident."[50]

This was all part of the "lynching mythology," as Donald Grant puts it, with the white southerner insisting that Reconstruction had fostered expectations of social equality among black men that gave them the idea they could have white women as they wished.[51] Beneath this lies the even more basic layer of the mythology, which is advanced as science by a writer like the German immigrant Frederick L. Hoffman, the statistician for the Prudential Insurance Company: that bestial black men, who are inherently immoral, criminal, and animalistic, are irresistibly and "strangely" attracted to the "foreignness" of white women, and their lust is not fully satisfied unless they butcher their victim after intercourse has been completed.[52]

Whatever we in restrospect might make of the southern white argument justifying lynching—that it masks a campaign for the restoration of social, economic, and political white supremacy; that it discloses serious psychosexual problems in southern white males; that it shows how both white women and black men were manipulated by white males[53]—it prevailed, and large sections of the white public in the North as well as the South tacitly or overtly concurred in it. Every black man became a potential rapist and every lynching a justified punishment of a rape committed or prevention of a rape attempted.

It is now an old story that not only are the accusations of rape nearly always false, rape is not even the most frequent charge against the victim by the mob. Ida B. Wells saw without too much trouble the falseness of the claim about rape. In *Southern Horrors,* she wrote that between 1884 and 1892 "only *one-third* of the 728 victims to mobs have been *charged* with rape, to say nothing of those of that one-third who were innocent of the charge." Walter F. White and Arthur F. Raper confirm that by far the majority of lynchings occur when a black man steps out of line, behaves in an insolent manner, or does in fact kill a white man, rather than when he is found raping, or attempting to rape, a white woman.[54] Even Theodore Roosevelt occasionally admitted "that 75 per cent of all lynching was for other reasons."[55] The African American counterargument flows from these convictions: (1) Blacks are not given to raping white women, (2) raping accusations are virtually always false, and (3) few lynchings actually are performed as the result of rape. More recently, Fitzhugh Brundage makes clear that, like everything else having to do with lynching, rape accusations lie in muddy waters. The southern white lynch mob tended to define rape much more loosely than did opponents of lynching. For the southern white man bent on keeping black men and white women apart, a mere glance, a playful nudge by a schoolmate, the asking of a question might be construed as rape, as well as the unwelcome truth that a southern white woman had actually entered into sexual relations with a black man voluntarily. When such definitions were used to identify the crime for which a mob lynched a black man, it is no wonder that "rape" could be said to be the cause of so many lynchings.[56]

The African American novelists of this period did not understand the economic, political, and psychological motives that are now believed to have lain beneath lynching. Even if they had, though, they would have had to take note of the charges made and accepted against the race, and to demonstrate that blacks are not what whites say they are, and that the southern justification of lynching is something other than what whites claim it is. The peculiar thing is that of the twenty-four novels dealing with lynching only two contain a direct attack on the charge of rape. In *Contending Forces* (1900), Pauline E. Hopkins presents a wide-ranging discussion in which her speakers express their version of the truth about rape and lynching. Rape, they say, is the most common accusation for which black men are lynched, yet not more than one out of a hundred accused is actually guilty of the act. Whites manipulate the truth about rape because it is "the crime which appeals most strongly to the heart of the home life" and hence arouses the most animosity in the populace. Hopkins makes no reference to the fear that black men threaten white men's sexual superiority. But she does base her rebuttal on the conviction that the southern white's stated reasons justifying lynching are not his real reasons. In a long speech to the American Colored League, one of her protagonists, Will Smith, points out the irony of white men as a group *"bewailing the sorrows of violated womanhood,"* who themselves violated black womanhood in huge numbers to create *"the mulatto race . . . by the very means which they invoked lynch law to suppress!"* No, says Will, almost articulating the economic and social motives behind lynching, rape is simply a pretext to justify the lynch mob, and lynching "is but a subterfuge for killing men . . . instituted to crush the manhood of the enfranchised black" (271).

Sutton Griggs, in *The Hindered Hand,* carries the exposure of the lies about rape to its extreme conclusion—that white men themselves do not believe them, that they cynically use the lie to cover over their unprovoked hatred of black skin and mask their brutal assertion of power. Thus, when a stranger asks a member of a lynch mob how it can be that Foresta Harper, a woman, can be lynched for the "one crime," that is, rape, he receives a cynical but truthful answer: "That's all rot about one crime. We lynch niggers down here for anything. We lynch them for being sassy and sometimes lynch them on general principles. The truth of the matter is the real 'one crime' that paves the way for a lynching whenever we have the notion, is the crime of being black" (136). This expresses the essence of the black novelist's perception of the motives that drive lynching. It is a sheer power play against the race, and the elevated rhetoric about saving civilization is, in the words of the truthful southerner, "rot." Griggs makes the point even more explicitly in *Overshadowed,* when his white politician Horace Christian trumps up a charge of rape against an anonymous black man. In a close race he needs the black vote, and gets it by pretending to come to the rescue of the falsely accused victim. His plan works and he is elected. He has taken advantage of the South's obsession with protecting white womanhood and made "it serve my purposes" (132).

But most of our authors pay little specfic attention to the issue of rape in their descriptions of lynching. If they can be said to attack the white claims of widespread rape as a justification for lynching, they do so indirectly, by citing other charges than rape. In our sample novels, just four out of the twenty-four cite rape as the charge against the lynched victims. If Ida B. Wells is correct in her claim that only 33 percent of the lynchings in the 1890s resulted from rape charges, then our authors use such charges at just half the documented rate, namely, 16 percent. If we counted all the lynchings referred to in these novels, the proportion would be even smaller. The accusations our novelists use range from no stated charge [57] to killing a rabbit on a white man's land.[58] Other charges are as follows: striking a white man *(Appointed),* defying a group of white toughs to protect a black child *(Hearts of Gold),* shooting a white man *(Contending Forces, The Hindered Hand, The Colonel's Dream),* killing a white woman—not rape *(The Marrow of Tradition, Light Ahead for the Negro),* gun possession *(The Quest of the Silver Fleece),* uppityness *(The Immediate Jewel of His Soul),* being too friendly with a white man *(Out of the Darkness).* This variety reflects the findings of most studies of lynching. James Elbert Cutler, who put the study of lynching on a scientific basis for the first time in 1905, found that the accusations actually made against the lynching victims do include rape, but more charges, as drawn from newspaper accounts, fall into such categories as murder, assault, theft, arson, and "desperadism." [59]

The more widely used technique for disputing the white stereotype of the black male as brute and black female as immoral chippy, and hence the whole argument legitimizing lynching, was the creation of models of black

deportment based on the Victorian manners and values of the white bourgeoisie. As Sterling Brown says, white people's lies about blacks called for
"propaganda . . . and propaganda [these novelists] gave, in good measure.
The race was their hero, and preaching a solution their business." They
hold up to the world "the millions of honest, God-fearing, industrious,
frugal, respectable, and self-respecting Negroes, who are toiling for the
salvation of their race." Against the white image of predatory savages on
the lookout for vulnerable white women, our novelists, as Brown puts it,
assert the image of the "talented tenth at its most genteel. The heroines are
modest and beautiful, frequently octoroon; the heroes are handsome and
priggish, and frequently black." [60] They argue, with "counterstereotypes,"
that African Americans are like whites and, like whites, observe the standard middle-class "virtues of industry, piety, and ambition." [61] Such counterstereotypes were intended both to underline the scandal of lynching
and to dismantle the caste system that made lynching possible. Virtually
without exception, the lynching victims are innocent men and women
who fall prey to jealous whites who cannot bear to see blacks successful
and create pretexts to destroy them, seeing rape in a friendly gesture and
murder in provoked self-defense. And when the counterstereotype is set
against the crude rednecks, with, we might surmise, tobacco juice dripping disgustingly from their brutish lips, the opposing sides are clearly
drawn. Thus, when beautiful light-skinned Elsa Mangus faces a howling
mob of cracker lynchers, in Charles Henry Holmes's *Ethiopia,* "virtue [was]
arrayed against vice; purity against foulness; justice and right against lust
and license" (84).

It was essential that the novelists' counterargument be believable, but
their evidence was often so appalling as to seem incredible. To avoid the
imputation of exaggeration, most of these writers describe lynchings with
the factual straightforwardness of journalism. They use the tactics of Ida B.
Wells, who made her case against lynching by quoting without comment
from prolynching southern periodical accounts of lynchings, accounts that
indicted their own authors.[62] They strive for verisimilitude, which they
practice much more faithfully when depicting a lynching than when telling
the stories of their romantic heroes and heroines. Verisimilitude is, in fact,
their main rhetorical weapon. In much the same way that the authors and
publishers of the slave narratives sought to establish the authenticity of their
stories, these novelists emphasize that the atrocities they describe are not
inventions sensationalized for commercial appeal. Sutton Griggs assures the
reader that "the details" of the torture of Bud and Foresta Harper "were
given the author by an eyewitness of the tragedy, a man of national reputa-

tion among the Negroes." And just as one of the conventions of the slave narrative came to be the suppression of some of the more detestable details of slave treatment in deference to the sensitive northern reader, so Griggs remarks that "Some of the more revolting features [of the Harper lynching] have been suppressed for decency's sake." [63]

Pauline Hopkins also carefully observes verisimilitude. To represent the reality of what is happening in the South as recorded by its own observers, she prints the article I quoted earlier, which she says comes from a southern white newspaper. Hopkins implies that no southern editor would invent such an account, and if the account is true, then surely it is evidence not of the success of lofty ideals of southern white supremacy but of the need to stop lynching. Like Hopkins and Griggs, W. E. B. Du Bois is concerned that people *believe* what he has written to be historically true. "In *The Quest of the Silver Fleece,*" he writes, "in no fact or picture have I consciously set down aught the counterpart of which I have not seen or known," [64] with the implication that the truth is so appalling it needs no invented fictions to amplify it.

With these factual accounts the novelists hope to enlighten whites who must be ignorant of the details of white violence against blacks in the South. If they were informed, it is inconceivable that they would sit by and do nothing. It is not threats of violent revolution that are used to stimulate white Americans to ameliorative action. It is logic and the evidence of brutality laid out before what the novelists believe to be a basically well-meaning people. Sutton Griggs, in *The Hindered Hand,* suggests that even the terrible lynching of Bud and Foresta Harper might have a positive result. Griggs's hero, Ensal Ellwood, extracts a promise from the sympathetic attorney who unsuccessfully prosecutes the Harpers' killers to help Ellwood in his campaign for black political equality. Ellwood wires to a colleague that the "Problem will now be solved," for the "better" whites, in control of the government, have gotten behind the campaign (293). This proves the superiority of Ellwood's nonviolent method over the violence of Earl Bluefield. Earlier, Bluefield symbolically kills himself as he unsuccessfully attempts to shoot Ensall (164). The psychic need to show heroic manhood through eye-for-an-eye retaliation does find its way into these pages. But moderation and restraint are the controlling emotions. The majority of African American novelists in this period criticize the lynch mob, but they suppose most whites to be good people simply waiting to be told the truth. And if they can, through their novels, bring that truth to the "better whites" in the persons of their sympathetic and respectable protagonists, violence will, perhaps, stop and equality reign.

MAKING THEIR OWN WORLD

It was novelist Thomas Dixon's white supremacist version of reality, of course, that gained sway over the white public mind and not that of the African American counterarguments and counterstereotypes. *The Leopard's Spots* (1902) quickly sold 100,000 copies and eventually went over a million.[65] D. W. Griffith's *Birth of a Nation* (1915) fixed the images of *The Clansman* (1905) in the popular mind for a couple of generations to come —shiftless and sinister blacks threatening white women and desecrating the noble old southern statehouses. Griffith's film is an example of the force of illusion conveyed with great artistic skill. Its morality in our eyes may be despicable, but its aesthetic power is indisputable. In her discussion of early black authors, Arlene Elder suggests that they were not more successful in gaining sympathy among white readers because they accepted the standards of white taste and once having done that could not be true to their people or vision.[66] But even had there been black authors to look at the African American experience with independent eyes—surely Charles Chesnutt was one—racial prejudice among American whites, predisposing them to endorse the stereotypes of Dixon and Griffith rather than anything so strange as a truly black human being, would have made them indifferent to the depiction of black victims and heroes. Besides, As Elder says, these novelists "were not composing belles lettres; they were manufacturing literary weapons."[67] In the end, the polemical counterstereotypes of the African American novelist did nothing to stall the move of white America to endorse either actively or by neglect the lynching of African Americans.

But even the makers of literary weapons need literary abilities, and except for Charles Chesnutt, Paul Laurence Dunbar, and James Weldon Johnson, our novelists lacked fundamental narrative skills. They had little feel for believable dialogue or incident, their plots tended to be confused and poorly paced, and they had not developed a sensitivity to mood and tone. Another problem is the way they folded the ugly reality of lynching into the well-bred romantic world of their genteel characters and enforced an unjustifiably positive ending. Most of the stories they write, in other words, are not about the tragic personal results of lynching but about the transcendence of those results through the success of their genteel heroes and heroines, who see in the refulgent morning sky the rising sun of the race. In the clash between the lynching and the romance lies an uncertainty of form in which the novel, the romantic melodrama, and the tract compete for dominance. This parallels these novelists' racial uncertainty. On the one hand, they create characters who claim their identity as African Americans and acknowledge their responsibility to help the race. On the other hand, the characters of these novels implicitly yearn for relief from the burden of race—at least the burden that comes from being linked by whites with the black lower classes. Some get relief by identifying with whites or white ancestry. Frances Harper's hero, Frank Latimer, carries "the blood of a proud aristocratic [white] ancestry" in his veins, and "generations of blood admixture had effaced all trace of his negro lineage"(*Iola Leroy*, 425). Pauline Hopkins suggests in *Contending Forces* that a reason "so many families of color manage to live as well as they do" is the "infusion of white blood, which became pretty generally distributed in the inferior black race during the existence of slavery." "Surely the Negro race must be productive of some valuable specimens, if only from the infusion which amalgamation with a superior race must eventually bring" (87).[68] By this means, many authors perform a metaphorical "passing." To be black, their novels suggest, is to be the victim of the real world of violence and prejudice. In that world, lynching is what happens to blacks as the punishment, in Sutton Griggs's words, for *being* black. To escape their vulnerability to that punishment is to escape the consequences of their color. These novelists manage that escape in their happy endings, their marriage rituals, their bright hopes for the future—all of which can be seen as metaphors for "passing." Their hidden agenda, though they declare their loyalty to the race, is to imagine a quasi-white world in whose refined culture they fit easily with, as a character in Holmes's *Ethiopia* puts it, their "genteel demeanor" (36).

The reality these writers faced was that neither they nor any other black could do anything about lynching if whites allowed the practice. Not only prejudiced public opinion but the numbers, the firepower, the law enforcement and judicial system, the state legislatures of the South, and a largely indifferent United States Congress were all arrayed against justice for the African American. In facing such daunting odds, the African American author had few options: realistic irony, tragic despair, optimism (even when reality mocked it). The last option tended to be the one most frequently taken. Their polemical goal was not only to change white minds by reassuring a white public uneasy about black people but to demonstrate to themselves the effectiveness of their heroes and heroines. To conclude in defeat would destroy their entire enterprise, and they needed victories wherever they could get them, even if they had to invent them. Some two-thirds, therefore, end their novels on a note of positive hope. In *Hope's Highway* (1918), Sarah Lee Brown Fleming creates an ideal counterstereotype in Tom Brinley, who survives the cruel chain gang, gets an Oxford education, and returns to his small southern town to bring his people learning. The rural blacks Tom returns to help will "never again . . . hear of the injustice of the Whites to the blacks," for Tom "had turned his people's steps away from the rough road of ignorance into the happy highway of hope" (156). Dr. Charles H. Fowler celebrates the achievements of the African American after the Civil War. In his *Historical Romance of the American Negro* (1902), he admits that the Klan spreads terror over the land with its lynchings and midnight raids, but the black people resist or migrate until the South comes to its senses. In his equivalent of Edward Bellamy's *Looking Backward* (1887), E. A. Johnson, in what is perhaps the most optimistic of all these plot lines, awakens his protagonist in a future 100 years beyond the novel's date of publication. Now blacks are accepted and free, and since lynching has disappeared, "a spirit of helpfulness to Negroes . . . permeates all classes." [69] J. A. Rogers's dialogues in *From Superman to Man* (1917), between a brilliant black man and a bigoted southern white, result in the latter's ceasing to be a prolynching racist and turning into a liberal ready to help through his influence in the growing moving picture industry.

The happy outcome seems contrived, inconsistent with both the conditions of the world as we see them in retrospect and as presented in the novels. That positive conclusion, however, is a hope for the future, a hunger for an end to the ordeal which defies and transcends all the evidence of the present, a kind of resurrection, to which one miraculously awakens after nightmare. These novelists do not consistently identify their protagonists with lynching victims or the lynching victims with the crucified Christ. But the vocabulary of the Passion is applicable. The equivalent of the Resurrection in these novels is the marriage between the protagonists, like the marriages in the white plantation novels, in which the superior male and female are symbolically unified in a ceremony of cultural victory. [70] The nuptials of the hero and heroine are certainly a convention in the traditional melodrama, but these early black novelists turn it into a sacred ritual. It is the rite of passage to a prosperous profession, a fulfilled life which is often devoted to racial uplift.

The married couple escape from the reality of lynching through honor, courage, loyalty to principles, and middle-class "refinement and intelligence." The new reality extending beyond the end of the novel, the one we never "see," holds out a promise that need not be followed up but lies in the couple's dedication to racial betterment. [71] The grotesque torture of black human beings may indeed take place in the real world, but for the middle-class protagonists, aspiring to higher things, life is driven by a force of good that is stronger than the cracker evil of the lynch mob, and that force of good is seen as the determiner of the race's destiny. Thus Lotus Stone and Clement St. John, in *Hearts of Gold,* happily contemplate their families in the golden afternoon sunshine of their New England estate.

Glowingly fulfilled, Lotus says to Clement: "After the clouds, sunshine, after the darkness, light, after sorrow, joy" (298). Having gone south, Iola Leroy and her husband, Dr. Frank Latimer, enter a life of public service, comforting the old, guiding the young. Iola's life "is full of blessedness," while the "Good Doctor" "abhors their deeds of violence, [and] pities the short-sighted and besotted men who seem madly intent upon laying magazines of powder under the cradles of unborn generations." More than that, he enjoys a "great faith in the possibilities of the negro, and believes that, enlightened and Christianized, he will sink the old animosities of slavery into the new community of interests arising from freedom" (461). Pauline Hopkins's Sappho and Will Smith, in *Contending Forces,* are "[u]nited by love, chastened by sorrow and self-sacrifice," and plan "to work together to bring joy to hearts crushed by despair" (401).

By circumventing the effects of the real world they refer to, these novelists reverse postbellum history. Black hopes had been aroused by Emancipation and heightened by the American dream of equality of opportunity and material success. By the end of the century, the freedpersons had been denied the early promises. Now their progeny invent the kind of world they want in their novels and superimpose a romance of completed hopes upon a reality of white malice and power. The middle-class blacks who set the form of the early novel stand in these years in an intractable predicament. They cannot return to the stoical world of their peasant/slave ancestors or resume the accepting temperament of emancipated parents and grandparents, for they have passed into another class and another set of conditions. Nor can they enter the world they are suited to by temperament, education, and sensibility. That world is controlled by whites and white prejudice keeps them out. Yet that is the world they themselves set as their goal for self-fulfillment. Like Theodore Dreiser's Carrie Meeber, they may dream such happiness as [they] may never feel." [72]

This is the atmosphere that produced the new ironic styles in realism and naturalism. Dreiser, William Dean Howells, Stephen Crane, Sherwood Anderson see their characters governed by disappointment. The yearnings of their protagonists cannot be met in their world. They are contemporaries of J. McHenry Jones, G. Langhorne Pryor, Pauline Hopkins, Otis Shackleford, but their disappointment with turn-of-the century reality is existential, resulting from the modernist view that God had "died," that the world could no longer be thought of as inherently meaningful, and above all that the breakdown in old social structures reflected what was happening morally and metaphysically. Our black novelists pay little notice to "modern tragic realism." [73] They face political and social disillusionment, and believe that the limits of their characters' fulfillment come from the color of their skin, not from the human condition. As William A. Sinclair says, The deplorable conditions existing in the South are not natural or spontaneous, but artificial. They are the direct result of the vicious and mischievous teachings of the leaders."[74] By exempting their heroes and heroines from the consequences of pigmentation, they achieve their American freedom, though only within the covers of their novel. This is commensurate with what seems to be their belief at the moment they write: that the position of the African American was the result of politics not of nature, a condition to be changed, not adapted to through a sense of the tragic. These early black American novelists have faith that such change is possible and that it is possible with a minimum of violent expense on their part. It is a faith that very little in their real world justifies.

[5]

THE LIMITS OF THE HERO: CHESNUTT'S *MARROW OF TRADITION* AND JOHNSON'S *AUTOBIOGRAPHY OF AN EX-COLORED MAN*

CHESNUTT, THE VICTORIAN

Charles W. Chesnutt's *Marrow of Tradition* (1901) and James Weldon Johnson's *Autobiography of an Ex-Colored Man* (1912) stand apart from the rest of the novels that deal with violence in the 1892–1922 period.[1] They also differ appreciably from each other in tone, attitude, and style. *The Marrow of Tradition* lingers in the Victorian age: moralistic, sentimental, and plot-heavy. *The Autobiography* is perhaps the first example of the realism of the Harlem Renaissance:[2] ironic, low-key, and underplotted. But on broader aesthetic issues, what can be said of one can be said of the other. Unlike most of the novels in this period, they make their racial points by fictional rather than polemical methods; they sound like novels rather than tracts. They illustrate how much more the novelistic art can say about violence and its ambiguous shadings, about people and violence's effect upon them, than can the polemical sentimental romance. More importantly, they acknowledge the limits of the hero's ability to produce change or bring about happiness. In these novels, both authors face up to the reality of the violent imaginary world with which they mirror the actual one. Indeed, they are the only two writers in this early period who build into their treatment of white violence against blacks a vision that acknowledges the full implications of the poisonous racial atmosphere of the times.

The Marrow of Tradition does have its weaknesses as fiction, particularly as we look back at these years of so much ferment in the development of the American novel, when new avenues of expression are opening up, and realism and naturalism have come to be useful tools of social criticism and analysis. Nevertheless, even with his taste for Victorian sentimentality,

Chesnutt is not only the first major African American novelist, he is also the first to explore, wisely and probingly, the full range of the debate over violence in terms of the nineteenth-century imagery: the warrior, the avenger, the forgiving Christian, and the principal forms they take. He asks the basic questions: What are the forces behind white violence? What are its effects upon African Americans? How should African Americans react to it? What action toward it can be called heroic in the southern context? How does it affect the prognosis for future black-white relationships? And he dramatizes these questions in ways his less talented African American contemporaries cannot match. Moreover, Chesnutt solves the aesthetic conundrum that bedeviled so many other African American novelists of the period. He makes the violence he explores part of the novel's main action, not an overlay upon the more important love affair between the hero and heroine. Romance belongs to the whites in his novel, not the blacks. Their lot is violence. It affects them directly and personally and produces the difficult moral questions they struggle to resolve. The book is thus an organic whole. Action, theme, and symbol are coterminous.

Early on in his own reflections upon the issue of race, Chesnutt takes his stand against violence. As a young schoolteacher in 1880, he declares in his journal that he wants to lead a "crusade" against the American caste system. It will not be "an appeal to force," however, "for this is something that force can but slightly affect, but a moral revolution which must be brought about in a different manner."[3] Just what that manner will be he does not say, but his contribution to the crusade will be a body of fiction that gives literary form to the search for the right kind of black hero to deal with white violence and that dramatizes the moral ambiguities embedded in the question of whether or not to use violence for self-defense or retaliation.

His short story "The Doll," published in 1912,[4] points up these ambiguities explicitly. Black Tom Taylor has gone north, become a barber, and carved out a moderately prosperous middle-class life. When he is confronted with the opportunity of avenging the murder of his father by an arrogant white southerner twenty years ago, he must choose between the satisfaction of redeeming his honor and maintaining the family he loves. A choice for violence would mean his imprisonment and his family's being left without protection. When his eye falls upon the doll his daughter had given him that morning to repair at the barbershop, he decides against the satisfaction of vengeance. The doll represents not only the Victorian cornerstone of civilized order, the family, but also the bond of love and affection that enforces that order. Only the highest type of evolved beings can override their coarse primitive passions with a more refined sensibility, a feeling for one's offspring and the race's well-being. Tom Taylor is the middle-class hero, sensible, socially responsible, able to control his violent inclinations without becoming a cowering weakling. He is not the humble, all-forgiving Christian; nor is he the avenger, who single-mindedly pursues a violent course regardless of consequences, or the warrior-hero, who sets about at the head of an army to redress the grievances of the race's victims. He is the hero who finds manliness in nonviolence and has faith in the power of civilized behavior to parry the violence he encountered long ago.

Chesnutt was himself a man of civility and culture. He went to school in North Carolina and taught in the country around Charlotte before he took his family north in 1883. He settled in Cleveland, where he had been born of free parents, was admitted to the Ohio state bar in 1887, and built a prosperous business as a legal stenographer and court reporter. He became one of the social leaders of the African American community. His daughters went to a good school and ordered their dresses from a seamstress. He and his wife joined social clubs and contributed to the cultural life of the city. He started writing early and by the 1880s was getting stories published by *McClure's, Family Fiction, the Great International Weekly Story Paper,* and, ultimately, the *Atlantic Monthly,* under the editorship of the most powerful arbiter of literary success in the nation, William Dean Howells, who saw in Chesnutt a new voice and encouraged him in his writing.

Like Tom Taylor, Chesnutt had a strong sense of family. He oversaw his children's education and leisure, had them attend dancing school, and sent them to summer vacations at Point Chautauqua. Race was an important element in his life. He and most of his family were light-complexioned enough to have passed for white, but, reinforcing the reality of the heroic behavior of the male characters I discussed in the last chapter, Chesnutt threw in his lot with the African American and devoted his writing, in fact most of his life, to seeking equality for American blacks. As a man concerned with anything that affected his family and his people, he communicated with major African Americans of his day—William Monroe Trotter, Booker T. Washington, W. E. B. Du Bois—and discussed with them the major issues facing African Americans.

THE BIG THREE: A CROSS-SECTION OF THE WHITE SOUTH

In *The Marrow of Tradition,* where he makes his major statement on violence, Chesnutt concludes that the race riot at the heart of his narrative, and the white supremacist rancor it symbolizes, can be but "slightly" affected by black retaliation in kind. While vengeance may sound gratifying and seem heroic, it oversimplifies the question and undermines the high ends of moral and social action. The goal must be the safety of the family and the secured future of the race. In *The Marrow of Tradition* Chesnutt puts this conclusion in a context that does full justice to the irreconcilable contradictions of the issue. He shows the source of the riot in the feelings of the whites and the state of affairs that conditions the blacks' response.

Although *The Marrow of Tradition* contains a near lynching, lynching is not the violence that raises the issue the novel addresses. That comes in a real happening which Chesnutt fictionalizes—the 1898 riot in Wilmington, North Carolina. The incident occurred in an area he had known as a young man and where he still had many friends. It was a power grab by white supremacist Democrats to reclaim control of the city from the Fusionist party, which showed too much leniency toward blacks. By giving the blacks the vote, said the Democrats, the Fusionist party had encouraged them to behave intolerably, keeping the better-educated and more deserving whites from decent jobs, bringing the city into near bankruptcy, and making the streets unsafe for white women. But the spark that specifically occasioned the outburst was the whites' determination to run a black newspaper editor, who had offended them in an editorial, out of town. The group that attacked the newspaper office turned into a mob that terrorized blacks all over town, frightening them off the streets, arresting them, beating them, shooting them. The white rioters achieved precisely the effect they sought. The black editor, together with a number of other black professional men, fled from the town, and Wilmington blacks were put on notice that Reconstruction was now truly dead and their voting days were over. In the process, the victorious white supremacists replaced the aldermen, who had been elected only a couple of days before, with their own hand-picked candidates.[5]

Chesnutt's narrative follows the historical facts closely, but he reduces the long and complicated story into a few characters whose interaction compresses the historical riot into a symbol for what had been happening in the entire South since the end of the Civil War. The riot results from the deliberate manipulation of public opinion by whites, who rankle under the "petty annoyances" of a few blacks in office. In the fictional town of Wellington, three white men, the "Big Three," conspire to exploit white resentment against "negro domination." The Big Three's campaign brings out a white mob determined to get rid of the city's black newspaper editor and wreck his printing presses. The members of the mob go on from there to terrorize the black populace, kill dozens of blacks, and drive several educated black leaders from the town, including the offending newspaper editor. Chesnutt analyzes the causes of the violence as a combination of ignorant racial prejudice, cynical greed for wealth and power, and a romantic but dangerous view of the southern myth.

The Big Three represent a cross-section of the southern power establishment, and in their conspiracy we see the tangled motives behind southern violence. There is the "Snopes" element, white trash like Captain George McBane, who have gained a certain wealth and power through unethical business dealings and make no effort to hide their coarse drive for power by putting down the "niggers." There is the old planter aristocracy, represented in General Belmont, former slaveowners who are used to authority and to condescending indulgently to the crudities of the South's McBanes. The one acts out of uneducated emotion, the other with an urbane and calculating cyncism. And there is the idealist like Major Philip Carteret, who believes in the nobility of the white supremacist enterprise, sees himself fighting a quasi-religious war, punctuates his thoughts and conversation with words like "crusade," "redemption," "prophetic," and speaks about the purity of the white race and its charge as the custodian of the "higher law"—just "a notch below Bourbon aristocracy," as Robert A. Lee puts it.[6] Carteret dreams not so much of profit and power as of a great noble line and sees the Big Three's plans through a lens of high moral purpose.

Chesnutt understands these white men with a true novelist's objectivity. But his most generous sympathy goes to Carteret's type. Rather than ridiculing Carteret's sophomoric but fatal idealism, Chesnutt acknowledges without scorn or irony the lofty principles with which Carteret purports to animate his action and the deep intensity with which he holds them. Carteret's type could do much good in a South bereft of solid ideals. But like William Faulkner thirty years later, Chesnutt sees that it is in the Carterets of the South where the sectional tragedy plays itself out in the contradiction between high ideals and corrupt means. Driven by his ideals, Carteret makes a pact with the cynicism of Belmont and the brutality of McBane and brings about a conflagration that sickens him, but for which he refuses to take any responsibility.

The bitter irony for a black author is that the aristocracy that Carteret seeks to preserve is intrinsically corrupt and even now in irreversible decay. Old John Delamere, the flower of the best of the southern aristocracy, has outlived his world and dies before the end of the novel. All that is left of his proud family is his grandson, Tom Delamere, whom Chesnutt calls "a type of the degenerate aristocrat" (95). Selfish, shallow, spendthrift, Tom murders his old great-aunt for money to pay his gambling debts but in the end inherits his grandfather's fortune. Carteret's own son "Dodie," for whose future Carteret joins the Big Three, embodies the malaise of the class, for as the riot reaches its climax, Dodie lies abed with one of his several serious illnesses, a "sickly blue-blood," in William L. Andrews's words, "in whose tenuous hold on life Chesnutt symbolized the equivocal spiritual condition of the South's aristocratic tradition."[7] Carteret's ideals are thus pathetically tainted by the liars, the cheats, the murderers, the "sickly blue-bloods," those in whose interests the riot violence is committed.

EVERY FINER INSTINCT

Against this background of white self-deception and dishonesty, Chesnutt explores the question of how blacks can and should respond to—how they can *stop*—such violence through a rich mix of black characters. He presents several forms of the forgiving Christian. Ignorant and obsequious syco-phants, like young Jerry Letlow, bow and scrape to the whites who hold them in contempt. Old retainers, like John Delamere's servant Sandy Campbell, remain doggedly loyal. In the young semiprofessionals, angrily jealous of their freedom and independence, like the Carteret's black nurse, Chesnutt introduces a new type, neither the forgiving Christian nor the warrior-hero. They often use rudeness to keep whites at a distance. Others put their skills to work in the community—lawyers work for racial prog-ress, journalists seek to educate the black social classes at the end of the century, doctors seek to make updated health care available.

Among these figures are three men for whom violence becomes a direct question, who embody various degrees of response to the white attack. Jerry Letlow illustrates what can happen to the forgiving Christian when his nonviolence is conditioned on cowardice and a failure of pride. Cring-ing and servile, when he suspects the Big Three are planning trouble for the blacks, he determines to "git in de ark wid de w'ite folks" (39). And as the riot starts, he goes not to the blacks for protection but to the whites, who, of course, in his "moment of supreme need," shoot him down like a "brute beast" (307).

At the opposite end of the spectrum stands the most appealing black character in the novel, the one who wants to fight back, the avenger. Josh Green comes from the lower classes, but he is no Jerry Letlow. Independent and industrious, he has the self-respect of an aristocrat and the willingness to defend it of a Teddy Roosevelt. "I ain' no w'ite folks' nigger," he says. "I don' call no man 'marster.' I don' wan' nothin' but w'at I wo'k forer, but I wants all er dat" (114). When the mob starts the riot, he gathers together a band of men to defend blacks and their property, "willing to die" to accomplish his purpose (113). His purpose is revenge. Twenty years ago George McBane shot his father in a Klan raid and drove his mother insane because of it. Josh has single-mindedly devoted his life to getting even, and he accomplishes his purpose. In the same melee in which Jerry

Letlow dies, Josh goes to his own death, taking his enemy with him. From Josh's standpoint, Chesnutt suggests, the black man's life is fulfilled; violence has worked for him, for he dies "with a smile still upon his face" (309).

Josh is a later version of Martin Delany's Gofer Gondolier. Like Chesnutt himself seems to be, we are powerfully drawn to Josh's courage and manliness. Chesnutt even sees that such a figure can be an advantage to the race. Dr. William Miller, the novel's black protagonist, reflects upon Josh's aggressiveness: "When his race reached the point where they would resent a wrong, there was hope that they might soon attain the stage where they would try, and, if need be, die, to defend a right" (112). But according to the values that prevail in Chesnutt's system, Josh cannot triumph, except as an example of undaunted but finally defeated strength of purpose. Chesnutt weights Josh's morality with too many encumbrances for the reader to accept it as a valid response to white violence. First of all, he is a man from the lower classes, and even though he has an unshakable self-respect, it is the self-respect of the peasant's crude passion. Second, Josh lacks a vision of the greater social good. He thinks in terms of his personal honor and the gratification of his hatred; like a priest, he is serving a consecrated purpose. He deliberately remains unmarried and childless, for no family man can honorably jeopardize a wife and children by putting himself at risk in pursuit of personal vengeance. Josh's narrow dedication to a violent purpose places him in the same category as his tormentor McBane, and significantly, McBane too comes from the lower orders of society. Uncultivated in the higher moral virtues, these men are a threat to both black and white society. Addison Gayle, Jr., cogently points out that "Green and McBane symbolize the poles of white-black anarchy."[8] In practical terms, furthermore, Josh and his kind are simply outnumbered and outgunned.

Moreover, for all his personal satisfaction, Josh dies a futile death. He has robbed his community of a strong man who could build a future. He is dead, while those who act prudently to save themselves and their families are "alive to tell the tale" (316). Reactive black violence also tears down the results of contemporary progress. Josh and his men retreat to the new black hospital, which had promised such "good things for the future of the city," partly for refuge and partly to defend the building from the white rioters. The hospital is destroyed when the whites go after Josh. In the aftermath of the fiery destruction of the hospital, the narrator reflects upon the smoking ruins, putting the issue, as Chesnutt did in "The Doll," into the evolutionary context. It was "a melancholy witness to the fact that our boasted civilization is but a thin veneer, which cracks and scales off at the first impact of primal passions" (310). The hospital encounter opposes primitives from both sides of the color line, and the result is destruction.

Finally, the Josh Greens give the whites evidence that they correctly see blacks as anarchist subhumans unworthy of "civilized" society. Chesnutt, more sharply than William Wells Brown does in *Clotel,* fully recognizes the absurd double standard, and he has Dr. Miller articulate the black frustration:

The qualities which in a white man would win the applause of the world would in a negro be taken as the marks of savagery. So thoroughly diseased was public opinion in matters of race that the negro who died for the common rights of humanity might look for no meed of admiration or glory. At such a time, in the white man's eyes, a negro's courage would be mere desperation; his love of liberty, a mere animal dislike of restraint. Every finer instinct would be interpreted in terms of savagery. (296)

No novelist seeking to cure diseased public opinion can afford to allow any nourishment to the virus that sustains it. He must emphasize those finer instincts. With any other color of skin, Josh would be a noble primitive. Black, however, he illustrates the self-canceling conflict of values Chesnutt struggles with between the honor in manly vengeance and the practical and moral values of the nonviolent Christian: patience and self-restraint.

WILLIAM MILLER: THE TRAGEDY OF REASONABLENESS

Dr. Miller insists that neither retaliatory nor defensive violence serves the higher purposes of the race. We must not see him, however, as a middle-class Jerry Letlow, for he is not a coward, either "morally or physically." His instincts are "manly," and they urge "him to go forward and take up the cause of these leaderless people, and, if need be, to defend their lives and their rights with his own" (282). But it is precisely those "primal passions" that, as a father and an educated man with civic responsibilities, he must resist. In his reluctant refusal to take up Josh's plea to lead the small band of militant blacks in self-defense, Miller advances what will become all the familiar reasons that violence will not work. "To what end," he rhetorically asks the black rebels, should they take up arms against the whites? Even if they did manage to cut down a few whites, their victory would be short and limited. The whites have vast superiority in firepower and numbers. History has given blacks "no territory, no base of supplies, no organization, no outside sympathy." There is a future, though, which, as Miller sees it, makes nonviolence both wise and practical, the kind of faith in social evolution that Frances Harper and others introduce into their novels. "Our time will come," Miller tells his skeptical audience, "the time when we can command respect for our rights; but it is not yet in sight. . . . Good may come of this after all" (283). If he is right, he and all the rest are more useful to the black community alive than dead.[9]

Miller's reasoning assumes the ultimacy of the family, the hallowed point of that highest evolutionary stage, Victorian civilization. These are the ingredients that compose the image of nonviolence that Miller projects. Chesnutt was a genuine practicing Christian, but he has Miller reject violence not because it is un-Christian but because it is impractical, bringing more negative consequences than good ones. Protecting the family, safeguarding the children, is the measure of civilized sensibility, and to do that, one must stay alive. That is why neither Miller nor the lawyer Watson will lead Josh's little *force de frappe*. They have families to think of. When he has Miller reject Josh's plea, Chesnutt flashes a message to any white who might be reading. Educated black leaders see the value of compromise, and that is a sign of their humanity, in the nineteenth-century sense, and their worthiness of membership in the larger body politic.

Implicit in the abjuration of violent retaliation is a kind of forgiveness. But when Chesnutt has the rioters, after killing men, women, and children, take Miller's only son, he changes the moral equation. And when he gives Miller an opportunity for a vengeance that requires no violence, he changes the moral question, showing the virtual impossibility of arriving at a satisfactory solution.

When the riot leaves Miller as the only physician to treat a seriously ill Dodie Carteret, the physician refuses his services to the white man who had earlier denied him entrance into his house on a similar errand and whose political manipulations had led to the riot that had killed Miller's son. Miller claims redress of his grievance by Mosaic law, an eye for an eye: "as you have sown, so may you reap!" he says portentously (320). The note of Victorian melodrama, with all its emphatic truisms and exclamation marks, may jar on the ear of the reader, but this is a high moment in the inner history of the African American and has been long awaited: appropriate vengeance against an oppressor. These two educated men play out the crude violence of the riot at a higher level. Neither commits any overt violence, but their actions contain the seeds of death: Carteret in his arousal of public anger to the point of riot, Miller's withholding of help that could save Dodie's life.

On the one hand, the law of melodrama dictates the conclusion, a last-minute tearful appeal, a last-minute rescue. Olivia Carteret goes to Janet Miller, and Janet Miller releases her husband to save Dodie. But beneath the melodrama lies a thoughtful meditation upon violence that shows Chesnutt the novelist-explorer working against Chesnutt the moralist-advocate. This accounts for the peculiarly ambiguous ending to a novel that contains so much moralizing.

Even the whites acknowledge the justness of Miller's refusal. Carteret, and the young white nurse and medical student called to treat Dodie, accept it "as pure elemental justice," even admiring the physician's citation of the ancient law (321–22). But Chesnutt's point is that this system of justice sustains the cycle of hatred and death, invoked now even by a black man who has suffered grievously under its hard inhuman terms. When the women come on the stage, Chesnutt seems to see some hope. The encounter between the two mothers, Olivia Carteret and Janet Miller, contains a probing of the values upon which violence rests. Olivia pleads that Janet break the iron law that justifies the taking of one life to pay for another and urge her husband to save Dodie's life. In this sensationalized scene, Chesnutt appeals to both sides. He seems to base that appeal not upon the virtue of Christian charity but upon the point that whites have always refused to grant, that blacks and whites belong to the same *human* family. Few whites have cared to discuss or acknowledge the long history of interracial sex that has bound them into a blood relationship with blacks. Chesnutt uses this literal family blood tie to symbolize the larger species tie, the rejection of which has made it possible for whites to regard blacks as subhuman. In the novel, this kinship is represented by the blood relationship of Olivia and Janet, daughters of the same white father. Until now, Olivia and her husband have refused to acknowledge the relationship with her father's "black" daughter, suppressing at the same time documents that would have proven Janet's legitimacy as well as her standing as a legal heir, depriving Janet of the dignity of respectability. Now Olivia desperately plays that card, acknowledging the direct family kinship and, symbolically, the species tie as well. "Sister," she cries (327).

That cry comes too late and too tainted by ulterior motives to restore the hitherto unacknowledged bond. Janet bitterly rejects Olivia's "sisterly recognition." Yet she sends her husband to save the white child, so Olivia "may know that a woman may be foully wronged, and yet may have a heart to feel, even for one who has injured her" (329). Janet thus suggests the possibility of breaking the vicious cycle of revenge, violence, and death that had corrupted race relations in America from the beginning. She stands to gain nothing from her generosity. Her motive seems to be her strong sense of belonging to the human family on her own merits and being capable of empathizing with the anguish of another human being. Here, suggests Chesnutt, is the answer to racial violence, a promise to whites that they need not fear a future in which blacks are recognized and violence abjured.

But does that promise, made essentially by the African American side, repair the destruction of the riot or forecast better race relations? William L. Andrews, Chesnutt's best biographer, argues with great force that the ending of the novel does make a case for a "historical evolution" in which Chesnutt has faith. Thus Olivia insists that her change of mind is more than superficial, and when Dr. Miller arrives at the bottom of the stairs in Carteret's house, he is urged to "Come on up," with the implication that both Dodie's illness and the South's racial sickness are, in Andrews's words, "an urgent but not an irreversible state of affairs." [10]

But this hopefulness is by no means unequivocal. It may be that the Carterets do recognize the Millers at the end of the novel, but Chesnutt has provided no objective correlative for that change of mind. No well-intentioned white man can stop the rioters once they taste blood. Josh Green's courage and Jerry Letlow's cowardice come to the same thing. The hospital that Josh's violent defense was supposed to preserve lies in "smoldering ruins." The son that Miller's nonviolence was supposed to protect lies dead. McBane is dead, but Tom Delamere, the "degenerate aristocrat," replaces his honorable old grandfather. General Belmont survives to falsify wills in whites' favor. And Chesnutt has his own narrator argue against the sudden conversions that make novels end happily. "More often, in real life, they do not change their natures until they are converted into dust" (304).

Everything we know about the Carterets and the white society they represent, therefore, urges caution in accepting their conversion at face value. When Miller enters the Carterets' house to save Dodie, the main feeling we get is not that, as the two symbols of black and white meet, a promising future course has been set. It is rather that Miller has yet once more stepped onto the old treadmill, as if he goes to his labor—in spite of Emancipation, in spite of his European education, in spite of his reputation as an eminent surgeon—like a slave in a world still controlled by whites. It is a white child, not a black, that is saved. It is a black, not a white, who makes the gesture of Christian support. The gesture does not guarantee an improvement of black fortunes, any more than Miller's refusal to fight staunches the flow of white hatred or saves his son. Indeed, no black man or woman in the entire novel performs a truly effective act. Josh in his militancy, Jerry Letlow in his cringing submission, Sandy Campbell in his loving service, the Millers and their life-saving decision—all are swallowed by white dishonesty, arrogance, and the apparently ineffaceable race hatred that is the marrow of the white tradition.

There is little doubt that Chesnutt *wants* to see a positive future. The last words he ever writes in a novel come at the end of *The Colonel's Dream* (1905):

But there are those who hope, and those who pray, that this condition will pass, that some day our whole land will be truly free, and the strong will cheerfully help to bear the burdens of the weak, and Justice, the seed, and Peace, the flower, of liberty, will prevail throughout all our borders.[11]

But, as in *The Marrow of Tradition,* nothing in the action of *The Colonel's Dream* justifies such hope. Colonel French, of the title, returning to his birthplace, the southern town of Clarendon, seeks to recover the "glory of days gone by" (102), believing that in the white southerners who remain, beneath the coarse demagogues and violent bigots, still run pure "currents of life" (90). Yet these whites burn a black man at the stake, resist the colonel's ethical business practices, and dig up the coffin of a faithful old servant he had buried in the white section of the cemetery, throwing the muddy box onto the colonel's lawn. Profoundly discouraged, and thinking now that he cannot change these people, he returns to his home in the North, defeated. Thus, the colonel's dream is only a dream, just as Major Carteret's invitation to Dr. Miller to "come on up" rings hollowly against the background of the devastating Wellington riot. I am inclined to go along with Hugh M. Gloster, who concludes that in *The Marrow* Chesnutt "prescribes no panacea for the ills which he exposes; and the implication is that he was not very hopeful for harmonious race relations in the Southern states."[12]

Chesnutt's conclusion to *The Marrow of Tradition,* like the last words of *The Colonel's Dream,* leaves the reader with an uninterpreted ambiguity which checks any unequivocal assumption. This is the only thing the artist can do. Such an ending does not, however, prohibit the novelist from expressing a preference. Cautious optimism, helpless pessimism—these are the materials of real experience to which Chesnutt the novelist must be true. And if he can find no evidence that black nonviolence will influence whites to a change of mind, he can still maintain that, of all the options, it contains the most promise. Anything more rigid and less equivocal falls outside the bounds of the novel form. The one certainty we have is that, though weighed down by grief, William and Janet Miller assume the familiar roles of nurturing and preservation and speak for permanent and life-giving values against life-denying violence.

LYNCHING AND THE "EX" IN "EX-COLORED MAN"

The Autobiography of an Ex-Colored Man is quite another kind of novel. To be sure, violent events bring about the most important turns in the plot. But Johnson is not concerned with finding the proper response to this violence in some kind of heroic action. He seeks instead to create a realistic world in which there are no heroes. The sentimental romancer of chapter 3 produces counterstereotypes of the most manly and dedicated nobility. If anything, Johnson creates the first black *anti*hero.[13] His narrator–protagonist does fantasize about "bringing glory and honour to the Negro race" (417). But when violence erupts in the black world where he has gone to seek his black identity, he does not react by selflessly leading lesser beings to political action or violent retaliation; nor does he affirm his devotion to the race and pledge his life to uplifting it. He runs to the sanctuary of whiteness and gives up his newfound black identity for white. He writes his autobiography in order to work out his own sense of uneasiness over running. Clearly he is no descendant of Chesnutt's Dr. William Miller or Harper's Dr. Frank Latimer, though he comes from the same mixed parentage and has the same fair skin. What, then, is he, if he is not a hero or an avenger or a victim? He is the first literary character created by an African American novelist to possess elements of the new realism and naturalism given impetus at the turn of the century by writers like Stephen Crane and Theodore Dreiser, and Johnson uses him to dramatize nonpolemically the difficulty of being black in America. Johnson subjects him to an intolerable tension. He is forced to choose between a rich black life, part of whose richness is its everyday hazards, and an attenuated and less fulfilling white life that is nevertheless secure.

Until he is ten, the narrator believes he is white. And for all intents and purposes he is. Though his mother is an ex-slave, his father is a white man through whose veins flows "the best blood of the South" (402). But from the time his teacher, in the mostly white Connecticut school where he gets his education, segregates him with the known black students in the class, he experiences an ambivalence about his status that is reinforced by the fact that his racial membership ultimately lies in his own choice. *The Autobiography* is mainly about the time between the shocking discovery of his racial origins and his decision to pass. It is the account of his attempt to discover "what my country considered me" (415) and "what it was to be coloured" (433). His quest takes the form of a search for his "hero–work," so to speak, a project that will make visible the beauty and the vigor in the soul of the black lower classes as embodied in their music. Success in this enterprise will allow him to conquer "the strong aversion to being classed with" (404) his black schoolmates he felt as a child and to accept his blood tie with the race as a whole without forfeiting his own essential membership in the middle class. That he does find his hero–work, and then abandons it, is the irony of realism. The hero of romance does not exist in the realistic genre of the novel. In *The Autobiography* we get instead the pathos residing in the gap between the ideals of the hero and "the dwarfing, warping, distorting influence which operates upon each and every coloured man in the United States" (403).

At the two points where he believes he has found his hero-work, the narrator is confronted with a violent event that destroys the psychological and material progress he has made. In the first incident, the narrator witnesses the shooting of a white woman by her black lover in the African American section of New York City. Fearing he will be the next victim, he flees to Europe with the assistance of a white millionaire friend. He does not renounce his black identity here but retreats to a place where it is benign. He leaves behind him the New York City where he first uncovered the real black soul. As I have said, it appears in the form of music, specifically in the new ragtime music. The nature of that music, like the nature of the soul of the black folk, is mixed. Its lyrics are "crude" and "vulgar" while the music is spontaneous and rhythmical. It is produced by the "natural musical instinct and talent" (447) of black piano players, untrammeled by set forms and traditions. Whites have already begun to steal this music from its originators and practitioners and make "small fortunes" for themselves. But Johnson presents it as quintessential black music, played by folk artists who can neither read nor write music. They are not rural peasants or the slouching street men of dark Atlanta. They come from a different class, and the audiences they play for are mixtures of black and white, the gamesmen of the city's gambling and theatrical culture and daring white women, often wealthy, who get their thrills by slumming. But they are very much the "popular" artists of the masses, who set feet tapping and hearts singing, without whose work the great formal art of high culture cannot exist (448).[14] Johnson does not endorse the world in which these musicians play—the gambling, the drinking, the avoidance of work and renunciation of the family. Many of the men the narrator meets have become addict-victims, their "will and moral sense so enervated and deadened that it was impossible for [them] to break away" (455). This, however, is the "dark" life from which ragtime comes, and the narrator senses that ragtime, ironically, could be the medium for bringing together the high and the low ends of the black community, making accessible a racial identity which the educated classes, to which he himself belongs, are in danger of losing as they reject what they see as the vulgarity of the lower classes. But, as yet, he has not clearly formulated how ragtime can become his racial work, and for the time being he seems content to surprise his white friend's guests at swank dinner parties and continue to drink in ragtime at the dives off Sixth Avenue.

Then his environment turns bloody, and he flees the "horrible nightmare" of the white woman's murder (461). The narrator does not, as I say, turn white. But he does enter a white world as if he were white. Certainly his millionaire friend treats him "as an equal, not as a servant" (464), and he never puts his observations of the cities he visits in racial terms, as Johnson does in his autobiography, *Along This Way* (1933), when he exults in the freedom he feels when he first visits Paris.[15] It is in Europe where his true hero-work is revealed to him, the concrete means by which he can distill the essence of American blackness into terms appropriate for audiences outside of the folk and realize his old dreams of glorifying the race. In Berlin, he observes a German pianist reversing the musical tricks he had been performing in New york. Instead of "turning classic music into rag-time, a comparatively easy task . . . this man had taken rag-time and made it classic" (471). With that display, says the narrator, "I clearly saw the way of carrying out the ambition I had formed when a boy" (471). He can overlay the art of the lower classes with the art of the classical tradition in which he was trained and thus preserve the music of the folk and infuse the sensibilities of the educated with the authenticity of its origins. It is useful to our understanding of this passage in *The Autobiography* to note that it expresses the germ of Johnson's idea about poetic diction which he more fully develops later in his preface to *The Book of American Negro Poetry* (1922), his poem-sermons in *God's Trombones* (1927), and his discussion of the subject in *Along This Way*. In the latter, he recounts how, when he was in New York in 1899, like the narrator in *The Autobiography*, the city showed him "a world of tremendous artistic potentialities," which started him groping "toward a realization of the importance of the American Negro's cultural background and his creative [and instinctive] folk-art, and [the possibility of] the superstructure of conscious art that might be reared upon them" (152). There is a close connection between this later material and *The Autobiography* as Johnson lifts whole groups of sentences on ragtime from *The Autobiography* and uses them verbatim in the preface to *The Book of American Negro Poetry*.[16]

The ingenuity of the German musician in showing the narrator how that "superstructure of conscious art . . . might be reared" upon ragtime impels him upon the final phase of his quest for the Negro musical soul, into "the very heart of the South," where he will go "to live among the people." There he will pick up his search for the musical form that predates ragtime, "the old slave song" (471). This is not a totally disinterested quest. Typically, the narrator's motives are deeply mixed. He follows partly a "selfish" aim for "a better future" for himself, and partly "an unselfish desire to voice all the joys and sorrows, the hopes and ambitions, of the American Negro, in classic musical form" (474). Above all, he believes that he has located the source of black identity. It has been the point of his entire odyssey, from the home in Connecticut in which he was raised to Atlanta, Jacksonville, New York City, Europe, and now at last back to Georgia, for his "first real experience among rural coloured people" (486). From the beginning, he has been troubled by the ambivalence he has felt toward the race of which his mother's blood made him a member, starting with the "aversion" I have already mentioned to being classed with his black schoolmates. As a youth of seventeen, he is repelled by the "unkempt appearance, the shambling, slouching gait and loud talk and laughter" of the Atlanta "lower class" (422). And as a more mature and experienced adult on his way from Europe to Georgia, he listens to a black physician inveigh against "those lazy, loafing, good-for-nothing darkies" who give the better elements of the race a bad name (479). Yet, he swells with pride as he watches his black friend "Shiny" present a stirring speech on Toussaint L'Ouverture at graduation (417). He argues that the "popular" underlies whatever is "great or enduring, especially in music" (448). And he reflects that it was the very types "the progressive element among the coloured people" now regarded with "condescension or contempt" who had "led the race from paganism and kept it steadfast to Christianity through all the long, dark years of slavery" (490). He frankly acknowledges his ambivalence, attempts to examine it, and in doing so manages to articulate the richness of the black experience as embodied in its song. His point is that the lower classes, from the Georgia rural folk to the sports living the dark life of the New York subculture, are indispensable to the self-definition of all African Americans. Uncouth, distasteful to more finely trained palates, they nevertheless are the seedbed of black American nature, in the same way that the morally deadened life of sporting New York—and before it Saint Louis and Chicago (447)—is the unique purveyor of ragtime. In the South, the narrator collects the materials that will allow him to express that identity, gathering the old musical forms "from the hearts of the people" in order to run them through the "alembic" of his classically educated sensibilities to produce a new form.

At the climactic point of his southern experience, a richly emotional black camp meeting, the narrator feels much different than he did in New York as a ragtime piano player. Not only are the black people in this rural area morally superior to the drinkers and gamblers and high spenders of the city, the narrator himself is clear about the moral path he is following toward the souls of black folk, for which W. E. B. Du Bois had already commenced to pave the way (486). Here, the sexual license and undisciplined jealousy that drove the citified black gigolo to murder his slumming white mistress do not cloud the perspective of the lives that Johnson's narrator has observed in his search through the countryside for material.[17] The black farmers and their wives and children who go to the camp meeting may be ignorant, even "negatively content with their lot," as the narrator says in another context (487), but in their "primitive state" (489) they effuse dignity. Their preacher rises to the "eloquence of primitive poetry" (491). Their religious faith and spiritual strength sweep the narrator along with an emotional power he has never felt before. He is, indeed, moved to tears by the fervor with which they sing the "old slave songs" (494). He emerges from this camp meeting "full of enthusiasm . . . in that frame of mind which, in the artistic temperament, amounts to inspiration. I was now ready and anxious to get to some place where I might settle down to work, and give expression to the ideas which were teeming in my head" (494).

At this point, southern violence permanently destroys his enthusiasm and drives him out of the community in which he had anticipated psychological and aesthetic satisfaction. The lynching that he witnesses in a small village near Macon, after the camp meeting, moves him to become the "ex-colored man" of the title, and is thus the mechanical and thematic pivot of the narrative.

The episode starts as an ominous disturbance in the atmosphere of the sleepy little town, late at night. It draws the narrator irresistibly out into the streets. There are "mutterings" and a vague "rumour" about "some terrible crime." Figures of grim white men materialize out of a shadowy indeterminate "background," their dreamlike quality intensified by the "orderly manner" in which they go about their business. But beneath their calm, excitement makes their eyes glitter. Stern and silent, they are bent on a lofty but not immediately defined purpose (496). When the victim is finally brought in, the terror of his situation has emptied him of human features, his "countenance" stamped with "every sign of degeneracy," a wretch "too stunned and stupefied even to tremble." The narrator traces the whole ritual:

A railroad tie was sunk into the ground, the rope was removed, and a chain brought and securely coiled round the victim and the stake. . . . Fuel was brought from everywhere, oil, the torch; the flames crouched for an instant as though to gather strength, then leaped up as high as their victim's head. He squirmed, he writhed, strained at his chains, then gave out cries and groans that I shall always hear. The cries and groans were choked off by the fire and smoke; but his eyes, bulging from their sockets, rolled from side to side, appealing in vain for help. Some of the crowd yelled and cheered, others seemed appalled at what they had done, and there were those who turned away sickened at the sight. (497)

Though we have read accounts like this before, Johnson constructs his symbol with a fictive skill unmatched by any pre–World War I novelist. Politics and polemics play no role here. The details are recorded because of their profound effect upon the narrator within the fictive world of the novel. Although Johnson's depiction of the lynching does argue strongly against the general practice, he presents it not in order to make that argument but to make vivid a decisive event in the narrator's life. He thinks he has found his true calling, which he can follow as a black man. He believes he has found a definition of his blackness in the folk of black belt Georgia. Then, in a sudden, shocking moment, he discovers a definition that overwhelms the religious ardor of the camp meeting, the poignance of the old slave songs, the rousing spontaneity of ragtime. The lynching answers the questions I alluded to above that set him upon his journey: "what my country considered me" (415) and "what it was to be coloured" (433). It tells him that, regardless of his education and good breeding, as a Negro he is never safe from the threat of violence. As Frederick Douglass did the beating of Aunt Hester during slavery, and with a high level of novelistic effectiveness, Johnson makes the lynching a central symbol of the African American predicament in the quarter century before World War I.

As in many of the novels of his contemporaries, Johnson's lynching victim has no personal connection with the protagonist. But Johnson employs this disconnectedness for a special effect. The victim's anonymity makes him an everyman, an embodiment of the collective African American. He lives out the potential fate of all African Americans. Guilt or innocence does not figure into the equation. Johnson made a definite aesthetic choice at this point: Instead of having the white mob accuse the victim specifically of "rape and murder," as he does in the manuscript,[18] in his final revised version Johnson has the mob subject the man to indescribable agony for a crime not even defined. The narrator reinforces this feeling by identifying with the man in the most powerfully emotional moment in the novel. He is "powerless" to turn away from the ghastly sight. Time telescopes for him, and before he realizes the ordeal is over, he is looking at the charred remains of what used to be a man. His mind is "dazed" and filled with "bitter thoughts," concluding that "Southern whites are not yet living quite in the present age; many of their general ideas hark back to a former century, some of them to the Dark Ages. In the light of other days they are sometimes magnificent. Today they are often cruel and ludicrous" (498). In this passage, Johnson departs from other novelists of the period in their confidence in the southern white aristocrat. The best of the South that might stop such barbarity instead "cower and tremble before 'Southern opinion'" (498).

In a way quite different from that of the characters in other novels of the period, Johnson's narrator deeply identifies with this victim. Robert Fleming maintains that "the narrator is distant and unsympathetic in describing the man being burned," that he lacks "hostility toward the white Americans who are burning the Negro." [19] The text I have summarized above quite contradicts this reading. The narrator is not acquainted with the victim, but he "knows" him, suffers with him. The subtext here in *The Autobiography* is expressed more explicitly in *Along This Way* in a passage that explains what Fleming calls the narrator's unemotionality. Writing for himself about the Georgia country folk whose offspring he teaches as a student from Atlanta University, Johnson says that "As I worked with my children in school and met with their parents in the homes, on the farms, and in church, I found myself studying them all with a sympathetic objectivity, as though they were something apart; but in an instant's reflection I could realize that they were me, and I was they; that a force stronger than blood made us one" (119). It is precisely such a feeling that governs the narrator's reactions during and after the lynching. The narrator says in *The Autobiography*, "I could understand why Negroes are led to sympathize with even the worst criminals and to protect them when possible. By all the impulses of normal human nature they can and should do nothing less" (497–98).

It is this same affinity that brings on the "great wave of humiliation" (497) that sweeps over the narrator as he attempts to recover from the shock of the lynching, the "shame at being identified with a people that could with impunity be treated worse than animals" (499). So long as the world takes him for a black man, he and the anonymous lynching victim are one in the flesh, and he, just as much as the anonymous victim, is vulnerable to such a fate. This is very much the other side of the hero from the Frederick Douglass who rose from "the tomb of slavery, to the heaven of freedom" by preventing Edward Covey from beating him, the fight that "revived" in Douglass a sense of his own "manhood." A passage I referred to from *My Bondage and My Freedom* in chapter 1 introduces a generalization about force and manhood that makes explicit what Johnson's narrator only implies. "A man, without force," says Douglass, "is without the essential dignity of humanity." [20] If the narrator of *The Autobiography* is "identified" with the wretched lynching victim, how can he not feel the absence of the "essential dignity of humanity"? And if he is not the Douglass hero who determines to die before he lets another white man humiliate him with unanswered force, neither is he the manly—though less violent—hero of the sentimental romances. He does not rise nobly to the occasion determined to lead an armed uprising in a fight for the race or suggest that the occasion needs romantic heroism. The tragic reality is that lynching and the attitudes it reflects lie beyond the will of the hero, beyond revolt or defiance or force. And so he decides that he will slip into the white world, neither avowing he is white nor disavowing he is black. He will "let the world take me for what it would" (499).

HOW CAN THERE BE A HERO IN A REAL WORLD?

Robert Bone says that the narrator's behavior reflects his "moral cowardice," which is "the theme that runs persistently through" the novel. Addison Gayle, Jr., finds the narrator more "willing to surrender the richness of his racial culture" than any "character" or "artist" "throughout history." And Robert E. Fleming sees him "indulging in self-pity and unable to accept his total identity and assume his position in a race for which he feels little sympathy or admiration." [21] These strike me as undeservedly harsh judgments of a character which was called by contemporaries of the novel a "composite" of "the Negro race in the United States." [22] Even allowing for a certain degree of authorial irony that Fleming rightly sees in Johnson's presentation of his narrator, a more balanced view, it seems to me, is that the narrator is a man of only average courage, who reacts like an average man. He is neither wholly contemptible nor utterly inspiring, neither totally self-sacrificing nor completely selfish. Johnson may not identify with him, but he understands and sympathizes with him. [23]

Johnson's treatment of his narrator reflects his uniqueness as a novelist in these years. He is the only African American novelist before Richard Wright who invents, as Wright describes his method in *Native Son,* "test-tube situations" to "work out in fictional form an emotional statement and resolution" of the character's problem. [24] The narrator of *The Autobiography* is no naturalistic titan like Frank Cowperwood or Wolf Larsen, ruthless players in a world where only strength counts. He is more like Henry Fleming and Sister Carrie, vaguely ambitious but relatively weak and possessing a tendency to drift, reacting rather than initiating. Johnson places his narrator in the predicament of an African American, gives him an escape hatch, and watches what he does when the pressure rises to its highest pitch. The escape hatch is a skin light enough to pass for white. That he takes advantage of it, finally, is not an indictment of his physical or moral courage, though we might cobble up such an indictment if we think in terms of the heroes of *Iola Leroy* or *As We See It.* Nor should we define his choice as a despicable betrayal of the race. It is Johnson's way of working out his point: The stringency of the racial situation for the African American is so great that, given the chance, some will sacrifice all positive satisfactions that the race affords to avoid what its members routinely have to suffer, the humiliation of being subject to the savage and violent whims of whites. He will give up the most substantial kind of fulfillment for security.

At the end of the last chapter, I suggested that the authors of the sentimental romances liberate their heroes and heroines of the real conditions projected in their stories by uniting their protagonists in happy marriages and promising them a future of devoted work to the uplifting of the race. I claimed that these endings were metaphors for passing into a quasi-white world where the characters were protected from the consequences of their color, a kind of hidden agenda for doing in fantasy what could not be done in reality. The life Johnson's narrator pursues after he passes is analogous to the life of the hero in the denouement of the sentimental romance, for it is marked by financial prosperity and a loving marriage. Johnson brings into the open the hidden agenda of the other authors, having his character undergo a literal rather than a metaphorical transformation into a white man. Thus he marries a beautiful woman, ironically "the most dazzlingly white thing I had ever seen" (503), and has white children who know nothing of their father's background. For Johnson, though, this is no ritual of resurrection and fulfillment. His narrator's escape is not into "better" but into safer whiteness. And with that safety he accepts a diminishment of satisfaction. It is not simply that his beloved wife dies prematurely and he never marries again, though that is a kind of emblem of the emotional contraction he has purchased. He has sold creativity and intensity of feeling for refuge. Both the narrator's black and white personas, the opposition between which will become the central tension of many of the novels of the Harlem Renaissance, exert a powerful draw on him. He is happy for his children that he has chosen to pass, for it liberates them from the particular limitations this country puts on blackness. On the other hand, he writes the account of his life because, as he tells us in the first paragraph, he suffers "a vague feeling of unsatisfaction, of regret, of almost remorse, from which I am seeking relief." Later, as he completes the telling of his story and his explanation of the reason for his uneasiness, he articulates the kind of realistic ambivalence that new white novelists like Crane and Dreiser had, more than a decade earlier, begun making a staple of their fiction. "I cannot repress the thought," writes Johnson's narrator, "that, after all, I have chosen the lesser part, that I have sold my birthright for a mess of pottage" (511).

The story of *The Autobiography* makes visible what he is forced to give up. And it explains the effect of violence on the life of a black man who cannot be a hero. It obviates satisfactions entailed in blackness. That is the radical truth of racial life in America before World War I, and no novel from this early period makes this incompatibility as clear as does *The Autobiography of an Ex-Colored Man*.

[6]

ART AND LYNCHING:
THE HARLEM RENAISSANCE
AND THE 1930s

JEAN TOOMER'S *CANE:* BEAUTY AND THE BEAST

In the years between the publication of Jean Toomer's *Cane* (1923) and
Richard Wright's *Native Son* (1940), African American novelists tended to
follow the lines of *The Autobiography of an Ex-Colored Man* rather than those
of *The Marrow of Tradition*. They seldom mention the lesser-known novel
writers like Sutton Griggs or J. McHenry Jones, or pre-Civil War novelists
or slave narrators. They have, in other words, few black models for the
literature they set out to create. As for the importance to them of *The
Autobiography*, it was not that they had read the novel, at least before 1927.
It was virtually unknown to the public until it was reissued in that year and
took its rightful place in the American and African American literary
canons. Johnson was simply the first African American novelist to write
the kind of realism that came to dominate the novel-writing art in the
twenties. The treatment of violence in the novels of this period derives
from this shift from Victorian moral romances like *The Marrow of Tradition*
and sentimental romances like Hopkins's *Contending Forces* (1900) or Herman Dreer's *The Immediate Jewel of His Soul* (1919). The Harlem Renaissance novelists reversed the method used by most of their predecessors for
representing violence by all but universally abandoning the polemical
stance. In the formative years of the Harlem Renaissance,[1] the novelists
turn to a self-conscious literariness. They do not drop lynching as a subject,
but they do cease to make it a cause. They no longer draw victims as pleas
for justice or search for a hero or heroine as initiators of race pride. Their
treatment of lynching is not, for the most part, a reaction to political
atrocities but part of their portraits of black life and, in some instances,

metafictional comments on the literary process itself. In these portraits, lynching and other violence tends to be a dramatic complement to black life rather than a condition novels are written to get rid of. Violence is used to define black life and becomes the subject of a well-shaped story, not proof of white injustice. This new sensibility produces real novels, great improvements over the well-meaning but floundering fiction of the earlier period.

The artists who make this shift in attitude belong to a new generation that migrated to the northern cities before and during World War I. There its members found themselves for the first time in large enclaves of black people, moderately prosperous and feeling an increasing self-confidence. Well-known European artists like Picasso and Matisse began discovering vital new material in African sculpture and design, reinforcing an already active interest in their race's birthplace by African Americans; blackness ceased to be a potential badge of shame; the slave past took on an unprecedented value; spirituals, folk songs, ragtime, and the blues acquired new status; and the "primitive" Negro became an object of interest for whites as well as other blacks. With the Harlem Renaissance, the first substantial African American art movement emerged. When the members of this movement came to the kind of violence that had preoccupied their parents and grandparents, they brought a new sensibility. Besides a transformed general atmosphere, two new conditions directly affected their approach. First, there was the novelists' increasing emotional and physical distance from lynching. In *The New Negro* (1925), Charles S. Johnson, the editor of *Opportunity,* expresses a point of which the artists themselves were aware: the "new voices" of the Harlem Renaissance stand "at a more comfortable distance" than their parents had from "the painful degradations of slavery" and, by implication, from the continued degradations and atrocities of the post-Civil War years.[2] Second, though some contemporaries state that lynching remains at the top of black concerns, and though it came to receive more public attention in the twenties and thirties than ever— perhaps *because* it did—lynching was gradually but definitely declining. By Robert Zangrando's count, the number of annual victims drops below fifty permanently in 1923 and is down to four in 1940—still more than enough for any time but many fewer than the 161 at lynching's peak in 1892.[3] This made it easier for the young and self-conscious artists to think of lynching as they thought of the other material out of which they made their art, as an aesthetic or technical issue rather than a polemical one. Thus one of the principal forces driving the literary representation of lynching in these years was the aim, as Alain Locke put it in *The New Negro,* to write "as" Negroes rather than "for" them (48).

No novelist better illustrates the change in the depiction of violence in the years 1923–40 than Jean Toomer does in *Cane*. The fictional work that ushers in the Harlem Renaissance, and certainly the most admirable and admired, *Cane* is an eccentric but deliberately organized collection of poems, plays, and stories, which Toomer orchestrates into three movements. Each movement has its own key, and each key is set by an account of an act of violence. These accounts differ greatly from each other in mood and function, but they are bound by a single intent, a preoccupation with art rather than politics or propaganda. Toomer's treatment of violence illustrates the profound change in African American novelists' attitude toward lynching and the role of the artist in matters of race that took place in these years. It was a shift from the perception of novelists as racial propagandists, politicians, and apologists to a claim for novelists as artists, whose responsibility to their art deeply modified their obligation to the racial struggle. Toomer's share in this claim was consistent with his stance toward his identity as a black man. Thinking of himself as both black and white, as a "new American," Toomer insisted that combining the two sides "has neither social nor political implications. My concern is solely with art." And when a magazine editor questioned him about his racial orientation, Toomer replied, "I used to puzzle my own brain with the question. But now I'm done with it. My concern is with the art of literature. Call me what you like." [4]

Toomer's preoccupation with his art determines his treatment of the classic lynching of Tom Burwell in "Blood-Burning Moon," the concluding segment of the first part of *Cane:*

A stake was sunk into the ground. Rotting floor boards piled around it. Kerosene poured on the rotting floor boards. Tom bound to the stake. His breast was bare. Nails scratches let little lines of blood trickle down and mat into the hair. His face, his eyes were set and stony. Except for irregular breathing, one would have thought him already dead. Torches were flung onto the pile. A great flare muffled in black smoke shot upward. The mob yelled. The mob was silent. Now Tom could be seen within the flames. Only his head, erect, lean, like a blackened stone. Stench of burning flesh soaked the air. Tom's eyes popped. His head settled downward. The mob yelled. Its yell echoed against the skeleton stone walls and sounded like a hundred yells. Like a hundred mobs yelling. Its yell thudded against the thick front wall and fell back. Ghost of a yell slipped through the flames and out the great door of the factory. It fluttered like a dying thing down the single street of the factory town. [5]

The content of Toomer's account closely resembles that of the descriptions that appear in many of the sentimental romances of the previous period, and that of Johnson in *The Autobiography*. But his highly literary manner reflects the degree to which he departed from his predecessors. His description is the third of three stages of style. The first is that of the middle-class strivers, whose sentimental romances are less works of literature than propaganda for their cause. Their lynching accounts often came verbatim from newspaper stories or, failing that, from alleged eyewitnesses. The point was to represent the literal truth of an actual event in order to create the greatest possible polemical impact. The idea that the description of a lynching should be artfully manipulated merely for the sake of the image seemed the very last thing in most of the novelists' minds. Johnson introduced the second stage. Compared with those of his contemporaries, his description of the lynching that drives his narrator out of the black race bears clear marks of literary intent. But compared with Toomer's account, Johnson's is the more emotional. The point of view is that of the narrator-observer, whose presence at the scene and whose reaction to the event are the fictive reasons for the lynching. It is as much an experience of the "I" as it is of the victim. "I shall always hear" the "cries and groans" of the burning black man. "I was fixed to the spot . . . powerless to take my eyes from what I did not want to see." "I was looking at a scorched post." "I walked a short distance . . . to clear my dazed mind." This highly personal description is intended to bring out the atrocity of the act, its ugliness and horror. In that respect, it takes its place among the polemical lynching accounts of the sentimental romance. But the aesthetic function of the passage is clear. The description must be powerful enough to justify the change the observation of the act causes in the narrator's life within the framework of the story and to convince the reader of the plausibility of his apostasy. It is this aesthetic quality that makes *The Autobiography* a forerunner of the new fiction of the Harlem Renaissance.[6]

Toomer's account of the Tom Burwell lynching completes the third stage of the change African American novelists go through in their movement toward a true novelistic art in the years after World War I. Even out of context, any reader can see the artistic care with which Toomer has crafted the description. The effect of that care highlights the key difference between Toomer and his predecessors. It is to throw the attention upon the literary act rather than the literal one, in the same way that slowing down film softens the harshness of a shooting or a boxing match. Toomer's style here, which he uses throughout, is a mask fitted over raw reality. The sentences are highly simplified. Each step of the lynching is separately framed. Key function words are artfully omitted from the sentences, fragmenting the action, individualizing and magnifying each bit of the scene, deflecting our attention from the terribleness of the picture itself. Toomer gets an eerie sound distortion as well. Just as a sound editor might muffle or filter out all but the crash of gunshots or the thump of blows, so that they occupy the entire auditory horizon, Toomer isolates the mob's yells in short, repeated phrases, the yells coming after a moment of uncanny silence. They echo each other, their volume gradually diminishing until, "like a dying thing," they subside back into the quiet of the southern night. This is not realism, as Sherwood Anderson wrote it, but imagism. All impressions are heightened, made more concrete and immediate. The brutality is lyricized without denying it.

Perhaps most important to the aesthetic effect of the passage is the withdrawal of a human observing eye. The narrative reporter is stylized, impersonal, unemotional. The feeling of horror that comes with the intrinsic inhumanity of the act is formalized and absorbed by the detached manner of the neutral eye. Inevitably, the eye, like a camera, selects and rejects. But the choices are made in the direction of a unified effect, which is more important to the artist than the moral one. The unifying eye tells us that we need not be involved in what we are viewing in a political way, that we can observe sympathetically but without making a social judgment, that we can see this in ways other than those which convention has taught us. The way Toomer sees it is as a mystical complexity, in which he finds a paradox. Art is the vehicle of that paradox. It transforms the lynching from an act of unrelieved ugliness and unforgivably brutal oppression into an image whose meaning cannot be expressed analytically. In that horror lies a terrible beauty.

The context in which the lynching takes place reinforces this paradox and the mystical effect it gives rise to. Bob Stone, scion of the town's leading white family, has made the mistake of falling in love with the family's black maid, Louisa. Tom Burwell loves her, too. On the fatal night, the two young men meet each other in front of Louisa's shack. They fight. Tom kills Bob, who manages to stagger to the white section and reveal his killer. We see all this in the mystic light of the blood-burning moon, which hangs over the landscape like a pagan god, a prophecy of the inescapable primitive ceremony to come. An old black woman sings, like a conjure-woman, a heathen priestess:

> Red nigger moon. Sinner!
> Blood-burning moon. Sinner!
> Come out that fact'ry door.

The words hint at some deep evil—Hawthorne's dark forests, Poe's decayed mansions—a blood ritual. But just as what Melville called "the power of

Blackness" was, in both Hawthorne and Poe, archetypal rather than theological or doctrinal, so "Blood-Burning Moon" touches sources of ancient terror. Some cosmic disharmony awaits an issue and nature trembles. Hounds, caught in the "tremor" of the song, prowl restlessly, begin to howl. Dogs bark, roosters crow, "as if heralding a weird dawn or some ungodly awakening" (53). With a Homeric inevitability, the two young men submit to their roles and play out the fate written into their southern script. They move like characters in myth, not so much by conscious will as by instinct and feeling—love, jealousy, race pride, race fear. Their vindictive gods, foreknowing the outcome, make them pay the price for their passion. Within seconds Bob's throat is cut and he is bleeding to death. Within minutes the southern mob transforms Tom's vibrant body into ash.

That there is beauty in this ugliness and pain is the paradox that lies at the heart of Toomer's treatment of violence. His perception of the lynching derives from his conception of rural black life in the South, and his account of it is his way of expressing that conception. The novel is full of references and images that express the paradox explicitly, each with its own contextual implications but all sounding the point. For example, the portrait of Fred Halsey's great-grandmother that appears in "Kabnis," the last section of the book: "On close inspection [of the photograph], her mouth is seen to be wistfully twisted. The expression of her face seems to shift before one's gaze—now ugly, repulsive; now sad, and somehow beautiful in its pain" (168). Similarly, Lewis, a northern black visiting the area, is struck by old Father John, who, deaf and blind and once a slave, labors to utter some sense of his life. Lewis, seeing from the viewpoint of Toomer, "seated now so that his eyes rest upon the old man, merges with his source and lets the pain and beauty of the South meet him there" (214). The most specific statement comes from Dan Moore, the artist figure of section 2's "Box Seat." When his prudish middle-class girlfriend, Muriel, tells him that she has tried to make people "happy," Dan reacts: "Happy, Muriel? No, not happy. Your aim is wrong. There is no such thing as happiness. Life bends joy and pain, beauty and ugliness, in such a way that no one may isolate them. No one should want to. Perfect joy, or perfect pain, with no contrasting element to define them, would mean a monotony of consciousness, would mean death" (112). These passages anticipate Ralph Ellison's comment on the blues as "an impulse to keep the painful details and episodes of a brutal experience alive in one's aching consciousness, to finger its jagged grain, and to transcend it, not by the consolation of philosophy but by squeezing from it a near-tragic, near-comic lyricism."[7] In Ellison's framework, *Cane* is a kind of blues.

Toomer perceives southern black life to be wrenched by contradictions and polarities. Ugly, crude, violent, it is also vital and vibrant, with moments of transcendent loveliness. These opposites give something of themselves to each other. They are so inextricably fused that they make up a single deep and complex object whose rich beauty would disappear were it to lose any of its elements. Sometimes, Toomer sees humor in these contradictions. In the first pages of "Kabnis," Ralph Kabnis, thinking of the beautiful poetry he could write, lies amid the barnyard clatter of scratching chickens in the shed next to his room. His angry brutality when he furiously wrings a noisy fowl's neck is in absurd contrast not only to his professed status as sensitive poet but to "the serene loveliness of Georgian autumn moonlight" (160). On the other hand, there is the ominous blood-burning moon that presides over the lynching of Tom Burwell as an analogue to his burning flesh, terrible and beautiful. Take away the violence, and the southern black experience stands fundamentally changed—for the worse, in Toomer's opinion, for part of the beauty of the experience is the lynching itself, the tragic sorrow of its pain.

Toomer's story of Tom Burwell does contain a substantial historical commentary. Bob Stone and Tom portray the all but imperceptible changes taking place in southern whites and blacks. Bob's "family had lost ground." Instead of entering the house, "as a master should," while black Louisa is at her chores and taking her, "direct, honest, bold," Bob has to sneak meetings with her in the cornfield and buy her pretty gifts (59). Tom is the bold one here, confident, manly. He is tragically imprudent when he pulls his knife in answer to Bob's own blade. But his act is not the desperate, frightened gesture of self-doubting Bob Stone. The whites still control the blacks, as proven by the quickness of the lynch mob to destroy this dangerous "nigger," but Toomer undermines even the mob's force by representing its members as rushing "ants" (65).

But these historical judgments do not operate as historical interpretation so much as an enrichment of the contradictory mix that imbues the passage with its aesthetic power, and a subtle statement of Toomer's perception of the South and the motive behind his writing. The point of the Tom Burwell passage is not to persuade readers to write to their congressmen about the Dyer antilynching bill. As the key-setter to the novel's first "movement," it epitomizes Toomer's aim: to capture a disappearing world. That is the burden, as the large volume of criticism and analysis of *Cane* makes clear, that his art must bear. All the traditions of what he believed to be authentic black life—the songs, the shouts and hollers, the stories— were being absorbed into "American civilization . . . American chaos." The new industrial culture was killing the pure Negro.[8] Civilization had become the enemy of what was valuable in black life, which was authentic only to the degree that it beat to the rhythms of the old folkways. The "pure Negro," said Toomer, was "the Negro of the folk song," which Toomer had first learned about in a three-month trip to Sparta, Georgia, in 1922. The old Negro had remained more intact in the South than in the North, but even there the type was being eroded. "It would surprise you," he wrote of some of the blacks among whom he had lived in Georgia, "to see the anemia and timidity (emotional) in folk but a generation or so removed from the Negroes of the folk-songs. Full-blooded people to look at who are afraid to hold hands, much less to love." These are the "Negroes of the town," says Toomer, middle-class people who, disdaining the soil, have moved out of the countryside and, hating the "folk songs and spirituals," listen to the blander popular music on their "victrolas and player pianos." [9] Toomer even seems angry that the descendants of slaves in some places have found a solution to violent conflict. He complained that in Harper's Ferry, West Virginia, "Life . . . has not the vividity and distinction of that of Middle Georgia. Racial attitudes, on both sides, are ever so much more tolerant, even friendly. Oppression and ugly emotions seem nowhere in evidence. And there are no folk songs." [10]

Toomer has come upon the evanescent world of the "pure Negro" at the moment of its waning. He focuses upon this particularly in the first part, to which "Blood-Burning Moon" is the climax. "In my own stuff," he wrote before *Cane* was published, "in those pieces that come nearest to the old Negro, to the spirit saturate with folk-song: 'Karintha' and 'Fern,' the dominant emotion is sadness derived from a sense of fading, from a knowledge of my futility to check the solution." [11] Toomer does not mean that there is total self-fulfillment in this folk-song world. Men do not understand women; whites do not understand blacks. Exploitation and oppression run through all relationships. Becky, a white woman who bears two dark-skinned sons, is cast out by both blacks and whites and dies, unseen, beneath the bricks of her collapsed chimney. Carma, "strong as any man," makes her husband so jealous that he knifes a man and lands on the chain gang. Fern's eyes desired nothing that a man could give. Neither North nor South, concubinage nor marriage, education nor ignorance can fill her emptiness. Nearly white Esther, disturbed daughter of the richest black man in town, is humiliated when she seeks out the charlatan preacher Barlo to father upon her a *black* child. Like Louisa, who is left alone at the door of her shack after both her lovers are killed, these women and the men they bewilder suffer pain and thwarted goals, but they feel intensely, live in a rural world close to the soil, bear the beat of the sun's heat, and sing melancholy songs beneath a moon whose brightness is not dimmed by the city's artificial light. The emotions that impel them baffle analysis. This is the "folk-spirit" that Toomer sees dying "on the modern desert," a spirit that contains for him a beauty dying a "tragic" death. "And this," he says, "was the feeling I put into *Cane*."[12] It is the beauty of Karintha, "perfect as dusk when the sun goes down" (5). Tom Burwell's lynching embodies all the passions of the novel's first movement, life lived at the basic level. It is part of Toomer's aim, by means of his art, to record for the future, while he still has access to it, the feeling of "pure" black life and the poignance of its passing. The poetry and narrative of the first part are dominated by the imagery of "sunset," "dusk," "evening," "night." And "Song of the Son" is an elegy to the old ways, addressed to the moment "just before an epoch's sun declines":

> Though late, O soil, it is not too late yet
> To catch thy plaintive soul, leaving, soon gone,
> Leaving, to catch thy plaintive soul soon gone. (21)

The keynote violence of section 2 is struck in the theater program of the "Box Seat" episode, when two dwarfs engage in a "heavyweight-championship" boxing match. It is a different kind of violence from the lynching of Tom Burwell, and it shows the different kind of sensibility that governs the lives of the middle-class theatergoers from that of Tom Burwell and the folk-song culture. In this violent encounter whites are not implicated. Moreover, we are made less conscious of the art with which Toomer shapes the episode than of the satirical social commentary. This reinforces the point of the novel, however. As a way of sharpening the profile of the southern folk, section 2 indicates what has happened to the dying culture of the old Negro in the South. The old Negro has metamorphosed into a new form in the cities, largely of the North. The fight between the dwarfs defines this new urban middle-class black culture. Pockets of Washington, D.C, and Chicago, where the sketches of this part are set, still contain elements of the spontaneous southern folk. Washington's Seventh Street, where southern black migrants have settled, "is a crude-boned, soft-skinned wedge of nigger life breathing its loafer air, jazz songs and love, thrusting unconscious rhythms, black reddish blood into the white and whitewashed wood of Washington" (71). But the black middle class, that "whitewashed wood of Washington" in whose stale sogginess the "wedges rust," are more concerned with dissociating themselves from this vitality and imitating the manners of the white bourgeoisie than living intensely and maintaining the habits of their old ways. Tied to middle-class possessions, without an inner life, unable to love, the citified northerners of

Washington, D.C., have lost their heritage, their natural emotions. The sound of their lives is metal clicking upon metal. The industrial culture that conditions their stilted behavior bolts them to steel runners. Walls, houses, chairs with imprisoning arms, asphalt streets, underground pipes—all appurtenances of modern living—replace living cells, red blood, flesh and bone, limiting their bodies as well as their imagination.

The boxing match between the dwarfs is the violence that characterizes this bourgeois sensibility. The significance of the episode is in the entire transaction between the dwarfs' fight and the audience that reacts to it, especially strongly middle-class Muriel. Our attention, in other words, is called less to its aesthetic qualities, as in "Blood-Burning Moon," than to its subject. Like Ralph Ellison's "battle royal" in *Invisible Man,* the match, which starts as an "act," soon turns serious; the two misshapen boxers suddenly become angry and begin to beat and bloody each other in earnest. And as in the "battle royal," the crowd roars with appreciation. As the audience is to the white world, the dwarfs are to the audience—"different" —and because of it are exploited for profit and pleasure. Muriel, who has come to the theater with a friend, is caught up in the excitement, too, in spite of her consciousness of the proper and correct: "Muriel pounds. The house pounds. Cut lips. Bloody noses" (125). Hers is the ambivalence of the crowd. They all have a trace of Seventh Street in them, a lingering southern folk intensity. Muriel has, as her boyfriend Dan believes, a "still unconquered animalism" (112) and feels an unexpressed desire for Dan to free her from the public opinion that rules her (110). In the theater she thinks to herself, "This damn tame thing!" (118). She wants to touch her real passions, and for a moment during the boxing match the atavistic impulse holds sway. But her concern for appearances and the limits of her circumstances fix her in respectability. The boxing match itself lacks the intensity to move her genuinely. The dwarfs are not victims as Tom Burwell was a victim. Their experience is neither fatal nor tragic. The whole setting is false, not dramatic art intended to preserve, or inspire, or enrich but crude vaudeville that entertains by mocking the abnormal. In the bloody battle between the dwarfs, no profound ritual grows, no pain or intensity, only tawdry, raw, cheap emotions of which Muriel will soon be ashamed.

This black theater falsifies even the real emotions of anger and the lust for violence. The fight abruptly stops, and the atmosphere incoherently shifts to a vulgarized blend of the religious and the romantic, confronting Muriel's bourgeois respectability with a distorted image of the folk. Still bleeding from the boxing match, one of the dwarfs, Mr. Barry, sings a romantic ballad. This is not the jazz or blues from Seventh Street but the kind of bland prudery observed by the whites that proper blacks try to imitate. The dwarf sings directly to Muriel, who sits in a box seat near the stage. As Dan sees it, his eyes speak with the expression of a modern Christ: "Do not shrink. Do not be afraid of me. . . . I too was made in His image" (128). The dwarf's mute appeal is the same as that made by blacks to whites. When the dwarf offers her a white rose, stained with his own blood, he is urging her to acknowledge her own past, which he in his deformity embodies. Muriel shrinks with revulsion, but the audience, viewing the situation through its own lens of middle-class conventions, urges her to accept the gift. When she gives in to the audience pressure, Dan sees a moral example which will inject him into the center of the tableau: "JESUS WAS ONCE A LEPER!" he exclaims, leaping to his feet. He reinforces the dwarf's association with the Savior and suggests that Muriel, bound tight in her middle-class fear of feeling and her revulsion toward the black folk, is repelled by the true Christian appearance because the dwarf does not meet her standards of gentility. She would have rejected the real Jesus before he was cleaned up by a history and theology in order to serve class distinctions rather than Christian charity. In effect, she renounces what embarrasses the black middle class in their past. Muriel's "young lady" fastidiousness is metaphorically one of the causes for the decline of the authentic southern folk.[13]

Mr. Barry as well, though, as are all the players in this scene, is tainted by the phony atmosphere. He ends his song accompanied by "a showy blare of orchestration." The scene is a burlesque, its emotions banal, its religious and social implications undercut by sentimentality and bathos. The audience, encouraging Muriel to take the flower from the dwarf, as I suggested above, sees merely a kind of Walt Disney version of Beauty and the Beast, Beauty sentimentally condescending to sentimentalized suffering. And Dan, a nutty redeemer, loses interest in his mission as soon as he speaks his big line. The grotesque comedy ends when, having forgotten the challenge to a fight he accepted in the theater, Dan wanders off hazily into the back alleyways. The black life that Toomer focuses on here has been devitalized. Even violence loses its immediacy and becomes material for soppy sentimentality. Each of the other stories that make up the core of the second section also ends in an aborted action. Rhobert slowly sinks into the mud of the conventions of unfulfilling jobs and house mortgages. Avey floats uncomprehendingly through a series of affairs and a life of prostitution, incapable of building up "an inner life against the coming" of another day (87). John, attracted to Dorris, who dances to get his attention, finally prefers a dream to her reality. Paul, believing that he has won something beautiful in white Bona, finds she has abandoned him. As George Kent says, these are stories about "the thwarted fulfillment of the soul,"¹⁴ unresponsive relationships gliding upon the surfaces of a metallic world.

Toomer's treatment of the Tom Burwell lynching is characterized by his intense consciousness of the literary process. His treatment of the dwarfs' boxing match reflects the same literary self-consciousness, this time to express his perception of how the primal experience of "Blood-Burning Moon" has become transformed into a meretricious exercise of commercial shallowness by an industrialized urban middle class afraid of direct emotion. Toomer arranges the two passages so that they express the part they appear in and reflect upon each other. The first part describes the folk-song culture whose passing the entire book mourns. The second dramatizes the forces that are undoing that old culture. In section 3, entitled "Kabnis," Toomer returns to the South, but it is not the world of Karintha or Fern. It is a culture in transition, and its dramatis personae ("Kabnis" is cast in the form of a play) extend from the old slave type like Father John, the blind old man living in the basement of the wagon shop, to the new class-conscious bourgeois like Samuel Hanby, the principal of the local girls' school. Toomer's consciousness of the literary process is as intense here as in sections 1 and 2, but here it produces not the tragedy of Tom Burwell or the satire of "Box Seat" but the irony of the old slave tale. The keynote violence is an account of a lynching-murder.

She was in th family-way, Mame Lamkins was. They killed her in th street [for trying to hide her husband], and some white man seein th risin in her stomach as she lay there soppy in her blood like any cow, took an ripped her belly open, an th kid fell out. It was living; but a nigger baby aint supposed t live. So he jabbed his knife in it an stuck it t a tree. An then they all went away. (178–79)

The man who tells this story, Layman, is a black preacher and teacher. His audience is his friend Fred Halsey, the village's wagon repairer, and Ralph Kabnis, the northerner who has come to Sempter, Georgia, to teach at Hanby's girls' school. Layman tells the story at the end of a conversation which takes place on a cold autumn Sunday afternoon in the parlor of Halsey's threadbare but comfortable house. The two born and bred southern Negroes try to teach the ingenuous newcomer how to behave in hostile territory. "[K]indly remember youre in th land of cotton," says Halsey. "Th white folks get th boll; th niggers get the stalk. An don't you dare touch th boll, or even look at it. They'll swing y sho. (Laughs.)" The metaphorical indirectness and the "half playful, yet somehow [deadly] earnest" (171) manner in which Halsey speaks set the tone for the rest of the conversation. Layman and Halsey are amused by Kabnis's assumption that whites would treat law-abiding and respectable blacks like themselves with greater deference than Mame Lamkins. They observe with a kind of condescension Kabnis's northern indignation, his desire to do something about it all.

They tell horror stories of white violence partly to frighten Kabnis for their own entertainment and partly as a serious attempt to warn him about what whites are really like and what blacks must keep quiet about. The incident Layman witnessed in which white men shot "an cut a man t pieces who had died th night befo" is the sort of thing "you neither does a thing or talks about if y want t stay around this away" (173). Layman exemplifies the point. He travels throughout the state, the narrator tells us, picking up and quietly filing in his memory examples of just how bad whites are to blacks, "and hence knows more than would be good for anyone other than a silent man" (169). That is why Lewis, the other northern visitor to the area, is going to "have t leave here soon, thats sho. Always askin questions" (177). Lewis particularly "noted" Layman's story of Mame Lamkins, "an that werent fer notin down" (177).

Unlike his technique in "Blood-Burning Moon," in this case Toomer places another character besides the narrator between the reader and the story. With Layman as the storyteller, the workings of the artist are laid bare. We see why he recounts Mame Lamkins's lynching (as an example for Kabnis of why he should avoid certain kinds of behavior), and we see how he does it. The purpose of the story dictates its form, part of which is its manner of telling. Layman delivers it with the casual objectivity of the skilled but taciturn raconteur. Its effect is ironic rather than tragic. Whatever rage Layman may feel, he curbs with understatement and irony, itemizing the most disgusting brutality with the nonchalance of a man used to the very worst. "A canebrake, murmuring the tale to its neighbor-road would be more passionate" (178), the narrator tells us about Layman's manner. He even ends his story with a calculated anticlimax—"An then they all went away"—designed to suggest to Kabnis that the slaughter of Mame Lamkins is part of the southern weather and that he should be prepared for its inclemencies without trying to change it.

The "lynchin" of Mame Lamkins is an atrocity; as Layman puts it, "Th worst I know of round these parts" (177). But Toomer does not use it to express social protest. It is a way of defining the position of Laymen and Halsey. They are transitional types. Having moved into the lower ranks of the southern middle class, they are still country people. They know their territory well and employ its forms of expression as a matter of course. They do not waste their time and energy in futile protest or angry diatribe. They do not even mourn poor Mame Lamkins's fate or that of her child. They accept their world for what it is and, without expressing *overt* resentment, devise ways to stay alive. By telling the story, Layman teaches Kabnis a way to survive in a hostile land.

Layman and Halsey resort to the folk idiom a couple of times to make their point, with stories about throwing a brick into a hornets' nest and killing "moren one rabbit" with a single shot. As with the story of Mame Lamkins, the manner is everything here. Halsey punctuates his advice about the dangerousness of the region with sardonic laughter: "Dont let th fear int y, though, Kabnis. This county's a good un. Aint been a stringin up I can remember. (Laughs)" (172). There is also the manner of the narrator in his stage directions and the effect he gains from the content and structure of the conversation. In counterpoint to the talk about violence, he alludes to the service going on in the church next to Halsey's house and the comments on religion in general the service evokes. None of them take religion seriously or show much respect for it. As Layman brings the conversation to a close with the Mame Lamkins story, all the themes come together in a virtual slapstick climax. Kabnis is at the height of his incredulity and nervousness, and as a "shriek pierces the room" from one of the excited worshipers next door, a stone, around which a threatening note is wrapped, smashes through the window. "Kabnis springs to his feet, terror-stricken. Layman is worried." It is a comic moment, like children listening to a ghost story in a firelit room on a dark night and jumping at the "boo!" one of them shouts at the moment of highest tension. Kabnis dashes "wildly from the room" in an excessive reaction, tears home, covers himself with mud as he scrambles for safety, and "knows" that the whites are pursuing him with hounds. It turns out, of course, that the note, warning "you northern nigger [to] Git along now" (179), not only did not come from whites but was not intended for Kabnis. Thus the violence of the episode, even the sickening lynching of Mame Lamkins, serves irony and comedy rather than tragedy. In fact, both Layman and Halsey seem proud of the danger with which they are confronted daily and enjoy the sense of superiority their own ease with it gives them over the anxious Kabnis.

Layman and Halsey employ the old slave-tale manner as the slaves themselves used it, as a self-defense in an intolerable situation. Toomer the literary artist employs that same manner to embody the mixed nature of the world between the folk-song culture of Tom Burwell and Louisa and the middle-class society of Muriel in Washington, D.C. Like the other worlds he draws, Toomer animates that of "Kabnis" with forces and counterforces. Its tensions are contained in the irony that exists between the deadly seriousness of Layman and Halsey and their playfulness. This irony is the form Toomer gives his vision of the black South in the final movement of his "swan-song." It is a modulated version of the tragic contradictions he expressed in his account of Tom Burwell's lynching in section 1. The opposition between the real danger that lies in white violence and the sardonic, even self-satisfied, tone of Layman's depictions of it is to Toomer a counterpoint whose melodies are part of a rich, interesting, and single whole.

Kabnis and Lewis present a similar opposition. They have come to Georgia for more or less the same reasons: to tie up with their past and find out who they are. But they are diametrically different in their behavior and responses. Lewis, an intellectual and "new Negro," admires and respects the culture he explores, but he is too educated and well bred to identify with it. He understands and reaches out but remains an observer who has come for information, not to throw in with a people who can be treated like Mame Lamkins. The local blacks are puzzled by Lewis. But they admire him, too, as Halsey does, for "knowin a bucketful bout most things" but being able to keep his mouth shut (177). But he has no intention of making his life in the South, and in the end he flees because he cannot bear the pain.

Kabnis longs to write poetry, to find beauty here in the South and to formulate it in beautiful words. But the conflicting stimuli disarm him, and he is frustrated because the words that he searches for will not come or are too ugly. The ignorance, dirt, and danger of the South frighten him. At the same time its painful beauty transports him. The dominant tone of irony in this part is especially emphatic in Kabnis's character. The reader can see in Kabnis what he does not see, his pusillanimity and his self-aggrandizing ways. He lacks Lewis's sympathy for and understanding of the life here. He is defensive and belligerent and believes himself in danger when he is not. He resents Lewis's cool, all-knowing manner. Yet, it is Kabnis, not Lewis, who enters the life of Sempter when he becomes the clumsy assistant to Halsey in the wagon shop. It is Kabnis who seems ready to grapple with his fear and anger in the presence of their sources. Toomer's most amusing trick is projecting himself in the character of the uncomfortable and not very attractive poet. "Kabnis is *me*," he tells his friend Waldo Frank.[15] In fact, as is generally assumed, Toomer seems to "be" both Kabnis and Lewis, using them as a self-criticism and a projection of his own deep and unresolvable ambivalence toward his material.

The tension between these and other counterpoint melodies repeat the tension between the ugliness and the beauty of the story of Tom Burwell's lynching, and between the priggish primness of Muriel's reaction to the bloody dwarf and her own smothered spontaneity. These opposites are bound together into an aesthetic whole by the force of art. It is their vital tension that gives the whole its life, not their resolution. This tension prevails at the end of "Kabnis." In the conclusion, the old Negro life in the person of ancient Father John seems to be reborn through the innocent respect of Carrie K., Halsey's young sister, who takes care of the old man in Halsey's basement. Section 5 of "Kabnis," indeed, opens with the image of the night as a pregnant Negro woman, and at the end of section 6 the night gives birth to the "sun" as a "Gold-glowing child" rising "from its cradle in the tree-tops of the forest." Its light is a "birth-song" sent to the village (239). Carrie K., the future, kneels before Father John, the past, in a pool of sacred light as the sun rises, as if receiving the benediction of continuity. Yet Carrie K. has been imbued with the same middle-class restraints on spontaneity and emotion as Muriel in section 2, for when Lewis holds out his hands in a gesture of healthy affection, "The sin-bogies of respectable southern colored folks clamor at her," and she avoids the man with "rigid gravity" (205). She is, as Lewis senses, "the nascent woman," yet "her flesh [is] already stiffening to cartilage, drying to bone" (205). As for Father John, there is something comic about him even when he seems most like the Negro of the folk song. Lewis sees the ambiguity, "A mute John the Baptist of a new religion—or a tongue-tied shadow of an old" (211), and labels him with tongue-in-cheek seriousness "Father John." The old man enrages Kabnis, who sees him simply as a rheumy-eyed ancient whose mind has gone. But he tantalizes even Kabnis with the possibility he possesses some tremendous knowledge that can come only from the past. When he finally does stutter out a few words about the whites' great sin in making the Bible lie, Kabnis laughs contemptuously and calls him an "old black fakir" (238). These ambiguities make the concluding birth imagery equivocal and thus call into question the possibility of the restoration in any form of the old culture. This equivocalness applies to the entire novel, and it reinforces Toomer's original perception: that the disappearance of the old folk-song world is irreversible, and *Cane* is its funeral elegy. It is Toomer's art that calls this world to our attention, his art that, like Keats in "Ode on a Grecian Urn" and "Ode to a Skylark," discloses the beauty that lies in death and dying.

THE AESTHETES: FAUSET, HUGHES, THURMAN, AND SCHUYLER

Toomer's emphasis upon artistic technique put an emotional distance between himself and the historical act of lynching. He was less dedicated to arousing his readers to political action to abolish the practice than to selecting the most aesthetically functional way of depicting it. The Harlem

Renaissance novelists who follow Toomer incline toward the same priority. Preoccupied with their presentation, they, too, create a distance between themselves and the lynching act. How the artists of the period see the world, of course, determines how they see violence, and they see the world through art. "The newer motive," writes Locke of the Renaissance "new Negro," "in being racial is to be so purely for the sake of art" (51). This reverses the "older motive" of being racial for the sake of the race—or, in the antonym to art, propaganda. The central argument of the Renaissance, indeed, was over the question of being racial and how "art" should deal with that identification, whether it should focus on aesthetics or propaganda.

There was no consensus on an answer, but the fact that there was a debate at all showed how different the literary climate in the 1920s was from that of the pre-World War I period. Some of the younger generation —Langston Hughes, Rudolph Fisher, Claude McKay—in revolt against the gentility of their parents, insisted that no propaganda advantage should interfere with the artist's free choice of subject or style. Older conservatives like W. E. B. Du Bois, William Stanley Braithwaite, and Benjamin Brawley, argued that all literature should be propaganda.[16] For the young radicals, the truth of the black experience lay in the lower classes, which had hitherto been minstrelized or ignored, and the most effective means of portraying them was realism. It was precisely the crude and uneducated folk that the conservatives sought to excise from literature and instead to play up those blacks who had reached the middle class and were seeking to live by white, not folk, standards.

The debate had an indirect but important effect upon the treatment of violence in Renaissance novels after the publication of *Cane*. One effect was negative. That is, the "primitivist" novels of the lower classes, like Claude McKay's *Home to Harlem* (1928), Rudolph Fisher's *Walls of Jericho* (1928), or Arna Bontemps's *God Sends Sunday* (1931), contain no lynching scenes or any other kind of white violence against blacks. The story lines all but exclusively follow black characters, urban and country. The conflicts are between the black characters, not black and white ones. What violence they do contain is intraracial, part of the color of the folk world: knifings, shootings, razor fights between men, hair-pulling fights between women. Such violence was the yeast that vitalized the dancing, gaming, drinking, and loving that went on among the carefree blacks.

The other effect of the debate was upon the way those novelists who did take up violence handled it. A line of quite dissimilar novels extends from *Cane* to Waters Edward Turpin's *These Low Grounds* and George W. Lee's *River George* (1937). The novels in this line exemplify the several Renaissance attitudes toward lynching and the question of whether it is to be treated as propaganda or art. The novels fall into two groups, which I will call for the purpose of easy reference the "aesthetes" and the "moralists." Each is affected by the preoccupation with art that marks the Renaissance. But each employs art in a different way. The aesthetes constitute the main school of "new Negroes" whose tendency is to give art priority over social concerns and to use social concerns to energize their art. The moralists regard art as the way to shape and energize their social concerns. Although there is some overlapping of the two, the aesthetes are the closest to the radicals in the theoretical argument about the subject and function of art. Without putting too fine an edge on it, the moralists are the closest to the conservatives.

If there is an earnestness in any of the lynching novels of the aesthetes, it comes not from the use of those novels to protest against lynching or create a heroic model of behavior but from the question of how best to portray the Negro *as* Negro. This links them, weakly, with Jean Toomer, though it is a linkage invidious to them, since none is as skillful or as profound as Toomer. These are "new Negroes" writing. They express an increased confidence in their African American identity and have freed themselves from the need to produce counterpropaganda and counterstereotypes.

The most characteristic feature of the aesthetes' treatment of lynching is to use it as a story within the story of the novel.[17] We have seen Toomer use this technique in Layman's account of the Mame Lamkins lynching. Toomer's successors use the technique as a kind of metafiction, to comment upon the way in which narrative transmutes real experiences into literary images. This produces a metaphor of the whole art urge in the period in which the lynching account is consciously, deliberately, placed in the spotlight as a little work of art within the larger one. Art is by definition not immediate experience. But there are degrees of removal from real life, and in the works I discuss here to illustrate the technique, we can see develop an increasing artistic distance from the world in which lynching really occurs. I do not mean that the authors grew indifferent or cynical about the practice but that they identified with it as artists rather than advocates.

In *Plum Bun* (1929), Jessie Fauset uses this strategy of the story within the story for the relatively traditional purpose of reinforcing two of her characters' commitment to their race. Both Anthony Cross and Angela Murray, angered and exhausted by the prejudice with which they are treated as blacks, pass into the white world. Anthony, after his black father is lynched in Georgia, moves with his Brazilian mother when she marries a white man. Like James Weldon Johnson's ex-colored man, Anthony drifts into whiteness, never denying or confirming his racial origins but living white. Angela herself had become disgusted with the race as well, with the talk "of rents, of lynchings, of building and loan associations," of sacrificing for the race, "the burnt-offering of individualism for some dimly glimpsed racial whole."[18] She, too, flees her origins.

When Anthony and Angela meet, they are drawn to each other, ignorant for the moment of the other's secret. But even when they discover their common background, they are kept apart by other commitments. Then, quite entertainingly, Fauset sweeps those other commitments away, brings the two together, and has Anthony, in the pivotal moment, tell Angela the story of his black father's lynching. Actually, it is the story of a story, for Anthony does not himself witness his father's death. The lynching is thus experienced several removes from the event. But the story has an effect upon both of them. As Anthony reconstructs the context of the tragic black past, he and Angela come together both personally and racially, an updated version of the pairing off of Frances Harper's Iola Leroy and Dr. Frank Latimer. And as if to counteract the decision of James Weldon Johnson's ex-colored man, Anthony declares, "I'm not ashamed of my blood." In fact, Anthony, unlike some of Frances Harper's and Pauline Hopkins's characters, who suggest that white blood can modify and improve black blood, believes that his black blood is "the leaven that will purify this Nordic people of their cruelty and their savage lust of power."[19] Through Anthony's story, Fauset permits these young "new Negroes" to absorb the pain and the humiliation that go with his father's lynching. Like the novel in which it appears, it is a safe, even remote, vehicle for confronting these two attractive people with the worst conditions of their color, which consolidates their affirmation of their black blood. Their own love is the result. They do not become a hero and heroine planning to devote their lives to upgrading the race. They enter a middle-class world, ready to enjoy the cultural riches of Paris, where they are safe from danger or embarrassing racial rejection.

Living up to his comments in "The Negro Artist and the Racial Mountain," Langston Hughes, in *Not without Laughter* (1930), uses a story of white violence to enforce the cultural richness of the black folk. This is a most satisfying novel. Its action is set in the small town of Stanton, Kansas. It deals with a broad range of characters that reflect a variety of classes and types—the puritanical but sympathetically dignified Aunt Hager, her lazy but good-natured son-in-law Jimboy, his hard-working wife, Aunt Hager's other two daughters, one who moves from prostitution to fame as a blues singer and the other who enters the Stanton middle class and becomes ashamed of her family. At the center of the relationships among these characters is the boy, Sandy, whose growth and development into an intelligent young man finally bound for college make up the spine of the novel. Sometimes Aunt Hager and her family and neighbors sit about at night on their porches and in the darkness tell stories about the past. In one such session Sister Johnson recounts her favorite anecdote, her own folktale about her experience as a slave, a freed girl, and a mother: " 'Well, it were like dis,' and the story unwound itself." It ends with the sacking of black Crowville, Mississippi, by a mob of angry whites, partly because they are denied the lynching of a black man when he escapes and partly because the Crowville blacks have prospered and become uppity.

The content of the story is less noteworthy than its tone and the purpose to which Hughes puts it. In the sequence of the conversation, Sister Johnson tells it to make the point that whites "are no damn good." Hughes, though, uses the story to deepen the colors of his portrait. Not only does it call forth the difficulty of black life lived among whites. It also illustrates the rich texture of the black community, its capacity for self-entertainment, its method for recording the tiny pieces of the racial past. This is oral history in the making. Hughes argued for just this subject in "The Negro Artist and the Racial Mountain," a sympathetic depiction of the way country and small-town blacks actually lived. It is also a demonstration of the power of the black vernacular, an impressive application of Hughes's poetic techniques to prose. Sister Johnson comes to her story's climax as the fire set by the whites reaches its most intense point:

An' de fiah light up de whole country clean back to de woods! You could smell fiah, an' you could see it red, an' taste de smoke, an' feel it stingin' yo' eyes. An' you could hear de bo'ads a–fallin' an' de glass a–poppin, an' po' animals roastin' and fryin' an' a–tearin' at dey halters. An' one cow run out, fiah all ovah, wid her milk streamin' down. An' de smoke roll up, de cotton-fields were red . . . an' dey ain't been no mo' Crowville after dat night.[20]

This exemplifies the point that artistic self-consciousness does not result in artificiality. In the power of its artistry, this passage runs a close second to Toomer's account of the Tom Burwell lynching—its impeccable rhythms, its vivid imagery. Hughes, though, adds the emotion of the storyteller. He also infuses into Sister Johnson's manner a dignity and humanity that dialect poetry or prose seldom captured from the folk in the years before Langston Hughes came to show everyone how.[21]

The lynching account as interior story is brought to its apogee by Wallace Thurman in *Infants of the Spring* (1932). His is the most self-conscious use of all, and done in an ironic tone very different from the Hughes passage. Thurman illustrates the very process by which lynching changes from a political and social problem to a subject for fiction. It is a process in which the focus shifts from the atrocity itself to the artist's perception of the atrocity. Thurman's take on the process is coincident with his satire on "the Negro artist" of the Renaissance. Euphoria Blake, for instance, is one of the self-congratulatory phonies who shoulder their way into the Harlem scene, self-consciously placing themselves on the edge of a movement that is torn between authenticity and fraudulence. At Niggeratti House, founded by Euphoria to stage her talents, the black and white artists confusedly pursue the intuitive and spontaneous, but the brainstorming sessions at which they are asked to be iconoclastic on cue are more contrived than natural, and the participants' intuition is more a matter of gin than of heart. Euphoria stars at these gatherings with her own life story, which she tells as the biography of a representative "new Negro."

Euphoria's significant experience, like that of Anthony Cross, starts with a lynching, the spectacle of a black man hanging from a telegraph pole in the small town where she arrives to start college. This experience shapes her life. She cannot get the image of the dead man out of her mind, and her cries in the night when bad dreams awaken her give her the reputation of a kook. From here on, she is a rebel and an outsider, but her story takes the form of Hughes's Sister Johnson in its move through a number of stages. She becomes a race woman, a Marxist-socialist, an agitator against the war and capitalism, and, for these activities, a jail inmate. It is a compelling tale. Nathan Huggins calls her story "a good sermon . . . pungent, forceful, and very moving." Such stories from "the Negro's own life and experience," says Huggins, "had the best chance of being effective art." [22] It is, indeed, how art gets created and becomes a powerful interpreter of human experience, with a strong potential for good.

There is, however, a "canker" here. It is the overaestheticized sensibility that "galls the infants of the spring . . . before their buttons be disclosed," as Laertes tells Ophelia in the passage from which Thurman draws his title (*Hamlet*, 1.3, 39–40). That is, the account itself is a canker upon the innocent experience. Euphoria moves her audience, step by step, from the immediate reality to the story of that reality. It is "art" rather than an engagement with an actual historical event. While Euphoria's story does evoke a certain pathos, as she takes us through her life after the lynching, episode by episode, we begin to suspect her sincerity. What happens to her happens to the new Negro of the Renaissance. After jail and a stint in the employment business where she exploited employer and employee alike and discovered that "Cowardice and conformatism ruled," [23] she decides that she must retreat from a rotten world to the insulated serenity of art. But since art depends on another canker, money, she determines to make herself rich so that she can give herself to art and protect herself from an imperfect world. Her life becomes the material of her art. By the end of her story, we feel the artificiality of her presentation and realize we have witnessed a highly polished performance, not an uncensored outpouring of spontaneous emotion. This is a story she has told "many times" and "embellished . . . with gestures and rhetorical ornamentation," a carefully orchestrated piece of theater. It is a glossy version of Sister Johnson's performance, which is also a repetition. But Hughes writes with affection and respect and captures the ingenuous dignity of the innocent folk storyteller. Thurman writes with a satiric bitterness that suggests in Euphoria a sophisticated self-centeredness. We feel that the reality we are dealing with in Euphoria's story is not the reality of that dreadful body hanging from the pole and its consequences but the story itself and the act of telling it. Art has gained preeminence and in the process, implies Thurman, has been cheapened. At the end, "Her eyes were afire. A twisted lace handkerchief unfurled in her lap" (90). Lynching has become for Euphoria not a practice full of terror and inhumanity but a "euphoric" aesthetic experience in which she is the leading actor.

That lynching, moreover, is going to fall into other hands for further use. Euphoria's story becomes material for Raymond Taylor, the troubled black writer. He wants to use it for his own novel, more interested in the lynching as good copy than as injustice. Thurman suggests that as lynching recedes into the past as a historical threat from whites, its immediacy diminishes, its political urgency softens, and the focus upon the real experience is replaced by a focus upon the aesthetic one. Earnest tracts and melodramas are replaced by stories about blacks' lives. In "being racial," which, as Locke says, is "the newer motive" of "the new Negro," for "purely" artistic reasons (51), passion and earnestness are confronted by the self-consciousness of the artist. But where such a transformation can enhance the representation of violence in *Plum Bun* and *Not without Laughter,* Thurman implies that artistic self-consciousness has, as the Renaissance comes to an end, become mere phoniness and exploitation. We can see it happening in Raymond. "I'd like to see [blacks] retaliate against whites in their own sphere," he says. "For every lynching, I'd like to see Negroes take their toll on whites" (218). This has the ring of the heroic age in it. But Raymond is not talking about the selfless courage of a Nat Turner or a Henry Blake. He is cynically speculating in the abstract. "I don't care about stray darkies getting lynched," he says, "but I do care about people who will fight for a principle" (219).

Raymond seems both innocent and decadent, working with both good and cynical intentions. This mixture characterizes the way art represents lynching in *Infants of the Spring*. This in turn reflects the problem with the entire new Negro movement. Thurman presents it as a movement torn apart by its own inner stresses and differences. Charles Scruggs calls *Infants of the Spring* "an appropriate conclusion to the entire period," for it discloses the "tragic insularity" of the movement, its abandonment of the "communal soil" for elitism and aestheticism.[24] In attacking the period's decadence, Thurman has himself come under attack for the same defect, for elitism, "self-hatred," shame of blacks, for having written a confused attack, and for the failure of the novel "to transcend the age it denounces."[25] No one can dispute the bitterness that *Infants of the Spring* expresses, the anger with what Thurman perceives as a failed movement. But the imagery with which Thurman buries the Harlem Renaissance (Bone calls him its "undertaker") is resonant and forceful, his symbolism rigorous and clear. Euphoria closes Niggeratti House. Ray's mistress, Lucille, has an abortion. Paul Arbian commits a futile suicide. In Thurman's handling, the Renaissance is over, an aborted infant of the spring, nine years after Toomer's "gold-glowing" sun rose from its cradle to shine on Sempter, Georgia. Like the Lady of Shalott, Thurman suggests, the new Negro expires in a kind of self-reflexive ivory tower looking at the world through mirrors. But because Thurman makes this criticism of his contemporaries does not mean that he, too, suffers from a self-destructive self-reflexiveness. *Infants of the Spring* is a good novel that makes its point with a stringent clarity.

George Schuyler's mordant parody of lynching and color madness, *Black No More* (1931), can be taken as a kind of coda to my discussion of the aesthetes' novels. Here a lynching takes place in a zany, impossible, pseudo–science-fiction world that anticipates Nathanael West's mad Horatio Alger travesty, *A Cool Million* (1934). However, Schuyler's satiric account is no retreat into the "tragic insularity" of the new Negro; it is a rollicking, blasting attack on the stupidity of the lynching horror, as well as a lampoon of color-obsessed Americans—black artists and con men (brothers under the skin), phony white politicians and businessmen, hyperbolically pious southern Christians. Turning the color conventions upside down, he makes his lynching victims a couple of burlesqued white supremacists, who, in a bizarre twist of fate, fall into the hands of the followers of the True Faith Christ Lovers' Church in the lily-white southern town of Happy Hill. Arthur Snobbcraft and Samuel Buggerie, whose names are half the fun, meet their fate through Schuyler's joyfully complicated plot, in which a black man discovers a method for turning black skin white. This sends everyone into a frenzy of skin-color changing, with blacks coming to look almost white and whites desperately searching for some color to maintain their distinction from blacks. In a dizzying sequence of color changes, we end up with Snobbcraft and Buggerie attempting to escape the country with their faces blackened for disguise, which, unfortunately for them, plays into the hands of the lynching-hungry Happy Hillites. Disregarding the fact that the two men are actually white, the Happy Hill church people proceed to "the ceremonies . . . according to time-honored custom," an allusion to Schuyler's perception that lynching was a formal ritual, like a church ceremony. The Happy Hillites are ecstatic; the victims, as "the flames subside," are just "two charred hulks." [26]

This is not light, knee-slapping stuff. Schuyler writes from a seemingly bottomless disgust, most of it directed toward the color system created by whites and carried to its extreme by the custom of lynching. He catches not only the absurdity of lynching that goes beyond outrage but the mob psychology, the hypocrisy that justifies the atrocity by invoking the name of Jesus Christ. Like its contemporaries, *Black No More* illustrates the distance the writers of the Harlem Renaissance have moved from the previous generation's treatment of lynching—of the whole color issue. It is inconceivable that anyone could have produced such a lampoon of lynching even ten years earlier. In 1921 fifty-nine blacks were lynched; in 1931, when *Black No More* was published, the number was twelve, evidence of a change in the atmosphere. Schuyler can now represent the ceremony of darkness in all its terrible ridiculousness. This expedition into an extreme satiric form is the single quality that makes it logical to treat *Black No More* with the novels of the "aesthetes." Otherwise, Schuyler's anger and his direct engagement with a lynching make him a "moralist."

THE MORALISTS: DU BOIS, JONES, AND WHITE

If I were using the terminology of Robert Bone, I could call the "moralists" the "rear guard," the novelists whose temperament and notion of the uses of the novel more closely resemble those of the previous generation than any other group of the Harlem Renaissance. They echo the deep preoccupation with lynching of that earlier period and keep open the question of the culture hero and whether he should use retaliatory violence. But, except for W. E. B. Du Bois and Joshua Henry Jones, the writers in this group belong solidly with the Harlem Renaissance and its aftermath in the Depression, for the novels they write are portraits rather than polemicals, and they extract from the act of lynching a tragic quality never before captured in the novel. In this respect, they are artists shaping their material. At the same time, like Schuyler, they intensely engage themselves with the issue. Oddly enough, their treatment of the questions raised by lynching goes counter to a general feeling of optimism and pugnacity in the years after World War I, a widely expressed certainty in the value of their black-ness and a refusal to accept passively any attacks against it. Marcus Garvey aroused the masses with his invigorating militancy. Black veterans of the war came home determined to get their due. Even the man on the street believed "The black worm has turned."[27] The black worm may indeed have turned, but in the black novel that deals with lynching this new Negro hardly appears. The avenger, for example, sympathetically portrayed in Martin Delany's Gofer Gondolier and Charles Chesnutt's Josh Green, takes on a much more negative tint. He is represented in some cases as a psycho-path whose hatred of whites warps his human understanding and distorts his judgment and perception. He loses sight of the ends of the racial struggle, reveling instead in the blood of his victims and reflecting, like the lynch mobs did in their highest frenzy, a pathological eroticism. In *Black Thunder* (1936), the story of Gabriel Prosser's aborted slave uprising, Arna Bontemps is one of the first novelists to draw the connection between sex and racial butchery. He shows bloodthirsty Criddle, Gabriel's lieutenant, wielding his great sword like a vengeful phallus.[28] Criddle and his near contemporary, Perigua, in W. E. B. Du Bois's *Dark Princess* (1928), recall the neurotic Iago or the plotting Cassius. We see them as lean and hungry, envious and unselectively vindictive, hating whites in the abstract, as whites are portrayed hating blacks, and acting with a vehemence far out of propor-tion to the situation—as Perigua does when he wants to blow up an entire train of Ku Kluxers in retaliation for the lynching of a railroad porter.

Similarly, the forgiving Christian is sometimes cast in an extreme form, unacceptably passive, even cowardly and dishonorable. Preaching restraint toward white violence, he is sometimes represented as a race traitor and provides occasions for expressions of the author's self-criticism or self-contempt. "We're tame tabbies," complains a character in Du Bois's *Dark Princess*, "fawning dogs." "You couldn't get one nigger in a million to fight at all, and they'd sell each other out."[29] In George Washington Lee's *River George* (1937), one character scorns those "niggers" who are "too scared an' too lazy fuh any use."[30] The object of this contempt is Do Pop, a whining town loafer just recently converted to religion, who, like Ches-nutt's Jerry Letlow, fears whites inordinately and urges blacks to avoid any act that would provoke them. "Dis aini' no time fur niggers tuh be talkin' 'bout zisting de white folks," says Do Pop. "It's just gwine git a lot uv dem lynched" (102). Later Do Pop, for a paltry reward, delivers the protagonist into the hands of the whites who want to kill him.

These extreme types, equally undesirable, suggest that the hero lies be-tween them, as in the novels of the earlier period, a man of courage who is not, at the same time, eager to shed blood. The two narratives of the post-1922 period that were composed on the model of the melodramatic romances of the pre-Renaissance years, do take the middle way, with the hard choices of an intransigent reality avoided rather than met. In *By Sanction of Law* (1924) Joshua Henry Jones, after an effective lynching scene, has his black hero manfully defeat the white supremacist villain at nonmortal fisticuffs and bring the villain's prejudiced white family to see the light. So successful is the hero, Truman Bennett, set from the old mode, that the oppressors give their blessing to the interracial marriage of the handsome, well-bred, light-skinned Bennett and their "white" daughter, who go off to Europe without rancor or desire for revenge. Jones manages to kill two birds with one stone, however. Not only does he crash through the color line by marrying off his hero and heroine, but he reveals through records at the county courthouse that virtually every "white" family in the region, so protective of its race purity, has some black blood in it, including the family from which the white heroine comes. Bennett is too noble to crow over his double victory. Instead, he reaffirms his loyalty to "our native land" and promises the reader a new day of comity between the races and lynch-free friendship.

W. E. B. Du Bois's *Dark Princess* approaches the middle way much more symbolically. A worldwide council made up of the world's people of color contains factions pro and con violence, one believing "only in Force," the other in "Peace and Reason." The hero and heroine are unable to decide which side to support. In the end, they back neither but suggest a solution in a kind of Marxist/Hegelian evolution toward an ideal mind: a "slow, sure, gathering growth of power and vision, expanding and uniting with the thought of the wider world."[31] When all other effective means of dealing with white violence and oppression are seemingly closed to them, hero Matthew Towns and the Dark Princess act to set this growth into motion. Like two symbolic gods in a sacred fertility ritual, they sequester themselves, couple sexually on a plane high above the merely erotic, and conceive a golden-headed savior with an East Indian name, the Maharaja of Bwodpur, a descendant of the Indian people's old gods through the African American "Kali, the Black One: wife of Siva, Mother of the world," who happens to be Matthew Towns's old peasant mother as well.[32] It will take time, but the little Maharajah will eventually right the wrongs of centuries and complete the plans of the world council of colored people. Thus Du Bois skirts a bloody and intractable reality with a kind of mystical deus ex machina. Du Bois is not "serious," though—that is, realistic. He subtitles his story "A Romance," by which he means a method of fantasizing rather than confronting, and his choosing that form illustrates his own bemusement over an intractable world, combined with his inextinguishable optimism in a form that mystically joins the parts of the worlds of color that he will turn to in a much more political way in the fifties.

These two romances, in which all is made right without very much trouble, are very much different from the three moralist novels that appear at the beginning and ending of this period. For them, the question of what to do about lynching and which culture-hero model to select turns more on the tragic implications of lynching than on any hope of ending or escaping it, through the middle or any other way. In these narratives blacks do not escape white violence or the life it symbolizes. Neither violent retaliation nor nonviolent acceptance will save them, and the ardent protagonist, working for the betterment of his community, must give up his life to the white mob. Escaping to the North with a beautiful bride to continue the racial work or exploiting a white skin to pass is not his option. His fate is to be a body hanging from a tree. This combines a political with an aesthetic sensibility. Racial and economic politics results in a lynching charged with tragic irony and pathos, possessing the kind of beauty that Toomer was the first to perceive. The hero is quasi-political, active but nonviolent, and his heroism is based on his own death or failure, which occurs because of his selfless devotion to the good cause. He fails in large part because the people he would lead out of their own oppression have not arrived at the point where they can collectively absorb the courage the hero would instill in them. One senses a faint light at the edges of the dark vision these novels present. The death of the hero, his failure, or both occur, though, before that light adequately brightens. Cruel and unscrupulous whites continue to set the circumference of the world and rules of behavior. The hero, by virtue of his courage and his zeal for his people, finds himself so far in front of the people he is trying to save that he stands in totally vulnerable isolation. The darkness remains so intense that even the light he would carry is quickly extinguished by his lynching or his failure, and the people remain benighted and divided.

Walter F. White was perhaps the most fully qualified of the Harlem Renaissance writers to transform the sentimental romance tract of the pre–World War I period into a true novel. He researched southern lynching for the NAACP and wrote up his findings in *Rope and Faggot*.[33] He thus knew firsthand the victims' families and the victimizers, and he became a tireless advocate of a federal law against lynching. The result is *The Fire in the Flint* (1924). Even though it is a strong advocacy novel, it stands next to *Cane* as a key text of the early Renaissance, but without *Cane's* polish and vividness. It is the novel of a man deeply involved in a social and political issue, but who is trying to think like an artist.

In *The Fire in the Flint,* White programmatically examines the way a lynching takes place. He sets two cultured and well-educated black men against a gang of ignorant southern rednecks. When the white men rape Bob and Kenneth Harper's sister, the act of violence confronts the two brothers with the old question. How should they react? Each brother follows one of the two options in the public debate over dealing with white violence, and White works out the novel's action according to the consequences that follow from the brothers' different decisions. Bob Harper shoots two of the rapists, but the whites form a lynch mob and Bob kills himself with his last bullet before the mob drags his body through the village streets behind an automobile.

Kenneth Harper, like Chesnutt's William Miller, is a well-trained doctor. Now faced with two outrages against his family, he tries to reason out the proper reaction. He moves through the familiar stages, from the "ungovernable hatred" of "the wild beast," who has cast off his civilized restraint, to the reasoned understanding of the social man who knows that fantasies of just one black man gaining revenge on an entire white community have their limits. After his first rage, when he believes, guiltily, that Bob "had been a man," he reconsiders, like Chesnutt's Dr. Miller, asking himself whether it "wouldn't . . . take more courage to live." [34] The note of combined fear and valid practicality slightly disappoints us in Dr. Harper, but his conflict is true and real, his emotion genuine. We believe him when he decides against violence and, again like Dr. Miller, rejects the opportunity for revenge against a white person by deciding to attend the sick wife of a white friend. But in Cross Roads, Georgia, black generosity is no virtue to lynch-minded whites. Harper's humane response to his friend's call only means to members of the same mob that raped his sister and forced his brother's death that he is a black man visiting a white woman's house. They seize him and put him to the flame on the charge of attacking the white woman who owes him her life.

It is true that White says that, in spite of the "personal tragedy and death for the hero, one senses that the spirit of revolt against bigotry which he symbolizes will be accelerated rather than diminished by his death." [35] But once again I am struck by the contrast between what the black author says about his text and what the text reveals. Dr. Harper's death calls into doubt *any* choice made by well-meaning blacks, for whether they choose manhood or cowardliness, fanatical revenge or humane generosity and forgiveness, the results are the same. This also forces us to question Bob Harper's unthinking response to the news of his sister's rape. How is Mamie helped or the black community uplifted by the purchase of his honor with his death? It only incensed the lynch mob further—to go after Kenneth. Is it honor, for that matter, or dignity to be forced to suicide crouching in a burning barn surrounded by murderous whites? Is it possible to bring under control or to find justice in an insane world by posing, as if they were options open to blacks, the questions of violent retaliation, Christian forgiveness, or nonviolent activism? In the end, the action of White's novel suggests that it makes no difference. The "fire in the flint," at first a metaphor for the noble courage of a true man who determines to avenge his own, becomes a symbol of the powerlessness of the southern black against a lynch mob, for the fire that leaps from the flint consumes the one in whose heart it was struck.

The Fire in the Flint is not about a solution but about a tragic fact in a tragic world. As a novel it does not argue a political or social point of view. It dramatizes a reality in which there is little hope. The Fire in the Flint is not a great work of fiction, but it is not a tract. It does not abstract from reality and argue a case. It dramatizes an experience in which a real social problem inheres but does not purport to solve that problem. Bob and Kenneth Harper, in differing ways, commit acts which, however understandable, set in motion the inhuman and inexorable process that can have only one outcome. This is a mechanism cast as iron necessity. White's predecessors avoided this view of their world, as if acknowledging the full scale of lynching's awfulness would have led to a paralyzing despair. Their optimism, however inconsistent with reality, operated as a survival technique. Their heroes and heroines, who escape the conditions of their world, who are not subjected to the same conditions as the lynching victims they try to help, reflect the novelists' determination not to give in to white violence. Only as the lynching figures gradually decline can a novelist like White allow himself to admit the tragic necessity of the chain of events that lead to the lynching. Such a perception comes only with artistic distance, which links the satire of Wallace Thurman and George Schuyler with the tragic realism of The Fire in the Flint. Both reflect the great changes occurring in the twenties and thirties in the relationship writers took up between their fiction and the reality that fiction interpreted. They also tacitly imply that, insofar as violence is concerned, the worst of the plague is over. Lynching has gone into irreversible decline.

FOLK RESIGNATION: LEE AND TURPIN

The novels that end this period more closely resemble The Fire in the Flint than the novels of main-current Renaissance writers. The action of George Washington Lee's River George (1937) and Waters Edward Turpin's These Low Grounds (1937) is grounded on the rigid inevitability of lynching. Like White, Lee and Turpin focus upon what Gloster might call "the experiences of the black masses of the cotton belt." [36] Their characters are realistic versions of the black peasants that Du Bois romanticizes in *Dark Princess.* At the same time, they bring in college-educated blacks who are driven by the desire to change a society in which lynching is possible. Unlike White, however, they view lynching through the eyes of the black peasant, the uneducated farm worker. For them, lynching is an element of the folk experience in the same way the seasons are, and the planting and harvesting of crops, and the system of tenant farmer exploitation by the white land-owners. The folk live harsh lives, but they deal with their difficulties sto-ically, transcending their condition with the kind of peasant resignation that we saw in old Abe Overley in Robert Waring's *As We See It* (1910). Lee opens *River George,* for example, with the sickness, death, and funeral of Aaron George's father, illustrating the way the folk bear the great sadness of the inevitable. Before the "magnificence" of their grieving but unde-spairing hymns as the casket is lowered into the ground, "terror fled, leaving only awe and a sense of the greatness of this messenger who had visited them" (19). They stoically respect the forces that govern their lives but that they cannot understand, and this confers upon them a dignity and a richness beyond politics or sociology.

Folk resignation is a highly modified form of the traditional reaction of the forgiving Christian frequently found in the sentimental romance. It has emerged from the process of the Harlem Renaissance as an affectionate and admiring reaction to the newly respected lower-class peasant. Aaron George, however, confronts that resignation with the impatient dissatisfac-tion of the educated over the way the white landowners treat the passive black sharecroppers. He has the main qualities of the hero: vision, spiritual and physical courage, and selflessness. He challenges the white supremacy traditions of his southern town by trying to organize the exploited ten-ants.[37] Lee takes this story from the tale of a real man, whose strength and militancy as a worker on the Mississippi River achieved the status of folk legend in Memphis.[38] But it is also an archetypal story, the native son returning to disrupt, with new ideas, the precarious balance between his people and their dangerous environment. Besides the cowardly warnings of Do Pop, George's loving mother Hannah intercedes with the same folk wisdom that has guided her her whole life through the threatening world of Holly Rock. She stays out of politics, confines herself to her house and garden, and follows the rhythms of the year. She warns her son about his political work. It is too much like white behavior, she says. Blacks have their own way of dealing with life, Lee's version of what Alain Locke calls the "race-gift." [39] "Niggers," she says, "got sumpin white folks ain' got. Dey kin res' an' be easy like in de[y] min's when white folks is frettin' demselves to death." Patience will deliver the future to the blacks, in what Du Bois called in *Dark Princess* "the slow, sure growth of gathering power and vision." Hannah prophesies that there is a "Great day comin'. It's niggers what try tuh push it too ha'd dat makes trouble. Yuh ain' got tuh try hurryin' t'ings too much, dat's all" (119). Lee does not associate Hannah's position with the sabotaging cowardice of Do Pop. In Aaron's mind, Hannah's is inspired faith, "a vision which could see in the future a glory coming to his people through the very force of their being, something which she believed must inevitably come about, without help or hindrance from such puny efforts as those which his committee might make" (120).

The degree of legitimacy Lee intends to grant Hannah's folk wisdom is unclear. On the one hand, when Aaron does not heed her warning against hurrying the onset of the millennium, the whites force him into a situation in which he accidentally kills a white man, and he spends the rest of the novel fleeing the lynch mob. When he tries to return home, the mob catches him. The process must complete itself in blood. George's mother and best friend find him, hanging from a tree, and Lee leaves the reader with the terrible but poetic image characteristic of the Harlem Renaissance and the Depression writers:

Then they saw it. Dark in the meager light of the stars it hung from a tree near the cabin door, tremendous, and heavy, and quiet, save that it swayed gently, and turned a little on the rope that held it. The legs hung straight, the great feet with toes pointed to earth, the long, ape-like arms, and huge hands, hung limp. The head was fallen forward on its chest. (274)[40]

On the other hand, the text does not support final advocacy of peasant resignation and Hannah's religious faith in a redemption of the black community sometime in a vague unspecified future. Instead, we get contradictions, and they suggest the same meaninglessness that comes in *The Fire in the Flint*. Aaron George's struggle against a repressive system is admirable; but he is killed without establishing a beachhead against the whites. His mother's way, for all its apparent wisdom, seems to provide no more effective solution. Her resignation was appropriate to the death of her husband, who died in the natural course of events, a man who had lived his life well to the end. Aaron's death comes prematurely and undeservedly, robbing the community of a future, and leaving Hannah personally bereft. Besides, she refuses to follow her way. Instead of absorbing the death of her son into the great sorrow song of her husband's funeral ceremony, she denies its reality. Aaron's face has been battered beyond recognition, and that gives Hannah the option of believing the lynched figure to belong to someone else. We are left with the futility of Aaron's death, of his work in the farmer's organization, even of Hannah's faith. We feel nothing of nature's irresistible process here, which at least promises new life, nothing of the awe and power of great forces at work. Indeed, lynching must not, Lee seems to say, be mistaken for some great messenger who carries off the appointed with sad dignity. It is a nasty act of unnecessary violence that grows out of "hate and greed and lust and terror" (268), a tragedy that results from the assertion of manly courage and the humanitarian wish to help the weak overcome their oppression. It finally reduces the very real heroic potential of Aaron George to total degradation, emptied of human identity, his face battered beyond recognition, his formerly powerful limbs transformed into the symbols of an ape, that animal that served whites so well in their relentless humiliation of the African American.

Most noteworthy is the image of Aaron George's dead body. Here Lee introduces an interesting modification in the traditional representation of a lynching. With almost no exceptions, previous novelists focused their attention upon the violence itself: the whole process of the lynching, the behavior of the white mob, what the mob does to the victim's body. Lee, reflecting the influence of Harlem Renaissance art, changes the tableau. The scene that Aaron's mother and friend observe is quiet, even peaceful. No yells echo off the trees. No white mob enjoys the spectacle. Only the stars look down, in the indifference of nature. We see the outcome rather than the act. The reference to the apelike body infuses the image with a strange pathos, a great and natural strength meanly and cruelly subdued. This is a darkly beautiful painting. It is, in fact, the best thing Lee leaves us, though we are not sure just what viewpoint prevails at the end. River George's dead body gives us no help except to show a powerful silence that perhaps speaks for itself.

These Low Grounds chronicles the lives of four generations of a black Maryland family from just before Emancipation to the middle years of the Depression. The frame of this chronicle is the cycle of seasons. Over the years of the four generations, Turpin illustrates the way in which youth turns into age, and white men, in every generation, kill black men. Winter comes, literally in the climate and symbolically in the lynch mob. The season of winter is not perpetual, but the lynch mob seems never to change. Just after the Civil War, black Jim Prince tries unsuccessfully to stop a lynching. His grandson, Jimmy-Lew Grundy, makes a similar attempt and similarly fails in 1936. The two efforts are tied together by the chain of events in which the members of the Grundy and Prince families participate. The repetition of the lynching episode demonstrates something of the same thesis that informed *River George*—that human experience repeats itself from one generation to the next, each, like "the woods and fields," flaming "in beauty before their annual submission to death."[41] Thus, Jimmy-Lew, young, ambitious to contribute to his people's development, seeing only the hopeful side of his world, is harshly taught how nature mixes life with death and how youth's beauty and strength are sapped by the drag of reality. He is taught to accept the "submission to death," the passive acknowledgment of nature's irresistible process.

His initiation occurs as he rushes toward the lynching he is too late to prevent, repeating his grandfather's failure three-quarters of a century earlier. Just as his grandfather had, Jimmy-Lew sets out to do something to prevent lynching in the future, trying to persuade the members of his community to sign a petition to the governor. And just as in his grandfather's time, the members of the community—out of inertia, fear, cynicism—refuse to take action. Jimmy-Lew feels the activist's anger at his people. In the novel's climactic scene with the young woman he is going to marry, Ellen Miles, he complains of their inertia, their cowardliness, the shame they make him feel for "being an American Negro." How can he marry and bring children into a world in which he cannot "act and feel like a man," in which he cannot give those children "protection from a lynch mob"? This is the nonviolent activist speaking in Jimmy-Lew, and his is a position we sympathize with. But Turpin undermines our sympathy, inadvertently, by allowing Jimmy's anger to become a kind of temper tantrum. Ellen, maternal and mature, resembling Hannah George and Matthew Towns's black mother Kali, comforts him with a quietistic explanation of the community's failure to act against the atrocity. "We're just people," she says. "And in our working, our loving, our sorrowing, and our dying we are making the America of Now and Tomorrow, just as we helped make it Yesterday."[42] Turpin gives her the strength of the all-accepting earth mother, and Jimmy-Lew is in this last scene like a child, burying his face against Ellen, unable to say more than "Maybe . . . maybe."

These Low Grounds seems a timorous equivocation, an unsuccessful attempt to hide quietism beneath authentic resignation. Neither Ellen nor Jimmy-Lew stands here as an admirable figure, yet Turpin clearly neither satirizes them nor subjects them to the awful fate of White's Harper brothers. Are we to grieve for the tragedy of the unpreventable lynching? Are we to subside into the all-accepting resignation of Ellen? Are we to rise up in anger and fling ourselves against the machinery of such injustice? Turpin does not seem clear on these questions himself. Nevertheless, in the evolution of literary history, *These Low Grounds* represents the state of the African American novel of violence three years before the publication of Richard Wright's epochal novel, *Native Son*. Turpin writes his novel after the Renaissance makes the folk a proper subject of fiction and lynching ceases to be the profound social problem it was in the years before 1923. The image of the hero gives way to the image of the folk living out a harsh life in a harsh environment. The middle-class dream of absorption into the white mainstream has changed to the artist's desire to depict a new black reality. For the African American novelist, lynching became, by the end of the 1930s, not an atrocity it was the duty of novelists to attack but an ingrained part of that reality.

AFTER WORLD WAR II:
LYNCHING, HISTORY, AND THE
SOURCE OF IDENTITY

A sense of identity is based on the experience of perdurance through shifting circumstances; and since all actual situations up to the present are, by definition, past situations, identity always has to be sought in the past. That is why continuing scrutiny of the real past is so important to human growth.

Gary Wills, *Reagan's America*

THE DISAPPEARANCE OF TRADITIONAL LYNCHING:
A NEW OPTIMISM

Between 1937, when Turpin's *These Low Grounds* and Lee's *River George* were published, and 1953, when James Baldwin brought out his first novel, *Go Tell It on the Mountain,* there seems to have been a moratorium on the topic of southern lynching in the African American novel.[1] It was as if the distortions of the war years brought on such changes that black writers concerned with the South and its violence had to pause and take stock. For that matter, the war seemed to have wiped the slate clean. No author of a pre–World War II lynching novel, except W. E. B. Du Bois, took up the subject again after 1945.[2] A new generation seized control of the territory. A new stage had been reached in black attitudes toward violence and in the creation of a hero for an age in which the nature of white violence was changing and the aggressiveness of blacks was increasing.

The major change was a reprise of the one thirty years earlier, after World War I, when the "new Negro" became more combative and determined that white oppression would no longer be tolerated without a fight. The reappearance of this temper in a somewhat different form suggested that the earlier one had not quite taken, or at the least was short-lived and had generated no major freedom movement. The failure of the hero in the novels of Walter White, George W. Lee, and Waters Edward Turpin reflected a perceived failure of the time. In the post–World War II period, the change I am describing was of a different nature from its predecessor, deeper and more substantial and, as events bore out, more effective politically. For the post-World War II lynching novel, the main change occurred in the temper of the black community. A general collective courage comes into existence conspicuously different from the isolated instances of daring that pepper the history of lynching. The symptom of this development appears in the African American novel in the emergence of a new hero. He is still selfless and loyal and may even die from white violence. But the black community now responds to his courageous example. If he dies, he is vindicated by the political activation of the group.

Change after World War II came slowly for African Americans, though. Jim Crow still confined them in special sections of public facilities, and they still went without the vote. In an area already behind the rest of the country economically and educationally, they were often used as emergency rather than as regular labor and kept out of white classrooms. White supremacist southern congressmen and senators could easily block any substantive civil rights legislation that might correct the situation. And white southerners did continue to attack blacks with a cruelty that reflects a continuing hatred and fear. Thirty-one blacks were lynched in the decade of the forties.[3]

But though this figure was appalling enough in those war years when the nation was fighting for democracy against fascism, it was a 74 percent drop from the 119 reported lynchings between 1930 and 1939. This was the largest drop by percent in a single decade since whites had installed the practice as the method of choice for keeping blacks "in their place." In the 1950s there was an even steeper drop-off in the count, an 81 percent change from the thirty-one in the forties to six in the fifties and then to three in the sixties. These figures signal an overall diminishment of white violence against blacks in the decade after World War II and the subtle new attitudes that develop in both races. Even widespread police brutality and the legalized "lynchings" made possible by unfair court proceedings indicated,[4] if in a backhanded way, a new consciousness in southern whites that at least the appearances of justice must be followed, that the old days of open season on blacks had gone. As Robert Zangrando says, "the mob no longer roamed at will" by the time the war was over.[5]

As lynching diminished, those lynchings that did occur were also profoundly changed. In the fifties and sixties, the classic public lynching disappeared. In the single year of 1955, the Reverend George W. Lee, Lamar Smith, and Gus Courts were all killed by "unknown assailants" for "racial reasons." The same thing happened in the sixties to Medgar Evers, Michael Schwerner, James Chaney, Andrew Goodman, Viola Liuzzo. Not all of these victims were black. But more to the point, none of them was publicly hanged, burned, or mutilated. Lee and Liuzzo were killed by shots from passing cars. Medgar Evers was gunned down by an assailant hiding behind a hedge. Schwerner, Goodman, and Chaney were turned over to a mob somewhere on a Mississippi back road, beaten, shot, then concealed in a grave. If we say these people were *lynched,* the word no longer produces a vision of epic festivals of torture that would attract entire towns, or the image of sheet-draped men boldly and blatantly parading their victim in the town square for the edification and pleasure of the local populace. In the new reality it suggests furtive ambushes by single assailants or small groups, and the classic lynching is replaced by simple murder.[6]

The change in the nature of the lynching party is matched by new reasons for which whites kill blacks—and black sympathizers. In most lynchings of the pre-1940s era, the victims were accused of assaulting a white man, or stealing from him, or not paying a debt, or being uppity, or raping or trying to rape a white woman. In the fifties and sixties, the majority of the killings occur because of political activity. Many of the victims are killed for organizing voter registration drives or trying to vote or participating in NAACP activities. Moreover, their deaths are not only a moral but a political scandal, all the media broadcasting the news to a disapproving nation.

Even the nature of the victim changes in the new era. The typical victim of the classic lynching normally tried to avoid arousing whites, and if he overstepped the racial boundaries, he did so unintentionally. At the same time, his or her powerlessness was the source of shame and frustration that so devastated the sense of dignity for blacks. Most of the victims of white violence during the fifties and sixties deliberately challenge the code and its boundaries. The victim converts into the hero.

Instances of collective courage increase. Seth Cagin and Philip Dray tell the story of a group of blacks rescuing Freedom Riders being attacked by a huge mob in Anniston, Alabama, in May of 1961. As the rescue party came into view, "The white mob could hardly believe what it saw. The Anniston police . . . stood open-mouthed in wonder at the spectacle of fifteen car-loads of Negroes rolling into town with shotgun barrels protruding out the windows."[7] In 1957, blacks in the town of Monroe, North Carolina, turned back a Klan caravan, breaking up the motorcade of shouting and jeering whites with "sustained fire" that sent the "robed men fleeing in every direction."[8] Neither the Monroe nor the Anniston action is unique to the post-1940s. Similar stories can be told about the pre–World War II days. But in the fifties and sixties these instances are more frequent, and they express a new political will taking shape all over the South.

The case of fourteen-year-old Emmett Till is a subterranean example of the change that is occurring in individual blacks. In the summer of 1955, his beating and shooting seem to announce to the world that the lynchers are still in command. Roy Bryant and J. W. Milam kill "Bobo" Till, visiting from Chicago, for allegedly affronting Bryant's wife. But interviewing them a year after the crime, southern journalist William Bradford Huie discovers that Bryant and Milam undertook their defense of their southern honor reluctantly and killed the black youngster only after he refused, with the same cockiness with which he had whistled at Bryant's wife, to acknowledge their superiority as white men.[9] That unobserved encounter on the bank of the Tallahatchie is a clash between the new black and the old white, though it had nothing to do with voter registration or sitting in at a lunch stand. Till defies the two white men, who seem more desperate than he, by showing that no threat of violence can force him to renounce his own self-esteem. The conventional smart aleck symbolizes a political movement that cracks the old forms. When James Forman went to Mississippi from Chicago as a fourteen-year-old in the mid-forties, he thought just like Emmett Till. Putting a hunting knife in his suitcase, he determined to use it on any white who started something. "Didn't matter what happened to me," Forman writes in retrospect. "I simply was not going to allow one of them crackers to hit me. Kill me, baby, but one of you will go down with me!" His own pugnacity is reinforced when he later sees a young black man, riding a bus in Memphis, defy the Jim Crow law and take a seat in the white section. A white man challenges him, but the black stands his ground. The encounter exhilarates Forman. "Yeah," says Forman to himself, "freedom was in the air. I felt good."[10]

The Emmett Till story also illustrates what is happening to whites. Bryant and Milam, who measured their own worth by an outmoded code, think they are honorably doing their community's will. But even though that community backs them during their trial and even though they are acquitted by an all-white jury a year later, they are pariahs in that same community. Their businesses are ruined by a general boycott of blacks who refuse to buy from or work for them. The white landowners who had contributed to their defense fund refuse to rent them land, and local bankers refuse to loan them money. The Sunflower County sheriff orders Milam to stop carrying the .45 pistol that county officers had previously ignored and with which he had killed Till. And local residents regard the two as "a tough bunch," of whom they "might as well be rid."[11]

Whites may have angrily opposed the civil rights movement, attacked marchers, got out the police dogs, set the fire hoses on demonstrators. But beneath it all was a growing disorientation and uncertainty. In the Nashville sit-ins of the early 1960s, the spectacle of polite, well-dressed black students from neighboring universities "who did not grovel or avert their gaze when a white man spoke" dismayed white Nashvilleans. "Groups of anxious white customers huddled together, confused and not at all sure how to react. Why were the Negroes doing this? What did it mean? Shouldn't someone call the police?" It was almost, a witness said later, "like a stock scene from a sci-fi movie when panic grips a city under attack by aliens or giant grasshoppers." [12] Even the Klan members of Monroe, North Carolina, seem put off their balance by this wave of black audacity. When the Klansmen hear that local black leaders are seeking to integrate the Monroe public swimming pool, instead of seizing them and hanging them from the nearest tree they circulate a petition calling for the removal of the troublemakers from the town. In the Montgomery bus boycott of 1956, says the Reverend Glenn Smiley, a white activist from the Fellowship for Reconciliation in New York, "Whites are scared stiff and Negroes are calm as cucumbers." "For the first time," as one of the participants said, "whites were confronted by Negroes who acted like men," and "All the threats which had been used to suppress the Negro had lost their potency." [13] Here were heroes patterned after the old model of the nonviolent activist.

In the new air of the South, violence in its old form is disappearing as a force for maintaining the rigid structure of white supremacy. Lynching as it used to be known becomes an anachronism, and blacks become stronger, more determined, and more defiant, but no more violent. "They beat us," says Diane Nash during the Freedom Rides through Alabama in 1961, "and we're stronger than ever. We can prove without sinking to the level of violence that the Negro cannot be intimidated." Blacks boycott Jim Crow facilities, sit in at segregated counters, ride buses through dangerous redneck territory to test the desegregation law, demonstrate in the face of vicious mobs, and subject themselves to arrest and jail sentences. Aggressive civil rights activities bring the southern African American "more self-confidence, more self-esteem, less fear of the white man's jail, and a more wide-spread commitment to eventual equality." [14] Speaking of community support of the Montgomery boycott in early 1956, Martin Luther King says, "A once fear-ridden people had been transformed. Those who had previously trembled before the law were now proud to be arrested for the cause of freedom." This reflects a new "feeling of solidarity." [15]

THE PAST AS IDENTITY: JAMES BALDWIN

With the virtual disappearance of traditional lynching after World War II, African American novelists' treatment of it changes, too. The distance from the event that the Harlem Renaissance writers introduced into their narratives widens for post–World War II novelists, and lynching becomes a historical affair, to which the novelists bring a contemporary sensibility and new conventions. The years that went before turn into a past, and the past into a history. And lynching is one of that history's defining features. Novels in which lynching occurs are thus forays into a past whose atmosphere is determined by the rope and faggot. They trek back into that past for a variety of reasons, but mainly their protagonists, discharged into a new age whose rules are changing and for which they have not been prepared, search for their identity. One gains the strength to face a problematical present by coming to terms with the ineluctable past. And since lynching is a definitive part of that past, accepting what cannot now be reversed means accepting lynching. The old tendency of the pre–World War I sentimental romance and the conservative thought of the Harlem Renaissance had been to deny the African American past, as if only by rejecting what some saw as the shame of subjugation and peasant origins could individual blacks acquire dignity and honor. Rightly or wrongly, this was associated with the bourgeoisie who became more class than race conscious. The countertendency has been to embrace that past with pride. W. E. B. Du Bois gave expression to that attitude in *The Souls of Black Folk* (1903). And the Harlem Renaissance "new Negroes" promoted "the folk" in their art. But there is an unprecedented historical sense that develops after World War II that only the full absorption of the pain of the past could give black America new life.

The classic expression of that feeling comes from James Baldwin. In *Go Tell It on the Mountain* (1953), Baldwin explored, with the imagination of a great poet, themes that some authors still found relevant many years later. Writing from the viewpoint of 1953, Baldwin sets his novel in 1935 Harlem. This "present" in turn stands against a pre–World War I past. A relatively small element of that past is a lynching that takes place in a small southern town just after the war. Small though it is—Baldwin describes it in less than half a page—it makes itself felt on every other leaf of the narrative.

There had been found that morning, just outside of town, the dead body of a soldier, his uniform shredded where he had been flogged, and, turned upward through the black skin, raw, red meat. He lay face downward at the base of a tree, his fingernails digging into the scuffed earth. When he was turned over, his eyeballs stared upward in amazement and horror, his mouth was locked open wide; his trousers, soaked with blood, were torn open, and exposed to the cold, white air of morning the thick hairs of his groin, matted together, black and rust-red, and the wound that seemed to be throbbing still.[16]

As George W. Lee does in *River George* in his description of Aaron George's lynched body, Baldwin omits an account of the lynch mob and focuses upon the results of its work rather than its acts. The victim is anonymous, but Baldwin shows us a glimpse of his grieving family and the frustrated rage of its men, "dreaming of vengeance." It is the feeling of humiliation and helplessness of the men that Baldwin's account particularly evokes. The Reverend Gabriel Grimes, a convert of many years from a sinful life in his youth, walks the hostile streets of the small town with rigid care after the lynching, forced to keep his anger suppressed and forcing himself to play his long-familiar role of "good nigger." But beneath his expressionless exterior lie feelings that even his piety cannot expunge, the dream "of the feel of a white man's forehead against his shoe; again and again, until the head wobbled on the broken neck and his foot encountered nothing but the rushing blood" (142).

Because he has no more than this fantasy, Gabriel develops an immense bitterness—toward whites, toward blacks, the world, the members of the family he acquires when he moves north to Harlem after his first wife, Deborah, dies. He refuses to accept what he is powerless to affect and in the process learns to hate himself and his race. But such violence gives African American history its unique identity, and descendants of its victims can achieve peace only by accepting it. How painful that acceptance can be is what we learn from the experience of Baldwin's autobiographical protagonist, fourteen-year-old John Grimes.

John learns bitterness from his stepfather. It is directed not only at the threadbare Harlem in which he lives but at himself as "nigger" and his father as unloving and hypocritical authoritarian. John's "niggerness" stands between himself and the dazzling white world of midtown Manhattan, to whose worldly entertainments he is irresistibly drawn but which he at the same time passionately resents for making him suffer. Here he goes to watch movies about white people, wicked movies, according to his stepfather's values. On the Saturday of his fourteenth birthday, John is confronted with a choice between those two worlds. The process of choosing takes place not in the movie theater where he first thinks of it (40) but within the walls of the structure that most forcibly symbolizes all that he fears and hates in Harlem, the storefront church in which his father serves as deacon and which all expect him to join. Essentially, it is a choice of perceptions. He thinks that the conflict stands between "the dust, and sweat, and urine" of Harlem, into which he fears he will be drawn, and the wicked but exciting pleasures of the glittering white stores and movie palaces of Manhattan. In reality, it is a matter of accepting what he is, of establishing his identity. John undergoes the ceremony meant to lead him to rebirth. Hitherto it was ineffective, but today is different. Today the past enters the present of the small church. It comes as the memories of his Aunt Florence, Gabriel, and his mother, Elizabeth. Their pasts are reenacted in the form of "prayers" they and the congregation use to bring John through his religious experience, the "Prayers of the Saints." The flashbacks to the memories of the three people closest to him particularize the collective black experience and present it as the racial womb in which John took shape: Aunt Florence's failure as a wife, Gabriel's Paulist change from a man of excessive self-indulgence to a man of excessive piety, Elizabeth's tragic love affair with John's real father, and the intense but deeply blemished relationship between them all.

It is in this past that the lynching takes place. John's relationship to the lynching comes indirectly through the frustrated personality of Gabriel. A victim of a South which literally and figuratively emasculates black men, Gabriel is divided into two warring parts, one weak and powerless before whites, another angrily jealous of his authority and religious zeal among blacks, especially his own family. It is John's task, as a member of the new generation, to make sure that he does not inherit Gabriel's doubleness but brings his own warring parts into unity. He does so on the "threshing floor" of the church as he goes through his religious experience. That experience is not simply finding God. It is acknowledging the past, and in it Baldwin poetically fuses John's personal struggle, the experiences of his immediate family, and the collective history of the race. The moaning of John's own voice joins with the moaning of the storm passing through Harlem outside the church, the voices of the "saints" praying over him during his ordeal, and the memory of the African American experience as dramatized in the stories of John's family.

For its beauty and its functionality, the passage in which this is all brought together is worth quoting in its entirety. No analysis can satisfactorily disclose the rich implications of this central passage of African American literature, with its evocations of history, the grand rhythms of the African American sermon, the sadness of the blues. As he lies on the "threshing floor" struggling to "go through," John hears the sound of murmuring. It is a sound that had "filled" his life:

He had heard it everywhere, in prayer and in daily speech, and wherever the saints were gathered, and in the unbelieving streets. It was in his father's anger, and in his mother's calm insistence, and in the vehement mockery of his aunt. . . . it was in the beat and jangle of Sister McCandless's tambourine, it was in the very cadence of her testimony, and invested that testimony with a matchless unimpeachable authority. Yes, he had heard it all his life, but it was only now that his ears were opened to this sound that came from darkness, that could only come from darkness, that yet bore such sure witness to the glory of the light. And moaning, and so far from any help, he heard it in himself—it rose from his bleeding, his cracked-open heart. It was a sound of rage and weeping which filled the grave, rage and weeping from time set free, but bound now in eternity; rage that had no language, weeping with no voice —which yet spoke now, to John's startled soul, of boundless melancholy, of the bitterest patience, and the longest night; of the deepest water, the strongest chains, the most cruel lash; of humility most wretched, the dungeon most absolute, of love's bed defiled, and birth dishonored, and most bloody, unspeakable, sudden death. Yes, the darkness hummed with murder: the body in the water, the body in the fire, the body on the tree. (200–201)

With these last words, we are brought around again to the lynching, represented as both an act of brutality with immeasurable consequences and an act of purification and renewal through the images of baptism and the Passion. The brutality of that violence, and the fear and degradation it carries with it, has embedded itself in the past that John, to resolve his own ambivalence about his blackness as well as that of his stepfather, must affirm. This image projects the collective experience and the oneness of John's own self. After it appears to him, he hears the voices calling on him to "rise up, Johnny," and he knows that "the night had passed, the powers of darkness had been beaten back" (206). He has bound himself to his people and he exclaims, "I'm ready. . . . I'm on my way" (221).

John does not flee. Through his mystical experience he joins together the ugliness and pain of the past and the present and finds in their fusion beauty and personal strength. At this moment in his life, John has won the fight against the meretricious attractions of downtown New York and the wasted avenues of Harlem. The external reality is still there—the littered streets, the filthy gutters, the signs of Saturday night's desperate excesses. But for now, that reality has, like John's soul, been washed clean by the thunderous storm that had swept through it in the hours of the early morning. John cannot preserve this state of grace without continually renewed effort. He knows that he will once again fall into fear and weakness. But he has now been through the fire, has lived the experience of his people, and has emerged as one of them, clear about who he is and unafraid of the knowledge of Ezekiel's wheel, the knowledge that out of sorrow grows joy, that joy brings strength, and strength gives the ability to bear sorrow (217). Having once attained transcendence through acceptance, he knows that he is forever changed. The collective black experience, lynching and all, is not to be escaped but to be affirmed as the trunk from which all limbs grow.

Ultimately, gaining one's historical identity has political implications, for it creates the black group that can successfully challenge all aspects of Jim Crow. Baldwin's later militancy as he becomes one of the major spokespersons for the civil rights movement, first in *Notes of a Native Son* (1955), then more aggressively in *The Fire Next Time* (1963), sheds light upon how to look at John Grimes's religious experience. On the personal level, what John at first denies and then embraces is that whole black identity that comprehends all aspects of the black experience. In his essays, Baldwin compresses that experience into a single simulacrum which he calls "this dark and dangerous and unloved stranger," which is "part" of the black person "forever." One can be free only by recognizing this reality and by making perpetual "adjustment" to it. Suggesting the historical nature of that "stranger," he says that "the past is all that makes the present coherent, and further . . . the past will remain horrible for exactly as long as we refuse to assess it honestly." We must accept, says Baldwin, or forever remain riven in parts.[17]

FATHERS AND SONS: RICHARD WRIGHT'S *LONG DREAM*

One of the important themes that Baldwin takes up in his novel is the father-son relationship. The emergence of this relationship as a preoccupation of African American novelists is one of the striking features of the black novel after World War II. Fathers and sons do appear in a few pre–World War II works, but their relationship lacks the intensity and the narrative importance that characterize its formation in the African American novel of recent decades. This relationship embodies the transaction between the past and the present that is the underpinning of the contemporary lynching novel. For Baldwin, the father-son relationship reflects simply the conflict between past and present. Gabriel Grimes represents what repels John about the past and the present. For others, the father is a symbol of the past they need to know. More often, the father—or father figure—becomes a source of courage for his son. The father's courage usually leads to his death, and the son draws from that death an example for his own political action.

Interestingly enough, Richard Wright is one of the first novelists to perceive the significance of the father-son paradigm. As a writer whose sensibilities and perceptions were shaped and articulated in the previous period, he views the violent past ambivalently, regarding with caution the changes said to have occurred during the 1940s and in progress when he writes *The Long Dream* in 1958. Yet, for all Wright's skepticism, the story of Rex ("Fishbelly") Tucker does contain traces of the more optimistic spirit of the times. Fishbelly's experiences—and those of his father, Tyree —in the 1920s and 1930s make him a rebel who successfully undermines one small instance of the southern system and then escapes to the freedom of Paris. Fishbelly's fate is influenced by two acts of white violence: a classic lynching and a political murder.

The lynching of young Chris Sims for sleeping with a white woman does not come unexpectedly in Clintonville, Mississippi, for it is a white supremacist bastion, and the time is the 1930s. Wright's account of the lynching, like those of Baldwin and George W. Lee before him, suggests a retrospective viewpoint. He does not install the reader in the center of a sadistic crowd of men, women, and children voicing their pleasure with their distinctive mob voice. Wright, looking back at an event that took place in a different era, becomes a historian who places the past under observation. We experience the lynching like Fishbelly does, by being at the elbow of the black doctor who informally autopsies the body. Through his commentary, we learn that Chris Sims has been subjected to the traditional lynching— hanging and castration:

"I'd say that the genitals were pulled out by a pair of pliers or some like instrument," the doctor inferred. "Killing him wasn't enough. They had to *mutilate* 'im. You'd think that disgust would've made them leave *that* part of the boy alone. . . . No! To get a chance to *mutilate* 'im was part of why they killed 'im. And you can bet a lot of white women were watching eagerly when they did it. Perhaps they knew that that was the only opportunity they'd ever get to see a Negro's genitals." [18]

In contrast to the voices of the mob that burns Bobo in "Big Boy Leaves Home" (1937), shouting across the hills in redneck accents, rejoicing in the ritual, in *The Long Dream* we hear only the subdued and bitter voice of the attending doctor talking to the mortician, Tyree Tucker, in an otherwise quiet room. The silence emphasizes the pastness of the event to the reader, while it has an immediate impact on Fishbelly in the world of the novel. Through it, he learns the absolute power of whites over blacks. Tyree uses the lynching to justify his own behavior toward whites. He plays the role of the obsequious manchild, cuts the white police in on the profits in graft, racketeering, and prostitution, and carefully avoids white women. If he fails to observe any of these rules of behavior, he pays the price.

Wright, with his connections to the pre-World War II years, is one of the few novelists writing after World War II who explicitly poses the question of how to respond to the classic lynching. Tyree answers it practically. Black men "ain't strong enough to fight back," so they must constantly compromise their manhood simply to stay alive. Tyree fawns deferentially in the presence of his white patron in the "syndicate," Clintonville police chief Cantley, despising himself for doing so. Tyree is divided by the same kind of psychic conflict as Gabriel Grimes. And Fishbelly, like John Grimes, seeks psychic harmony. He is a member of a new generation, and Tyree's "wisdom" disgusts him. Fishbelly's dream, the "long dream" of the title, is to create a life in which he can be natural and live as one self rather than the two that white force requires of him.

But when Chief Cantley has Tyree killed for trying to expose the white man's illegal dealings with Black Town graft and prostitution, his father becomes a model for Fishbelly, showing him not only that he *can* fight but how to fight, even if it means his own life. Tyree is a transition between the old and the new, surviving as long as he played the old game with which he was familiar but giving up his life when he attempts to burst out of his own historical category. Fishbelly is the new generation, incapable of playing his father's game of convincing the white man of his humility. He is, as Chief Cantley says, "one of these new kind of niggers," which white men no longer "understand" (365). Cantley justly suspects him, for Fishbelly completes the destruction of the police chief and his world begun by his father. Through the cleverness and courage of his father's example, by manipulating some signed checks as a way of exposing Cantley's illegal business dealings, Fishbelly disempowers the old system that had been propped up by lynching, breaks out of his racial bonds, and escapes from Clintonville altogether.[19] Historical conditions make this possible. It is just after World War II, and Fishbelly flees to a Paris which like himself has just been liberated. For both it is a rebirth, a joining of two disparate parts forced into separation by a cruel regime, the unity of self that Fishbelly longed for.

In Fishbelly, though, Wright does not celebrate the new Negro of the civil rights movement or interpret the emergence of the Emmett Till character in black America. He expresses his own lifetime struggle, carried on in precisely the terms in which Fishbelly thinks of his contradictory "desire and dread" of the white world. Fishbelly does just what Wright himself did at the end of World War II when he, too, took voluntary exile in Paris. Instead of confronting the racism of the Clintonvilles he knew, Wright fled from it. This marks him clearly as a member of an older generation. He does accurately sense the new atmosphere of the 1950s, in which a character like Fishbelly can be juxtaposed to a character like Tyree. And he does reflect one of the trends in postwar African American fiction. Fishbelly refuses to live under the old aegis, and he does survive, experiencing a denouement impossible a generation earlier, a plausible rescue from the white lynch mob. But Wright does not seem to feel in himself as the creator of Fishbelly and Tyree the personal spiritual, even religious, strength that black writers a generation younger than he celebrate in the "new black," a strength they give characters that allows them to find themselves and stay the course. The source of their strength is the very blackness that stigmatized their parents and grandparents and made those ancestors perpetually vulnerable to the lynch mob and the exploiting landowner. As a member of the older generation, Wright seems to regard flight from blackness the only plausible solution to a Clintonville America. The younger generation, coming of age in a time when the traditional lynching and all it implied has practically died out, sees pride in its blackness and affirmation of its past as the means by which it will transform that Clintonville.

FATHERS AND SONS: THE REDEMPTIVE COMMUNITY FROM JOHN O. KILLENS TO RAYMOND ANDREWS

Five representative members of that younger generation, covering the decades of the fifties, sixties, and seventies, project an optimism far less equivocal than Wright's: John Oliver Killens, in *Youngblood* (1954); William Melvin Kelley, in *A Different Drummer* (1962); Ernest J. Gaines, in *The Autobiography of Miss Jane Pittman* (1971); Leon Forrest, in *There Is a Tree More Ancient than Eden* (1973); and Raymond Andrews, in *Appalachee Red* (1978). For them, the violence of the past explains a great deal about the present, even acting as a propellant for present action. They develop the new hero figure to its definitive point. It is essentially a two-part image. In their vision, the father becomes a sacrificial martyr whose death creates in the son a secular messiah, the activist shaper of a new world. Moreover, they depict a reformed and unified society. Through the example of the father, the son, or both, the black community is finally pulled into a whole capable of action, bringing a specific change from novels of the pre–World

War II period like *Fire in the Flint* (1924), *River George* (1937), and *These Low Grounds* (1937). The novelists I refer to thus project into fiction the spirit of the civil rights movement, the willingness of many older people to expose themselves to white anger and the determination of the young to consolidate and advance the gains their elders have made.

The ideal of unity in particular seizes the minds of these younger African American novelists. It is the same ideal that pervades the movement in the fifties and early sixties, an unprecedented feeling of comradeship and family.[20] So powerful and widespread is the feeling that the members of the original Student Nonviolent Coordinating Committee, in their "statement of purpose," formulate it in biblical terms, finding the base of their authority and power in "the redemptive community."[21]

The stories that these five novelists tell show this new unity rising from the ashes of the past. The images of the father and son, the concepts of the redemptive community and the messiah, and the history to which the present is connected become central to the novelists' treatment of lynching and other violence and the long-standing questions of how to deal with it. They are reference points for exploring the old divisions and the new unities, the old pusillanimity and the new courage, expressing the novelists' new vision of the past: that it was the years of black suffering and enduring that finally killed white violence against blacks and made possible a new African American pride and activism. The early twentieth century they deal with in their novels is not the early twentieth century of Pauline Hopkins or Walter F. White or even Waters Edward Turpin, who himself attempted to explain the present through the past. The pictures of lynchings, shootings, and beatings drawn by these early writers are like the sites of crucial battles, now visited by the contemporary heirs of the fallen to relive the terrible experiences, to pay tribute to the martyred soliders, and reinforce present resolve.[22] From the old ceremonies of violence a new liberation emerges. What was once a bleak termination, a charred body hanging from a tree and frightened blacks cowering behind locked doors, becomes the tragic foundation of a new optimism.

At the center of that historical process these novelists place a violent act, the killing of the father figure. He is not a victim in the old sense, though. He dies because he rises in courage against the oppressor, and in this act he becomes a kind of messiah and creates the redemptive society. The son rejects vengeance and becomes a hero of nonviolent activism rather than violent retaliation.

Killens's *Youngblood* is significant as one of the first novels of the postwar period to make the connection between past white violence and current black strength. It is a political interpretation of the black past, a history of the unification process of one community as it grows to the point of its readiness to take action. It is a "big" novel, covering two generations of the Youngblood family in the plantation town of Crossroads, Georgia, from about 1900 to just before World War II. The black life of *Youngblood* is a struggle with an arrogant white world made up of ignorant and vicious crackers and an unfair justice system. Injustice is heaped upon injustice, as sneering white sheriff's deputies legitimize the exploitation and humiliation of earnest, worthy, and industrious blacks. Killens's black characters are models of middle-class moral uprightness. They do not drink, at least to excess; they do not swear, at least around girls or ladies if they are men, or at all if they are girls or ladies; and they have a strong repugnance toward immodesty or sexual promiscuity. But though Killens makes no attempt to hide the ponderous machinery of propaganda, or the sentimentality, the oversimplifications, even the stereotyping, *Youngblood* is a moving book. We, too, feel Killens's sense of outrage over injustice.

In the novel's pivotal act of violence, Joe Youngblood strikes a white man and is gunned down. From the beginning, we know that the moment is inevitable. The white system fears Joe, his size and strength, his moral probity, his untrained intelligence. Joe's bosses systematically humiliate him, calling him "boy," assigning him to work beneath his abilities, ignoring his superior qualities. In turn, Joe's son Robby is jailed for fighting white boys who taunt him and utter obscenities to his sister. And repeatedly over the years, the mill paymaster cheats Joe of his rightful pay, adding economic exploitation to psychological humiliation. Finally, as the decade of the thirties nears its close, Joe refuses the whites any further encroachment upon his integrity. He questions the paymaster's calculations, and when the white man, infuriated, reaches for his gun, Joe knocks him down. Instantly, other armed whites are ready, and one of them shoots Joe down.

But Joe's death is a beginning, not an ending, leaving, as the preacher says at Joe's funeral, "a strength and spirit and determination that will bring together the God-fearing freedom-loving people of Crossroads, Georgia," in a "union of strength."[23] Writing from the perspective of a moment in which African Americans are poised to begin the most effective civil rights movement in their history, Killens can look back to nearly the same historical point at which George Washington Lee ended *River George,* with that terrible image of the black body hanging from a tree, and reconstruct it, live it another way. Because fifteen years later Killens can see a different world taking shape, he can make a reality in which the murdered black man does not die in vain. Not only does Joe inspirit his community with determination, he stimulates his son to make his own symbolic gesture: joining a union where he works. History does not stop with the killing of a black man or woman. African Americans may die at the hands of white supremacists, but each death strengthens the community's power to endure and resolve to act, loosening the hold of white supremacy and making white power slightly less absolute. Singly, these changes are imperceptible. Cumulatively, we can see the great historical currents to which they give impetus.

The new world that comes out of Joe's death is not the middle-class paradise of Frances Harper or Pauline Hopkins, either. Killens rejects the middle-class white values espoused by so many of his predecessors. He has absorbed the movement of the Harlem Renaissance toward an Africanization of the black American folk and transformed it into a politicization of the black American working class, strengthened by its folk heritage but increasingly sophisticated and determined to have its rights in America. He also comes out of the Marxist protest movement of the 1930s. *Youngblood* is a proletarian novel in which the clash between white and black resembles that between the working class and the economic imperialists of the Depression-era social protest novel. The people become the hero, and they struggle for the Good against the Bad of a white bourgeoisie.

Implied in his Marxist sympathies is the suggestion that only when the black folk accept their class, affirm their worker identity, can they come together in community. Aspirations to middle-class status are inherently divisive. And only as courageous proletarians can they force whites to abandon violence. For Killens, history is a Marxist-Hegelian evolution toward this more effective black type.

Killens completed *Youngblood* before the Supreme Court ruled against "separate but equal" education. Even so, the atmosphere of the early fifties seems to have energized the optimism of his novel. President Truman officially integrated the armed forces in 1948. The South abolished the white primary. In just a couple of years, the Montgomery bus boycott would begin, and Eisenhower would enforce the new integration law in the Little Rock public schools. Consequently, Killens cannot take us beyond "The Beginning," which he entitles the last part of his novel.

William Melvin Kelley, in *A Different Drummer* (1962), writing when the movement was in full swing, strikes a much more militant note. He imagines an entire county of blacks simply moving out on its white landlords and overseers, accomplishing a wish-fulfillment revenge that only a justly angry mind could have conceived. The source of Kelley's title in Thoreau's *Walden* suggests that every individual not simply step to the beat of his own drummer but, as Thoreau says in the same work, "mind his own business, and endeavor to be what he was made." This spirit evokes Emerson's "Self-Reliance," too: "What I must do," says Emerson, "is all that concerns me, not what the people think." *A Different Drummer* seems, indeed, as Robert L. Nadeau has noted,[24] to be Kelley's attempt to appropriate a larger American tradition, transcendentalism, to the purposes of the new black consciousness in its rebellion against the white status quo. It calls upon the new African American to break with the old customs, to act rather than talk, to throw off the imprisoning past just as America threw off its European dependency, to put the integrity of the self above the oppressive power of the white man, just as the colonial immigrant, searching for autonomy, fled the suffocating European class system.

As a token of his desire to move to a new beat, Kelley resorts to fable rather than the realism of mainstream African American fiction. Though the focus of the narrative is upon the present, it is a present that seems like a dream of current reality interwoven with its own history. To understand the fabulous significance of Tucker Caliban's behavior in the present, we must know his origins, and they go back to a primordial father figure, an African king whom the whites cannot enslave and therefore must shoot. True to the pattern of these novels, Tucker's story, the story of a modern messiah, commences with a murder. The African, combining immense physical with mental strength, poses far too great a danger to the white enslavers for them to allow him to live. When he refuses to be enslaved, they kill him. But he is the seed from which Tucker's line springs, and of which Tucker is the last member. His task is to put to rest the slave past and start a new "kingdom" in freedom, to escape the social structure that has kept blacks imprisoned for generations. Tucker dismantles all signs of the slave heritage, destroys the farm he has bought from his old employer and the old clock that had come over on the same ship as the original African. He then departs the imaginary Willson County for the North, and in him the free African is born, all bonds dissolved.

Since Tucker marches to his own drummer, he rejects the role of leader. Speaking in epigrams, quietly, laconically, he does what he does because he has to, as if some ancient power impels him, not because he assumes the mantle of a movement. In his private messianic strength, however, he infuses the black community with strength, and it is ultimately through the combined power of the individual members of the black community that they triumph over white oppression and rise above the dangers of violence. Kelley suggests that every black person has access to Tucker's power source, and to be free they must tap it. They must decide they need no leader to "give" them freedom. "I can do whatever I want for myself by myself."[25] Stimulated by Tucker's example, every black person in the county departs, leaving the whites, who had used the blacks to build the county, without a future. The whites remain, like Roy Bryant and J. W. Milam, mired in a moribund tradition, suspended in a silent wasteland of their own making. And also like Bryant and Milam, Kelley's whites turn to traditional violence in their attempt to preserve their crumbling world.

They set out to lynch the single black remaining in the county, the Reverend Bennett Bradshaw. A more or less well-meaning, limousine-owning preacher who has come back to Willson County from the North where he became rich, Bradshaw, like lynching, has become obsolete. The blacks in this fabled county no longer need guidance or exhortation, and Bradshaw's death, a reversal of the Crucifixion, constitutes the necessary pain that accompanies the birth throes of the new consciousness. Brad-shaw's lynchers are a group of poor whites who laze around the porch of their leader, Mr. Harper, listening to his philosophizing about life and race relations. Harper's confinement to a wheelchair suggests their paralysis. Their white line has come to its end, too, but they have no strength for renewal and rebirth. "Yes," says Harper, "I feel sorry for my men. They ain't got what those colored folks have." [26] After at first sneeringly ap-plauding the departure of the silent blacks, they finally realize what the emigration means to them. They are losing the single source of energy and work they had. Their move to lynch their "last nigger," therefore, is des-perate rather than preservative, a conclusion, not a new beginning or continuation.

As with the black inhabitants of Joe Youngblood's Crossroads, so with the black residents of Willson County. An act of violence, a murder of a black man, is the original impetus that propels them out of their bondage. The murder of the African is given a necessity by Kelley that works as a metaphor—the seeds of black liberation were planted on the day of black enslavement. The point at which the county blacks' newly won self-reliance turns into action is marked by an old-fashioned lynching, the last one ever to be performed in Willson County. The saga of bondage that began with the destruction of the great African ends with the destruction of the traditional apologist for that bondage, the preacher. Thanks to the example of Tucker Caliban and the exertion of the community of Willson County blacks, lynching and dependency have been killed, too.

Kelley's blacks do not answer violence with violence. They free them-selves with unified action and take certain selected whites with them into the new age of freedom. The Willson family of *A Different Drummer,* the white dynasty that parallels that of the Calibans, has undergone the familiar decay. Kelley makes them well-intentioned in their aristocratic sense of noblesse oblige. But they have developed in the reverse of the Calibans. Unlike Tucker and the other contemporary blacks, the contemporary Will-sons are either morally or practically weak, afraid to love, unable to deal with the real world. Their marriages founder, their youth have difficulty growing up, their women are either dominant or emotionally frustrated. David Willson, the epitome of the "good white," weak and immobilized by the South's rejection of his liberal views, has spent his life isolated in his study from his wife and his son. Tucker saves these people. Naturally wise, Tucker teaches young Dewey Willson the rites of adolescence, advises Camille Willson on her relations with her husband, senses the desires they all hide from each other, and formulates for them homely aphorisms that produce solutions to the most complex problems. On the day that Tucker declares his freedom from the long tradition of white oppression, all the solutions to the Willsons' problems drop into place, their family unity is restored, and they look with optimism upon the future.

Kelley suggests with Killens that a bright new day is awaiting not only blacks but those whites capable of accepting the black way. Both Joe Young-blood and Tucker Caliban bring natural cycles to an end and assist in the renewal of life, Joe by dying, Tucker by striking out on his own. They have the moral power to save a white America whose belief in black inferiority betrayed its own professed creed, and a white South whose continued insistence on violence reveals its increasing desperation and decadent rigidity. They can carry the white American back to his original virtues and salvage the American dream, and those whites incapable of joining the black redemptive society will, like Harper, remain figuratively tied to a wheelchair, abandoned by history.

Killens and Kelley see in the past the story of the evolution of the black leader and the unified black community, and the devolution of the white culture and the violence by which it maintained its supremacy. Since the growth of the blacks is irresistible and irreversible, these novelists do not raise the issue of retaliatory or self-defensive violence as a matter that requires discussion. Their hero does not worry about his manhood or agonize over whether to meet violence with violence. Favored by an evolutionary process that is both moral and social, blacks simply need to act according to their nature in order to achieve independence from the disintegrating whites. This perception of black history vindicates that tendency in black thought that goes back to the nineteenth century and the Reverend Henry M. Turner's insistence that "When the white race reaches decrepitude, the Negro will have reached his prime, and being in possession of all he has and will acquire from the whites, and his genius and industry to manufacture more and lift him to a higher civilization, he will stand the wonder of the ages." This is God's plan, and it requires no "bloody conflict." African Americans need only wait "patiently . . . till God broke their chains." [27] Although we can deduce from *A Different Drummer* that Tucker must not subside into quiescence but must act, we also need to remember that this novel does not contain any blueprint for action. It fabulizes Kelley's sense of the African American state of mind in the early sixties, the belief in self-reliant action and the inevitability of a black triumph.

In his landmark novel *The Autobiography of Miss Jane Pittman* (1971), Ernest J. Gaines conducts his survey of the black past through an almost foolproof device, the voice of a crusty and tenacious little old lady who lived the story she tells. It is hard to imagine any more fitting character for personifying the new optimism than this hardy, persistent, stubborn woman, tough as a piece of aged leather. Gaines divides her story into four parts, each one chronicling a phase in Jane's life and an era in the evolution of the southern black. The engine of change from one phase to the next is the death of a black man at the hands of whites. In the beginning, "the war years" and "reconstruction," the whites are strong and vicious, the blacks eager but disorganized and weak. The whites use violence freely, and the blacks adopt protective behavior. Over the century that we follow Jane's life this state of affairs gradually reverses itself, until Jane, over 100 years old, joins forces with the young blacks whose history she embodies and uniquely voices, defies her threatening plantation landlord, and marches off to open the voter registration campaign in Gaines's fictional Bayonne, Louisiana.

Gaines, however, differs importantly from his predecessors. The worlds of Killens and Kelley, for example, are constructed of unnatural and tempo-rary social and political patterns, and the issue is how to destroy those patterns and replace them with more natural and intrinsically moral forms. The action in their novels, therefore, takes its shape from the politics of the times rather than from an attempt to grasp the larger and less parochial rhythms of human life. Gaines is sensitive to the same political issues, making them the foundation of his story lines: the social and economic oppression of blacks by whites, the use of poor whites by wealthy whites, the racial sexual myths, the whole apparatus of white supremacy. But he sees these issues in a more comprehensive context. The other novelists seem to regard reform as a need limited to their time and created by artificial conditions, the force which will bring an end to conflict and establish permanent justice. Gaines perceives the reforming impulse as an expression of constant change and growth, hence a permanent feature of nature, human life and society. He makes his stories out of that impulse, blacks and whites in conflict over change and resistance to it.

When, for example, Sidney Bonbon kills Marcus Payne, in *Of Love and Dust* (1967), we get an illustration of the conventions of white supremacy at work. Marcus is the "uppity nigger" who refuses to abide by the rules of the plantation in both work and love, for he wins Bonbon's white wife away from him. But white supremacy is not strictly the subject of the episode. The subject is the way the forces of change and conservatism, acting through the reluctant Cajun overseer, constantly struggle against each other. The narrative does not tell the reader that the Sidney Bonbons must be got rid of in order to bring about a better world. Bonbon himself is a prisoner of a rigid tradition which he has unconsciously internalized. Nor can we expect anything lasting by removing white plantation owner Marshal Hebert from the picture, even though he is the most destructive of all the actors in the book. The narrative tells us that all change and all efforts to bring it about carry with them a conflict that gives human life at its heart its tragic pathos.

Gaines does not easily identify the good blacks and the bad whites. Some of his most sympathetic characters side with the whites who oppose change. Aunt Charlotte in *Catherine Carmier* (1964) and Aunt Margaret in *Of Love and Dust* both hold to the old ways, honor their "white folk," and fear the dismantling the apparatus which, for all its oppressiveness, makes the two old women feel secure. And they are warm, loving people, with a courage and durability we cannot help but admire. The workers of change, like Jackson Bradley and Marcus Payne, have none of the heroic certainty or divine intuition that we find in Joe Youngblood and Tucker Caliban. They are troubled, shortsighted, imprudent young men, who fail in their immediate task and leave their world unchanged—at least on the surface. Gaines suggests that both characters have started something, but he draws back from saying that change in either social forms or black attitudes comes suddenly or dramatically. The old forms resist every step of the way, and much of the time blacks resist with the same intensity as whites. Change is both inevitable and necessary, but it also destroys much that we cherish.

In *Miss Jane Pittman,* white violence blocks change and steals from Miss Jane her best and brightest men, whose deaths are payments exacted from her for growth toward more auspicious conditions of freedom and autonomy. With their violence, the whites expect to make the blacks fearful and malleable, continuing to acquiesce in their own exploitation. The courage to die, therefore, becomes for blacks, as it has for all other oppressed people, the instrument for effectuating their revolution, the best strategy for undercutting the effectiveness of white violence. It produces admirable heroism but also great grief, and its advances are made only at high costs, so high that we might wonder whether the advance compensates for the loss. Yet we know that the alternative is even worse. Even though it is an inevitable natural process, it is no easier to bear.

Jane, although she never bears any children of her own and does marry legally, suffers the losses that go with this process: of her common-law husband, Joe Pittman; her first "son," Ned Douglass; her putative white son, Tee Bob Samson; her "grandson" Jimmy Aaron. Her sons die from racial causes, Ned and Jimmy being killed for their civil rights activities, Tee Bob committing suicide because he cannot bear the artificial barriers between himself and the mulatto girl he loves.

Joe Pittman is the symbolic father and grandfather to Ned and Jimmy Aaron, bringing with him the kind of courage necessary to meet white malice and violence without losing one's self-esteem, and establishing black manhood on a nonpolitical foundation. Joe's credo combines a love of life with a sense of personal honor, stoicism, and necessity. We all sign a "contract" to die, he tells Jane, and "one of these days I'm go'n lay down these old bones." [28] The inevitability of this limits people's choices. But though they cannot choose to live when the machinery has brought them around to die, they can choose to live proudly the life they do have by choosing a thing to do and doing it well, by stamping their mark upon their world, however faintly.

Manliness is the courage to accept the tragic conditions of life and to live uncompromisingly by the thing one does well. Joe breaks horses. He might have been a farmer. It would have been his first choice, but the conditions were unacceptable. He would have been required by the white plantation owner to give up his dignity and independence. Breaking horses exposes him to the danger of death, but it is a limit that does not compromise his manhood. Once he has made his choice, Joe must, as he tells Jane, "keep going," until he is removed as the "Chief" by means of one of the natural mechanisms of change. Joe is removed by the great black wild stallion that Joe and the men capture. Jane, fearing what the almost mystical beast means, tampers with the natural mechanism. Driven by her need to "save" Joe, she frees the horse and it kills Joe when he goes after it.

There is no shame for Joe in thus dying. His collision with the stallion, purified of any political intent, gives meaning to his life. There is also a subtle gain for the community, because Joe becomes the father figure for Ned Douglass, and Ned, back at the turn of the century, begins the civil rights work that will result in the changes of the 1960s. Ned even sounds like Joe: Since one must die eventually, he tells one of his black students, "wouldn't you rather die saying I'm a man than to die saying I'm a contented slave?" (112). When, after doing with his life what he needed to do —urging resistance, struggle, even retaliation if necessary—Ned inflames the local whites, he accepts that he must die. Refusing to be intimidated by threats of white violence, he calls upon himself his own death and starts the acid process that eventually causes the system to crumble.

Signs that the process is under way do not appear until the generation following Ned, in the 1920s and 1930s, and then they show up in the scion of the white South. Tee Bob Samson falls in love with the daughter of a proud mulatto family. The son of Robert Samson, who owns the plantation on which Jane works, Tee Bob is prohibited by every kind of southern taboo from treating the girl respectfully as a sweetheart. When Tee Bob commits suicide as the only way out, he seems to be a failure for the line from the traditional white viewpoint. From the black viewpoint, however, Tee Bob displays a certain courage. Just as Ned Douglass will not live in a world in which the "rules" stop him from speaking freely to his students and moving freely as a man, so Tee Bob refuses to go on under a system that will not allow him to love where his genuine feelings lead him. In this sense, he is the same sort of rebel as Ned Douglass for, held in by tradition, he gives his life to escape. Tee Bob is not the future that the white Samsons hope for. But alive or dead, he illustrates the cracking of the tradition.

With Tee Bob's death we are brought to the final stage of black growth, the end of the process begun with the swamp massacre of a group of Jane's friends just after the war and the dispersal of the black community. The focal point in this stage is Jimmy Aaron, a latter-day Ned Douglass, who returns to the plantation for the revolution that is sweeping the South in the late fifties and early sixties. Jimmy, born and bred among them, carries the people's hopes as "the One," a savior who will one day drive through the quarters in a divine chariot and carry them all away to the land of their long-awaited reward. The change Jimmy brings, though, is not what they expect or want. Like the whites, in classic Gaines style, they are conservative, frightened of change, anxious about new things. When Jimmy steps into the pulpit and speaks to them about education and law rather than sin and redemption, they are angry and refuse to understand him. In the familiar move, they oppose unity and reject the leader they themselves educated.

At least at first—for on the surface, not much has changed since the massacre in the swamp and the murder of Ned Douglass. The fourth stage of the postbellum history of the world Jane lives in seems to recapitulate the first. The southern whites who fought against change during Reconstruction and won are still fighting against it and apparently winning. Just as Colonel Dye appears on his plantation house balcony after the war to tell the newly freed slaves either to accept the return of the old rule or get out, so Robert Samson takes a similar platform and warns his black workers not to follow Jimmy Aaron in his civil rights protest if they want to stay on his plantation. But we have seen what happened to Tee Bob, and there is something hollow in Robert Samson's threats. The blacks on the Samson estate may be conservative and fearful, but they are different from those childlike people to whom Ned Douglass had spoken half a century before, tougher, less likely to scatter under threats of violence. The whites, too, have grown weak in their rigid refusal to change. Paradoxically, they show just how weak they are by shooting Jimmy Aaron.

As in all these novels, the shooting of the messianic protagonist, in this case Jimmy Aaron, takes place in a context in which new historical conditions hold. It is an act of desperation rather than of absolute authority. More significant, the return to traditional violence does not have the old effect. Instead of frightening the plantation blacks away from the civil rights demonstration that Jimmy had planned, his murder tends to consolidate the group and make them more determined. Indeed, before the shooting, they were holding back, fearful and divided. When word comes that Jimmy is dead, a wave of anger and distress ripples through them, and the climactic confrontation occurs. As the blacks cluster around Miss Jane, their longtime center, she faces Robert Samson, the black capacity to survive through growth and change confronting the white tradition of reaction. Samson once again tries to hold them back. But Miss Jane has from the beginning been on the move, and once more she refuses to stay put. Carrying with her the collective black intention, she gives us the last sentence of her autobiography: "Me and Robert looked at each other there a long time, then I went by him" (244).

Miss Jane does indeed pass Samson by, with the implication that in just this way blacks are passing whites by all over the South in the early sixties. Jane's role has been to connect the disconnected lives of her men, the fathers and the sons. And, with Jane, Gaines is one of the first novelists to celebrate the tremendous binding and integrating force of the black woman, weak in body, tough, tenacious, and enduring in spirit.[29] With her as the historical continuity, we observe how the stages of development are tied together, how one leads to another. In her experience, we see the disintegration of the great slave family into discrete parts and witness the slow process by which it reintegrates in the new form of the redemptive community. As her men act courageously against the threats to their lives and help to unite the black group against those threats, Jane contributes to growth and change with her own courage and penchant for action.

In the 1970s, during the decreasing effectiveness of civil rights activism, a kind of decadence creeps into some of the black novels dealing with white violence, an increasing preoccupation with style over substance. Raymond Andrews's *Appalachee Red* (1978),[30] for example, has the same narrative structure and political foundation as the novels of Killens, Kelley, and Gaines—the father figure who dies at the hands of the white man, the son who inherits the father figure's independence and courage, and the whites who collapse in the face of the son's indomitable personal power, leaving the black community unified and strong. But he sees all this through a lens of humor. Andrews stages the murder of Big Man Thompson by white sheriff Boots White like an amusing cartoon, a scene out of *Tortilla Flat* or *My Name Is Aram*—picturesque, folksy. Even the names of the characters—Big Man, Little Bit, Baby Sweet—suggest a kind of camp version of the folk realism of the thirties. Boots White, the alleged white master of Dark Town, is also a parody, perhaps of Faulkner's fascist Percy Grimm. Boots prides himself on "stomping niggers" but seems totally harmless, a buffoon, which makes the blacks' fear of him baffling. We do not believe in his menace, any more than that of a cartoon character. In fact, the attitude we might take toward these characters is suggested by the illustrations drawn for the book by Benny Andrews, which show lovable stylized slouches, like the fondly caricatured figures in the animated series of Bill Cosby's *Fat Albert*.

Big Man's putative son, Appalachee Red, arrives ten years after Big Man dies, and after twenty years of training his Dark Town people and frightening the whites, he manages to reverse the relationship between black and white. And why not? He is "Red the Risen, the Way, the Truth, the Light," as the converted black toughs of Dark Town call him.[31] Thus, on the day Kennedy is shot, Red shoots Boots "through his one good eye" and himself almost magically disappears from town with his white half sister, comically putting the cap on years of miscegenation. Had this happened twenty years earlier, all of Dark Town, fearing white vengeance, would have "quickly got off the streets" and taken "to their homes . . . as had all the generations before them" (102). But after the years in which the redoubtable Red has instilled pride and courage in the Appalachee blacks, it is the whites who cower in fear, connect their sheriff's death with Kennedy's, and "quickly got off the streets and took to their homes . . . where most of them sat imprisoned beneath their own roofs, listening silently and uncomfortably to the eerie sounds . . . like the beating of tom-tom drums. The pendulum had swung" (283).

But it is disingenuous for Andrews to write in the late 1970s of such total victory, even in his sardonically sentimentalized style and even with his fictional town of Appalachee. In 1978, to be sure, blacks no longer needed to fear the southern lynch mob, and thus freed they had achieved many important gains in voting rights and desegregation. But in jobs, in schooling, in property ownership and wealth, in the more subtle forms of discrimination, the "pendulum" may have moved a bit in the right direction, but it had not "swung." Andrews wants to tell us something serious, but his ironic, condescending style has the effect of trivializing its own subject.

In a similar sense, Leon Forrest's expressionistic rhapsody, *There Is a Tree More Ancient than Eden* (1973), is stylistically topheavy. This is an art novel, a mix of Faulkner (principally *The Sound and the Fury*), Joyce (both *Ulysses* and *Finnegans Wake*), Shakespeare, Dylan Thomas, Greek and Roman mythology, the Bible, spirituals, sermons. As experimental fiction it strikes me as a bit passé. Forrest does not condescend with satiric caricature, but he is so busy with allusions and stream of consciousness and omission of punctuation that we are distracted from the story he clearly wants to tell us.[32] Beneath the obfuscation is a valid study of the confused and yearning black mind of young Nathaniel Witherspoon, who, having lost his mother, searches for who he is. *There Is a Tree* contains the same obsessive brooding over the persistent questions of the past as well as the metaphysics of the everyday that we get in Quentin Compson's monologue in *The Sound and the Fury,* an obvious model for Forrest. Nathan, however, is more like Molly Bloom. He survives, in moderate triumph, after trekking through his own brief past and that of Western civilization and the race, back to the Crucifixion, the middle passage, slavery, the Civil War, and lynching. The Crucifixion and lynching go together, for the man on the cross becomes a black man and the cross becomes the hanging tree, the "tree more ancient than Eden." Forrest's point seems to be that, just as Christ needed to be crucified before he could be resurrected, so the African American must suffer the symbolic lynching before he can be redeemed. In Nathan's vision, therefore, the Crucifixion becomes a classic lynching: castration, dismemberment, immolation. But when the victim's bones are gathered in sackcloth, symbolizing both the collective suffering and the collective penance of the black community, they go through a spiritual transmutation. The shawl explodes and the man on the cross, the "nigger," rises *"Upwards* and seemed to be TOTALLY COLLECTED INTO HIS ORIGINAL FORM."[33]

Having passed through the crucifixion-lynching experience, Nathan can now rise to the final stages of what we finally recognize as the mystical ascent, first the "dark night of the soul," then unification—all worked into an allegory on the failure of Reconstruction and the ascent to the civil rights movement. Finally, Nathan awakens into his own individuality and strength to stand alone. His is not a political triumph, nor does he lead his people against white oppression. It is religious, personal, and psychological. But as a black everyman he embodies both the messiah, whose "father" died on the cross, and the collective community, and Forrest renders symbolically what Killens, Kelley, and Andrews render pictorially. Like them,

Forrest suggests that by reliving the past his protagonist finds out who he is. Like the other novelists in this group, Forrest represents lynching as the painful birth throe of the contemporary African American.

DOUBTING THE FATHER-HERO: W. E. B. DU BOIS, WILLIAM MAHONEY, AND SARAH E. WRIGHT

In the novels I have been looking at, lynching is what happens to an ancestor, a father figure. No longer a horror occurring in real life, it is an ineluctable part of the past, flowing into the black experience like irrigation water, strengthening rather than destroying the black character. The picture of the inspiring messiah shaping the fractured and weak black community into a politically effective unity to fight white violence and injustice expresses a powerful optimism. By turning back to the past in which they find the origins of black strength, these novelists depict how blacks have come to give up their infighting, resentments, and jealousies, and overcome their fear of whites, and join together not only to face the dangers besetting their movement for justice but to turn the tables on whites, making *them* afraid. The civil rights activity of the fifties and sixties gave them what seemed to be a historical confirmation of their fiction. The names of black communities whose citizens unified to bring about basic racial change have become part of the American legend: Montgomery, Birmingham, Selma, Monroe, Jackson, McComb, Philadelphia. And the organizations that coordinated the marches and the sit-ins and the voter registration drives have given their acronyms as bywords of the American vocabulary: SCLC, SNCC, CORE. Yet, the novels tend to idealize the achievements of both the leaders and the people and to exaggerate the degree of their unity. *Youngblood, A Different Drummer, Appalachee Red, The Autobiography of Miss Jane Pittman*—all dramatize the point at which black people come together and suggest that their community has finally achieved the unity required for successful revolt against their condition. Joe Youngblood, Tucker Caliban, and Appalachee Red possess unlimited tolerance for their own people and express virtually no resentment or envy or self-justification.

Not all accounts of the civil rights movement in the South and the communities involved in them give the same picture. In their autobiographies, James Forman of the Student Nonviolent Coordinating Committee (SNCC) and James Farmer of the Congress of Racial Equality (CORE) speak repeatedly of the conflicts between the leaders of their groups, the ideological and tactical disagreements between them that weaken their ability to act. David J. Garrow and Taylor Branch, in their accounts of Martin Luther King and the Southern Christian Leadership Conference

(SCLC) give example after example of pettiness and resentment between the various groups, the sensitiveness of local leaders to the encroachment of visiting organizations, the frequent unwillingness of local communities to march. This is not to play down the unprecedented achievements of the movement, or the real changes novelists like Killens and Kelley and Gaines reflect, without which no civil rights victories could have been won. It is simply to say that people are human and driven by human motives, not capable of godlike self-control over their feelings, that the very real idealism driving the movement was often mixed with a not so noble need for ego satisfaction.

The novelists who express this view counterbalance the uncritical optimism of the novels I have been looking at. They are ambivalent about the past, skeptical that a redemptive community exists, and doubt the transforming power of the pain of lynching. Willard Savoy, for example, in *Alien Land* (1949), has his protagonist, Kern Roberts, light-skinned son of a black father and white mother, reenact the experience of James Weldon Johnson's ex-colored man. He hates the humiliation that living black brings him. When he witnesses the lynching of his uncle, he does not set about organizing the community to break out of the white stranglehold. He goes white, leaves the South for the North, finishes in a white college, and marries a white woman who accepts his family background.

Most post–World War II skeptics, while acknowledging the heroism in black history, see it mixed with weakness. Their leaders are not messiahs but limited human beings who tend toward self-doubt, and their communities contain cantankerous eccentrics who refuse to blur into a homogeneous background. They are not sure that the present is much different from the past. Their novels focus on the ambiguities of the past's relationship with the present and ask more questions about the father-son relationship and violence than they answer. They see no heroes in their reality, but neither do they see the helpless victim of tradition. If there is a triumph in their fiction, it is in surviving the suffering and learning to live with, but not to conquer, the pain.

A surprising figure in this group is W. E. B. Du Bois. He is to these novelists what Richard Wright was to Killens, Kelley, Gaines: a member of an older generation, trying to assess the new era. Much more than Wright, however, Du Bois is part of a previous period, for when he published the first volume of his Black Flame trilogy in 1957, *The Ordeal of Mansart,* he was eighty-nine years old and had been at the heart of the struggle for black rights since before the turn of the century. His two earlier novels, *The Quest of the Silver Fleece* (1911) and *Dark Princess* (1928), reflect the optimism of relative youth and the artificiality of their time. Now, however, at the end of his life, when grounds for optimism appear so much firmer, he seems doubtful about the effectiveness of his life work.[34]

The Black Flame trilogy is both a chronicle of that work and an outline of the history of the years between 1876 and 1956, the life span of the trilogy's central character, Manuel Mansart,[35] whose birth occurs at precisely the point of the collapse of Reconstruction with the Rutherford B. Hayes sellout. Mansart, as a member of that educated "talented tenth," devotes his life to the true liberation of African Americans after they had been reenslaved at the end of Reconstruction. His sense of duty is spurred on by the murder of his father by the Ku Klux Klan for assisting a white woman. At this precise moment Manuel is born and is baptized as "Black Flame" in his father's blood, which carries with it the obligation of racial activism, for in Mansart his father is reborn: "Three cries rent the cold night; a howl of death, the scream of birthpain, and the wail of a new-born babe."[36] Mansart does not have the success that Tucker Caliban or Appalachee Red had. Struggling in the economic and political currents of the national life, observing the lynching figures gradually drop, experiencing the heady optimism of the 1945 Pan-African Congress, Mansart nevertheless arrives at the end of his life with very much muted emotions. His grandchildren have suffered racial discrimination in the war, and he himself has absurdly been called before a congressional committee on charges of participating in a Communist conspiracy. Nor does lynching produce any inspired or inspiring messiah. It simply intensifies black pain.

Du Bois does show that the nature of white violence changes, and the attitude of the blacks with it. And by the end of the novel we do have a different world. White violence has diminished and black pugnacity has increased. One of Mansart's younger grandchildren, freer than his grandparents had ever thought of being, cries out "I want to fight." Yet the status of blacks falls far short of Mansart's hopes for them fifty years earlier. As he lies dying in 1956, Mansart's loved ones gather around him and wonder aloud at the limitedness of their progress. "Save me my children," exclaims Mansart with his last breath. "Save the world!"[37] Just how that is to be done remains unclear. The Black Flame trilogy does not serve up the defiance and anticipation of the contemporary black revolution. Du Bois had seen all the cycles, had himself experienced previous periods of optimism and expectation, and had been an active participant long enough to witness the glacial slowness with which progress was made against white racism and indifference. And Du Bois himself had become almost irrelevant, having joined, after a lifelong courtship, the moribund American Communist party and surviving principally in the work he had done before 1930, eventually being embalmed by the movement as a symbol of early militancy. Mansart, a thinly disguised Du Bois, sounds like an exhausted soldier, who has fought more battles than he can remember. He still believes in his cause and would drag himself to the trenches again if physically capable but does not fool himself that there will ever be an end to the war, much less the promise of a new era.

One novelist of the younger generation, William Mahoney, was an activist himself, a student at Howard University and a participating sit-in rebel, as well as a Freedom Rider in Alabama in the early sixties. By the end of the sixties, it seems his idealism had been diluted by what he observed. He does not become cynical, any more than Du Bois does, only sadder, older, and wiser. *Black Jacob* (1969) is the expression of his hard-won knowledge, a novel about politics, election campaigns, and the reality of the perversity of the ignorant, the educated, the well-meaning. In it Mahoney studies the risk assumed by blacks in the sixties who have the brass to run for a congressional seat against a white man in the South. Dr. Jacob Blue, running against the incumbent, John "Whiteman," feels the danger that has saturated the air for years, volatile, familiar. It hangs in "the darkening sky, the swamp, the shadows of the courthouse," and it rises from "the hundreds of shot, lynched, mangled, consumptive, worn-out, deceased, pickled bodies he'd examined."[38] There is a reason other than tradition for Dr. Blue to feel this way. His political allies expect to be killed, and the sheriff intimidates potential black voters.

Yet Mahoney, too, like Du Bois, acknowledges that things have changed. Blue's candidacy itself demonstrates that. A white man says there "Ain't no more Klan" (72), and a black woman says, "These are new times" (59). But these changes promise no new world for blacks. Things may not be "done that way no more," but "things" are done. When a Medgar Evers or a Martin Luther King shows up in a character like Jacob Blue, he is, in the world that Mahoney has seen, taken care of. But now the tragedy lies not in the stern Klansmen whose aim is to save civilization but in the absurd comedy of continuing pointless violence. Blue loses the election and then futilely, ironically, is gunned down by a redneck flunky seeking favor with the sheriff, an ignorant sycophant who hardly knows what the word "civilization" means.

Sharing the fault for Blue's death are the blacks themselves. They do not welcome their saviors—Dr. Blue, the civil rights workers from their own group. They stumble in genuine bewilderment over conditions they cannot fully understand or affect, selfish, disunified, resistant. Blue grieves that they cannot achieve a "common viewpoint" among them, some "common greeting or common words" that "would indicate the existence of camaraderie" (28). They fight each other in Fats' poolroom when they should be having a good time. A dirty, surly old man begs Jacob for some food, then resentfully criticizes him. These people know only what hurts them, not how to make it stop. The picture hurts, but Mahoney draws it well.

Black Jacob is an unusual act of self-scrutiny in those revolutionary times, and it looks with an unwavering, unsentimental eye at the black group that more optimistic observers call the redemptive community. Dr. Blue looks upon his own community from a distance, resignedly laboring to ameliorate the problems they themselves refuse to deal with, skeptical about the efficacy of most action, yet deeply enmeshed personally in the web of human relationships in which he has willy-nilly been caught. Blue has no messianic effect upon the townfolk or even his friends, even though Mahoney includes all the paraphernalia of the optimistic novel that produced such an effect—the lynching of Blue's father, for example. Far from being the inspiring work of violence that liberated Joe Youngblood or Appalachee Red, it is a shameful secret kept by Jacob Blue's mother, too embarrassed to let her son know it. It had been a dirty little lynching, based on lies and false accusations, and retained no nobility for the present. And it makes Dr. Blue skeptical of his entire background.

Yet we admire Dr. Blue, regret his meaningless death, and ultimately believe in his commitment to his election. It is just that Mahoney allows us that feeling only as skeptics made doubtful by reality. We do not end as cynics, only as observers saddened by the unavoidable. And Mahoney plants in his last pages a sense of renewal, invoking the imagery of fertility and rebirth for the blacks when Jacob's long infertile wife finds out she is pregnant. In contrast, the whites engage in sex that is purely mechanical and sterile. The novel does not promise a new world, but at least we end with life.

In this period of revolutionary enthusiasm, as revolutionaries themselves, Du Bois and Mahoney read the African American experience as a continual drain upon the strength of those who would do good. This view especially colors the treatment of the past in its own right, rather than as the precursor to the present, when it is seen vividly for its own sake rather than as the shaper of the contemporary world. This is the case with Sarah E. Wright's version of the past in *This Child's Gonna Live* (1969), an exceptionally fine piece of folk realism, rendered in the language of pre–World War II blacks on Maryland's Eastern Shore without a false or affected note. In *This Child's Gonna Live,* Wright pays tribute to the black women of this time and place, not as bearers of political or social change but as sufferers of the eternal condition of the downtrodden and the unlucky. These are the women who bore up under the most trying circumstances, aching to escape a bleak rural existence with no future, but going on when they were needed. Lynching is part of the hard Tangierneck life, and two lynchings pervade every other action of the narrative, one a father lynched in 1875, another the son lynched in the 1930s.

These lynchings are strictly a matter of economics, a pure grab of black land by whites, for both of whom it symbolizes power and independence. But the land also reflects the conditions of black life on Tangierneck. The season seems always to be winter, the air always cold, the ground cracked and barren from frost. In this inhospitable climate, what nature does not confront the blacks with, the whites do, limiting them to a life of disease, poverty, deprivation. Beneath this weight, the black people are not shining examples of patience and tolerance. They are suspicious of each other, angry, frustrated, mean. They do not often pass decent words among themselves, nor do they have hope of bettering their material lives. Death is a constant occurrence, from automobile accidents, tuberculosis, pneumonia, cancer.

The whites kill and blacks die for land that is as stony as the people, in a tragedy as absurd in its futility as the murder of Jacob Blue. The black males see in the possession of the land a fulfillment of their lives, while the black community in which they live sees it as a source of potential communal use. But Mariah Upshur, married to one of the men for whom the land is everything, dreams only of escaping. The Tangierneck black community does not provide her with warmth and support. Most of the ladies resent Mariah for bearing, several years before, a child out of wedlock, and her father-in-law has never reconciled himself to his belief that his son married down when he married her. This personal alienation is what the land means to her, what black men risk dying for. Her husband, Jacob, is trying to buy back from the whites the twenty acres his family once owned. For Mariah this simply means more hardship and estrangement for her and greater dangers for her children, and her determination is, as the title tells us, that the child with which she is pregnant is "gonna live."

The child does live, but in a way quite different from Mariah's hope. The Tangierneck community, rent by petty discord, does have a survival instinct that could be called unity. When the Crawfordville white men descend upon Jacob's cabin and threaten him and his family, the Tangierneck blacks come to their rescue. And Mariah's friend Vyella is the heart and soul of the community, caring for its children and overseeing the building of a proper schoolhouse. At her death, Vyella begs Mariah to carry on in her place, caring for the family she is leaving behind, taking over the building of the schoolhouse, becoming the cement that holds the community together—in short, assuming the ancient burden of the black woman. Mariah is hardly a messiah or the iron rail that guides blacks that Jane

Pittman is. She does not accept the burden Vyella places upon her except with tears of reluctance and loss of hope. Nor does she inherit a black community ready to follow her. But that is precisely Wright's point. We do not feel the kind of conventional optimism or release from tension that the other novelists give us. Indeed, Mariah nearly commits suicide in contemplating the bleakness of her future. But there is an inspiring strength in her that she can draw on even at the extremity of her pain and desolation. And it is not so much that we admire that strength as stand in awe of it.

In Wright's acknowledgments we learn where Mariah Upshur comes from—from Wright's "seemingly invincible mother and grandmothers, and aunts, and sisters, and cousins."[39] "Invincible" is the key word here, linking the experience the novel covers, between 1875 and the early 1930s, with the period Wright had to have observed as she wrote, the 1960s. We need find no overt expression of it in *This Child's Gonna Live* to understand the connection between Mariah Upshur's invincibility and that of, say, Rosa Parks or Fannie Lou Hamer or Coretta Scott King. One does not seek the occasion for demonstrating one's invincibility. But when the occasion comes uncalled, the Mariah Upshurs just "got to keep marching," not to the sound of silver trumpets and the applause of multitudes but to the dissonant strains of one's own disappointment. In the end, Mariah surrenders her escape money to Jacob so that he can complete the payments for the land even while she undertakes the care of Vyella's orphaned children and husband. Personally, Mariah affirms her bond with the black community but at the same time locks herself into her prison without promise of reprieve.

Wright's historical novel explains the toughness of the post–World War II black woman. Wright implies that any more optimistic picture of the past would diminish the true heroism of those Tangierneck blacks. Like Mahoney, she does not praise the messianic charisma of the unusual leader or the effectiveness of the unified group but admires the grit of the ordinary person.

Among the novelists of the post–World War II years who deal with lynching, the believers in the redemptive community outnumber the doubters. The black past, with its history of lynching, charges the post–World War II community with its strength and provides its members their identity. In taking white violence against blacks as their subject, their work coheres with the novels of racial violence produced during the half century before World War II. It shows these novelists reflecting their own time, with more aggressive protagonists and a greater optimism about specific political success. Yet even the majority of these protagonists, like their forerunners, reveal a skepticism about the use of retaliatory violence and rely more upon strength of character and a sense of their own moral rightness than upon giving back blow for blow.

With Bigger Thomas, Richard Wright changes this picture. Bigger's two murders in *Native Son* (1940) produce a new equation. Bigger is the first in a line of fictional characters that turn the flow of violence around, from white-upon-black to black-upon-white. This is a fictive line that develops from the desperate seeker after self-esteem and autonomy that characterizes Bigger to a full-blown, totally self-confident violent hero, the black nationalist revolutionary. The novels in which this character appears and changes appear concurrently with the fiction I have been discussing in this chapter and reflect in a perverse way the same political optimism. Their authors seem in a subtle way to take heart from the changes in the racial climate that occur, first imperceptibly in the thirties, then more overtly in the forties and fifties, and finally the explosion in the sixties. But they express a very different view of racial violence. They display an unusual readiness to write plots in which black characters kill whites. To be sure, there were avengers like Gofer Gondolier, Josh Green, and Perigua, as well as respectable and educated retaliators like Abe Overley in Waring's *As We See It*. But our perception of them was always modified by the more reasonable and conciliatory hero or heroine. What we get in *Native Son* and its progeny from 1940 on is a whole species of novels in which the character who does violence is elevated to the role of protagonist, without any ameliorating influence of a compensating hero. The characters in these novels undergo an evolution from the desperate Bigger Thomas to the ebullient Black Power revolutionaries of the late sixties and early seventies, and then turn in a new direction with the figures of Milkman Dead and Guitar Bains in Toni Morrison's *Song of Solomon* (1977). Morrison's book brings the development of the novel of racial violence to a close, or at least to a temporary stop, for we can only speculate where it will go from there. In fact, as we will see, she transforms not only the entire question concerning racial violence, and the way it is answered, but also the way it is put. For now, though, I turn to the novel of black-on-white violence.

IMAGES OF REVOLT:
BLACK VIOLENCE AGAINST WHITES

RICHARD WRIGHT AND
BIGGER THOMAS:
GRACE IN DAMNATION

Of all the African American novelists who have explored the issues raised by violence, Richard Wright is the most probing. It is therefore fitting that he comes to us *in medias res.* In the person of Bigger Thomas, and in the features of his own personality which he puts into Bigger, Wright projects the most fundamental of the ambiguities residing in violence, and in the figures of the victim and the hero, and therefore provides the pivot in the history of the African American novel of violence. The story has become part of American lore. Bigger Thomas, hired as chauffeur by rich Chicagoan Henry Dalton, finds himself cornered in the bedroom of his employer's daughter, Mary. He has assisted the girl to her room after chauffeuring her and her boyfriend around town while they get drunk and try to make friends with him. When Mary's blind mother enters the room, Bigger smothers the girl to keep her from giving him away. Later he kills his black girlfriend Bessie Mears, figuring he cannot take her with him in his planned escape and cannot leave her behind to expose him. He tries to flee, is captured by the police, convicted of murder, and on the last page of the novel sits in his jail cell awaiting his execution. These two murders are the pivotal acts of violence in the African American novel, and Wright's meditation on their effect upon Bigger is the subtlest comment on violence to be made by a black novelist up to 1940.

Before *Native Son,* the typical pattern of events in African American novels dealing with violence started with whites. A group of southerners would rape a black woman, lynch a black man or woman, or riot against vulnerable black citizens. The novelists would expose the injustice and dastardliness of the violence and then consider whether the victimized blacks were morally justified in using counterviolence in retaliation or self-defense. Usually they decided not. Their characters were too morally upright to descend to such savagery and would opt instead for forgiveness and nonviolent activism to counter white brutality. Wright reworks the pattern profoundly. When Bigger kills he is not reacting to any specific act of white violence. No rapes or southern-style lynchings occur in *Native Son*. It is Bigger's *black* violence that we are concerned with, an extreme act of self-defense, embodying the contradictory, even self-canceling, elements of the victim, the hero, and the pariah. Bigger is Wright's statement about the impossible double bind in which the black man finds himself in "the presence of the white man"[1] and the narrow options left him for heroic action and a sense of dignity.[2]

If we look at the novel as social protest, Bigger's extreme reaction might be mitigated by the truly threatening situation he finds himself in. His sense of personal vulnerability in Mary's room when her blind mother gropes her way in grows out of his conditioning by the racist environment in which he has been raised. The white culture of Chicago may not be as overtly violent as that of the South, but it still makes perfectly clear the danger any black runs when he or she oversteps the racial limits. Thus an argument could have been made by any social liberal at the time that, while Bigger's deed was bad and he should not have done it, it was a racist, class-driven society that made him do it. And indeed Wright does suggest that society bears a portion of the blame. The white racism that closes off to Bigger avenues of achievement and growth that are taken for granted by whites creates an atmosphere in which it will be only a matter of time before a young hothead like him will do just what he did. Even before the murders, he feels "like something awful is going to happen to me." And after them he says that he had really killed before.[3]

But Wright introduces into his narrative a number of elements that make it difficult to see the novel simply in terms of social protest. The murder of Bessie, for one thing, shatters any justification for absolving Bigger of guilt because he is a victim of racism. Killing white Mary Dalton, however awful, is understandable. She is a symbol of everything that has kept Bigger back. Killing a black woman and feeling good about it complicate the issue beyond simple protest against white bigotry. Then there is the difficulty with Bigger himself. Although we may mitigate Bigger's actions because he has been shaped by a narrow and stultifying social system, he brings few endearing qualities with him. Not only does he frighten his own family and friends, the murders he commits are impossible to justify by most readers' moral standard. We cannot say that he is defending the lives of his family or his honor as a man, or that he is justly retaliating against a particular white outrage upon a black victim. He is hot-tempered and brutal. He is a petty thief with only enough courage to rob other Negroes. He cruelly teases his sister, bullies his own friends, and resents the helping hand extended by a benevolent, though hypocritical, white man. Even his own mother says he will come to no good. Mary Dalton tries, however clumsily, to befriend him; Bessie Mears trusts him. He murders them both for their trouble. We cannot warm to Bigger and cannot condone his violence, in which there is nothing we could call admirably manly. In this respect, Wright achieved his stated resolve to avoid the pathos of the stories in *Uncle Tom's Children* (1938, 1940) and write a book that "would be so hard and deep that [the reader] would have to face it without the consolation of tears" (xxvi). By making him murder Bessie as well as Mary, by making the murders the seedbed out of which Bigger's sense of esteem and identity grows, by making Bigger less than attractive, Wright undercuts the view of *Native Son* as social protest. He obviates much of the sympathy we might have for Bigger as a social victim and thumbs his nose at the traditional black middle-class insistence upon morally unblemished protagonists. He produces instead a totally problematical hero who not only takes full responsibility for the two heinous crimes but experiences total exhilaration for having committed them. Bigger's quiet certainty in the rightness of his violence at the end of the novel strikes horror into the heart of Mr. Max, because Bigger has created for himself a morality in which murder is a good.

It is this moral paradox and Wright's disappointing all expectations of what convention requires in a black character that make *Native Son* so different from any earlier African American novel. Moral paradox, indeed, characterizes the violence of the novel, both Bigger's murders and his own pending execution. More specifically, it characterizes the two moral systems that seek to control our attitudes toward that violence—Bigger's system and the one represented by the Daltons and State Attorney Buckley. The two systems, in polar opposition, nevertheless mirror one another. Violence is at their center, along with the question of whose violence is the legitimate one, which system controls violence and maintains the power to define it as virtuous or criminal. The tacit assumption here is that violent acts are morally neutral. They take on a moral charge with the attitudes we have toward them. Wright deals with these issues not as a polemicist, moralist, or philosopher, by formulating a discursive argument with a reductive conclusion, but as an artist. Through the design of his action and imagery, he dramatizes the inherent ambiguity of any morality that seeks to legitimize violence. Like any good novel that takes on such a basic, explosive topic, *Native Son* is made up of a conflict that is inherently inconclusive at the same time that, as a novel, it is morally revealing and aesthetically satisfying.[4]

The conflict originates in Bigger's attitude toward the murders themselves, through which Bigger acquires his unprecedented sense of self. After he kills Mary, he feels reborn; after Bessie, he feels whole and empowered (101, 226). Bigger also comes to believe that through his acts he redeems his family and friends.[5] Throughout the novel, he sees *them* as victims, not of any literal physical violence from the white world surrounding the South Side Chicago ghetto where they live but of their own timidity. They have sold out to the racist social and moral system which demands not only that they should be what the system says they are but that they affirm that identity as natural and right. They have accepted the racial limits imposed upon them and agreed to be satisfied with the seedy "corner" of the city to which they have been assigned. They thus pay "mute tribute" to the tremendous and intimidating "force" of the white world (109). As he contemplates his family the morning after he murders Mary, Bigger feels in them "a force, inarticulate and unconscious, making for living without thinking, making for peace and habit, making for a hope that blinded" (102). They acquiesce in the mental and moral darkness in which whites force them to live. The entire black community cowers, muffling its pusillanimity through drink, as Bigger's girlfriend Bessie does, or rationalizing it through religion, as his mother does (226). The black church music he hears when he is a fugitive hiding in the empty tenements of the South Side whispers to him "of another way of life and death, coaxing him to lie down and sleep and let them come and get him, urging him to believe that all life was a sorrow that had to be accepted" (237). This "was his mother's world, humble, contrite, believing," requiring that he lay "his head upon a pillow of humility and [give] up his hope of living in the world. And he would never do that" (238). The murders he commits turn out to be a way of executing his determination to "never do that," of finding and then asserting an autonomous consciousness that can work in the favor of other blacks. In the end, as his family, his friends, and a black minister all crowd into his jail cell, feeling sorry for him because he is "guilty," Bigger suddenly sees that he has saved them from the shame of their victimization:

They ought to be glad! It was a strange but strong feeling, springing from the very depths of his life. Had he not taken fully upon himself the crime of being black? Had he not done the thing which they dreaded above all others? Then they ought not stand here and pity him, cry over him; but look at him and go home, contented, feeling that their shame was washed away. (275)

But the moral system reflected in this attitude is no less flawed than the system that Bigger fights. The white racist morality is tyrannical, oppressive, and unfair. Bigger's requires victims, too—Mary and Bessie. Yet Mr. Max can, with accuracy, call Bigger's murders an "act of *creation*." The two murders do indeed open Bigger up to consciousness, meaning, knowledge. His fear and shame had heretofore kept him from using processes which these acts of violence now put into motion. As he seeks to hide his crimes, he calls into service senses and intelligence his environment had previously blocked. His feeling of being present in life is heightened to incandescence. He becomes more finely aware of his every move, brings every muscle and nerve into play.[6] His body trembles with a mix of frenzy and clarity. He is a new man, and the world he returns to is new. After he murders Bessie, he sums up the meaning of his acts: "In all his life these two murders were the most meaningful things that had ever happened to him. He was living, truly and deeply, no matter what others might think, looking at him with their blind eyes" (391–92, 224). Bigger now has a sense of being that living in the kitchenette with his family or planning robberies with his friends had never given him. And by the end of the novel, as Bigger waits in his cell to go to his death in the electric chair, he interprets his violence by the revolutionary moral system Mr. Max refers to and which Bigger slowly develops in the course of the novel:

"What I killed for must've been good!" Bigger's voice was full of frenzied anguish. "It must have been good! When a man kills, it's for something. . . . I didn't know I was really alive in this world until I felt things hard enough to kill for 'em. . . . It's the truth, Mr. Max. I can say it now, 'cause I'm going to die. I know what I'm saying real good and I know how it sounds. But I'm all right. I feel all right when I look at it that way." (392)

When Bigger attacks Gus in the pool hall before they are going to rob Blum's delicatessen, his violence is simply that of a bully brought to the boiling point by frustration and fear. It is not an act that engages the larger world or makes him more than he is. When he murders Mary Dalton, however, Bigger takes on more powerful forces. He approaches the forbidden, at first with dread and then, when the barrier has been scaled, with exaltation. The one absolute good that Bigger senses at the moment he commits the first murder is his own existence. Only later, after reflecting upon his deeds, can he explain what the killing was "all about": that if his existence is good, what supports it has to be good (392). This does not mean that either we or Wright must endorse Bigger's point of view. In fact, we must not. On the other hand, we must not assume that we have reached the final answer by being brought to see the flaws in the larger white system that made inevitable this "new form of life" (361).

Instead, we must submit to Wright's art, which foregrounds the conflict between the two systems, not the resolution of the conflict; emphasizes the paradox rather than a solution. Wright does not ask us to approve or disapprove of Bigger's violence but to feel the quandary in the situation: two opposing systems each containing goods embedded in bads. Bigger's independence and self-esteem, which we presumably value, grow in a character we do not especially like through acts we cannot condone. The racist white moral system victimizes blacks, it is true, yet it embodies a high good in its theoretical prohibition against murder. Simultaneously, it seems to exploit this high good as a way of curbing Bigger's self-creating revolt. Both systems contradictorily assign both high and low value to human life. They base their assignment of value on an unstated selection criterion that gives some humans higher value than others. This criterion justifies violent acts toward one group, which are considered criminal when committed upon another. Both systems abuse human life to achieve their ends of celebrating and protecting human life. Thus Wright troubles us with a moral dilemma in which tacitly accepted goods (the cultivation of personal identity and the protection of the sanctity of individual life) are entailed in systems containing tacitly accepted bads (the suppression of personal identity and a disregard of human life). Each system claims violence as the means for protecting the higher good as its supporters define it.

The impact of the novel, of course, is not in the abstract explanation but in the concrete drama, and in that drama Bigger has a unique role. At one level he has the effect on us of the outlaw-hero. He breaks laws we know are right, but we are drawn to him for doing it. We agree that he has to be punished but regret it. Houston A. Baker, Jr., puts a slightly different spin on this view. Bigger, he says, is the black culture hero—the courageous slave who revolts against his bondage; Nat Turner, who leads a rebellion; the folk hero Stackolee, ambivalently admired among blacks for his fearless meanness. Baker reads Bigger from a virtually untrammeled racial point of view. Bigger destroys the symbol of white purity and superiority in Mary Dalton, says Baker, and becomes "a strong, Satanic figure determined, at whatever cost, to have his freedom."[7] The Satan identification strikes me as exact. It defines in a single image the clash between the two moral systems that I have noted. White authority reserves violence for its own exclusive use and stigmatizes any unapproved use of it. The murders Bigger commits, therefore, are not simply acts that gain him freedom. They are in themselves free acts. They are Bigger's refusal to submit to a system that demonizes the only means it has left him to achieve his definition. That those acts are in themselves morally indefensible makes the paradox all the tighter and the reader's perplexity all the more intense.

The paradox also heightens the drama. Bigger steals the gods' fire, so to speak, and this starts up the implacable mechanism of authority's self-defense and punishment of disobedience. His liberation entails his annihilation, for authority cannot tolerate his autonomy and remain authority. Bigger is a doomed rebel who, even while he revolts, acknowledges the validity of the punishment he must receive for trying to find himself. Wright does not have him insist that the moral system that makes murder for him an "act of creation" should supersede the moral system that says those two murders are crimes. Instead, he speculates about giving it a parallel validity and then bringing it into collision with the majority system. For it all to work, Wright must be able to induce in the reader at least an understanding of the logic of Bigger's moral system, though not acceptance of it. So he confronts the reader with a hero who is willing to take on the white world and undergo destruction to achieve self-discovery.

The genesis of this hero in Wright's mind is indirectly described in his autobiography, *Black Boy* (1945). Here, Wright explains that violence was ubiquitous in the South of his youth. It was used to thwart his attempts to grow out of the limits set for him by his world. Even though he himself experiences only minor instances of white violence, he sees the evidence of its terror all around him and knows men whom whites kill.[8] It has a powerful inhibiting effect on him: "My sustained expectation of violence had exhausted me. My preoccupation with curbing my impulses, my speech, my movements, my manner, my expression had increased my anxiety. I became forgetful, concentrating too much upon trivial tasks" (171).[9] In the concluding pages of *Black Boy,* he reflects that "as I had lived in the South I had not had the chance to learn who I was. The pressure of southern living kept me from being the kind of person that I might have been" (227). Violence is the pervasive impediment to the achievement of a spontaneous autonomous self-identity.

This impediment was not limited to whites. The pattern of violence in the larger white world is repeated in the black world of his family, his school, and his neighborhood. In his telling, his family, like Bigger's, conforms "to the dictates of the whites above them." The slappings, the spankings, the beatings his older relatives administer are an extension of white discipline intended to force him to be "what the whites said I must be," a compliant nullity (227). Wright's description of two famous beatings his mother gives him as a child makes the link explicit. Each causes a fever during which, in his delirium, he sees "monstrous white faces suspended from the ceiling, leering at me," and, much more symbolically, those often-cited "huge wobbly white bags, like the full udders of cows, suspended from the ceiling above me." [10] The family violence is mixed in his fevered unconscious with the all-pervasive white danger. The black as well as the white seek to stifle the growth of Wright's youthful personality. He is constantly in conflict with some institutionalized "naked will to power" that seeks to force him into submission (119).

In his neighborhood and at school, though, he meets violence under different conditions. Bullies and gangs try to initimidate him and subject him to their command. They threaten him, steal his money, take his lunch, try to bend him to their will. Whenever he changes schools or moves to a new neighborhood, he has to prove himself by fighting or be forever relegated to anxiety and limited freedom of movement. But this conflict has a much different effect upon Wright than that between himself and his family and white people. These fights become a way of defining himself, of establishing who he is and achieving the admiration of his schoolmates. Once he has proven himself in a fight, the other schoolchildren accord him the kind of individual respect that he needs to be whole. He feels a mild contempt for the "docile" students in the Seventh Day Adventist school he attends who have had all the spunk taken out of them in their submission to the religious strictures of their families and churches. They lacked "that keen sense of rivalry which made the boys and girls who went to public school a crowd in which a boy was tested and weighed, in which he caught a glimpse of what the world was" (90). This is the only violence for which Wright expresses a positive feeling. It is clear why that is so. Both the contestants and their audience understand what is expected of each. The best man wins in this healthy competition. Unlike the other violent structures to which Wright is subjected, that of the neighborhood and school-yard provides a satisfactory outlet for his sense of his own importance. It embodies a mutual respect and a basis for self-respect that the other structures withhold. Most important, the violence of the neighborhood and schoolyard is not clothed in the hypocritical moralizing of self-serving piety or backed by social or familial institutions. The power struggles are naked and straightforward. There is only one moral system, and its rules are transparent, universally observed, and equally applicable to all.

Not so the moral system of his grandmother's household and the white world it mirrors. There the moral rules are unequally applied. It is God's will that all members of the family have a sacred right to punish the young Richard when he seeks to go his own way, or that whites are morally authorized to kill blacks when blacks seek to claim equal rights. This system does not authorize either young Richard or blacks in general to fight back. When Richard does fight back, he does what Bigger does. He asserts a

moral system of his own. Wright fights back against the corporal punishment of his family with the same physical vehemence with which he fights
to protect his autonomy in the schoolyard and neighborhood. When he
gets old enough and big enough, he returns violence for violence or
threatens to defend himself with violence if attacked, sometimes grasping a
knife and holding off an aunt or an uncle with grim recklessness. But there
is no pleasure in these encounters, or sense of achievement, or even ground
for self-esteem. Every fight results in intensified bad feelings, resentment,
anger, and increased alienation, rather than a heightened sense of autonomy
or regard for a former competitor.

The story Wright tells in *Black Boy* is essentially one of his struggle
against a violent, suppressive environment to become the person he can
spontaneously be. The first episode, about four-year-old Richard setting
fire to the curtains of the family cabin and the punishment that follows,
epitomizes the rest of the narrative, as well as many of Wright's fictional
narratives. The passage contains a group of images that cluster around the
core of much of Wright's writing: fire, the rebel; the conventional and
timid observer of the rules (Wright's little brother says, "Don't do that,"
when Richard first sets the broom straw afire [4]); the rebellious crime
(setting the curtains afire); the flight of the criminal (Richard hides under
the house); the pursuit by authority (his parents go looking for him);
punishment; and his reflection upon the "meaning" of the episode.

The act springs out of the conditions that Wright always hated, con-
straints against his free search for light, knowledge, and experience. He is
feeling restless under the orders of his mother to remain quiet and avoid
disturbing Granny Wilson, lying ill under a doctor's care in the next room.
He looks for something to do. He is resentful of the limits forced upon
him, of being expected to suppress his natural animation, of the fear he is
made to feel about defying his mother's authority or disturbing the fierce
matriarch, his grandmother. Light and fire attract him—knowledge and
power. The "glowing coals" in the fireplace fascinate him. He lights a few
straws from the broom he finds. But unsatisfied, he moves his eyes to the
curtains. They are "long," "fluffy," and "white," a description he mentions
twice. They are expressly and specifically "forbidden," outside the approved
set of playthings that his brother dutifully confines himself to, and mark the
boundary of his containment. Beyond that fluffy white purity is the street,
in which he dreams of "running and playing and shouting."[11] Instead, he is
cooped up in a cheerless room. He touches the burning broom straw to
the curtains, they flare up, the house catches fire, and Richard tries to
escape by hiding under the house. Bedlam breaks out, screams, frantic
movement, then fire wagons. He is terrified. His father, finding him curled

up next to the chimney, drags him out by the legs, and his mother beats him.

But it was all "an accident," says Wright. He had only wanted knowledge. "I had just wanted to see how the curtains would look when they burned" (4). That is, in the midst of limiting conditions, Richard was curious about what lay beyond. He looked for "illumination," needing to find the meaning the curtains conceal. Even threats from authority could not dampen that need. Wright's little brother, out of fear, cooperated with that authority, obediently rejecting whatever knowledge it is that the adults forbid. As for Richard, he seized the only experience authority has left him. From the viewpoint of that authority, he looks like a disobedient brat. For a personality that needs liberty to live, he does what he has to within the conditions imposed upon him. The fire was an "accident" he had not intended. This is the same way that Bigger speaks of his crime. "I really never wanted to hurt nobody," he tells Mr. Max. "I didn't mean to do what I did. I was trying to do something else" (388). But for better or worse, both Richard and Bigger, all by themselves, transformed the world that had controlled them. Had authority allowed them some other avenue of self-expression and exploration, both Wright in *Black Boy* and Bigger in *Native Son* might have taken it without violence. But it is the nature of the kind of authority that Wright sees ruling the world to prohibit self-knowledge as a threat to its power and to punish those who violate the prohibition. The words Wright uses to describe the beating he receives from his mother imply that prohibition. The whipping causes him to lose "consciousness," he says. "I was beaten out of my senses." (6). This is not surprising since consciousness and sense—how the curtains would look—were the states of awareness that Richard lit the fire to attain. His mother, in this case Authority Enraged, beats him to put out the light he tries to ignite with the flame. His punishment is the violent obliteration of the consciousness he had sought. I do not mean that Wright the four-year-old conciously and intentionally set out to acquire "knowledge," only that Wright looking back imbues this episode with a kind of mythic order that is a prototype of many of his other narratives.[12]

Wright comments on the discovery his experience brings to him: "Each event spoke with a cryptic tongue. And the moments of living slowly revealed their coded meanings" (7). Richard is driven to seek the coded meanings uttered by the cryptic tongue of the curtains. It is naughty mischief, but Wright is a naughty and mischievous child, who *should* be punished. At the same time, we admire his exasperating insistence upon his own will. It is the same ambivalence we feel toward Bigger Thomas's punishment.

Not all the knowledge Wright attains in *Black Boy* is dangerous or calls him to the attention of the "gods." But when he does encroach upon the gods' ground, when, say, fire itself is an issue, they use no restraint in going after the challenger. This is primordial myth and religion, a stage on which is acted out the ambivalence of the human being toward consciousness, its attractiveness but its dangerousness as a form of revolt. Consciousness, understanding, knowledge, awareness are precisely what the jealous gods of so many myths do not want the upstart humans to acquire. When it comes to fire and consciousness, it is too tempting to resist invoking Prometheus,[13] whose story suggests many elements in the typical Wright narrative: the argument among the gods (authority) over the amount of knowledge humans (blacks) should be allowed (consider the discussion Mr. and Mrs. Dalton have over Bigger's "education"); Prometheus the rebel bringing humans the fire of technology and understanding; the punishment of both Prometheus and humans by the jealous gods; the simultaneous destructiveness and creativity of fire.[14] When translated into English, the language that Aeschylus puts into the mouth of Prometheus suggests Wright's language. To the Chorus, Prometheus says,

> Before I gave them *sense and understanding,*
> Men were like babies, like figures in a dream;
> Eyes they had, but didn't *notice* things;
> Ears they had, but couldn't *distinguish* sounds.[15]

The fire that Prometheus steals from the other gods and presents to humans is the light of understanding and knowledge that Bigger seeks through the murder of Mary and Bessie, and that young Richard ignites the curtains to acquire. "I opened [humans'] eyes to the stars," boasts Prometheus, "And what they signify" (line 462). To steal the gods' fire is to claim a right to awareness, and that is an autonomy the gods cannot tolerate. For such a theft, the Prometheus figure must be punished. He must be taught "not to rebel against Zeus" (line 10). Adam receives punishment for the same offense, acquiring forbidden knowledge. There is a certain rightness in those punishments. As Milton puts it, "Die [man] or Justice must" (*Paradise Lost,* 3.210). Social harmony still depends in large part upon the observation of "degree, priority, and place" (*Troilus and Cressida,* 1.3.86). At the same time, it is in the nature of the seeking self to see authority as tyrannical, and revolt as the only way available to preserve full existence. And often, even objective onlookers bring only an ambivalent respect for authority and applaud the rebel for doing what they themselves would not.

The Richard Wright who sets the curtains afire to see how they would "look" is a kind of Promethean rebel, an Adamic seeker after knowledge, impatient with his own ignorance. From his viewpoint, the "system" (his mother, acting in behalf of Granny Wilson and the rest of the family) overreacts with punishment out of proportion to the alleged crime. Michel Fabre speculates that much of Wright's adult anger stemmed not from his racial problems but from the beating he received from his mother. It was an "incomprehensible punishment for a transgression he did not accept as such, an experience which long predated his first encounter with racism." [16] Fabre speculates that this might have been the original betrayal. We have also seen how Wright connected this beating with the kind of violence he faces in the white world. What we might call his self-pity becomes a sense of grievance against an unjust world that Wright carries with him to his grave, aggravated in his last years into a paranoiac conviction that the Central Intelligence Agency was pursuing him and planned his death. [17] All of his main characters are "innocent," even though they might have performed acts defined as crimes within the values of constraining authority. In his dying words, Cross Damon, after killing no fewer than four men in *The Outsider* (1953), says that "in my heart . . . I'm *innocent*. . . . That's what made the horror." [18] We get the same feeling about Bigger Thomas, and it lends legitimacy to the rebel's individual moral system.

For Wright the *raison d'être* of the narrative is in the drama of the rebel challenging the tremendous power that will inevitably crush him. When he steals the gods' fire, the rebel sets himself ablaze and draws the attention of the universe to himself. He puts himself into the cosmic spotlight. An easy target, now, for the pursuing furies of authority, he becomes an object of awe and terror to the timid who fear to strike the spark. One of the more revealing images in *Black Boy* embodies the nature of the drama for Wright. It appears in another typical story of revolt, in which Wright recounts how, when he publishes his first short story, "The Voodoo of Hell's Half-Acre," in the local newspaper, his family and schoolmates are baffled and uncomfortable. The "dream" that story represents was something "the entire educational system of the South had been rigged to stifle" (148). In Wright's mind, his family, friends, and acquaintances, like Bigger's, collaborated in their own oppression, refusing to contemplate any act or thought outside approved bounds. When they discover that Wright has struck through those bounds to unapproved *consciousness*, they warn him that he is going past the limits set for him by the racial culture, just as his little brother had warned him about the fire and the curtains. The metaphor contains all the elements of the hero's struggle against darkness and oppression, together with the grandeur of a defeat that is also a victory.

In me was shaping a yearning for a kind of consciousness, a mode of being that the way of life about me had said could not be, must not be, and upon which the penalty of death had been placed. Somewhere in the dead of the southern night my life had switched onto the wrong track and, without my knowing it, the locomotive of my heart was rushing down a dangerously steep slope, heading for a collision, heedless of the warning red lights that blinked all about me, the sirens and the bells and the screams that filled the air. (148) [19]

It is this sensational readiness to risk the wrath of the powers that be for higher consciousness that rules Wright's narrative and dramatic interests. His heroes, including himself in *Black Boy,* stride across a vast stage, the center of attention, the object of all apprehensive eyes. They ride the wild locomotive, hurtling through space on a disastrous but resplendent course. All existence condenses itself in their act. They are Prometheus, Satan, Ahab, the Byronic hero—America's romantic individualist defiantly taking on the forces of oppression and death, striking through the pasteboard masks to forbidden awareness and knowledge, saying "No!" in thunder. Alone, they blast through the night, doomed, but ready for their fate, for in their damnation lies redemption, in failure, glory. Their crime is a thrust for freedom. Wright seeks for them not authority's grace or society's approval but tragedy, heroism, fame; he craves attention and admiration; he wants them to flame out in an unprecedented gesture of defiance that stimulates the world to awe. With their destruction they willingly pay for the priceless prize of illumination, consciousness, and autonomy. Like Hemingway, Wright sees the world rigged against the individual. But unlike Hemingway, he makes no separate peace. Wright's prototypical story —his autobiographical writings and much of his major fiction—is an account of the way he and his protagonists refuse to submit to these forces: "Ought one to surrender to authority even if one believed that that authority was wrong?" he asks in *Black Boy.* "If the answer was yes, then I knew I would always be wrong, because I could never do it" (144). For him, the fight is everything. It is the vehicle of the consciousness and autonomy he must seek for fulfillment.

Bigger Thomas and Richard Wright revolt as black men against a white world. But they are more than a black folk hero or an instrument of social protest. Neither is a "victim," surely, like a slave who is whipped, an accused black man who is lynched, or an urban citizen run to ground by a mob. Nor is either a "hero" in the sense that they mobilize a following to try to make a difference in the world they live in. What makes them unique in the history of the African American novel of violence is that they are the first black figures to take on the authentic features of the traditional American romantic individualist.[20] At the same time, like the rebel Albert Camus imagines over a decade later, Richard Wright and Bigger Thomas find the meaning of their life in revolt against dehumanizing limits and show how the African American can be seen as a metaphor of modern existential man.[21] Bigger is the first black character to reject all aspects of the white moral system and to substitute his own. Unlike such notable nineteenth-century rebels as William Wells Brown, Frederick Douglass, and Henry Bibb, who carefully stayed within the limits of Victorian sexual morality and attitudes toward thievery and violence, Wright has Bigger insist that his own value justifies actions that whites call crimes. He declares black independence in a way no black protagonist had since Martin Delany's Henry Blake. He sums up half a century of black novel writing about racial violence and lays the foundation for the half century to come.

[8]

THE REBEL STIRS:
TEMPORARY INSANITY AND
CREATIVE RIOTS

AFTER BIGGER THOMAS

Bigger Thomas has his antecedents in the avengers I have so often referred
to: Martin Delany's Gofer Gondolier, Chesnutt's Josh Green, Du Bois's
Perigua, Bontemps's Criddle. And as we have seen, considerable attention
is paid by the novelists of racial violence to the question of asserting black
manhood and getting back at whites by retaliating in kind. But as I have
already suggested, the earlier killers tended to be secondary characters, and
even when they were protagonists, their violence was set in the context of
the question of answering one act with another. Bigger has not been
threatened with a lynching, nor has he seen any friend or relative lynched.
The white girl he kills has attempted to befriend him. His act springs out
of quite a different background from that of, say, Josh Green, who killed to
avenge another killing. Moreover, those novelists who wondered about
retaliating against whites mostly inclined against violence. With Bigger, it
is as if the African American has reached the end of his tether, and violence
against a white person is his or her only recourse.

Before 1940, black novelists' hesitancy about violence perhaps had something to do with a general sense of jeopardy; an apprehension that the
African American did not yet see himself, in the collective, as not yet a real
actor in the violent racial drama but only a passive victim. Wright's treatment of Bigger's violence reflects the awakening of a new mind-set, a more
aggressive activism commencing to flow through black consciousness. And
the spirit that Wright picks up evolves eventually into the civil rights
movement of the fifties and the black nationalism of the late sixties. We can
read Bigger as a metaphor of that nascent aggressiveness.

As he had antecedents, Bigger also has successors, and those successors are the subject of this chapter, for they confirm Wright's perception of a shift in the thinking and feeling of the African American community. William Attaway's Mat Moss in *Blood on the Forge* (1941), Ann Petry's Lutie Johnson in *The Street* (1946), Chester Himes's Jesse Robinson in *The Primitive* (1955) are just three of a number of characters who, in the two decades following *Native Son,* kill whites or white surrogates. All the killings can be traced to socioracial causes, which press the characters beyond their endurance. It is the way they react to this pressure that produces their distinguishing trait. They are driven into a kind of derangement, a temporary insanity of the sort we saw in Solomon Northup's slave narrative in Chapter 1.[1] They explode out of their normal controlled, even law-abiding, behavior and attack those they feel to be responsible for their intolerable condition. The morality they violate with their act is the very morality that has kept them and their people in bondage since Emancipation. It has told them that any violation of the restrictions they are placed under is a terrible crime. And literally, like Bigger's, the murders they commit *are* terrible crimes. But as metaphors of the inchoate civil rights movement, they illustrate how novelists begin to think of breaking the taboo against any black move against white hegemony. To defy the system is the equivalent of committing murder. The metaphor begins to emerge only when we see this group of novels together and realize how different they are from their predecessors of the first four decades of the century.

The metaphor is grounded in the social protest that permeates the novels. They all take place in a northern city, usually a ghetto. Thus the characters are not bucking the southern system as it is controlled by lynching and other violence. In their new context they are controlled, as Ann Petry puts it, by the North's lynch mob—the "kitchenette,"[2] the shabby streets and rundown apartments, the absence of jobs with a future. The ghetto lynches them figuratively; it *does* something to them that makes their killings inevitable. Wright speaks of how this cause-and-effect relationship became clear to him when he discovered some statistics on Chicago's black population in the University of Chicago's sociology department. These gave him his "first concrete vision of the forces that molded the urban Negro's body and soul," he said, and to write accurately about black urban life, black writers had to understand that the ghetto provides an experience so low in quality, so crude and brutal, that it can result only in explosive behavior: "It is distinctly possible," he contended, "to know *before it happens,* that certain forms of violence will occur."[3] Thus we get Bigger Thomas, whose mind is warped by a lack of education, whose aesthetic sense is dulled by the cracked cement and decrepit buildings on Indiana Avenue, whose ambitions are thwarted by his color, and whose movement is constrained by the space in which he is forced to live with three other people. The ghetto comes to determine the dominant style of African American life, and Bigger is a model of the ghetto man. But unlike the southern black who is vulnerable to lynching, Bigger has the option to strike. Rightly or wrongly, under extraordinary circumstances and in an unprecedented frenzy, Bigger kills a white person—partly to protect himself, partly because he had been subliminally thinking of it for a long time.

Wright and his successors begin making a consistent connection between the inner city and this particular kind of sudden, explosive, racial violence only after they recognize the ghetto *as* a ghetto. In *Blood on the Forge,* William Attaway chronicles with great power and poignance the process by which a southern black man who comes north is destroyed when urban and industrial forces push him into violence. The novel has the quality of fable, condensing the great migrations before and during World War I into the story of the three Moss brothers, whose reasons for going north from their small Kentucky farm reflect the combination of motives that must have moved so many southern blacks to abandon their familiar way of life. They want a better life, to get free of the sneering condescension of white trash. But the immediate cause of their flight is Mat's killing of his white riding boss for insulting the name of his dead mother. In the North, however, there is little more dignity than in the South, and this leads Mat to the act that will destroy him. For the Moss brothers the North is steel mills, symbols of capitalist industrialization that suck the soul out of men. To the accompaniment of the prophecy by a crippled mill hand that "Steel gonna git somebody,"[4] it does "git" all of the Moss brothers in one way or another. Only Mat dies by violence, however, and his death comes about through the whole pattern of northern life that develops in the industrial culture. The city springs from the steel produced by the mills, and in that city Mat is trapped, isolated from the more natural ties he had in the South, from his wife, Hattie, and their close marriage. Anna, the Mexican whore he takes up with, is like the steel. She allows no man to get close to her. She saps Mat of his manhood, and he tries to get it back the only way he knows how, through his physical strength. When the mill workers go on strike, Mat, instead of joining them, accepts a temporary appointment as deputy sheriff. Mat thrills with a sense of new importance, a black man with authority over whites, and he sees this as the way he can impress Anna, who would "know that he was a new man . . . that he was a boss" (255). In his new identity as "boss," Mat gets the same sensation from beating on the white strikers as Bigger does from murdering Mary and Bessie, "a sense of becoming whole again" (250).

Also like Bigger Thomas, Mat is turned into a monster by conditions he did not create, with violence the only thing society has left him for maintaining his integrity. Mat, too, has been cut off from the sustaining life forms, such as the hills of his southern home, which are like a fertile woman in his mind, renewable, natural, needing attention, bearing new life. In the mills he loses his sense of participating in the natural process, as he loses his feeling of manliness with Anna. Like Bigger, he seeks "to heal his ruptured ego," as Attaway puts it, with "a sense of brutal power" (249). Attaway does not give Mat the self-awareness that Bigger has. Instead of insight, his violence brings his final disintegration. He has turned himself into the same kind of hater as the whites who made his life miserable in the South. The employers' gunmen called out to deal with the strike are like southern posses, who are "struck with blood lust, not wanting to quit until they had made a kill" (223). The state troopers that the governor calls out to quell the rioting make a religious rite of violence: "There was a fierce, almost religious ecstacy in them as they landed blow after blow" (252). When Mat arrives at a "complete kinship" with the troopers and the deputies, he reaches the nadir of his decline, maddened by the terror of his victims and eager to fling himself upon them and drag them to the ground for the kill.

Attaway does not reject violence in itself. Its moral acceptability depends upon the motives of those who use it. Mat's defense of his mother's good name and his personal dignity make his killing the riding boss condonable according to a certain rough justice. The joy that he feels in hurting others as a deputy signals his total moral deterioration. Besides, the moral mechanism produces self-corrective forces. As Mat had acted to kill cruelty when he struck his riding boss, so a new power rises to kill Mat, in the figure of a young Slav, who, hating what he is doing, clubs Mat dead in an encounter between union and owner forces. Mat is no hero, clearly. He could have been one: He has a sense of honor, and he is strong and fearless. But he is no match for the tremendous industrial powers that dehumanize him. For Attaway the enemy is these industrial powers as they collect in the great mill cities. For others of the school of Wright, the ghetto is the villain.

THE DEVELOPMENT OF THE NORTHERN GHETTO

African Americans did not become city dwellers with urban problems until the 1890s, when southern farming became less productive for them and their disfranchisement became complete. Then a slow drift off the farm began, and by 1910 a million or more blacks had moved into northern urban centers, commencing the great shift of the African American demographic center that would not be completed until the 1960s.[5] The first concern of black novelists and other observers in the early days of the migrations, however, was not about a black ghetto as a segregated enclave that prevents its inhabitants from joining the prosperity and enjoying the freedom of mainstream America or deprives them of the opportunity for spiritual fulfillment. It was the classic worry of the rural moralist over what the wicked city would do to the simple black people from the farms and the villages of the South, when the innocent hayseed was accosted by the city slicker with a scheme, when the wide-eyed young farmer found himself in the sweet arms of vice and gambling. In *The Sport of the Gods* (1902), Paul Laurence Dunbar suggests they disintegrate morally and stoop to the worst of all crimes. When Joe Hamilton comes to New York City from the South, he turns to drinking and gambling and his sister runs off with a dancing company. But Joe's final degradation is his murder of his girlfriend. This does not result from racial oppression, nor is the violence a retaliation against injustice. It reflects the final breakdown of what Dunbar saw as the old southern black morality.

In the nearly forty years between the appearance of *Sport of the Gods* in 1902 and *Native Son* and *Blood on the Forge* in 1940 and 1941, there is an evolution in the nature of the black urban experience as well as in the way the black writer perceives it. In the beginning, except for the moralizing voice of Dunbar, few people pay much attention to the growing black areas in northern cities. By 1913 the ghettos have already started upon their irreversible growth, and a more hermetic segregation than anything known in the South was taking place. Except for faint and ignored voices like that of George Edmund Haynes, director of the National Urban League, who in 1913 worried that "a distinct Negro world" was growing up all over the country, "isolated from many of the impulses of the common life and little understood by the white world," no one seemed to be complaining.[6]

Most whites in the years when the ghetto was undergoing its early growth regarded it as simply another source of stereotypes and recreation. For them, Harlem in particular became the symbol of play in the 1920s. Black writers saw it as the incubator of the first generation of real African American artists—writers, painters, musicians. Half a dozen black novels are set in Harlem: Claude McKay, *Home to Harlem* (1928); Wallace Thurman, *The Blacker the Berry* (1929) and *Infants of the Spring* (1932); Rudolph Fisher, *The Walls of Jericho* (1928) and *The Conjure-Man Dies* (1932); Countee Cullen, *One Way to Heaven* (1932). Langston Hughes, in *Not without Laughter* (1930), looks at black Detroit and Chicago. Out of these comes a composite picture of the northern ghetto, with Harlem as the flagship: speakeasies, the crowded drawing rooms of a new colored social and artistic elite, the lively and benign world of all-night gambling and tavern hopping, the Sunday spectacle of well-dressed blacks parading after church on Seventh Avenue, likable goldbrick characters who spend much of their time avoiding work, sleeping during the day, and partying at night. This atmosphere does not crush blacks' self-esteem or drive them to murder. Black characters do complain about racial discrimination, but there are rent parties and charity balls most nights to lighten the sting. And these novelists see no violence in their world they need take seriously. The unsuccessful rape attempt in *The Walls of Jericho* and the murder of the medium's assistant in *The Conjure-Man Dies* seem little more than a cosmetic accent of the primitive, only hinting at the fever under the glitter. The ghetto was a new phenomenon, more an object of curiosity than of social concern, arousing an interest in the folkways of a new city culture. The black writers who take it as their setting display a kind of local-color interest in the features of the place and the people who give it its uniqueness. They express no anxiety and make no prediction that Harlem is turning into a social problem. It is different from other towns and cities in America, not because it is becoming isolated and run down but because its people are black, interesting for their own exotic styles of living. The streets the characters walk are generally well lighted, and the buildings they enter seem in good repair, not the abandoned husks that look upon Bigger Thomas like ominous skulls or the incubators of disease that Ralph Ellison's Dupre will burn down in *Invisible Man* (1952).

With the Depression, Harlem ceased to be a white amusement park or a generator of a vital new African American culture. It was revealed, as Alain Locke writes in 1936, as "a nasty, sordid corner into which black folk are herded." Locke suggests that the success of the Harlem artistic Renaissance obscured what was happening underneath, and the Renaissance writers were powerless by themselves to halt the deterioration their own images were unintentionally concealing. "There is no cure or saving magic in poetry and art," says Locke, "for . . . precarious marginal employment, high mortality rates, civic neglect."[7] Sterling Brown has the same hindsight, remarking that the literature of the Harlem Renaissance failed because it failed to give the whole picture: "the lines of the unemployed, the overcrowded schools, the delinquent children headed straight to petty crime, the surly resentment—all of these seeds that bore such bitter fruit in the Harlem riot [of 1935]."[8] This is the northern black city that Wright and his followers make the environment that stimulates their characters' violence.

A NEW CITY FICTION: STRIKING OUT BLINDLY

The novelists that carry out the start made by Wright and Attaway put the finishing touches on the ghetto as destroyer and purveyor of violence. Their protagonists struggle against the brutality of racist policemen, the filth and shabbiness of their living quarters. They try to leap over the white barriers preventing them from getting decent jobs, to evade the predators both black and white that put them in constant danger, and they break free of their confinement to options that impoverish and degrade them. They are, in general, driven by the conventional values of white America: material possessions, a clean living space, adequate security, and a sense of personal worth. But the entrenched conditions of the ghetto prove intractable, or the efforts of the protagonist appear too weak. As their attempts to break out of the ghetto or achieve a satisfying self-esteem fail, and as they see their failure as coming from white oppression and the faceless racist system, they explode violently against the symbols of authority and injustice, both white and black.

In Carl Offord's *The White Face* (1943), for example, Chicagoan Christopher Woods becomes psychologically sick from white abuse and humiliation. Blinded himself by racism, he is sent to prison for beating a Jewish lawyer. He hates everyone, finds the "white face" everywhere. He is enraged at the thought "that he should live and die by it, without smashing it, without cracking it, without even bruising it!" [9] When he attempts to get revenge "of his own making" against a prison guard, he is instantly killed. In Curtis Lucas's *Third Ward Newark* (1946), a white bar owner in Newark's inner city becomes for the female protagonist "a symbol of all that was wrong, a personification of all the prejudice and ugliness and grief she had ever known." [10] But she fails in her attempt to kill him and is herself killed in the process. In *Knock on Any Door* (1947), Willard Motley puts white characters in the role of the ghetto victim. Nick Romano, a nice boy who is driven to theft by the conditions of the slum he lives in, develops a running enmity with an Irish cop, a sadist who enjoys arresting the young street men and beating them. He represents the authority of the system that makes it hard for ghetto youngsters to survive legally, and Nick acquires a powerful hatred for the man after a particularly brutal beating. In a later confrontation, Nick empties his pistol into him, kicking the dying man in a delirium of exultant revenge.

Not all of these protagonists win our sympathy. When Taffy, in Philip Kaye's novel of that name (1950), explodes in a temporarily insane rage, it is hard for us to feel the understanding we give to Mat Moss and Nick Romano. Taffy, too, is a victim of the ghetto, in both Harlem and Brooklyn, but he behaves with a meanness and pettiness that goes beyond forgiveness. Like Studs Lonigan, Taffy dreams of seducing beautiful girls, receiving the adulation of the masses, making millions of dollars, and parading along the street in his fine new threads with a strut and arrogance he has not earned. Limited in abilities and weakened by pusillanimity, Taffy cannot win the respect of the young men he would like to lead or conquer the resistance of the snobbish Brooklyn coquette he wants to date. He is affected not so much by the shabby environment of the ghetto as by the constant humiliation that environment subjects him to, the limitations whites impose upon blacks, the subservience required of them. Checked on all sides by conditions and character, Taffy finally loses control of himself when he holds up a white insurance collector. Tasting power for the first time in his life, Taffy falls into "the grip of an unreasoned excitement," like Nick Romano with the cop. He stabs the terrified little white man and then slits his throat. At first he is dazed at what he has done, but then, gloating, he evokes the symbolism that justifies his crime: "White sonofabitch!" he exclaims. "Stealing our money. Served him right. . . . They've been after me all my life. That's one white prick that won't ever bother me or yell 'nigger' again." [11] But like the other characters he resembles, Taffy gets his punishment. A policeman guns him down when he runs away from his arrest, and his end is as ignominious as his balked life.

THE STREET: THE NORTH'S LYNCH MOB

By the 1940s, clearly, black writers were on the attack against the ghetto. Most of them put into play two sets of values: those of the white world against which straight blacks measure their own degradation, and those of the ghetto, of the pimp, the prostitute, the numbers man, the dope dealer, the youthful gang. The one holds out the dream of freedom, cleanliness, respectability, safety. The other threatens filth and degeneracy, constant trouble with the law, and a diseased life cut short by violence on the street or in the electric chair. The ghetto leads inevitably to violence, the corruption of the soul, and the suffocation of the self. It is a death trap in which the protagonist longs for recognition, self-esteem, or escape. It is the elusiveness of these goals that frustrates the characters and drives them into their violent and self-destructive temporary insanity.

Ann Petry draws this pattern in its fullest expression. Much more straightforwardly and single-mindedly than any of her contemporaries, she designs the narrative of *The Street* (1946) to demonstrate that the necessary outcome of the ghetto experience is an enraged, self-destructive attack against the symbols of white oppression. When Petry looks at the ghetto she sees the degraded underside of "Nigger Heaven." She comes to Harlem with a New England upbringing and the experience of a reporter who has covered the ghetto. Much more the sociologist even than Wright, she draws a portrait of the inner city containing most of the now conventional images. Black men lounge on street corners because they cannot find jobs. They are humiliated by having to rely upon their women, who can always get domestic work with whites, even though they are normally underpaid. With the mother gone, the children fail to receive proper care. The home falls apart, the men flee, the children take to the streets. And underpinning all this is the poverty, from which there is no escape. Yet, Petry's characters try. They immerse themselves in illusion, hating the white man, hiding in the blurred world of liquor and the false love of prostitutes. Some adopt the code of the streets and turn to crime; some pursue wealth and power by selling out to the white jailers they hate. But all these are typical fantasies, and to Petry's protagonist, Lutie Johnson, each reflects a surrender to the street. She determines to fight and to make a real escape with her young son, Bub.

But the street is much too powerful. The web it spins entangles its victims in inescapable determinism and strangles those who struggle. As the characters pursue their fantasies, they act upon each other, nearly always adversely, because those fantasies involve each other. When the characters collide and are hurt or destroyed, the reader finds the cause in the street and, beyond that, the white society that is responsible for the street's existence. Famished for love and dignity, money and power, or merely a place to stay that is halfway secure, they prey upon each other, lose their sense of decency and community. As the web entangles Lutie, thwarting her attempts to get money, landing Bub in jail, and exposing her to the predatory Boots Smith, she acquires a profound hatred of the white world that keeps her down. Boots Smith becomes a symbol of that world, for though he is black, he serves the white man who dominates the street. Thus, when he refuses to give Lutie the money he has promised her to get Bub out of jail until she sleeps with him, she loses her grasp of reality. She ceases to see him as Boots Smith or a black man. And when she seizes a candlestick and hits out at him, she strikes "not at Boots Smith, but at a handy, anonymous figure—a figure which her angry resentment transformed into everything she had hated, everything she had fought against, everything that had served to frustrate her." She does not kill a black man when she kills Boots Smith; she kills "the white world which thrust black people into a walled enclosure from which there was no escape." As it is with Bigger Thomas, her murder of Boots is only the outward manifestation of a feeling long present in her, an "impulse to violence" that had for years been "growing, feeding, until finally she had blown up in a thousand pieces."[12] Her hope for herself and Bub dies with Boots. No matter how assiduously the ghetto dweller pursues the dream of escape, or how deeply she believes in the values implicit in that dream, the street will destroy it.

THE PRIMITIVE: THE NIGHT OF THE LONG KNIFE

In the 1950s, Chester Himes, whose early fiction is often associated with the school of Wright, transforms this perception of the effects of ghetto life and white supremacy into its most powerful imagery. But in *The Primitive* (1955), he takes the violent act out of the context of the ghetto and places it in a downtown New York apartment, where black Jesse Robinson stabs to death his white mistress, Kriss Cummings. He kills her because she is white, and because the world he lives in as a black man is like a ghetto, slowly driving him beyond his mental and physical limits. As with Bigger Thomas and Lutie Johnson, Jesse's violence has been long in the making, deriving "perhaps from the first time they ever hurt you for being born black."[13] He commits the crime in a psychic daze that is deepened by alcohol. His plea before the court, therefore, will be "temporary insanity," Himes applying for the first time this explicit label to this uncontrollable act. The emotional atmosphere does indeed vibrate with insanity, for Himes encloses us in the stifling thought-world of Jesse rather than the naturalistic world made up of other people. There are other characters, to be sure, but they all, including Kriss Cummings, seem more emblems, projections of rage and hurt, than rounded people. Thus, in the pattern of the other novels in this group, we are more intrigued by the effect of the murder upon Jesse than moved by what happens to Kriss. Jesse follows the familiar process: immediate reaction, then a kind of explanation. At first, Jesse's stupefied mind refuses to admit his crime, but when he does he recognizes "the body of his victim as the final result of his own whole life. 'End product of the impact of Americanism on one Jesse Robinson—black man' " (158).

The conventions are all there—the violent effects of white racism on the black man raised in the ghetto, the unbalanced state of mind in which the violence is committed. Himes broadens the source of Jesse's violent psychosis from the impact of the ghetto to the way African Americans are treated at large. Jesse lives in Harlem, but we see little of its streets or its people. Most of the time, we are confined in Kriss's small apartment in Gramercy Park, far south of Harlem.

After his first four novels—*If He Hollers Let Him Go* (1945), *Lonely*

Crusade (1947), *Cast the First Stone* (1952), and *The Third Generation* (1954) —critics enrolled Himes in the school of Richard Wright and labeled him as a "protest" writer. In *The Primitive,* he tries to slip out from under those associations. He set out "to write about the deadly venom of racial prejudice which kills both racists and their victims," thus striking "a great blow against racial prejudice" (1). He saw only later that what he had really done was to show how, in a country whose social relations are governed by racism, "one comes to feel the absurdity of life." [14]

That absurdity governs the conventions dominating sexual relations between white women and black men. Jesse sees Kriss as a white woman to sleep with; Kriss sees Jesse as a weapon against the white men who have rejected her. By controlling him through her color she can demean all men. But they are both battered by white male supremacy, are both "outcasts," "lost and lonely." They need each other, physically and psychologically, even though the only thing they share is a mutual hatred (55). Kriss can avoid "feeling like dirt" only by sleeping with black men. Jesse can get back at white men by sleeping with their women. But the system is so efficient that they end up destroying each other rather than the white man they resent. The cause-and-effect mechanism that churns toward murder goes into motion when Jesse learns his novel is rejected. It is "social protest," and social protest isn't selling. Feeling sold out once again by a racist system, he gets drunk and blearily focuses upon the white woman, the occasion of racial sexual taboos and the symbol of prejudice. "Something's got to end," he says (101). Ominously, he "stabs" his manuscript, a projection of himself, the racist world, the reality that makes no sense. From here on he moves through a dead world. Even his whiskey bottle is "dead," and Jesse, "half-laughing," mumbles "Kill 'em all' " (102). The imagery of death and violence increases. In the two-day orgy of drunkenness, Kriss and Jesse raise the volume on their racial battle, Jesse becoming convinced that "This bitch wants me to kill her" (112). Jesse becomes more and more obsessed with killing. He dreams about it, cries out in his stuporous sleep "Kill you!" (122, 124). And before Kriss's visitors leave, Jesse has threatened first one of the guests and then Kriss with a butcher knife he wields drunkenly. His brain "blazing," and his "accumulated rage" bunching into menacing hatred, he exclaims with not a little self-pity, "I'm gettin' good and goddamn tired of these hurt white bitches takin' it out on me" (148). Later, in a psychic blackout, he kills Kriss.

In *The Primitive,* Himes adds a new angle to the crazy quilt of the psychotic reaction to white racism. The "temporary insanity" into which conditions have driven these killers is not a simple response to the crude conditions of a subpar ghetto. It reflects the destruction of what is best in the African American. Before racism destroys him, Jesse is a "primitive," a creature without prejudices or the pretensions of a developed code of manners. Himes takes the old stereotype of the black man as ape or savage and turns it into a biting irony. Jesse kills Kriss not because he is a primitive but because America has turned him into a "human," after all those years of rejection. Killing is the most human of all behavior, thinks Jesse with the "lacerating" humor that characterizes his last hours. "Human beings only species of animal life where males are known to kill their females," he mumbles to himself drunkenly. The "Alchemy Company of America" has filled him with "principles, integrity, honor, conscience, faith, love, hope, charity, and such." America "purged" him of the innocence of the primitive. The action and dialogue of the novel, of course, have shown that the principles by which Americans claim their elevation to the exalted level of human being are simply cover-ups for their true character. The real human being is without conscience, brutal, indifferent to others' suffering, bigoted. The true human being is what Jesse is when he stabs Kriss. Himes thus bitterly spits back the long-made argument by African Americans that they are as human as white Americans. Jesse has "made it into the human race" by killing, a product, as he says, of America (158–59). He is now a fallen human being in a fallen world which "he no longer understood" (49). What *can* make sense when prescient chimpanzees predict the future in the surreal images of the television set? It is the "Chimpanzee" being interviewed by TV personality "Gloucester," in fact, that "predicts" the apprehension of Jesse and the plea he makes to the court of "temporary insanity" (14–15, 152 ff.). Himes never "explains" this phenomenon. It is part of the absurdity in which the old associations no longer make sense. When it is all over, Jesse cobbles up the traditional "one crime" memories that so upset the southern lyncher by calling the police, identifying himself as a "nigger," and saying he had just killed a white woman.

Into the sixties and early seventies, some black writers still depict characters driven to pathological acts by white prejudice in general and the ghetto in particular. Young Martin Williams, in Bryant Rollins's *Danger Song* (1967), kills a wealthy Boston businessman when he is driven to insanity by the white man's malice. And Shadow, the protagonist of Nathan C. Heard's *Cold Fire Burning* (1974), oddly identifying an insolent young black revolutionary with "every embarrassment and every frustration I'd ever suffered . . . every white person/cop in the world," [15] gives the radical a terrific beating, freeing himself from his sense of inferiority and, momentously, making it possible to complete coitus with his white girlfriend. But these characters are so shallowly, even confusingly, conceived that it is hard to take them seriously, and I only need to note them here in the context of their more convincing and aesthetically superior antecedents.

Taffy Johnson, Lutie Johnson, Jesse Robinson—three very different figures, but all exemplify the effects of white racism and urban degradation. They may be called prerevolutionaries, for although they perform their acts in a desperation bordering on insanity, they do take action, striking out at the white racism and ghetto conditions that cause their frustrations. They are metaphors of the new aggressiveness in the African American consciousness, a negative form of the optimism at the basis of novels like John Killens's *Youngblood* (1954) and William Melvin Kelley's *Different Drummer* (1962). They are, in fact, relatively simple characters and pose relatively straightforward questions about the racial injustice that drives them to commit their crime. There is no moral conundrum in their crime. It is made perfectly clear that murder is wrong. That these otherwise law-abiding and sympathetic characters commit such violence serves only to show the true difficulties of their plight. Their desperate act is the result of social oppression, but it is not a vehicle for higher consciousness. Unlike Bigger Thomas, the characters do not discover themselves through murder, and unlike Wright, their creators do not ask us to contemplate two contradictory moral standards as productive of both moral good and bad. The racial system that warps them is unquestionably bad. But the act they commit in response is also bad. These characters are victims forced into immoral action, not heroes asserting a higher morality. They belong to that long tradition in African American history of abiding by the Euro-American moral system and feeling guilty when violating it. Wright's superiority as a writer to his followers lies in his perception that Bigger's real independence came when he violated the Euro-American code without guilt.

The difference between Wright and his followers contributes to a structural difference in their novels. Wright's action essentially begins with Bigger's murder of Mary. The consequences of that act of violence for Bigger, both positive and negative, make up the central issue of the narrative. The violence in *Blood on the Forge* (except for Mat Moss's killing of the southern overseer that motivates his move north), *The Street, Knock on Any Door, The Primitive,* and other novels in their class comes, on the whole, near the end of the action. The central issue of the narrative is the unjust conditions that lead to that violence. The weight of the story is more sociological than psychological or ethical. For Wright, violence is both an effect of oppressive social conditions and a cause of intensified consciousness. For his followers, violence is purely and unambiguously an effect of racism, particularly that racism which creates ghettos.

INVISIBLE MAN: TEMPERING RAGE WITH IRONY

Readers may well ask what a novel like Ralph Ellison's *Invisible Man* is doing in the company of these essentially American social realist works. It is symbolic and surrealistic, psychological and mythic, existentialist and European. And it differs from the novels of the Wright group in literary quality as well as in literary style. But because it is contemporary with those novels, and because it explores some of the same features of violence as they do—though producing new and different effects and conclusions—I am integrating my treatment of it into my discussion of the school of Wright.

Invisible Man is probably the single most widely read and respected novel by an African American. It has been the subject of criticism and analysis, essay collections, books, periodical articles. They examine its narrative structure and its patterns of imagery. They point out the significance of parallel scenes, the suggestiveness of its metaphor and allegory. And they especially delve into Ellison's extensive use of jazz, the blues, and African American folklore and oratory.[16] Some deal with the violence in *Invisible Man,* but only as a secondary or tertiary interest. Stephen B. Bennett and William W. Nichols address the issue directly, usefully seeing the violence in Ellison's novel in the context of their thesis about African American fiction in general. In that fiction, violence can be a way of achieving a sense of dignity and power in the face of ages of humiliating oppression. They call this "creative violence" and find it in Tod Clifton's attack on the policeman, who then kills him.[17] Their article is a short one, briefly exploring "an hypothesis," and *Invisible Man* is only one of several novels they refer to. Their discussion of necessity excludes not only lengthy examination but violent elements in the novel that tend to modify their findings. My perception of Ellison's attitude toward violence differs considerably from that of Bennett and Nichols, as the following discussion will show.

Invisible Man introduces us immediately to an act of violence. It is an act, moreover, that resembles the familiar concluding encounter in the novels of the school of Wright, in which the African American protagonist is pushed by racist conditions beyond his or her rational control. The Invisible Man, the novel's narrator, becomes enraged when a white man he accidentally bumps into on the street curses him instead of apologizing. For a moment he falls into "frenzy" and "outrage," and he beats the man bloody trying to get him to "Apologize!" Then he pulls his knife and gets ready to slit the other's throat.[18] When thus described, this sequence seems to reflect the general pattern of the other school of Wright novels. The incident itself is merely the occasion for the blowup. Its causes lie in the narrator's past. We might infer that they are the conventional ones, social oppression and racial injustice. Although these causes do enter into Ellison's thinking, his principal subject is more complex. His narrator is driven by more cerebral, less sociopolitical motives—by ontology, so to speak, metaphysics, existential identity issues. The white man, says the narrator, "had not *seen* me" (4). The narrator's multilayered self is invisible to the white man, who covers it over with a simplified image in his own mind. It is this "phantom," the narrator suddenly realizes, that "had sprung out and beaten [the white man] within an inch of his life." He had been "mugged by an invisible man" (5). The insight occurs to the narrator just as he is about to draw his knife across his victim's jugular. But the realization is too ludicrous for such a serious act. It calls for hilarity, not murder. And so he pockets his knife and walks off into the night laughing so hard he is afraid he will choke.

It is not simply the Invisible Man's pulling back at the last minute that differentiates him from the killers of the Wright group. It is his pervasive sense of ironic comedy. Such an ironist can never give in fully to his "frenzy" or feel a sense of grievance so powerfully as to commit murder to redress it. His immediate motive for his attack on the white man is not to gain racial vengeance or rid America of racism but to dispel his feeling of invisibility, to make himself feel he exists in a world that does not see *him* (4). The laughter into which he explodes in the midst of murder is a sign that his consciousness is too acute for him to expect success from violence. The point is that he can depend only upon his own awareness to give him a warrant of his existence. He confirms the radical freedom at the heart of that existence by recognizing himself as an "invisible man," not by vengefully taking a life.

At this point, it looks as if the decision has been made *against* violence as a solver of either the social or the existential problems of the narrator. "Most of the time," he says, "I am not so overtly violent. I remember that I am invisible and walk softly so as not to awaken the sleeping ones. Sometimes it is best not to awaken them; there are few things in the world as dangerous as sleepwalkers" (5). The "fight" he has undertaken against a world that does not see him can be carried on more safely and effectively without violence. He has found that the age-old slave method of trickery and deceit, which his grandfather and the vet at the Golden Day urge upon him, is a more effective way of securing his identity.[19] Therefore, in a metaphorical jest Bigger Thomas could never have understood, he steals "power" from the Monopolated Light & Power Company. With it he illuminates the underground hole he fell into at the end of his memoir and acquires the power to "see" and thereby know himself. Light, not violence, is the form this power takes, and it "confirms my reality, gives birth to my form" (6). This light-power, though, is analogous to the overt power that goes clothed in violence. Overt power can also result in illumination. The narrator's violent attack on the white man transmutes into the perception of himself as an invisible man and then turns into the illumination of the hole which is brightened by nonviolently stolen power.

But this does not make violence a sign of either virtue or vice, or the ground of heroism or victimization. And lest we assume that the narrator saw himself as taking the moral high road because he sheathed his knife instead of spilling the white man's blood, we must note that at the end of the prologue, in which this whole reflection upon violence occurs, the Invisible Man has second thoughts. Perhaps he *should* have killed the white man, who, after all, is the dangerous one, the sleepwalker, the blind man. Getting rid of him would have protected "the higher interests of society" on three counts: It would have made this dreamer and sleepwalker "pay the price" for refusing to awaken to the truth of human identity; it would have destroyed the dreamer's "dream world," which excludes blacks; and it would have carried out the narrator's "responsibility," as "invisible victim," for "the fate of all"—for those both within and without the sleepwalker's dream world. Had he killed the white man, he would have been a hero who put his overt power to the service of society, enforcing punishment upon the wicked who would stultify the identity of his race and opening a wider community for blacks.

Why, then, does he not kill the white man? What lies behind his "irresponsibility" in refusing to take on responsibility for "the fate of all"? The problem with expecting answers to such questions from the novel is that the novel is designed to pose questions and demonstrate paradox, not to state answers or resolve contradictions. The reason the narrator gives in response to these questions evokes more questions than it answers and makes bumpy what otherwise might be a smooth explanation of his problem. His problem is, unexpectedly, his feeling of guilt, his sense of "shirked . . . responsibility" (14). On one page, he cites the ludicrousness of the situation as his reason and implies that no amount of violence could awaken the sleepwalker to the Invisible Man's reality (4). But, just ten pages later, he says he did not commit the murder because he was a "coward." He had "become too snarled in the incompatible notions that buzzed within my brain" to rid the world of the sleepwalking white man. Ambivalence produces paralysis, or "cowardice" (14).

Are we to assume from these lines that murder is a viable, even heroic, method for dealing with the situation of the African American and that not to use it is cowardly? No clue in this passage tells us not to assume that.

Yet the moral code that we bring to our reading of the novel and which we share with Ellison questions the point. More than that, the narrator's suggestion that it was his responsibility to kill the white man does not square with the point he writes his memoir to express: that the world is diversity, and that to understand this is to be free. The difficulty lies in the phrase "incompatible notions." The incompatibility of "notions" is an analogue to the idea of diversity, and diversity is used by the narrator in the epilogue to stand for the openness, possibility, and contradictoriness of his true self and the real world. If "diversity" and "incompatible notions" are analogous, the narrator seems to be saying that what makes him a coward at the end of his prologue makes him free at the end of his memoir. By this logic, to be free is to be a coward. And to be a coward is to be afraid to use violence. Here is another bump in my attempt to find coherence in the attitude toward violence in the prologue. In the course of the memoir, the narrator never demonstrates any fear of using violence. In fact, he seems to emerge from his violent episodes, not as a coward, or even one paralyzed by "incompatible notions," but as one convinced that nonviolence better serves the true condition of the world.

As I say, this apparent equivocation on a relatively important phrase makes it hard to pin down Ellison's position on the kind of violence over which the school of Wright novelists expended such anguish. Paradoxically, it may be the very feature of the narrator's character that gives him aesthetic coherence that accounts for the shift in meaning of "incompatible notions" —his tendency to intellectualize. Where Bigger Thomas, Lutie Johnson, and Jesse Robinson *feel,* and react emotionally *in extremis,* Ellison's narrator *thinks.* Anguish does not enter Ellison's picture. He tells us at the end of the novel that by going into his hole he "whipped it all except the mind, the *mind.*" It is true. The narrator reflects, meditates, philosophizes. He calls himself a "thinker-tinker," one who plays with theories and words. The result is a narrative voice that is ironic and detached, addicted to inconclusiveness and contradiction. He ends his narrative with only his attitude changed but the world remaining the same: "just as concrete, ornery, vile and sublimely wonderful as before, only now I better understand my relation to it and it to me" (563). Yet he remains "confused" (566), unable to make any headway on the great issues. "When one is invisible," he says, "he finds such problems as good and evil, honesty and dishonesty, of such shifting shapes that he confuses one with the other, depending upon who happens to be looking through him at the time" (559). Nor has studying "the lesson of [his] own life" helped him to interpret the ambiguous advice of his old grandfather on his deathbed. He finally gives up: "I can't figure it out; it escapes me" (562). He has come to see the world as inherently contradictory and chaotic but made up of "infinite possibilities." This is reality, and because what is real is healthy, "only in division is there true health" (563). The "health" he speaks of is both political and psychological; at least one dimension of the narrator's thesis is understandable enough: "Whence all this passion toward conformity anyway?—diversity is the word. Let man keep his many parts and you'll have no tyrant states" (563). Thus the narrator speaks in paradoxes and contradictions: "now I denounce and defend. . . . I condemn and affirm, say no and say yes, say yes and say no . . . I hate and I love" (566).

In what William James might have seen as a "buzzing, blooming confusion," the equivocation on the "incompatible notions" that supposedly make the narrator a coward fits into the picture. And his calling himself a coward can be seen as both serious and ironic, in the same way that suggesting murder to be the responsible course is perhaps valid philosophically but questionable as a course to follow in the real material world. This gives us a mind that, having fundamentally changed, now contemplates from a philosophical and artistic distance his sometime passionate engagement and sees his treatment of that engagement in the terms of the kind of intellectual game that best fits reality as he has come to see it. His is the kind of mind calibrated to measure the diversity of reality. His memoir, in its twistings and turnings, brings us finally to his discovery of this self and to an answer to the questions the narrative tacitly asks: What type best enhances the free and diverse world? What type best illuminates its liberating contradictoriness? It is hardly necessary to say that this type is not a warrior-hero, whose identity lies in his capacity to inflict harm upon the enemy and for whom violence is the medium of his heroism.[20] The enemy, as finally defined by the Invisible Man, is the "gang" that seeks to put "the world in a strait jacket" (563). It is Bledsoe and Ras as well as the southern whites at the smoker and the Brotherhood in New York. This enemy is best fought by the mind, by its understanding that the definition of the "world" is "possibility" (563). This is achieved by awakening from the sleep of the straitjacket, not by overpowering an opponent.

INVISIBLE MAN: IRONY OVER VIOLENCE

The process of awakening is acted out in the Harlem riot, from which the narrator graduates into his final state of knowledge. In the concluding act of the riot, the narrator explicitly raises the question of whether or not to react violently. Ellison avoids making it a racial matter, presumably in order to universalize his metaphysics of diversity. The immediate conflict is between the narrator and Ras, the black nationalist who has changed his name from "Exhorter" to "Destroyer." Bellicose and excessively race-conscious, for whom violence is an important weapon, Ras takes advantage of the uproar of the riot to enlist enraged ghetto dwellers in a revolution. Like the avenger in earlier novels, he has tunnel vision, thinks only in terms of enemies and friends, and since the Invisible Man is not with him, he is as much an enemy as the hated whites and so must be destroyed. Ras urges his followers to hang the narrator as an Uncle Tom. Caught in the vortex of the self-destructive riot and confronted with death for not being radical enough, the narrator decides that the proper response to it all is not Ras's belligerence "but a few simple words, a mild, even a meek, muted action." The point is "to clear the air. To awaken them and me," not to obfuscate further with blood (545).

With this conclusion, we are back to the sleepwalkers and dreamers of the prologue. Now, though, they are not white men cursing phantoms on dark streets but the narrator himself and a group of fanatical blacks using the wrong way to throw off oppression. These must not be punished, as were the sleepwalkers and dreamers in the prologue. They are to be *awakened*. And the weapon is language, not violence. These are just the people whom the narrator needs to reach with his new understanding of the world, to instill in them the insight and self-knowledge that disclose their own individuality and psychological freedom. They need to see that the riot is not an occasion for revolution but a plot to draw black blood in Harlem for the Brotherhood's propaganda machine.

But once again, as with the white man in the prologue, the narrator is "no hero," nor is he the leader that he would like to be. He is ahead of his people only "in the stripping away of my illusionment" (546). This is not enough to convert Ras's followers or to calm Ras. He must fight physically to save himself—not against white racists but against black ones. By thus shifting the focal point, the narrator strips his central point of all distracting elements. It is a matter of metaphysics, of world view, not of race. Ras is as blind and as dangerous as Jack and the Brotherhood, for he, too, tyrannically forces oversimplified identities upon people. The narrator's situation is reduced to its simplest form, literally fighting for his life. He is in a position analogous to that of the characters in the Wright school novels, except that he maintains his sanity and is not driven by frustration and a sense of victimization. He seizes Ras's own weapon, the African spear, and, to prevent the man from hanging him, flings it at Ras, locking his jaws and shutting up the advocate of race war. This is not what one would call a "meek, muted action" by a nonhero. But the narrator makes nothing out of his reversal of course, the resort to violence after suggesting that nonviolence is needed. Indeed, it is one more instance of several in the novel in which the narrator's violent act gives him, like Bigger's murders, a new life: "I let fly the spear and it was as though for a moment I had surrendered my life and begun to live again" (547). But it is not the act in itself that operates with such symbolic effect. The renewal of life is literal; the narrator, by throwing the spear and then fighting off Ras's men, escapes the lynching they have in store for him. This is not the violence of a great leader, either, guiding his people out of oppression into freedom. This is an individual's struggle "to live out [his] own absurdity [rather] than to die for that of others" (547).

Nevertheless, with his new perception of reality, this nonhero understands the would-be hero of violence. Dressed in his Abyssinian animal skin, armed with his African spear, and riding his huge horse, Ras is a "madman," "real and yet unreal" (546). He is both "funny" and "dangerous." More insightfully, the narrator finds Ras "wrong but justified," a phrase that could be applied to Bigger himself, or to Mat Moss, Lutie Johnson, or Jesse Robinson. The phrase shows the narrator's special awareness derived from his experience and the frustrating contradictions that beset anyone trying to make moral sense out of the anger racism has created or the violence it has cultivated—"wrong but justified, crazy and yet coldly sane . . . funny and dangerous and sad" (552).

The conflict between violence and nonviolence the narrator poses during the last encounter he has with Ras and his men carries no moral lumber. The narrator does not struggle with his scruples before he throws the spear and fights his way out of the mob. His act is purely mechanical, a measured response to a threat, not the result of vengeance or emotion. The narrator does not explain why he prefers soft words and meekness over violence to clear the air during his encounter with Ras. But given his discovery of the diverse and contradictory world, we might draw this inference: The moral struggle in that world does not transpire between justified and unjustified violence, or even between black and white, but is between the straitjacket gangs and those whose liberty lies in an awareness of their invisibility. Nonviolence works better for taking up the attitude that sets one free. Violent action blocks from the mind the subtlety and irony needed to understand reality and to tolerate the contradictions that must be held in suspension without giving in to paralysis.

INVISIBLE MAN: THE HERO AS IRONIST

Ellison does not make violence the basis of his narrator's identity. It does not have the creative importance that it has for Bigger Thomas, or the tragic effect it has for Lutie Johnson and Jesse Robinson. But violence is everywhere in the novel. The imagery and action are saturated with it. It appears not as a heroic recourse for an unjustly besieged people but seriocomically as an agent for change in human social and psychological life, and as a metaphor of how wrenching change is when it does occur. This is the narrator's "boomerang" theory of history. It is important enough to the novel's theoretical framework that Ellison defines it in the prologue after describing the narrator's encounter with the white man. The imagery expresses Ellison's basic conviction about the nature of reality, its illogicality. "[T]he world moves," says the narrator, "by contradiction. . . . Not like an arrow, but a boomerang" (6). History is always doing something unexpected and irrational. It cannot be fully explained or controlled.

The Brotherhood, the proto-Marxist group that the Invisible Man falls in with in New York, insists upon the contrary: that history operates according to a logical and orderly set of laws of which it is the sole custodian and executor. Those who refuse to accept the authority of the Brotherhood and its laws fall outside history and into "chaos," losing meaning and relevance as the Brotherhood defines those terms. The Brotherhood attempts to manipulate chaos for its own ends by replacing it with its version of "historical" reality. It is a "gang" that tries to force upon the world's crazy and chaotic diversity the Brotherhood's vision of its puppet identity. The northern embodiment of southern white supremacy, the Brotherhood embodies this universal tendency to put the world into a straitjacket, vested interests forcing roles upon people from the outside. In his argument against this view, the narrator insists that chaos is precisely where true history lies, the unrecorded instances of anonymous personal experience, propelled by chance and human emotion, out of the control of any single power, eluding logic and rational explanation. The world does not hide this important knowledge about reality from us. In fact, "reality is as irresistible as a club" (559). Events are constantly swinging around, like the boomerang, and hitting us in the head to make us notice, when our attention drifts. This is why we must "Keep a steel helmet handy" (6).

At each stage of his progress, the narrator is moved along by an equivalent of this boomerang, some violent situation that boosts him to the next phase of his education. The historical boomerang operates to jar us out of our mental straitjackets. In delivering its knocks, it demonstrates the sham of the authorized view, the safe and logical group. The blows that true history imparts force the consciousness into new areas of perception, demolish old systems, and clear the way for new visions. Violence is thus part of the atmosphere of the Invisible Man's journey to self-discovery. Each material change that violence brings about is an expression of a psychological one: the battle royal, the riot at the Golden Day, the explosion of the boilers in the paint factory, the shock therapy at the paint factory hospital, the fracas at the eviction scene, the murder of Tod Clifton by the policeman.

These violent eruptions all have some political content, but this simply shows that political action, like violence, is part of the natural human process of change. Without it history calcifies and grows a shell. The stimulus of political violence can occur on either side of the color line, too. Thus the murder of Tod Clifton impels the narrator along a new course of reflection that brings about another awakening (433).

The death of Tod, the most popular member of the Harlem Brotherhood, involves the traditional white-against-black violence. A white New York policeman shoots him dead on Fifth Avenue when he strikes the cop during his arrest. The narrator is a witness to it all. Ellison does not use the incident to advertise the injustice of the racist system. Instead of expressing outrage at a traditional atrocity, the narrator becomes curiously remote. He observes the scene from a distance, and he presents it to the reader like a silent movie, dreamlike, apolitical, unslanted. Every detail is recorded objectively, as if the narrator had no emotional stake in the event, or was too stunned to show feeling. He passes no judgment on the action but numbly informs the police he is Tod's friend. The atmosphere contains no racism. Pedestrians gawk, but they are more shocked than gloating. They show concern and admiration, not satisfaction. A white man yells something in "protest" (426), and a young boy exclaims over Tod's strength (428). The police reaction is similar, ironic rather than racist. They call the narrator "Junior" and "Mac" and seem more tired than gratified (427–28). The narrator's first reaction is an intellectual one, cast in the framework of the Brotherhood's philosophy. Instead of seething with indignation at white oppression, the narrator wonders about "history" and why Tod had plunged out of it. It troubles the narrator that Tod was killed in a chaos of anonymity, that his death was futile because he made no contribution to the Brotherhood program.

As he has done several times after a particularly important transitional event, he descends into the womb of the subway. He speculates upon other young black men who like Tod wander outside of history, "transitional types," as he calls them, drifting without plan but living out events hidden from the likes of the Brotherhood. As for history itself, perhaps it is "not a reasonable citizen, but a madman full of paranoid guile and these boys his agents, his big surprise" (431). Only when he begins to think of political strategy, of how he and his Harlem brothers and sisters can put Tod's death to some use through a public funeral, does he cast the incident in traditional racist terms: "It was provocation and murder!" he tells the young black workers who gather in his office after Tod's death. This is "anger" he finally begins to feel as his numbness disappears, but it is also exploitation (437). "We must strike back," he insists (438). He begins to load his language more heavily in his funeral elegy, suggesting that the cop who had killed Tod had called him a "nigger," an inference for which the narrator's description provides no evidence (446). And when he defends his decision to put on the funeral in opposition to the critical Brotherhood central committee, he declares that Tod was shot "mainly because he was black" (458). He would be alive if he had allowed himself to be pushed around. In this entire process, the traditional racial angle is played down. The important effect of Tod's death is upon the narrator's awareness. Within thirty pages, he twice "awakens" from a "dream" (433, 465). The historical boomerang is doing its work.

The Harlem riot that stands at the climax of the narrator's experience is the most complex and prolonged instance of the boomerang theory. The resentment over Tod's murder and the cynical withdrawal of the Brotherhood from its Harlem activities are its immediate causes. More fundamentally, it results from the environment of the ghetto. Therefore, we may regard it as another form of the temporary insanity that produces the murders in the novels of Richard Wright and his followers. Here a whole city rather than an isolated individual throws off normal controls and reacts to many years of intolerable conditions. The scale of the riot's violence is much larger than anything the narrator has been put through up to now, and Ellison uses it to sum up all that his narrator has learned about diversity, contradictoriness, and the boomerang of history. It is the last phase of his education. The reality he enters from the calm downtown Manhattan where he has been staying is violent and chaotic. Time "bursts"; the air "explodes"; people appear in "tearing movement"; there is "the crashing of huge sheets of glass"; the sidewalks "shimmered like shattered mirrors." Policemen stride in black shirts, like fascist storm troopers in a surreal despotism, their "flaming pistols" thrust before them. A shadowy figure falls to the pavement. Dark shapes crouch in doorways. The narrator is felled by a policeman's shot. Looters suddenly materialize when the police pass; they seize stores, put them to the torch. It is a spectacular picture of Ellison's diverse world, a chaos of contradictory moods: frenzied, festive, electrified with desperate excitement and elation, alarm and fear, exuberance. No weak historical form rationally formulated in abstract words can exist for long here. Reality's club shatters everything familiar: "All the street's signs were dead, all the day sounds had lost their stable meanings" (523–25).

For a while, even the Invisible Man makes no attempt to counter with speech this hurricane of unloosed feeling. But the "transitional" types take hold, those like Tod and the three subway zoot-suiters who create a reality outside of "history." Their action, though, is not aimless. Two of the men who helped the narrator, Dupre and Scofield, have a "plan," insist upon "some organization." As they proceed to execute their plan, the camera of the swinging narrative stabilizes, and the focus fixes upon one symbolic action. Deliberately, systematically, Dupre leads his rioters in the torching of the disease-infested tenement that he and other blacks are forced to live in, paying more money than the space is worth to a white landlord who makes no effort to keep the building in repair. It is where Dupre's child died of tuberculosis. The only objection to burning the building down comes from Dupre's pregnant wife who wonders what she will do when her time comes. Dupre is determined that no more babies are "go'n be *born* in there" (534). The rest of the group backs him up. "Goddam you rotten sonsabitches," says Dupre to the absent owners. "You didn't think I'd do it but there it is. You wouldn't fix it up. Now see how you like it" (535). In these words lies one of the rationales for the riot violence, an attack against a hated system symbolized by the rotting structures. No new start may be made until the old world is destroyed. White power will never do it, so black power must.

As Dupre's tenement burns, the narrator slips into the crowd, "a black river ripping through a black land" (537). At this instant he is "one with the mass," all moving in the same direction, history in flow, illogical, unpredictable, but together. This entire riot is a series of boomerangs, of changing perspectives and meanings, of gunshots and blows, flames and blood, death and birth. It does not move in a straight line toward a clear destiny. The rioters are like the country "yokel" the narrator speaks of in the prologue, who steps inside the professional boxer's sense of time and knocks him out. Just so do the Dupres and the Scofields step inside the Brotherhood's sense of history. The paradox of their behavior is the constructive destruction of the degrading, death-dealing tenement.

Inside the framework of looting and drunken partying, a grim seriousness of purpose informs the action of the transitional types. As Dupre wants vengeance against his landlord, Dehart, who suddenly turns up in the narrative, wants to be wherever a fight breaks out against the white police, "where there'll be some fighting back" (540). Dehart and Dupre are potential heroes, hungry for redressing their community's grievances and courageous enough to risk their lives to do it. We are drawn to both of them for the brief moment they are on the stage. But in Ellison's world, they are more victims than heroes. The narrator suddenly sees an appalling flaw in the exhilaration of Dupre and Scofield and then, especially, Dehart.

As he realizes how few guns the Harlem rioters have to carry on their fight, he discovers a meaning in the riot that had not been clear to him before he hears Dehart demand violent confrontation. The riot, he comes to believe, results from the Brotherhood's deliberate maneuver of pulling out of Harlem and leaving the ghetto without resources for struggle. Jack and his committee expected such a reaction and encouraged it for propaganda (545), so they could attack the racist police who shot down innocent people. The riot, reasons the narrator, is therefore not "suicide," the self-destruction that comes when the helpless turn their fury inward. It is "murder," a lynching bee, created to make black and white kill each other. In the bloodshed and confusion, the Brotherhood could step in with its straitjackets in the name of restoring stability. It is the classic white supremacist strategy, the supreme gang working its straitjacket gambit.

In the narrator's case, the gambit backfires. The riot cracks the hard shell of the system, and self-awareness escapes, like light. Both the Brotherhood and Ras's nationalism—white and black—threaten the identity of the individual self. At the point he comes to this awareness, the narrator himself falls out of history, dropping into the complete darkness beneath the man-hole cover as he flees the three white men chasing him. It is the final darkness which he now illuminates by destroying his past. To see in the darkness, he sets fire to the symbols of his old selves, which were also shells that contained clues to the truth it takes him the entire narrative to learn —his diploma, one of Tod Clifton's Sambo dolls, an anonymous letter, a slip of paper with his Brotherhood name on it. Their destruction feeds the flame that illuminates his new vision. He has stymied the intentions of the Brotherhood and avoided the fate Ras had intended for him. Underground, he reflects upon what he has experienced and comes to his final understanding of the "infinite possibilities" of "multi-implicated reality."

When he began writing *Invisible Man,* says Ellison, he had been reading Lord Raglan's *The Hero* (1936) and was "concerned with the nature of leadership, and thus with the nature of the hero. . . . Thus it was no accident that the young man in my book turned out to be hungry and thirsty to prove to himself that he could be an effective leader."[21] But the action of the novel suggests that precisely this hunger made him vulnerable to what he calls the straitjacket gangs that use him for their purposes (563). Learning to resist such groups and retain his own identity is, of course, the point of his memoir. It is a story of how he gradually changes from willing acceptance of the limiting identity the gangs give him to a perception of himself and the world he lives in as containing "infinite possibilities" (563). The hero of this quest is not the traditional hero, the warrior, the man of force, or even the determined self-sacrificing Founder of the narrator's southern college, whose legend is reverently recounted by the blind Barbee. He is, paradoxically, the unheroic ironist, whose clarity of vision and objective stance replaces the blood-obscured sight of the irrationally passionate and the messianically fervent. For all his lurching after the role of silver-tongued race leader, the true self the narrator finds at the end of his quest is less dramatic even than a character like Bigger Thomas, less needful of the spotlight, more reflective and meditative. Violent action may reveal truths about the real world, but ultimately it works against the kind of mental activity that suits him (and his creator) best—peaceful contemplation. It is for this reason that he is neither "hero" nor "victim" in the old sense. And it is for this reason that during the years of the most radical black nationalist movement Ellison was regarded as a conservative.[22]

The Invisible Man does not renounce violence across the board. But while it has a deep role to play in his world, it does not resound with the racist implications, both black and white, that it does in most African American novels. Here, the intellect is the hero, and the intellect stays on course. But there is still a resemblance between Ellison and the novelists of the school of Wright. They are all developing new ways for blacks to battle out of their psychosocial jail cells, creating characters that anticipate the full-blown revolutionaries of the sixties and the seventies, for whom killing whites becomes one of their most troublesome theoretical questions.

[10]

THE RISE OF THE
BLACK REVOLUTIONARY:
THE MAKING OF AN IMAGE

There is a society. It's made up of a few men who are willing to take some risks. They don't initiate anything; they don't even choose. They are as indifferent as rain. But when a Negro child, Negro woman, or Negro man is killed by whites and nothing is done about it by *their* law and *their* courts, this society selects a similar victim at random, and they execute him or her in a similar manner if they can.

Toni Morrison, Song of Solomon

THE CREATION OF THE BLACK POWER MOVEMENT

Although Toni Morrison's *Song of Solomon* (1977) does not belong with the novels I deal with in this chapter, her description of the Seven Days Society quoted in the epigraph gives the reader a good idea of the imagery that emerged in the mid-1960s in the African American novel of violence. At that point, the organized revolutionary group becomes a popular way to express the anger of many black Americans. These groups occupy a late stage in the evolution of the violent hero and avenger developed over a century or so of African American fiction: the single-minded fanatics like Martin Delany's Gofer Gondolier that go back to his 1859 novel *Blake; or, The Huts of America;* the educated black man who went out to avenge the latest southern white atrocity but fell before the overwhelming mob, like Walter White's Bob Harper in *The Fire in the Flint* (1924); the prerevolutionary figure like Wright's Bigger Thomas and Himes's Jesse Robinson in *The Primitive* (1955), exploding out of hatred and frustration, striking out blindly, desperately, sometimes hysterically at the racist world that hemmed them in; the rioter, like Ellison's Dupre and Scofield, not organized or premeditative but able to seize the occasion for which they seem to have been waiting in order to burn down the white-owned tenements that killed their children. The new revolutionists are the logical and lineal descendants of the proviolence side of the long-standing debate in the black community over how to retaliate and defend against white violence and oppression, the warrior-hero in full bloom.[1]

In fiction, the first hints that such a hero model is in the making appear when the nonviolent civil rights movement is beginning to fracture and violence begins to appear in northern cities. Ronald Fair, for example, writes a "fable" in *Many Thousand Gone* (1965) in which the blacks in a southern county rise up against their white oppressors in a spectacular show of revolutionary mass murder. Fair's novel is always verging on the grotesque and the hyperbolical, but at its intentionally exaggerated heart lies conventional protest, a militant anger over social conditions imposed by white supremacy. In this fable, the racial world is made up of extremes: The blacks of Jacobs County, Mississippi, are still living, in 1965, in virtual bondage, kept totally ignorant of the outside world. The whites live in splendor off the labor of their black helots. It is a condensed version of the national racial situation as Fair sees it. When the Jacobs County blacks finally discover that the outside world differs from theirs, that the whites have exploited and lied to them, they achieve a new self-consciousness and become a revolutionary people. They set fire to the mansion of the county's white patriarch, killing everyone in it, then burn down the town and the surrounding woods, immolating the white population. In the context of the spiritual from which it comes, the title, *Many Thousand Gone,* refers to the abused Africans and African Americans who have come and "gone" in their painful American experience. Fair jocularly turns it around as he constructs his own fantasy of what blacks would like to do to whites. Few novelists have dispatched their oppressors so handily or caused a conflagration that is so much fun. One hardly feels there are people dying in those flames. At the same time, the note of bitterness is unmistakable, and we think of George Schuyler's magnificent lynching party in *Black No More* (1931), for both novels rise from anger.

Fair must be credited for sensing, in 1965, the turn the civil rights revolution was about to take toward Black Power and a cultural nationalism that consecrated color, and for giving a boost to the descendants of Wright and Ellison. Three years earlier, William Melvin Kelley had imagined a similar black uprising in a southern city in *A Different Drummer,* but his Willson blacks, led by Tucker Caliban, use no violence against the whites themselves, only against the land that symbolizes slavery. Fair suggests the increasing willingness to fantasize in public about blacks killing whites wholesale. The civil rights climate had for a decade favored nonviolence. Martin Luther King, the early Student Nonviolent Coordinating Committee, the Nashville group led by divinity student James Lawson had all spoken out for nonviolence, committing themselves to a saintly campaign of Christian love and humility. They marched, throwing their bodies against southern hate. They went to jail singing and blessing their captors. They integrated buses and schools and restaurants and public facilities. They transformed voter registration patterns in dangerous counties. They won victories that exhilarated them and drew the world's admiration. They cracked, and finally changed, the South's system of Jim Crow and racial disfranchisement.

But gradually the early successes of nonviolence began to diminish. Places left to integrate and voters left to be convinced they should register dwindled. The new goals of the movement became confused and ambiguous. And trying to love their oppressor, as their Christian ideals of nonviolence urged them to, took a psychological toll on the activists. Psychiatrist Alvin Poussaint, who treated movement workers, reported that though they did not strike back at the police who restrained them they fought each other, both verbally and physically. "While they were talking about being nonviolent and 'loving' the sheriff that just hit them over the head, they rampaged around the project houses beating up each other. I frequently had to calm Negro civil-rights workers with large doses of tranquilizers for what I can describe clinically only as acute attacks of rage."[2] And Robert Weisbrot concludes that "By 1965 it was evident that people were tired of professing love for brutal sheriffs and racist mobs. The mass saintliness that had sustained the nonviolent revolution was at last giving way to more common if less admirable human responses—frustration, blind rage, and, perhaps inevitably, racial hate."[3]

It was just in these midyears of the sixties, too, that the northern ghettos began to erupt. Between 1964 and 1967, dozens of cities each year felt the shock of the riot. Rochester, Paterson, and Philadelphia went up in 1964, Watts in 1965, Cleveland in 1966, Detroit and Newark in 1967—and these were only a few of the worst. The northern riot marked another major change in the civil rights movement, the shift of momentum to the North, to the ghettos. But there the problems were more complex than in the South, and the aims more blurred. Eventually, the civil rights movement foundered, then broke apart on the obdurate rock of the black ghetto. But for the time being, in the mid-sixties, the riots were a backhanded effect of the early optimism, partly a matter of disappointed expectations that had been aroused by events in the South. The southern movement had focused the attention of the nation on the condition of the African American, and it seemed as if everyone was concerned, even Congress, for it passed a major Civil Rights Act in 1964. But what SNCC and SCLC and CORE achieved in the South, the North already ostensibly had: the vote, more or less; integration, by law if not in fact. The most obvious grievances of the ghetto were "legacies of the past," according to Joseph Boskin, such as "a high percentage of unemployment, poor housing, crowded living conditions, and economic exploitation." [4] But much more immediate was simply that "the ghetto itself was a monstrous evil," as Benjamin Muse puts it. "Until Negroes should be able to find homes elsewhere, until whites should be ready to accept Negroes as neighbors, there could be no lasting peace." [5] Indeed, the ghettos seemed to produce an anger and hostility that were more intense than in the South and hence more susceptible to violent revolutionary thinking. SNCC's John Lewis noticed the difference when he went to Harlem in 1963: "I saw a crowd of people on the street corner in Harlem chanting and raving about what they were going to do to whitey. . . . The boarded-up buildings, the chains, the grates on store windows—it was very different from what I'd seen in Alabama or Nashville. It was despair." [6]

The voice of the ghetto became Malcolm X, who put into words the feelings that the riots expressed more explosively. His fiery rhetoric drew crowds at Harlem street corners who wanted to hear their anger expressed. The white man was their enemy and had to be fought like an enemy, and one used all means for such a fight. As early as 1963, Malcolm X advanced the notion of the urban riot as revolution. Desegregating parks and theaters and restaurants, he said, was no revolution. "Revolution is bloody, revolution is hostile, revolution knows no compromise, revolution overturns and destroys everything that gets in its way." The "Negro revolution," he said, is a matter of getting "control [of] the politics and the politicians of our community" by any means necessary. [7] Without using the phrase, Malcolm X meant Black Power.

The riot was said to be one of the "collective styles of life" in the ghetto of the 1960s, reflecting the attitude caught by Ellison in *Invisible Man*, nonideological anger. The conflagration in the Watts section of Los Angeles, for example, was called an "expressive" riot, based on anger rather than ideology, and participated in by virtually every class. [8] As its philosopher and prophet, Malcolm X stimulated a younger generation of southern civil rights workers waiting to replace their older nonviolent brothers and sisters. When they did, they changed the temper of the movement completely. The symbolic, if not the literal, moment of change occurred in June of 1966, when Stokely Carmichael used the phrase "black power." [9] Some believe the introduction of that phrase split the movement. Some believe it was a symptom of a movement in the process of falling apart. [10] Whatever it was or did, it gave a label to what Malcolm X had preached before his assassination in March of 1965. And, with that phrase, the civil rights movement of the 1960s gave birth to a new phase of the old proviolence argument, renewing it with an unprecedented vigor and defiance. Wright and Ellison had brought the argument out of the closet and to the attention of the nation a generation back; Stokely Carmichael made the new position media-attractive in a way it had never been before, with a simple slogan tailored for television's oversimplified coverage of events. Just as television had stimulated the sympathy of the nation for the early movement with its images of vicious police dogs attacking well-dressed young blacks, now it evoked white alarm with its images of threatening new faces demanding "black power."

Carmichael hinted at reprisals and rebellions:

We've got to bring [the whites] to their knees. We've got to build a power base that will be our protection. That if they touch one black man in California while he's taking his wife to the hospital, if they touch one black man in Mississippi while he's walking down the highway, if they touch a group of black people riding their horses on their day off in Detroit, that we will move to disrupt the whole damn country.[11]

In August of 1967, H. Rap Brown, Carmichael's cruder and blunter successor as chairman of SNCC, inflamed black college students in Cambridge, Maryland, with his demands for violence: "Burn this town down," he said. "When you tear down the white man, brother, you are hitting him in the money. Don't love him to death. Shoot him to death."[12]

Heretofore, the movement's leaders had started from the premise that the conditions in which African Americans lived were degrading, unfair and unjust, and that the reason those conditions existed was that whites willed it so. Changing those conditions lay in the power of whites, so the aim of African American political and social action was to move whites to effect needed change. With the introduction of the Black Power debate into the equation, the premise of action shifted and the ends altered. The new premise was that whites would never change, and the new end was to get what blacks wanted in spite of whites. Embedded in this position were several positive side effects. Carmichael recalled the arguments of the warrior and the avenger, the Teddy Roosevelts, positioning African Americans in a drama in which they were the protagonist and not a lower-class secondary character. He projected the image of courage as well as defiance. As Benjamin Muse suggests, writing from virtually within the maelstrom in 1968, the concept of Black Power did tend to promote Negro self-respect and self-reliance. It helped increasingly to stimulate interest in Negro history and culture, and a healthy pride in *negritude*. To the general public the label served to identify the growing number of activists who followed the anti-white-man, anti-integration, and anti-nonviolence line. It came to be applied vaguely to the whole trend toward Negro violence. Whatever it might mean—and however little it might mean—"Black Power" had a grandiose and war-like ring that emboldened many Negroes and intoxicated some.[13]

Malcolm X, too, had spoken of arousing the people "to their humanity, to their own worth, and to their heritage."[14] The Oakland, California, Black Panther Party for Self-Defense took Malcolm and Carmichael at their word and presented the dual image of the warrior and the nationalist as concerned with working with the black community as with challenging whitey. To be sure, uniformed in sleek black leather jackets and black berets, a paramilitary organization, the Panthers provocatively brandished shotguns in the state capitol and insisted upon their constitutional rights. But they never went to war literally against the Oakland Police Department, though they sought with their guns to give the impression that they were ready to. Blacks found that *readiness* bracing, and the whites found it threatening. At the same time, the Panthers searched for black pride and neighborhood welfare. As Malcolm had urged, they sought control of their own community. They attended to the poor and the deprived, distributing food to the hungry and establishing a free breakfast program for black schoolchildren. They published a newspaper which they said gave their side of things and exposed the distortions of white media.[15]

But the positive side of the Black Power movement got lost in the glare of its provocative side. The white press paid much more attention to the latter, and the white public reacted negatively to the inflammatory rhetoric of the new movement and the flames of the northern ghettos. The national white willingness to make concessions had already begun to weaken with the passage of the 1964 Civil Rights Act, and whites' resistance to further accommodation increased as the Vietnam War took up more of their money and their attention. Partly because of the stiffening of white resistance and partly because of increased competition for visibility, the ambitious spokespersons shaping the concept of Black Power became, in the second half of the sixties, more and more radical and pushed the limits of its meaning to greater and greater extremes. Not only did they continue to hint at violence, they encouraged the principle of separatism. Carmichael said, "We are going to move to better our schools by ourselves. Yes, Lyndon

Baines Johnson, we going to go it alone, because that's what we've been doing for lo these four hundred years inside your country. Don't you be ashamed to tell them we going to go it alone." [16]

Black Power as defined and practiced by the Black Panthers, SNCC, CORE, and other groups was more complex and less confrontational than it was represented to be by the white media. In their attempt to define the principles which the phrase expressed, Carmichael and Charles V. Hamilton spend only a few sentences on violence. The rest of their book, *Black Power: The Politics of Liberation in America* (1967), concentrates upon the need for political power through effective organization of the black community. And in his discussion with Erik H. Erikson at Yale, Huey Newton speaks of the Black Panthers' Maoist aim to rid the world of war: "the Black Panther Party is against violence and works for the day when it will no longer be necessary. We want to abolish all guns and all wars because we believe it is better for people to resolve their differences without violence." [17] The white press tended to neglect the nuances and complexities of the new rallying cry and spent more time on the threats than on the appeals.

White reporters especially found the drift toward black nationalism and separatism to be an affront. And, indeed, the isolationist rhetoric does lend itself to reporting. Much of the Black Power rhetoric expressed a later version of the "redemptive community," the ideal for which was first articulated in SNCC's statement of purpose and which applied at that time in 1961 largely to the southern movement. In his Detroit speech, Carmichael lays out the principles of the new "community" which would get along by itself, and it sounds amazingly like those that William Melvin Kelley created for his messiah, Tucker Caliban, in 1962. Carmichael renounced the role of "leader." Whatever power he had, he claimed, came to him through the Student Nonviolent Coordinating Committee, which was the embodiment of the black people, and the black people possessed the ultimate source of Black Power. The inspiring idea was the mystical power of the black "folk."

But once the "folk" is conceived of as a mystical community, maintaining its purity becomes an important aspect of its action. Whites can never be members of the group, of "the club," as John Killens calls it. They are incapable of understanding or helping. The black masses, already isolated, by this reasoning are called upon to celebrate their isolation as a strength. It is a reversal that Black Power rhetoricians constantly employed. If whites sneer condescendingly at instinctive black rhythm or blacks' hard heads or their natural speed, what appeared to be comic features of a comic figure, and handicaps to older middle-class blacks, are turned into desirable attributes possessed exclusively by a special people. From this vantage point, blacks can in turn sneer condescendingly at whites for *not* possessing these qualities.

In the friction generated by the white backlash and intensified black pugnacity and separatism, one question about violence long debated was answered: Could small groups stand up against the white establishment? They could not. The Black Panthers lived a robust life only for a couple of years before J. Edgar Hoover's Communist-hunting cohorts, alarmed by what they insisted was a major threat to the national security, weakened them by fomenting internal friction and encouraging the police in cities like Oakland, Chicago, and New Haven to gun down some and jail others of their leaders. H. Rap Brown, the last really militant chairman of SNCC, became a fugitive in 1967 and was eventually jailed, when he encouraged his young black audiences to destroy property and burn buildings.[18]

That black activism posed any kind of threat to national security appears in retrospect to be laughable. And one feels embarrassed for the country's senior domestic undercover officer marshaling the full force of his gigantic organization to stamp out these pitifully small and pitifully powerless groups. But by the mid-seventies they were all but gone, and the Black Power movement was forced from its storefront offices and street corners to the high school and college campus, and its political activism retreated into cultural nationalism. The creation of images replaced the formation of programs. Students gained pride not by shouldering weapons against the National Guard but by demanding black cheerleaders, soul food in cafeterias, no school on Malcolm X Day, black studies courses.[19] In other areas, black academics, critics, and artists kept the Black Power motive alive by incorporating its ideals into the principles of a "black aesthetic."

The Black Aesthetic is the articulation of the traits of a pure black art. In 1941 Nick Aaron Ford had spoken of the responsibility of the black writer to be a "propagandist" for African Americans, to present them both to themselves and to whites as respectable citizens.[20] And in chapter 3 I pointed out how the early novelists, for propaganda purposes, advanced admirable counterstereotypes against the ludicrous stereotypes created by whites. The theory of black literature and art that appears in the 1960s still has propaganda as its cornerstone, but the images that propaganda projects are not of respectable black people acting like middle-class whites. Black writing calls for funk and defiance. The thesis of Addison Gayle's highly readable history of the African American novel, *The Way of the New World* (1976), is that the best—the most "truthful"—novels written by African Americans are the "blackest" ones, those that present the image of the black American as a revolutionary. We applaud the writers of these works,

Gayle says, because they refuse to let white aesthetic values dictate the "images" they create for black readers. At the center of the struggle between the black artist and critic and the white artistic establishment is the question of who controls the image-making machinery.[21] The revolutionary black writers and critics identify themselves as authentically black by rejecting all white images, criteria, and judgments. The Black Aesthetic, says Gayle, is "a means of helping black people out of the polluted mainstream of Americanism."[22]

Black things should be reserved for black people, and let the whites keep their corrupting hands off of what does not belong to them. Gayle has nothing but scorn for the white critics who discuss black art: "one does not waste energy," he says, "on the likes of Selden Rodman, Irving Howe, Theodore Gross, Louis Simpson, Herbert Hill, or Robert Bone."[23] The Black Aesthetic critics see this cultural nationalism as the source of their identity and reality. Aside from leading to different literary judgments about the quality of specific works of art, the Black Aesthetic criteria for judgment seem no different from what one might call the white criteria. Gayle, for instance, applies terms like "overwriting," "character development," "repetition of incidents," "plot focus," to his discussion of black novels. He calls John O. Killens's *The Cotillion* (1971) a good book because it is relatively "free of overwriting, drawn-out scenes and incidents." On the other hand, it has minor weaknesses, a plot that is "too slight to support a major satiric venture" and some episodes that "receive inadequate attention." Even the phrasing reflects the academic ponderousness of the then white male-dominated Modern Language Association and its journal, the *PMLA*.[24] The Black Aesthetic leads to his political conclusion, though, that the important thing about *The Cotillion* is that it shows black people throwing off their middle-class illusions and recognizing their own black beauty. The Black Aesthetic thus legitimizes the criterion of social and political effectiveness in judging a work of art. It is the particular, authorized result that the work of art produces that is important. It should incite its readers to action, advance the approved moral values, and imbue the people with the proper revolutionary ethics. This leads to some peculiar judgments by the purists. For example, Ron Karenga, the leader of the radical US group, rejects the blues as "invalid," not because they do not express a deeply black mentality but because "they teach resignation, in a word acceptance of reality—and we have come to change reality." "Black art," says Karenga, "must expose the enemy, praise the people and support the revolution."[25]

Cultural nationalism raised new ends and mobilized against new enemies. It stopped the search for concessions from whites and integration into the mainstream and espoused—on paper and in words—the creation of a totally black system. Part of this aim was to recognize and preserve cultural purity. As more energy was spent on defining authentic blackness, more intellectual resources went into protecting the cultural group from contamination, searching out the inauthentic and rejecting the undoctrinaire. When the authentic culture had been defined and its celebratory rituals and icons established, all means for protecting it and advancing its interests were automatically sanctified and validated. This meant that the certified black was morally authorized to commit violence against the group's enemy —the white man—with full theological support, even though such action could not be mobilized in the real world.[26]

The black revolutionary image that grew out of these attitudes touched the string to which young ghetto blacks in particular vibrated. In *Brothers and Keepers* (1984), John Edgar Wideman records his brother Robby's response as a high school student to the outspoken black militants of 1968. "This was when Rap Brown and Stokely and Bobby Seale and them on TV. I identified with those cats. Malcolm and Eldridge and George Jackson. I read their books. They was Gods. That's who I thought I was when I got up on the stage and rapped at the people." You could feel everywhere, says Robby, the belief that "no way they gon turn niggers round this time."[27] Nevertheless, except for the ghetto riots, black violence driven by ideology occurred only on the printed page, and there was some pushing and shoving to see who could be the most inflammatory. The Black Aesthetic movement anticipated the "politically correct" activism on today's university campuses, which assumes all culture and its literature exist as manifestations of dominant power groups.[28] For the Black Aesthetic group, whoever rejected the principles of cultural nationalism fell into the category of middle-class Uncle Toms who had abandoned the people and could not therefore be trusted as combat brothers and sisters in the revolution.

WISH–FULFILLMENT FANTASIES IN FIVE BLACK POWER NOVELS

It was virtually impossible for any African American novelist writing in the years between 1967 and 1977 to ignore the well-publicized proclamations of first the Black Power advocates and then the cultural nationalists. And many of them seemed moved by the same exhilaration and hope that Robby Wideman felt. The open talk of violence was heady in itself, but to watch a white nation tremble at their threats—that seemed, for many, an irresistible stimulant, and a number of novels appear in these years in which the rhetoric of Malcolm X, Stokely Carmichael, H. Rap Brown, and others is embodied in the characters and action of fiction. Much of this fiction, however, reflects the same exultant fantasy of the most extreme Black Power speakers, a fantasy that borders on comic-strip images. The most egregious of this group is Julian Moreau's *The Black Commandos* (1967) in which a total reversal of the South's racism occurs through wholesale black violence. The hero, superhumanly brilliant J. Denis Jackson (Moreau's real name), possessor of many degrees, speaker of many languages, master of abstruse scientific principles, and author of important books, scientifically trains his black commandos in hit-and-run guerrilla tactics and undertakes a campaign of merciless slaughter of hundreds of southerners, mainly cracker Klansmen and policemen. Jackson's motives are both personal and public, those of the messianic hero and those of the enraged avenger. When he was a child, his father was killed by a white policeman and his mother dedicated him "to the cause of black folk." And when he was nine years old and a white sheriff brutally kicked him, he declared savagely, "One day, white man—you won't be so big." [29]

With this hero, Moreau illustrates how things have changed since Chesnutt's Josh Green gave his life to kill George McBane and Lutie Johnson turned her dream into a nightmare when she bludgeoned Boots Smith to death. Jackson wants not only revenge but to improve the lot of his people, which he will do by forcing concessions from whites by any means necessary. And the necessary means turn out to be the kind of violence that so many of Moreau's predecessors yearned to mount. By killing off whites in daring raids brilliantly planned and executed, Jackson succeeds in pushing the "white power structure" to the verge of collapse, then negotiates an agreement favorable to African Americans. He does not seek the destruction of American society. He only wants "a country every citizen can be proud of regardless of his skin color" (219). The agreement expresses a serious attempt to say what African Americans need after three centuries of oppression. For thirty years, they will live as a "privileged group. Then after the inequities were washed away, the races could 'gradually' become equals and go on from there to challenge the universe together" (225). Moreau's belief in racial unity carries him beyond the anger he expresses in his novel and separates him from the most voluble Black Power activists. His notion of privilege even hints at the affirmative action programs that will be instituted in the late sixties and seventies to redress the inequities he talks about. Though the novel is more tract than art, it speaks with a voice that other, better novels assume and in its crude oversimplifications highlights the superstructure of the Black Power sentiment.

Other novelists writing out of the Black Power ideology are only slightly less implausible than Moreau. They articulate overtly what is merely hinted at in the statements made in front of the television cameras and in the newspapers by opinion shapers like H. Rapp Brown, Floyd McKissick, and Eldridge Cleaver, the warning that blacks will rise up and destroy whole cities, even the nation, if things do not change. Indeed, these violent revolutionaries intend, like Dupre and Scofield, to force the creation of a new world by destroying the old. Their narratives show how black revolutionaries will bring on apocalypse, wreaking vengeance upon whites in massive upheavals by armed black militants or retaliatory mass assassinations by ideological Mafia-style groups of grim black revolutionaries. In *'Sippi* (1967), John O. Killens's hero, in one sense a descendant of Joe Youngblood, finally realizes that whites do not "respect" nonviolence. He joins a black organization called the "Elders," which anticipates—is perhaps the model of—Toni Morrison's Seven Days, a group that has armed itself to protect the black community and bring into being the inevitable change for the better. When an admired young civil rights spokesman is gunned down by whites, the Elders retaliate by killing whites and throwing their dead bodies on the porches of southern churches, an allusion to Thomas Dixon's "indomitable" white revolutionaries in *The Clansman* (1905), who throw the body of a black "rapist" on the lawn of the scalawag state lieutenant governor.

This, however, is only one result of the young leader's murder. It also brings about a worldwide rebellion against racist America by the peoples of color. "All over the world in every corner of the earth, American Embassies were stoned and set afire. . . . Outraged demonstrations everywhere, especially in the colored nations of black Africa and brown Asia. Pitched battles between black and white Americans in the rice paddies of Vietnam." "Hundreds of thousands" of black people from Europe, Africa, and Asia, as well as from all over America, come to view the body and "go away perhaps changed forevermore." [30] By joining the Elders and throwing in his lot with the Black Power movement, protagonist Chuck Chaney comes to maturity. We are left not with an agreement with the white power structure as in *The Black Commandos* but with Chuck's determination to help bring that structure down with further violence. In *King Strut* (1970), Chuck Stone locates a similar action in Washington, D.C. When the president of the United States and the homosexual director of the Federal Bureau of Investigation order the assassination of a black congressman for crossing them politically, a guerrilla team from "Blackland," disguised as middle-class tourists, kills and wounds some thirty congressmen in retaliation.

Sam Greenlee used the idea of turning street gangs into revolutionary guerrillas the previous year in *The Spook Who Sat by the Door* (1969) and brings the black revolution to an even more apocalyptic end. His hero, Dan

"Freeman," a northern J. Denis Jackson, trains a tough street gang to be urban guerrillas and leads them in robbing banks and stealing from well-protected armories, which they do with incredible ease and to amazing profit. *The Spook Who Sat by the Door,* however, does not exemplify a method for establishing a new society. It simply asserts the determination of blacks to use violence and thus warns the white populace of what is in store for it. Creating an image of a heroic warrior is more important to Greenlee than considering the practical effects of the warrior's methods. Thus, in the riot that ends the book, the guerrillas take to the roofs, machine-gunning young white National Guardsmen who are turned out to quell the upheaval. Himself, mortally wounded, a sacred sacrifice to the cause, Dan mentally urges his freedom fighters on: "Go on you black-ass Cobras, go get your own."[31] His dying glory is illuminated by the world he leaves in flames.

By the seventies, the Black Power novel has absorbed the philosophical and psychological justifications of violence that made its advocacy so attractive. Violence itself is a powerful cathartic. For example, Bayard Rustin argued that the riot violence was for many an end in itself, a means of freeing the feelings of anger and frustration long suppressed.[32] Frantz Fanon, the black psychiatrist from Martinique who treated rebels in the French-Algerian war and to whom some Black Power theorists had turned for an intellectual underpinning to their ideas, had made a similar point at the beginning of the sixties. His analysis of the relationship between the colonizer and the colonized acted as an analogy to the African American's relationship with the white American. The settler, Fanon writes in 1961, imposes both a psychological and a physical control upon the native, to the point where the native, collaborating with the settler, turns his anger inward in self-hatred. Only violence can free the native from self-destruction in his psychic turmoil.[33]

In *Operation Burning Candle* (1973), Blyden Jackson, basing his plot on the fantasies of the extreme Black Power position, reflects not only a reading of Fanon but much that happened and was said in the 1960s. Once again the familiar image appears: Black guerrillas assassinate twelve southern senators in a well-planned undercover action. As thousands of Harlemites watch the carnage on television (the bloodshed takes place at the Democratic convention in New York City), they shout joyfully, "They're killing the honkies!" Jackson's hero, Aaron Rodgers, a veteran of Vietnam, explains the function of his group as an exercise in "collective psychotherapy" through "creative violence." Violence is creative when it does more than "simply represent revenge or anger." It must force "white folks . . . to acknowledge our humanity in the only terms they can understand or have ever responded to—violence," and "help us as a people move forward." Like Greenlee's Dan Freeman, Aaron dies for the cause, knowing, however, that he has "altered the political balance of the nation . . . back to the left" and has brought on a transformation of the country.[34]

These novels have the quality of the comic-strip potency fantasy. Their hero, the ideal warrior, has mastered psychology, art, literature, the martial arts, terrorist tactics, and good manners (as a smoke screen). Like the hated symbols of white macho, John Wayne and James Bond, they are superstuds with an infallible masculinity, fitting them to blow up communities, change the world, and give women unprecedented satisfaction. In *The Militants* (1974), Nivi-Kofi A. Easley's protagonist, Nick, has put together the Coordinated Organization of Nationalists, otherwise known as COON, which has an agenda that is impressively inclusive: "the overthrow of the government, Capitalism, and Honkyism in general."[35] They blow up several bridges, machine-gun a few gas stations, explode a bomb in a crowded white discotheque, drop a grenade in a subway car, shoot down several whites at random on dark streets, and threaten to kill one policeman a day until the white world accedes to its demands. Concessions are swiftly forthcoming, and Nick smashes the nation's entire racist system.

Just as effective for demonstrating Nick's well-rounded capabilities are the series of minutely described sexual encounters he has in which he displays his superhuman powers in bed. His white girlfriend in particular is made ecstatic by his incredible potency and size. In the end, Nick's goals turn out to be both sexually and economically modest. He takes the two women who adore him, one black and one white, to live in a co-op apartment that overlooks "the Throgs Neck, Bronx Whitestone and Triboro Bridges" (155). And with this ménage à trois, Nick is confident that "with three salaries paying the bills there's nothing in the world we can't do if we really want to" (156). It is a declaration of faith in his sexual power, a good income, and capitalism (regardless of what COON says about it) to solve the racial conflict after violence has done its work. In their new apartment in the new world, the interracial threesome anticipate hours of shared sex, endless climaxes, and glorious ejaculations.

Easley's callow hyperbole illustrates how strong is the need for an effective hero to smash the system that has humiliated the black male. That hero is the revolutionary, who stimulates black pride and encourages an identity with the ghetto's African roots that give it dignity and nourishment, *because* rather than in spite of its location outside the majority white culture. Thus Aaron Rodgers, the planner of "Operation Burning Candle" in Blyden Jackson's novel, promises his Harlem listeners an end to "four centuries of separation from each other. We shall no longer be alone, dying, crying, by ourselves, unable to reach out to each other" (127). Later, dying from the wound he got in the attack on the Democratic convention, he struggles toward the playground at 116th Street and Lenox Avenue, where he played as a child. As he drags himself along the rough pavement, through the "empty brown bags and cigarette butts," he hallucinates his racial past, seeing his attempt to return to the security of the playground as an analogy of an attempt to get back to the African village of his ancestors before the slavers capture him (220–21). The sign of his successful return to the tribal sanctuary is the appearance in every Harlem window of a burning candle, suggesting a unanimous endorsement of his guerrillas and a massive gesture of identification with their violence. It is the symbol of a new racial unity and an indication of the creative force of Black Power.

By Addison Gayle's standards in *The Way of the New World,* these images come from the truest and the most aesthetically admirable novels, for they "deal openly with anger and resentment expressed in unabashed terms," and their creators, functioning as the "amanuensis" of the black revolutionary, "record this desire for violent change."[36] Other readers might find these particular revolutionary novels to be stiff and implausible. No more than their real-world cultural nationalist counterparts are the fictional revolutionaries allowed by their creator to reflect upon the possible contradictions in their course. Neither the youth gangs nor the urban guerrillas in these novels exhibit any doubt about their choice for violence. They undergo no internal struggle over its morality. The conflict is between them and evil white stereotypes. Thus they do not see the irony in their reversal of the white myth of stereotyped black brutes slavering over delicate white female bodies. The Cobras, the Black Commandos, the Vietnam veterans are the black equivalent of the white Ku Klux Klan, justifying their mayhem with the same self-righteousness that white supremacists used to defend theirs, which was always the logic of the antiviolence side in the ongoing debate. The attraction of participating in the fantasy, however, is irresistible during a time when advocacy of violence carried its own radical chic and gained entrance into some of New York's most fashionable penthouse fundraisers, when judges were being shot by young blacks in daring rescue attempts, and martyrdom, when headlined in the press, seemed of all things the highest fate.

JOHN A. WILLIAMS AND THE REALIST'S DILEMMA

The contradiction does strike hard at the more able writers of the period. The expectations that had been so bright at the beginning of the sixties had tarnished by their end, and the conventional black wisdom responded by more openly recommending violence. The serious African American novelist who felt constrained—by public events and the conspicuousness of the Black Power movement—to address the issues everyone was talking about had a difficult time avoiding the pitfalls of tract writing and the oversimplification that seemed to attend any treatment of violence. Good men and women were confronted with what many saw—with much supportive evidence—as an implacable and indifferent white world. Killing seemed to be a dead end, yet whites seemed to react only to violence. But to employ the method of their oppressors meant a capitulation to what the black community had long objected to in whites.

John A. Williams best expresses the dilemma in *The Man Who Cried I Am* (1967), one of the best American novels of the decade, which came out just a year after Stokely Carmichael had commenced exploiting the mediagenic phrase "Black Power." For Williams, the optimism of the black revolution turned sour fairly early, for the apocalyptic endings of both *The Man Who Cried I Am* and *Sons of Darkness, Sons of Light* (1969) resound with a bitterness quite different from fantasies like *The Spook Who Sat by the Door.* His tone is neither pugnacious nor swaggering but grieving, an expression of mourning for the failure of the movement's dream. *The Man Who Cried I Am* is the chronicle of the emotional progress of the mainstream black intellectual during a professional life that climaxes in the 1960s. It is also a sensitive and intelligent treatment of the movement's issues as they affect the reflective man. Williams does not deal with the specific political and social problems that fueled the civil rights activism of the sixties—segregated facilities in the South, voter registration and participation in elections, the southern system of injustice—or with the riots of the northern cities or their background. They simply form the racist atmosphere in which his characters move.

Williams was born in the South but raised in Syracuse, New York. Schooled with white children, he made the mistake of thinking they all had the same relationship to America and to each other. He did not discover his error until he was a teenager, and from then on his struggles with the world become not merely those of a young man growing up and trying to find a place commensurate with his abilities but those of a black male growing up.[37] All of his fiction of the 1960s deals with the constant pressure of a not-so-subtle discrimination which makes him more and more paranoid. Lynching a black man in the South was something even whites could see. The enemy of the black intellectual often does not realize that he is an enemy, or refuses to admit it if he does realize it, as with the white magazine editor who let Williams go and the white man who withheld the literary prize for which Williams had been unanimously recommended. One can agitate for a law against lynching or fight back in a riot, but one cannot knock down the director of the Academy of Rome because of suspected discrimination. In his 1960s fiction, Williams is at his best when he writes about these conditions, about the black intellectual, a projection of himself, caught in invisible but palpable racism, which saps his creativity and limits the range of his observations. Williams himself and his best characters are not activists. They reward us most when we see the drama of their inner life as they respond to the racial problem, as they fight their own subtle emasculation.

His first three novels—*The Angry Ones* (1960), *Night Song* (1961), and *Sissie* (1963)—deal with racism in the world of music and literature. *Sissie* is the best of the three, showing how a black playwright finally accepts the truth of his situation by concluding that his paranoia is not pathological but practical, a rational response to the reality of life in America. By 1967, with the heating up of the civil rights movement and the advent of the Black Power concept, Williams was evidently no longer content to dramatize the process of discrimination. Like those of many other black intellectuals, Williams's frustrations led him to consider theoretical violence, and he used *The Man Who Cried I Am* and *Sons of Darkness* as laboratories for his investigation.

The Man Who Cried I Am is one of those works of fiction in which a writer's special abilities happen to fuse with his best themes in a harmony that seems as much chance as plan. This is the story of Williams's own intellectual and racial life as well as a history of the period the novel covers, 1940–66. It is also the story of the black writer's life during the years of Wright, Baldwin, Chester Himes, and of how white racism affects their emotions, their attitudes, and their writing. Africa breaks its colonial bonds; black Americans discover their beauty and their political power; the status of the black writer improves. But the gains are only external. Underneath, white supremacy remains as the foundation and prevents any real progress toward eliminating those racial barriers that can be perceived only by an African American. One of Williams's main convictions is that African Americans must, in order to survive, acknowledge the full truth of their place in the white scheme of things and understand with absolute clarity the true nature of white prejudice. They must, like Ralph Ellison's Invisible Man, achieve a higher consciousness, which will function not to reform the system but to provide psychological liberation. Much of "true" white prejudice is bound up in people's mannerisms, the inability to uncouple their unconscious belief in black inferiority from the artistic judgments they make of blacks' artistic work. This produces a tacit conspiracy to keep black writers or painters or musicians out of the main media of dissemination, the refusal to accept black intellectuals on their own ground.

To give all this an economical form, Williams devises a clever metaphor. European racism is embodied in an "Alliance Blanc," in which the white nations of Europe agree secretly to prevent black Africa from taking charge of its own destiny and enjoying the profits of its own resources. The American arm of the Alliance Blanc is the "King Alfred Plan," which white authorities have developed for use "in the event of widespread and continuing co-ordinated racial disturbances." [38] The plan calls for the mobilization of all federal, state, and local law enforcement units to detain, imprison, or contain as necessary any black person thought to pose a danger to whites in an armed insurrection. The lives of the characters in the novel illustrate that such a plan has always existed in America, that it is simply a codification in writing of the measures that whites have always used in their suppression of African Americans. The experience of the protagonist, Max Reddick, is a movement toward a discovery of the actual existence of this plan, developed step by step as he moves through white America and Europe in the novel's action.

In the hours before he is killed, ironically by two black CIA agents, novelist Reddick reads a long letter from his fellow novelist, Harry Ames, a Richard Wright figure. Harry's letter documents the existence of the Alliance Blanc and the King Alfred Plan. As he reads, Max relives his own life, moving back and forth from the present to the past. As the letter unfolds the information about the King Alfred Plan, flashbacks unfold the course of Reddick's life and his fragment of African American history. Thus the evidence exposing white racism accumulates on two parallel tracks, the past and the present, which reflect each other. In the end, Max reads the letter straight through. By then, with a knowledge of the past in his mind, the reader realizes, and so does Max, that the King Alfred Plan is a logical extension of historical American policy. Even so, it is suddenly and vividly illuminating. "I'd spent so much of my life writing about the evil machinations of Mr. Charlie," writes Harry, "without really *knowing* the truth, as this material made me know it" (369). That Williams puts this knowledge into the hands of two novelists indicates his conviction that the role of the black writer is first to perceive and then to articulate the truth about the white world as they see it. *The Man Who Cried I Am,* as a novel, does what its characters do in the story.

Max himself is not a violent man, nor are any of Williams's intellectuals. But Williams suggests that the white world surrounds them with violence to suppress them, and this forces them eventually into violence themselves.

Whites preach nonviolence and human rights but forcefully repress attempts by unauthorized groups to exercise those rights. The black person who would discover and then disclose the truth about America endangers himself. In *The Man Who Cried I Am,* every statesman or artist who exposes the elaborate institutional framework by which whites rationalize their crimes is killed, either literally or figuratively. Knowledge is a terminal disease, a "pain in the ass," as Max calls the rectal cancer from which he is dying. The cancer commences at the same point that Max begins to learn the truth, a few hemorrhoids, some irritating discomfort, a bloody stool or two. It develops slowly, until the time Max starts reading Harry's letter with only a little while to live. As the African American rises toward the goal of existence, understanding, he also moves toward death—and not a natural death, either. This is the fatal illness of being black in America. Max moves through his last hours in a cloud of pain, able to cut it only in the classical way that many black men have used to cut the agony of their lucidity, through liquor and dope.

Williams identifies too closely with the activist spirit of the decade, however, to leave it at this. Understanding may be a worthwhile goal in itself, but there are things to be done and a world to be changed, and finally it is the question of how change may be achieved that confronts Max Reddick in the final pages of the novel. It is impossible not to write a political novel in these years. But Williams addresses the question with skill and a writer's sensitivity. *The Man Who Cried I Am* is not an opportunistic exploitation of a chic market fashion, nor is it a puerile fantasy. It is an attempt to make meaning out of a set of events that Williams would rather not have to face. He attacks the problem on the personal and the political levels. Max Reddick is the man who cries "I am," asserting both his personal existence and a political determination to act as a catalyst of change. To act in this way is to exist. His political act is to make public the King Alfred Plan before he himself is killed for possessing his knowledge. He makes the decision reluctantly, for he knows it will begin a civil war, a suggestion that requires a weakening bit of melodramatic fudging by Williams. Yet, in the uncertain atmosphere of those times of riot, the possibility did not seem all that remote. Black people, Williams suggests, have always been resourceful in finding reasons for not acting. The voice of those reasons is "Saminone," Max's other side, who appears to him at critical times in his life. Saminone is all the Uncle Toms and cynical hipsters wrapped into one. To Max's desperate "I am," Saminone counters with a sardonic and bitter humor: "You am whut, you piece of crap? Turd" (187). Max's assertion defies the white man's negation of the black. Saminone finds in that defiance a contemptibleness that causes him to laugh bitterly, as well as a little nervously. You are only a black man, he says in effect to Max, believing in his own inferiority. What can a black man expect to do to the forces arrayed against him? Saminone is the profoundly fatalistic strain in the black character, and Max struggles to defeat it. His decision to disclose Harry's information is another way of saying "I am." To discover and then reveal the truth is to assert one's black existence. To the tradition of black rebels like Josh Green and Perigua, Williams brings a humanizing depth and discloses another aspect to the heroic but desperate logic of "if we must die" poetry. Not to act, though the act will inevitably bring Max's own death and the death of others, is to place no value on his own and other blacks' lives, to allow whites to make what they will: a Saminone who has internalized a paralyzing cynicism and pessimism. To fight, and to accept death as a probable consequence—even if nothing is gained by it— is to create one's own value. No white value system can supersede that.

The Man Who Cried I Am is Williams's adaptation of the rhetoric of Black Power. It is a gloss upon a sentence in his *This Is My Country Too:* "Today the strength of the contemporary Negro is in being ready to die." [39] There is no stereotypical black militancy in this novel, however. Williams does not resort to simple reversal or get any vindictive pleasure in imagining the deaths of whites or the superior ability of blacks to kill. Melancholy pervades this novel, not heroic anger or righteous resentment or revolutionary fervor. The violent ending, in which Max is gunned down after he has made a civil war in America certain, cannot erase the sorrow that dominates every scene, a sadness over the tarnishing of America's promise. And after the political implications in the failure of whites to live up to their professed creed comes yet another discovery that makes the novel so complex and effective. African Americans can be as petty and self-serving, grasping and self-centered, as anyone else. Like America itself, every relationship carries with it warm human possibility, and every promise dissipates in the air of human frailty and the deficiency of conditions. No motive is pure, no act untainted with bias. Blacks as well as whites display greed, jealousy, duplicity, opportunism. Even the authenticity of Max's decision to risk death by exposing the King Alfred Plan is undercut by the fact that he is already dying of cancer.

But no more than many other black writers can Williams relinquish all hope. The civil war that Max's disclosure makes inevitable implies a violent revolt of blacks as they set about defending themselves against King Alfred. No black commandos are introduced to stand in glorious silhouette against the flames of a burning America. This is an apocalypse of pain and loss, but one in which some future lies. The issue is not the right to kill; it is whether America is worth the agony of this rebellion.

Max's successor in *Sons of Darkness,* Gene Browning, also believes that America is worth saving, and he also concludes, only with reluctance, that violent confrontation is necessary. Blacks have exhausted every other recourse and want desperately to make their country healthy, to heal the division between races. Violence is like the shock treatment one authorizes for a beloved relative. That it *is* his country is a conviction from which Williams never wavers; the problems of the African American can only be solved in America, and only violence, reluctantly used, can solve them.

BLACK POWER AND THE POWER OF ART:
ALICE WALKER'S *MERIDIAN*

As I have said, the Black Power concept, in which this advocacy found its main home, died a fairly quick death in the public sphere. One by one the radical black militants—Stokely Carmichael, H. Rap Brown, Eldridge Cleaver, Huey Newton, Fred Hampton—disappeared from the scene, victims of police shoot-outs, fugitives from justice, or simply soldiers who surrendered peacefully to wealth and material comforts. Riots, too, became dated. Even by 1968, according to a report released by the Department of Justice, "the scope and intensity of racial riots" had declined.[40] By the 1970s, what seemed like an urgent, long-range truth to Max Reddick disappears completely from the field of vision of Ralph Joplin, who reappears in Williams's later novel, *The Junior Bachelor Society* (1976). The survivors of the fifties and sixties, solidly ensconced in their middle-class or working-class ruts, older and wiser, gather for a reunion of the old gang in an attempt to re-create the former illusion of good fellowship and passionate purpose. Except for a vestige of old ties, every one of the old Junior Bachelor Society has slipped into a life in which they concentrate on themselves rather than on a larger social good or acts that will bring about social change. What Williams has retained from those sad but vital years of the 1960s is the theme of the destruction of illusion, placing himself squarely in the main tradition of American fiction. The feverish final moments of *The Man Who Cried I Am,* in which Max Reddick tries to crack open American racism with a blast of civil strife, testify to the fervor of his hope for America. It was something worth dying for, as well as living for. The members of the Junior Bachelor Society have lost that zeal. Even the reunion of the society is one of those fleeting things, only half successful. And Bubbles Wiggins, who has engineered it, knows "they would not do this again, ever."[41] It is Williams's epitaph on an exhilarating time when change still seemed possible.

The Junior Bachelor Society does not put the quietus on the revolutionary novel. The speculation upon the image of the heroic revolutionary who can bring change through violence is still a factor in the African American imagination, expressing a persistent anger, illustrating a state of mind not easily changed, reassuring militant African Americans that, in those years of declining militancy, militancy can still be imagined. One of the more probing of those imaginings is Alice Walker's *Meridian* (1976), a book about two kinds of revolutionists, feminist and black, in equal parts. Like *The Man Who Cried I Am,* it explores the relationship between revolutionary violence and art and approaches the turbulence of the high revolutionary period retrospectively, remembering that period with reverence and respect. Walker's novel is about the education of an innocent black woman into the realities of the American racial scene, explicitly considering the role that black violence can play in the African American reaction to that scene. Over the course of the sixties, Meridian Hill, Walker's faintly autobiographical protagonist, finds an ambiguous answer to her question about violence through her participation in the civil rights movement and the black revolution. As the movement proceeds through its phases, Meridian matures and learns. She finds that the heart of the revolution is violence and that the functioning revolutionary must be able to commit to that violence. She herself, however, cannot make that commitment, and coming to terms with this unchangeable part of herself is what *Meridian* is about.

In the 1960 world Meridian lives in, men oppress women and whites oppress blacks. In this atmosphere, to live she must rebel. (Walker read Camus avidly.) As long as she allows herself to exist under the dominion of either men or whites, she can have no full being. And so she searches for the means of freeing herself of that dominion and confirming both her color and her gender. She starts with her pre-1960 nonidentity, a womb of vaguely dissatisfied ignorance, a sexual object for men, and a mother of a child she does not want. She is a racial as well as a sexual prisoner through her own uninformed sloth and indifference. When the civil rights movement comes to her town and penetrates that womb, she awakens into the larger world, and in growing consciousness she throws herself into the struggle for the liberation of her people and herself. As she becomes a more effective worker, she becomes more independent of the old influences. She learns to live without men and to fight white supremacy. The result is the genesis of a surpassing strength, which she employs against oppression in the service of the poor and the powerless. She "cleanses" herself of "sickness," reconciles herself to her "ambivalence," and becomes "strong enough to go," as her onetime lover Truman Held puts it when he realizes he can no longer "hold" her. From the old Meridian he once knew, a "new" one issues, "sure and ready, even eager, for the world." If she is alone, it is only in the sense that she has no family or lover. She is part of others who are also alone and who, she says, "will one day gather at the river. . . . And in the darkness maybe we will know the truth."[42]

At the center of the truth for Meridian lies a reconciliation with the one requirement of the revolutionary that had precluded her fully entering into that fraternity, the ability to kill. Others seemed to find it too easy to declare they could "kill for the Revolution." Meridian sees more than rhetoric in the question. For her it is rent flesh and dripping blood. This is no judgment against violence as a necessary weapon in the revolution but the statement of a problem that Walker says she herself faced, as she worried that she was not "more violent."[43] How could she be a part of the great epochal forces working their fundamental change if she could not make the contribution of a revolutionary? For Meridian, the answer lies in a new understanding of the relationship of the past, art, and the revolution.

It is her attachment to the past that blocks her from slipping into the easy vows of her friends. They are intoxicated by the new black aggressiveness. But Meridian remembers too affectionately the images of peaceful old black men and young choir girls singing in a country church for violence to come easily. In those long-existing rural and village communities resides the heritage that gives the present its richness.[44] She cannot imagine those old men and those young girls committing murder. Beneath Meridian's anxiety is an unstated assumption that the revolution is forcing her to choose between what she sees as a peaceful past and a necessarily violent present. She wants to be a part of the present without giving up the past. The students who so easily come to witness for violence regard the past as a drag upon those working for the new utopia. To be part of it, Meridian must submit to the movement's orthodoxy. Unable to throw off her past, Meridian feels ashamed and guilty.

Past and present must be reconciled. For Meridian, that reconciliation comes about in a country church where the two meet in a painful clash. A parishioner's son has been killed in the civil rights movement. The father is inconsolable, but the congregation has been transformed. Its members have determined never to let such an atrocity happen again and have promised to replace their customary inaction and piety with action and ardor. The vehicle of this transformation, in which the congregation joins their past with the all-demanding present, is their church songs. They are the "ritual" that links the bereaved man with the church, not, as the narrator tells us, the specific denominational church but the "communal spirit, togetherness, righteous convergence" (199). The church music is the spiritual glue that binds the members of the community to each other and the community to its supporting past. This is not a religious thing. In the birth of its revolutionary spirit, the congregation has turned secular. The old stained glass window of "the traditional pale Christ with stray lamb" has been replaced with a picture of "a tall, broadshouldered black man," a guitar strapped around his shoulders and his raised arm clasping a bloody sword (198).

The alembic of the new church music and the militant figure on the stained glass window work its chemistry upon Meridian as well. In a kind of alchemical transmutation, she first concludes that, since the value of her own life depends upon her willingness to fight for it, her identity with the small congregation requires that she fight for it, that "she *would* kill, before she allowed anyone to murder [the old man's] son again" (200). But the opposite pull of her ambivalence continues to work upon the solution's float, and she realizes still that she cannot kill. This leaves her out of the front lines of the revolution, "listening to the old music." But if so, that gives her a role in the revolution she had not understood before—as a singer-recorder of the racial memory, the equivalent of the ritual church music upon which the little congregation founded its own new militancy. Her songs will fortify the revolutionaries with the sustaining past. "For it is the song of the people that holds them together, and if any part of it is lost the people suffer and are without soul. If I can only do that, my role will not have been a useless one after all" (201). She, the artist, may not be the revolution's warrior, but she will be its soul.

This is a much different aesthetic from that defined by the cultural nationalist. Walker's most ingenious and effective metaphor of the way art functions in the revolution is the Sojourner tree, which stands on Meridian's college campus. It had been planted long ago by a slave, Louvinie, an artist, a storyteller from a storytelling family in Africa. When her owner cuts her tongue out she buries it, the instrument of her art, under her young magnolia tree, and the tree becomes the mute bearer of her tales to future generations, sending its roots into the past and its branches into the future. The music group to which Meridian belongs names it the "music tree," linking storytelling with songs. When the tree is threatened by a new building, the students save it, but they cannot save it from themselves. In a riot to assert their rights in the age of the incipient black revolution, they destroy the great old tree. A revolution that tears down elements from the past that should be saved along with those that should not is a rudderless revolution. Art preserves and is necessary to revolution, which is potentially aimless in its destructiveness and inherently blind to what is rich and venerated from the past. While the artist may be unable to join in the destruction, he or she remains vigilant against its excesses and, preserving the past, gives direction to the future.

Meridian illustrates the weaknesses that revolutions are prone to, defects in the human being rather than in the revolutionary process. The people with whom Meridian lives and works lack the sincerity of the church congregation in which Meridian reaches her reconciliation. Activists Truman Held and Tommy Odds are hardly admirable examples of the good revolutionary. Truman is a selfish male chauvinist who comes to heel only after seducing a young and inexperienced Meridian, pursuing the white girls from the North and marrying one, then, after ten years of this, pleading with Meridian to take him back. Tommy Odds is a psychotic hater of whites who rapes Truman's fragile white wife. Similarly, the most revolutionary of the young students who urged Meridian to pledge to kill has cooled off considerably now that she has married well and has money. Instead of inflammatory and supportive revolutionary art, she now writes poems "about her two children, and the quality of the light that fell across a lake she owned" (201). She was a revolutionary for show, preoccupied with style and the figure she cut.

The artist who saves the best of the revolution must make clear the distinction between the posturers and the authentic, like the son of the bereaved father and the determined congregation. This is where Meridian must go for her portraits of heroes like the indomitable black man in the stained glass window. From them she will draw her songs that celebrate the unconquerable spirit of "slain martyrs," poems that disclose "the gentleness at the heart of the warrior" (196–98). *Meridian* the novel is just such an expression, delineating the process in which past and present, killer and artist, join and make possible Meridian's individual strength for carrying on the people's fight. That is how we leave her. She has rejected the orthodox revolution for her own, and life with a male chauvinist for life on her own with the people to whom she devotes herself. Art, Walker shows, is the mortise that joins the conservative past and the revolutionary present. This is not a principle of the cultural nationalist movement that provoked the writing of novels like *The Spook Who Sat by the Door* and *Operation Burning Candle*. It is a statement about the general process of revolution, not as it gives indiscriminate approval to both false posturing and genuine sacrifice in the specific years of the sixties but as it shows that true revolution is the same in all its forms. In *Meridian* Walker finds a meaning in both "the" revolution and revolution. Writing in 1976, she takes her place in a new time that at last can view the turbulent sixties from a certain artistic distance. What she sees is the inevitability and necessity of violence in revolution and the indispensable idealizing force of art.

THE WANING OF BLACK POWER'S POWER: ERNEST J. GAINES AND JOSEPH NAZEL

Meridian also shows a shift of setting that occurs as the decade of the seventies winds down, from the northern ghetto back to the southern countryside. It is as if the African American novelist, after a journey to the North in search of the desirable revolutionary image, returns to an ancestral home with that image modified. In addition to *Meridian,* two other novels appear in these later years whose hero is not an individual warrior but a group of black men. In *Black Uprising* (1976) and *A Gathering of Old Men* (1983), Joseph Nazel and Ernest J. Gaines, writers of fundamentally different visions and talents, create a pattern of revolt that illustrates how much changed the old perceptions of the militant revolutionary are. At the height of the Black Power movement, even just two years before Nazel's book comes out, the ideal rebel, acting alone as a powerful leader, worked underground to develop a guerrilla combat team which would strike at northern police and National Guard troops in what was essentially war. This reflected the adversarial attitude of the cultural nationalists and the principle of separatism upon which they started their campaigns. When the novelists return south in 1976, with *Black Uprising,* the notion of apocalypse had dropped out of the picture. What remained was the old traditional preoccupation with manhood and the possibility of achieving it through violence.

The actions that Nazel and Gaines contrive to dramatize this concern are virtually identical. In Nazel's Crossroads, Alabama, and Gaines's Louisiana delta country, the old southern system of justice still holds. In part, the black men themselves are responsible for this state of affairs because they have submitted to it. They have held back from seizing their independence for various reasons: timidity, misdirected piety, fear, personal relationships that prevent action. But when whites push them too far, they undergo a complete change. They get their antiquated guns, organize themselves for combat, and set out to defy their traditional masters.

At this point, an intriguing change takes place from the earlier revolutionary novels. Instead of going underground and opposing the duly constituted law enforcement agencies of the white establishment, these new southern black rebels team up with the local sheriff. In both novels, the sheriff reflects how different things are from the way they were in the fifties and early sixties. Now these law officers are sympathetic, straightforward men, more interested in preserving order and serving the law than in maintaining white control over blacks. It turns out that the black revolutionaries revolt not against a justice system rigged against them but against rogue whites who have taken the law into their own hands one time too many. Blacks join with whites to enforce justice. This obviates any threat to the general order from the revolutionary collective, and in this form their violence does not pull down society or engulf it in holocaust. It rids society of the distorting elements that would crack it open.

In the armed encounter between the blacks and whites, both blacks and whites are killed, but the blacks show a courage and tenacity hitherto unknown to either side. In *Black Uprising,* even the church joins the new world, after advocating nonviolence for so many years. It is the Crossroads pastor, in fact, who organizes the posse that helps the sheriff break the defense of the outlaw band of whites. He himself uses his old shotgun on the most vicious of the white men. "A man can't hide himself away in a church and let the Lawd do all his work for him," says the pastor. "He's got to stand on his own two feet sometime." [45] In doing so, he and the rest of the black posse not only forge a new manhood for themselves but also restore order and justice.

Nazel's characters incline to stereotypes, the whites in particular—except for the beleaguered sheriff—playing the role of unrelieved wickedness. Gaines always shows an understanding of tradition, and of the emotions of both whites and blacks. His Cajuns, who determine to avenge the death of one of their own at the hands of a retarded black man, are moved by a sense of honor. We respect their leader, an aging patriarch who suffers from the passing of the old ways and anguishes over the conflict between the honor he feels he must preserve through vengeance and his children who want to do things the new way. Gaines, furthermore, gives his old rebels, determined to prevent the Cajuns from doing business as usual, a past which shows us the personal weaknesses they hope to compensate for. When the old Cajun patriarch decides to give up vengeance and an arrogant hothead leads a number of his good-for-nothing friends into the black camp, the old men stand their ground when the firing starts. They have been changed by the collapse of the old system and the onset of the new and reverse a lifetime of shame by this climactic gesture of octogenarian courage. "Don't never be scared no more, Dirty," Charlie tells the narrator before he goes to his death. "Life's so sweet when you know you ain't no more coward." [46]

In this image of collective heroism we see a continuing belief in the strength of the southern redemptive community by which its black populace won so many victories in the early civil rights movement. The shotgun-toting men, furthermore, have traveled a great distance from the Crossroads, Georgia, congregation grieving for the dead Youngblood in John Oliver Killens's novel, and the temporarily insane ghetto murderer like Lutie Johnson and Jesse Robinson. Here, the black man, perhaps frightened, perhaps even desperate, is nevertheless in control in a way he never was in the novel of those earlier decades. And control is at the center of the manhood that Eldridge Cleaver insisted that "we shall have." In 1968, however, when Cleaver said, "We shall have it or the earth will be leveled by our attempts to gain it," he was ready to tear the world apart. A decade later, the heroic collective seems ready to put it together.

[11]

THE FALL OF
THE REVOLUTIONARY:
THE IMAGE DISMANTLED

THE MORAL AND PRACTICAL DRAWBACKS OF
RETALIATORY VIOLENCE

The novels I deal with in this chapter form the last stage of the long
discourse on violence and its heroes and victims that began with the first
African American novel, William Wells Brown's first version of *Clotel,*
published in 1853. The same questions that gave that discourse its shape lie
at the bottom of these novels as well. Should African Americans engage in
retaliatory or revolutionary violence against the white majority system that
impedes their free search for life, liberty, and happiness? Is the true African
American hero the figure that fearlessly employs such violence? Should the
victims of white violence be avenged in kind? Is the use of such defensive
and retaliatory violence even plausible given the situation of the African
American?

   The novels I am now going to explore appear in the twenty years
between 1967 and 1987, enclosed between Ishmael Reed's *The Free-Lance
Pallbearers* and John Edgar Wideman's *Reuben.* They show that, as in every
other period, unanimity was never reached even in the hyperactive sixties
and seventies on the desired hero image to be projected by the African
American novel. While Black Power novelists were idealizing the urban
guerrilla leader of small revolutionary bands that bring apocalypse to racist
America, these other novelists were at work undermining that image, re-
shaping it in other implicitly critical forms: the doomed violent gang
leader, cautious practicalist, gentle Christian, steely-spined pragmatist and
nonviolent activist, disenchanted skeptic, buffoon. The composite figure
that emerges from these re-formed characters embodies the practicalist

doubt that lay broad and deep in the black community beneath the head-line-grabbing Black Power defiance, doubt about both the morality and the logistics of violent revolution. The subtext of these novels is the question of the relationship between fictional narrative and reality. Even a novelist like John A. Williams pushed to the borderline between fantasy and reality, asking the audience to take something very like fantasy as reality. Certainly John Oliver Killens, Sam Greenlee, and Blyden Jackson write "realistic" narratives that mirror reality only in the sense that we recognize the details of the world in which they move. The uprising they depict calls upon the reader to exercise a powerful willingness to suspend disbelief, and to believe at the same time. The novels I take up in this chapter, however, focus upon the probable rather than the wishful. And for most of them, the gap between the probable and the wishful is so great as to call forth reactions that are of various grades of irony and doubt.

In the public debate, the main spokesperson for this doubt (though not the irony) before his assassination in 1968 was, of course, Martin Luther King, Jr. Though he died before the revolutionary hero had been fully outlined, he formulated the logical argument inherent in the counterimage. Dr. King's was an argument built on deep religious faith, an old-fashioned confidence in the moral potential of the human being, and hardheaded practicality. Those who advocate "overthrowing racist state and local governments," he wrote, "fail to see that no internal revolution has ever succeeded in overthrowing a government by violence unless the government had already lost the allegiance and effective control of its armed forces." The United States government had not. Nor have any "violent revolutions been successful unless the violent minority had the sympathy and support of the non-resisting majority." [1] The black minority had not. In fact, to use violence against whites is a sure way to self-destruction. The Black Power novelists had seen such self-destruction not only as gloriously heroic but as the necessary first step to change. Dr. King's view is that the glory is chimerical and that violence not only does not bring change, it hardens the opposition by the beneficiaries of the status quo.

The function of the civil rights movement of the fifties and sixties, he says, was to create moral power through the nonviolent strength of a unified and activist black community integrated with white sympathizers. For King, in other words, black unity does not mean the separatism of the black nationalist; rather, it means the ability to work cooperatively as a group, which will only be effective when it is consolidated through "constructive alliances with the majority group." [2] King seems to have no illusions about whites. Some can be trusted, some cannot. But the inescapable reality is that whites control the social structure of America, and if the black is to ameliorate his own condition he must enlist the help of those in control.

For Black Power advocates the end often lay in the means, since manhood and ethnic pride seemed in many cases to take precedence over more jobs and better living conditions. The proviolence advocate said that threatening the system with guns promoted social advances by promoting a sense of self-esteem. When the system continued to resist such advances, violence could at least make a man feel like a man. This thinking informed the most extreme fantasies of Black Power novelists like Sam Greenlee and Blyden Jackson, for whom martyrdom in their imagined worlds was a high and holy fate. The exuberance of their books came, perhaps, from the release always felt when bars to self-expression fall and formerly prohibited thoughts become thinkable and forbidden images are projected. King, however, kept his eye not on the imagery of heroism but on the socioeconomic improvement of African Americans, and eventually of all poor Americans. King's advocacy of nonviolence was based partly on a quest for political power, for he believed that political power came from moral power. He did not take the position of the traditional nonviolent Christian, whose advice was always "to wait on the Lord," and wait for the white gateman to open the door unasked. His way is nonviolent but activist. He would pound on the door but never shoot the lock off. As Harold Cruse said in another context, it is more difficult than some revolutionaries think "to succeed in shooting one's way into voting rights, jobs, and 'desegregated' public facilities."[3]

If King projects an image, it is his own—the exemplar of nonviolent activism: courage in the face of white mobs, humble strength under police cruelty, eloquence in the pulpit, always animated by the highest and most unquestioned of motives. However close this is to the "real" Martin Luther King—and there are revisionists who question its accuracy—it is an image conveyed by the television camera. Of all the pictures that appeared on the nation's TV screens in the twelve years of King's public life, that of King himself is the most indelible—marching peacefully, being accosted by white law officers, and, above all, intoning his "dream" in what surely is the most eloquent adaptation of the black sermon on record before thousands at the Lincoln Memorial in 1963. But oddly enough, the novelists do not attempt to draw the King hero as they react to the Black Power revolutionary. Instead, they tend to draw the black revolutionary image but to render it in terms of its weaknesses and dangers and its inevitable failure rather than its glorious martyrdom in which the black community can take hope and pride. They try to show the illogicality of the moral and practical argument underlying this character, in whose actions and statements and fates we see, rather than the figure of King himself, certain aspects of his argument worked out.

This character appears in unexpected places. For example, "black experience" writer Donald Goines illustrates King's point that the violent revolutionary can only expect counterviolence, not a new world based on fairness. His revolutionary is Kenyatta, whose fortunes Goines, under the pseudonym of Al C. Clark, traces through four novels: *Crime Partners* (1974), *Death List* (1974), *Kenyatta's Escape* (1974), and *Kenyatta's Last Hit* (1975).

Kenyatta operates in the ghetto, whose people are corrupted by drugs and oppressed by racist police. Revolution for Kenyatta is to move against the institutions that underpin these degrading forces. He aims, therefore, to take back the ghetto from the police and rid it of its predatory drug lords, both black and white. Thus Kenyatta the black nationalist is pitted against the two groups most responsible for the debased conditions of the black community. His cause is just, for he is no gangster. His behavior is selfless. The battles he fights against the drug lords and the white police (whose one token black police detective makes their racism all the more obvious) are warranted by his black nationalism and his concern for black youth. The moral tone is caught in the fourth volume of the tetralogy, *Kenyatta's Last Hit*. Kenyatta has fled Detroit to Los Angeles, where he gathers around him "a growing number of young, idealistic blacks" to fight the increasing drug traffic. "They had known that the government, the law enforcement agencies and the supposed poverty programs were not working. Kenyatta had told them that the situation was in their hands, that they were the force behind the ghetto, and that they would be the ones who could make it better for their brothers." [4]

But Kenyatta's methods doom him to failure. In fact, his failure is tragically built into the conditions he seeks to improve. In this world, violence is the everyday way of doing business, and few conduct their business as effectively as Kenyatta. An outsized version of the Black Power nationalist, Kenyatta is brutal and unforgiving, totally ruthless and utterly without fear. He hires psychotic gunmen to kill his enemies and trains paramilitary armies who engage in pitched battles in which men and women on both sides are torn apart by shotgun blasts and large-caliber bullets. It is bloodshed and human damage at its most sensational. Neither Kenyatta nor the male and female soldiers in his highly trained guerrilla army have any compunction about killing whites, whether they are police or not, or about gunning down members of black dope rings. In turn, they receive no quarter themselves. Kenyatta's vicious methods lead only to relentless police pursuit and retaliation by competitors. The Detroit police mercilessly clean out the "farm" where he trained and indoctrinated his soldiers. His last battle takes place in the Las Vegas office of a white dope dealer. When he goes after this kingpin as part of his campaign against the drug trade, he is outwitted. As the drug lord makes his escape, Kenyatta and his two-score gunmen are slaughtered. Kenyatta has achieved none of his goals. The police remain inveterately racist, and the drug trade continues unabated.

The Kenyatta tetralogy makes up about a quarter of the total number of pop exploitation novels Goines wrote between 1970 and 1974 for Holloway House publishers in Los Angeles. Violence is their basic motif, meant at least in part as an attraction to their no doubt largely black male readership. But there is an element of the morality tale in them, too, so that exploitation lies in tension with moral disapproval. The Kenyatta novels must be seen in the context of these other novels, though he is the only black revolutionary character among them. They are not fantasy, though they are perhaps exaggerated fiction, for Goines lived in the world in which the Kenyatta story is set. He was a Detroiter by birth, a dope addict, a sometime bootlegger and street player, an ex-convict. He belonged to what was in the Black Power movement's eyes the only truly authentic black community and was the type that the Black Power novelist would have respected and admired, at least from a distance. He carried on the battle, so to speak, on the front lines of the ghetto, scorning whitey's world, defying the conventions of the majority, seeking to make it on his own. He thus writes from the perspective of the mean streets of Detroit and Los Angeles.

The cynical ending of the Kenyatta tetralogy derives, surely, from his experience of this hard world and not from any idealism about nonviolence. Goines's view of Kenyatta's violence is that of a self-educated street man. He was born into a middle-class family, who were alarmed by his preference for the attractions of the street over education and respectable behavior. But he joined the army early, where he contracted an addiction to morphine and then heroin, and returned to Detroit to make his way in the street world of gambling and crime. His experience of violence was firsthand, unidealized. He neither romanticizes nor softens Kenyatta's ruthlessness. For all his good aims, Kenyatta's indifference to other lives is still ruthlessness, and he has the impervious hardness of a diamond. His single-minded dedication to his cause, his unshrinking courage, his charismatic leadership—all suggest his potential for heroism. But the violence he so readily employs is the sign of a moral void, and the sordidness of his defeat at the hands of the essentially inferior white dope dealer undercuts any nobility that might have accrued to his "last hit." Goines senses this deep ambiguity in his character and manages to convey it. Kenyatta goes down in the good fight, but the triumph of evil calls all in doubt. We are not sure that nonviolence would work in this savage world. But Goines suggests that, when the methods of the enemy are deployed against the enemy, the enemy tends to win.

Goines's sixteen novels, written in the short span of four years, show the marks of an amateur writer but a born storyteller. But in the Kenyatta novels, we are lucky to have his contribution to a type of behavior that few of those who wrote about the violent revolutionary knew firsthand. Working from his own ambivalence toward his material in the Kenyatta series, Goines packages King's warning in a profusion of brutal vendettas and gun fights with a pessimism that borders on nihilism. The macabre part of Goines's story is that he himself, like King, died violently. For reasons still unknown, two white men whom the police never identified shot him at his typewriter in his Detroit house. He had put all of the finishing touches on the last novel he ever wrote.[5]

Less exploitational novelists argue King's position in terms of the moral implications of violence, its ethical logic, and its dangerous effects upon black people. Arnold Kemp and Bill Webster, for example, bring out novels in 1972 in which they tell the reader that the black revolutionary is now simply claiming the right to employ the kind of violence he has always abhorred and resented, and at great cost to the African American community. In *Eat of Me, I Am the Savior,* Kemp addresses the problem of internecine violence raised in the assassination of Malcolm X in 1965. Kemp himself was in Sing Sing at the time and a follower of Islam, of Malcolm in particular. *Eat of Me* is a fictional account of the killing of Malcolm's look-alike, Nicholas Said, and the battle for power that led to it. Just as many claimed at the time about Malcolm's murder, in Kemp's novel the white man stands behind the scenes cleverly playing upon the frustration and disappointment of blacks to set them against each other. His death provokes even greater turmoil and, eventually, more blood, especially black blood.

Trying to fight it out with the white man toe to toe is an exercise in futility, for it is a simple matter of firepower and ownership of resources. Yaquii Laster learns all this after his leader is killed, and because of it he himself wants "to kill everybody, the whole world." Working against the whites, trying to bring unity to his Detroit groups, Yaquii is involved in a sequence of bloody but futile shootings and bombings. Finally, in a dreamlike conclusion, Yaquii receives a summons from the aging Prophet to lead the Nation. Artistically, this is much too abrupt to be clear or convincing, but it does enable Kemp to assert his conclusion. The Prophet, instructing Yaquii in the language of Islam, says that though the younger man "must stay and fight . . . guns alone cannot destroy the unhuman creations of

Yakub." For this, says the Prophet, putting a Muslim twist to King's Christianity, Yaquii and his people need unity and "spiritual help."[6] Attempting, as Yaquii does, to give whites their own medicine produces more black deaths than are worth it and afflicts blacks with the same disease as the whites.

Yaquii Laster changes from a vengeful revolutionist to a nonviolent activist. Bill Webster shows this conflict in two opposing characters. In the figure of Vernon Peel, he embodies his attitude toward the admired Black Power revolutionary we saw in chapter 10. He distantly modeled Peel on Oakland Black Panther leader Huey P. Newton, who in 1967 was accused of killing a policeman. Newton steadfastly claimed his innocence of the deed, and eventually a higher court threw out a lower-court manslaughter conviction. In *One By One,* Vernon Peel is a distasteful young man whose revolutionary defiance comes to look like self-promoting boasting. He, too, is brought to trial for the killing of a policeman. But instead of challenging the system he has treated with such scorn, Peel admits he shot the policeman but claims innocence on the ground of a "racial-induced mental disorder," justifying murder on the grounds that he had a bad life in the ghetto where he grew up.[7] This is a defense Tatty Johnson, Lutie Johnson, and Jesse Robinson do not think of claiming. And Webster sees it as moral waffling. Peel and his lawyer are cynically playing the system in order to save the revolutionary's skin, admitting the system's legal authority, and seeking loopholes in it through which they can escape. Moreover, Ben Waddell, Webster's prosecutor protagonist, maintains that such a defense, given credence, would excuse even the atrocities of whites against blacks, on the grounds that the whites were subjected to a conditioning that made them racially prejudiced and hence not legally responsible for their acts. Instead, we all must accept personal responsibility and be tried "one by one."

SATIRIZING THE VIOLENT HERO: ISHMAEL REED AND OTHERS

A number of novelists expand Webster's disapproval and draw the revolutionary as a cynical self-promoter, manipulating ghetto dwellers and playing upon their idealism and their longing for leaders they can admire and trust. The revolutionary role becomes a refuge for scoundrels, unscrupulous supernationalists, whom the novelists attack through satire and direct invective. Roosevelt Mallory's Leroy Johnson, a Malcolm X character in *Harlem Hit* (1973), joins a "volatile religious group" when he gets out of prison and advocates "a separate nation for people of color, and violence for violence." Leroy pretends to "clean up crime" in the ghetto but really plans to take over control for himself. "And his followers believed him to be benevolent," the sarcastic narrator tells us.[8] In Omar Fletcher's *Walking Black and Tall* (1977), Malcolm Lumumba independently struggles against both the Mafia and a radical black revolutionary group, the Muslims. He concludes that "The Muslim leader was as ruthless in his way as the mafia *patrone* was in his."[9] And the Reverend Truman Blood, creator and leader of the Church of the New Day Revolution, in Joseph Nazel's *Street Wars* (1987), is simply out for power and money, not a reformation of society for his downtrodden ghetto dwellers. In searching for a large sum of money to conduct his organization, he brutally kills innocent people, even the mother of one of his church's members. And in her widely unnoticed short novel *Francisco* (1974), Alison Mills expresses a hip California opinion about revolutionaries. Her young woman narrator says she hates them: "they all turn out to be movie stars in this country anyway, or the government puts them in jail and fucks with their brains through some drugs producing chemical changes then releases them when they can't see straight no more, seems like most of the breakthroughs have been broken up. seems like almost everybody has been bought."[10]

Yet other writers undercut the image of the revolutionary on the basis of one of the oldest positions in the literature—that blacks are simply incapable of organizing and staying together long enough to make any kind of effective violent campaign possible. If the revolutionaries are not bought, as Mills's character insists, they meet the implacable indifference of the black public. Barry Beckham's *Runner Mack* (1972) is a funny–sad, surrealistic little book in which the innocent naif of a hero is converted to revolution by Runnington Mack, a charismatic leader who believes fervently in violent revolution for freeing American blacks. Not interested in starting small, they decide they have to bomb the White House first and take over the whites' resources so "we can start getting our own black thing together." But when only five people show up at what they expected to be a huge meeting to kick off their campaign, the sincere but naive planner of the affair, Runnington Mack, hangs himself in despair. "We keep trying and planning," he says before his suicide, "and it doesn't mean anything. History keeps going and we keep trying and nothing happens."[11] Fate itself works against optimism. Mack's "student" in revolution, Henry Adams, deliberately named to suggest the growth of Henry from innocence to understanding that *The Education of Henry Adams* depicts, gets hit by a truck after discovering Mack's dead body. The failure here turns not so much on an impeding world as on the black public's rejection of action, the inability of the community to do what is necessary even in its own behalf. "When the deal goes down," says Beckham, commenting on his ending, "there's no one there, although we've had all these plans and so much enthusiasm has been shown for the project." [12]

The pathos of *Runner Mack* also contains an element of bitter humor, and this puts it with the distinctly minority voices that satirize rather than celebrate the violent guerrilla revolutionary during the Black Power years. Ishmael Reed, writing a few years earlier, also refused to take the Black Power revolutionary seriously. As for that, Reed's first novel, a fictional satire called *The Free-Lance Pallbearers* (1967), takes nothing seriously. Bukka Doopeyduk and his wife Fannie Mae, the Reverend Eclair Porkchop, Judge Whimplewhopper, Arboreal Hairyman, and Harry Sam, the democratically elected dictator of HARRY SAM, all get battered by Reed's satirical club. They come out of America's zaniest traditions: *Mad Comics,* Max Schulman, the Nathanael West of *A Cool Million* and *The Dream Life of Balso Snell.* Bukka himself starts out as a young man piously devoted to the myths about hard work, thrift, and blacks keeping their place. Ungrammatical dictator Harry Sam promulgates these values cynically to control the populace. But after being divorced by Fannie Mae, roughed up on stage while working for Entropy Productions, and falsely quoted as advocating violence in overthrowing Harry Sam, Bukka abandons his gee-whiz awe of Harry Sam and himself leads a bloody attack against Harry. "We tore the Swiss guards to pieces," writes Bukka in euphoria, and when Harry's gnomes come to his defense, "they were no match for my greasy stompers who mashed them as if they were so many pesky little bugs." [13]

The Black Power movement is not Reed's exclusive target, but all people who thirst for power, all *systems.* Like Ralph Ellison, he has a deep aversion to any institution that would bend people to its beliefs. That is why he ridicules the heroic revolutionary and his insistence that he and his violence represent the liberating power. As Bukka pushes Sam into the noxious poisons of the Black Bay, which Sam himself has created to protect himself, Bukka now crows that *he* will take over the country. "NOW I WAS DA ONE," says Bukka in that peculiar truck-driver patois in which Reed has his characters speak. "ME DICTATOR OF BUKKA DOOPEYDUK." Like all dictators, Bukka sees the nation over which he hopes to rule as simply an extension of himself (112–13). But systems seem to have a life of their own, and instead of ruling his, Bukka gets hung up on meat hooks by it, while the "next-in-rank on the Civil Service list" gets sworn in to head the country. This makes no difference in the end, though, since the Communist Chinese, who have been infiltrating the land from the beginning of the narrative, take over, and we are to assume that this entire story has been "WRITTEN IN CHINESE NO LESS" (116). Against world-class revolution, the small-bore Black Power figure, which Reed locates in the middle of the minstrel tradition, hasn't a chance.

Instead of advocating nonviolence, Reed shows how absurd is the revolutionary who borrows the same means for his liberation as has been used for his suppression. The Western white man has systematically beaten down his opponents with violence, says Reed, made victims of us all, imposing on us a view of the world and a sensibility that excludes all mystery from our lives, all magic, all laughter, joy, singing, dancing, aesthetic pleasure. The proper weapon for freeing ourselves of this view is not more violence and more systems but disentangling from the suppressive tentacles the values that will give us life. Reed's villains in *Yellow Back Radio Broke-Down* (1969), for instance, are western cowboys with their blazing six-guns and the eastern establishment with its anachronistic ray guns, who destroy themselves and others in mind-numbing battles that parody the conventional notion of the West. His hero is their opposite, the "devil incarnate," the Loop Garoo Kid, joyful and fun-loving, a master of hoodoo and the spirit of art, the supporter of nonviolence. Loop survives a vicious conspiracy against him led by outlaw John Wesley Hardin, remaining alive to receive the pope, who comes after him to persuade him to go back to the old homestead in the sky. In *Mumbo Jumbo* (1972), set in 1920s New York City, Biff Musclewhite and Hinckle Von Vampton symbolize the white killer tradition. They attempt to staunch the flow of African American spirit entering the country in the form of "Jes Grew," the irresistible impulse to dance, for it threatens the long-faced seriousness of white rationalism. They personally kill several of the blacks working to ease Jes Grew into the land. Papa Labas, one of Reed's favorite characters, opposes them through nonviolent means like those used by the Loop Garoo Kid: intelligence, the old religions, and the powers nature gives to us, rather than through the great upheavals fomented by the Black Power revolutionary. And he thinks more of the people than of promoting himself. In the end, he is moderately successful, exposing the true criminals, but without the power to establish Jes Grew permanently in America.

JOHN EDGAR WIDEMAN: THE DARK SIDE OF THE BLACK POWER HERO

John Edgar Wideman's satire on the heroic revolutionary in *The Lynchers* (1973) takes quite a different tack. Wideman paints the image in the dark colors of sadness. Certainly the satiric element is there, but his would-be revolutionary is too weakened by the system he talks about overthrowing for us to laugh at him or feel anything but the pathos in the gap between his desire and his ability. Like Beckham, Wideman was, in the early seventies, looking for a new way of expressing the frustration in the black community as the black revolution was winding down and the nation was beginning to pay attention to issues other than the civil rights movement. That *The Lynchers* is part realism and part fantasy suggests, like *Runner Mack,* that the real world is too crazy and incoherent to be accurately depicted realistically.[14] Wideman loves words, and in *The Lynchers* he speculates on the relationship between the words of his characters and the reality with which they struggle, and he finds that there is very little there. His revolutionary is mostly words and little reality.

The wordsmith of *The Lynchers* is Willie Hall, otherwise known as "Littleman" on South Street, Philadelphia. Littleman is far from being the gigantic sexual power that some romantics admired. The legs attached to his dwarfish body are so weak that he has to wear braces. He compensates for these twin deformities, as well as for his color, with intellectual pride and an outpouring of fevered analyses of the racial situation. Willie Hall does not speak for Wideman in the way that Max Reddick speaks for John A Williams. Willie's physical disabilities are metaphors for the African American revolutionary's weaknesses in an impregnable white world. He has only his words left, and Wideman seems as interested in those, and the motives behind them, as in his statements about the treatment blacks receive at the hands of whites.

One of Willie's problems is that for him words are reality. He is very good with them, but he cannot seem to get beyond them to action, and this frustrates and depresses him. As he looks around South Street, he perceives it in terms of how it affects him. "This street means they are killing us, whittling away day by day, a man, a woman, a baby at a time." This makes him "weak and sick." To preserve his balance, all Willie can do is believe that some day the "scab" of this city will be "peeled back so air can get to the wounded land."[15] Unlike Wideman's first two novels, *A Glance Away* (1967) and *Hurry Home* (1970), *The Lynchers* contains all the elements of the racial protest novel—the citation of the general white crime against black people, the expression of anger, the articulation of what needs to be done. It is, however, a negative image of the protest novel. Wideman puts something in Littleman's speeches—which is usually the form his conversation takes—that hints at all this being just talk, and this hint gives the novel its distinctive flavor and separates it from such inferior Black Power novels as *'Sippi* and *The Spook Who Sat by the Door.* Littleman *is* a little man. That and his blackness drive him to seek the grandeur of which his condition deprives him. The interior view that Wideman gives us of this mad ghetto-created Napoleon is a more devastating comment upon the puerility of Greenlee's Dan Freeman or Jackson's Aaron Rodgers than any critical argument.

Littleman has a plan for pulling the city down. It calls for lynching a white policeman. No specific occurrence has aroused Littleman to this scheme, no desire for vengeance. Any such passion would contaminate the enterprise. To be valid and to demonstrate that blacks now have the same power over whites as whites had over blacks in the old southern lynching days, this city lynching must be symbolic and ritualistic, like the traditional southern lynching, "brutally and arbitrarily" performed. "A great artist must have conceived the first lynching," he says, and he envies the man. For the victims among his own race he expresses little sympathy. It is art, not pity, he is talking about: "You better believe that poor lynched darky blinks his message like a lighthouse through the misty countryside" (61). To equal the artistry of the South, Littleman and the co-conspirators he enlists must lynch the specifically innocent but generally guilty cop in the midst of an approving crowd, while black policemen look on benignly.

This is Black Power distilled of any social aim or impurities of emotion. Through the lynching, Littleman seeks to mark their understanding of and break with the imprisoning past. It will express their decision not to fear what they have always been taught to fear. It will introduce a new black, defined by his refusal to be humiliated. That in turn will mean the achievement of a separate communal identity, for the black community will sanction the act, just as the southern community did. The white world would get the message: that blacks are now the equal of whites, that there will be "no more battles in which only one side is allowed to fight" (118). Here are all the old expectations of the romanticized guerrilla fighter: the need to change white minds about the manhood of blacks, the fantasy of sudden, apocalyptic change. Littleman has all the old philosophical answers about communal unity and some of the new ones about violence. Blacks have hitherto failed to rise up in violent retaliation because they have been afraid to die, preferring "the worst [the whites] can do to death" (118). This terror has in the past isolated them from each other. Now that isolation must be overcome. Blacks must take back the only significant choice they have, to give something value by choosing to die for it, a "decision to make some arbitrary event or choice worth your life" (119).

Richard Wright and John A. Williams, among others, take this argument seriously. But Littleman is a rhetorician who loves to talk, who revels in logic and language. The correspondence between his language-fantasy and reality tends to be fragile. For much of the novel, he lies in a hospital bed, injured when he fell down a flight of steps (how the mighty have fallen!)

during one of his extemporaneous harangues outside a junior high school. From his bed, he spins dreams in his glorious cadences to anyone who will listen, like slow-witted Anthony, the black hospital attendant, who is puzzled but awed by the vain little black man in the all-white room. But Littleman has his successes. He has attracted three other men to his plot. All of them, however, in this asylum of cracked pieces of black humanity, are unstable in deep ways, suspicious and contemptuous of each other, hiding their weaknesses and their fears.

For much of the novel, dense with the florid and convincing oratory of Littleman and the details of the others' lives, we believe that its true reality lies in the validity of the lynching plan, and we await its execution. Wideman substantiates this belief with a series of quotations listed without comment at the beginning of his narrative, pointing to the violence with which blacks have been treated in America, including a long list of names of blacks who were beaten or killed by the Klan and other organizations after the Civil War. The list comes from a petition to the president for laws to protect the newly freed slaves. The deep silence surrounding the petition, both Wideman's muteness and our own knowledge that no laws were passed to aid such victims, throws into relief the evidence that explains how Littleman could be moved to devise such a plot as his and justifies his carrying it out if he can.

But the conspirators who would execute the lynching have been psychologically disabled by the system they dream of destroying. It has conditioned them to a sense of inferiority and helplessness, the defect that African American literature has worked hardest to eradicate. Thomas Wilkerson, neurotically preoccupied with a father who, as Thomas sees it, has given up, wants to weep for all the would-be revolutionaries who can live only in their "puny dreams," "lying, cheating, even killing to avoid the simple truth" (144). To others, the plan is "insane," "ugly and sick." And finally, on the designated night, one conspirator shoots another, and Littleman, the leader, drifts off into a paralyzed stupor on the verge of death. In an interview, Wideman suggests that, though Littleman and his colleagues fail to carry through their plan, they have become different people. They have won something. "It doesn't make any difference," Wideman says, whether the conspirators pull their plot off and bring America to "Armageddon" but that they "are changed," apparently for the better, "more by their imagination than they are by actual external events." [16]

It is difficult, however, to draw anything positive out of this novel except the fact that Wideman still retains enough hope to write it. In it, no objective relationship holds between words and reality, rhetoric and deeds. It throws doubt on the possibility that black men can act effectively at all.

Moreover, it negates that period of optimism about black capabilities that commenced with *Native Son,* when Bigger Thomas instinctively threw off the psychological bonds of total white domination. Wideman passes no judgment on the morality of violence or its validity as a weapon blacks might use in opening up a closed racist society. But in this mirthless and merciless satire, his primary comment seems to be upon the *rhetoric* of Black Power, and the quality of dream and abstraction that pervades the thinking and the proclamations of its advocates. In *The Lynchers,* Wideman reduces the stars of the radical sixties to four neurotic bunglers who do more harm to each other than to their enemies. He turns the heroism of the black warrior into the ineffectual self-destructive posturing of four failures, psychically deformed by a racially oppressive society. And he turns the novel to a literary rather than a social use, since for Wideman it is the imagination of Littleman and his co-conspirators and the way those imaginations were shaped that are important.

Wideman is still concerned with the issue of retaliatory violence and the rage of the ineffectual black man fourteen years later in *Reuben* (1987). The protagonist of that novel is Wally, a basketball recruiter with his base in Pittsburgh. Like Littleman, he has a *theory* of vengeance. It guides him in his one-man campaign of murder against white men. It is the theory of "abstract hate." Wally starts with the classical African American victim, the man lynched by the Ku Klux Klan, the woman raped by her husband's killers. Driven insane by the trauma, the woman kills her children. The white men who perpetrate this atrocity hated in the abstract and kill in the abstract. Wally thinks like Littleman: For his revenge to be perfectly reciprocally balanced, he must retaliate in the abstract, kill white men as abstract representations of the race that killed blacks. "Nothing personal, you dig. Letting off steam in a way." The main thing is that "You free yourself from the burden of what they've done to you." [17]

Wally tells a story of such a revenge killing, in which he anonymously kills an anonymous white man, like a private member of Toni Morrison's Seven Days Society or John Killens's avengers in *'Sippi.* We cannot tell, however, whether the events he recounts really took place, whether the victims of the southern lynchings were Wally's family or not, whether, even, he actually tells the story. Layers of fantasy intermingle with layers of objective reality. In the story that Wally might be telling Reuben, the killer is a basketball recruiter, a thin masquerade for himself. But when he is finished, Reuben, Wally's friend and the dwarfish character who gives the story his name, asks what the reader must ask: "Is the story true?" [18] Wideman's answer perhaps would be the same as his comment on *The Lynchers.* It makes no difference whether it is true or not. The important thing is what it shows about Wally, the depth of his hatred, the images that hatred moves him to contemplate. Judging from what he says of Littleman, Wideman would see Wally's story and his theories about killing whites as working changes within him that are just as important as the effects of any overt urban guerrilla campaign upon American racial relations. This validates novel writing, imagining rather than doing. Fantasies may not build buildings, but they change people, and when people change inside, their overt lives change, too. A novel's words have the power to affect how we think about things, keeping alive the sense that profoundly frustrated people persist in imagining violent solutions to their frustrations.

But the net effect of both *The Lynchers* and *Reuben* is the futility of black vengeance and the impossibility of carrying out the programs of Black Power conceived in the days when almost everything seemed possible. Wideman's tortured characters show not a liberation from white suppression but an intensified sense of imprisonment within the psychic bars racially imposed, and an increased paralysis that results from it. The 1987 date of *Reuben* suggests that pockets of frustration over violence still exist in the black community and in the African American novel that would give voice to the community's feelings. Those novelists who dismantle the heroic revolutionary's image express a sense of failure that is immune to Black Power optimism. They seem to acknowledge reluctantly that, if they cannot harness violence to their goals, manhood and their goals are lost.

[12]

IT ENDS IN BROTHERHOOD:
TONI MORRISON'S
SONG OF SOLOMON

They were as true as steel, and no band of brothers could have been more loving. There were no mean advantages taken of each other, as is sometimes the case where slaves are situated as we were; no tattling; no giving each other bad names to Mr. Freeland; and no elevating one at the expense of the other. We never undertook to do anything, of any importance, which was likely to affect each other, without mutual consultation. We were generally a unit, and moved together. Thoughts and sentiments were exchanged between us, which might well be called very incendiary, by oppressors and tyrants.

Frederick Douglass, My Bondage and My Freedom

ECONOMIC AND FEMINIST FORCES BEHIND
THE DISSOLUTION OF THE BLACK POWER HERO

During the decade or so that Black Power was a provocative force on the American scene,[1] African American imagery was dominated by a heavily male sensibility. Stokely Carmichael, H. Rap Brown, George Jackson, Huey Newton, Eldridge Cleaver—their language, both visual and linguistic, set the definitions of the period. They brought to a climax the view that authentic manhood and heroism were the prime object of the black male's search, that those qualities were defined in contest with white men and their institutions, and that they were based upon the readiness to draw white blood. Of all issues, they suggested, these were the ones that most urgently needed to be addressed. And for a while, to judge from the attention they got, the public and many black novelists seemed to agree with them. Between 1968 and 1972, the high years of the movement, the *Reader's Guide to Periodical Literature* listed nearly 80 articles under the heading of "Black Power," and some 140 under the "Black Panther Party," the most conspicuous organization embodying the movement's principles. In the history of the African American novel of violence, the Black Power period was a logical outgrowth of over a hundred years of artistic and political grappling with a wide variety of images of victims and heroes. It was a conclusion in which the focus of the argument narrowed to the image of the violent hero.

The dismantlers of this image, whom I dealt with in the last chapter, did not kill it. Its obliteration came at the hands of other forces, which were accumulating even while Black Power advocates seemed most in control of the public debate. In reaction to the challenge of the Black Power organizations, the nation's various police groups drove the most active purveyors of the movement underground, forced them into exile, or killed them.[2] With the most noticeable agitators out of the way and their organizations disempowered, cries of "police brutality" ceased to command headlines. Extralegal white vigilante strikes against blacks, long in steep decline anyway, disappeared. More blacks took public office. In Congress the Black Caucus was formed. Complex socioeconomic changes were also taking place. The social programs of the "Great Society," in the opinion of some, helped bring about an expansion of the black middle class and its flight from the ghetto.[3] With the migration of this group, and under the pressures of unemployment, illegitimacy, drugs, and crime, the deterioriation of the black inner city, already well under way in the 1950s, accelerated. Inflation, the oil embargo, the first signs of the white middle-class wage earner's losing ground, and an increasing white resentment at perceived racial favoritism—all of this drew attention away from Black Power as a significant feature of the consciousness of both the black and the white public. By 1977 interest in the generic revolutionary guerrilla band and its proper definition had dropped sharply. Between March 1977 and February 1978, just three items on the Black Panthers appeared in the periodicals indexed by the *Reader's Guide,* and none on Black Power. National attention had shifted from the student protests connected with the Vietnam War and the civil rights movement to other concerns. John Edgar Wideman's *Reuben* (1987) exemplifies some continuing interest in the old-style racial violence in the African American novel. But in the seventies, new authors appeared with different concerns, reflecting the new directions of the general public.

Black women in particular began writing novels in unprecedented numbers, and they introduced a whole new sensibility that had a special bearing upon the theme of heroic violence. A correlative of the Black Power position during its high years was the role the revolutionary hero expected women to play: satisfier of men's sexual urges and server at their table. On the surface, the black woman seemed to accept these criteria for establishing her racial validity: subservience to black men and the glory of rhetorical violence. With all the stridency of an Eldridge Cleaver or H. Rap Brown, Nikki Giovanni wrote "Nigger / Can you kill / Can you kill / Can a nigger kill / Can a nigger kill a honkie?" Black Panther Elaine Brown felt that the high point of her life was when she became Huey Newton's "queen," at least until she suceeded him, very briefly, as the leader of the mostly male party.[4] Even a nationally known black woman like Angela Davis, for all her radical brilliance and independence, seemed a kind of handmaiden to the men.[5] And black men certainly outnumbered black women in the production of novels. The sexism both overt and implicit in the Black Power movement brought to the surface a gender antagonism that had hitherto seldom been the object of attention, an antagonism which combined with other forces to cause the demise of the Black Power hero. Before the mid-sixties, the tribulations of race and the exigencies of the labor market tended to draw black men and women together. Certainly, some women novelists attacked black male chauvinism, as Zora Neale Hurston did in *Their Eyes Were Watching God* (1937) with her devastating portraits of Logan Killicks and Joe Starks. Nella Larsen gives us a depressing picture of Helga Crane's entrapment in her life with the coarse Reverend Pleasant Green in *Quicksand* (1928). And Calvin Hernton, in *The Sexual Mountain and Black Women Writers* (1987), argues persuasively for Ann Petry's *The Street* (1946) as a feminist exposure of the injustice with which black women are treated by their own men.[6] But, by and large, there is no sustained gender antagonism before we get into the late sixties and early seventies. Both Toni Morrison and sociologist Robert Staples speak of the "comradeship" of black husbands and wives in administering their households.[7]

With the appearance of the Black Power hero and the explosion of white and black feminist activity, that sense of solidarity and equivalence was, at least in the public discussion, greatly weakened. The heroic image that black men projected as a means of improving life for African Americans came to be perceived by some women as a device for aggrandizing black men, with no significant place left for women in a movement that not only was potentially violent but whose leadership was almost exclusively male. Alice Walker acknowledges the gender division in *Meridian*. She defines the ambivalence the division produces in women who believe in the larger revolution and wish a part in it but are blocked by those black men, as Walker implies, whose demonstration of masculinity consists of talking inflammatory rhetoric and bedding as many women as possible, especially white ones. Meridian's anxiety that she cannot be violent is a personal concern no Black Power male ever expresses. Her decision to march *behind* the men who make up the revolutionary vanguard, bloodying their hands in the gore of the enemy and endangering their own lives, is a resolution no male character makes, and it fits in with the expectation the Black Power male has of his women. Meridian concedes the necessity of violence in the revolution, and she can imagine noble black male heroism in the form of the figure in the little country church's stained glass window. But she personally encounters no such males, nor does she experience revolutionary violence. The men in her world seem only to seek to exploit her as a woman rather than free her as an African American.

Walker was among the first new women writers resolved to reform the terms in which the images of black men and women were explored fictively. As early as 1967, she was writing what she later came to call "womanist" short stories, collecting them in *In Love and Trouble* (1973). These are tales, she says, about black women, "mad, raging, loving, resentful, hateful, strong, ugly, weak, pitiful, and magnificent." The women in them are not defined in terms of their black men, who appear distinctly unheroic. They are on their own, and they are, for Walker, "the most fascinating creations in the world."[8] In 1970 Walker publishes *The Third Life of Grange Copeland* and joins the reaction to the Black Power movement, which began to tilt perceptions of blackness in new directions. From this start, an unprecedented number of novels appeared between the mid-seventies and mid-eighties by black women asserting their own notions of who they were and what it was important to write about. Even black males began to complain about male chauvinism. In *Scarecrow* (1974), Calvin Hernton has one of his female characters criticize black men for using black women the same way white men use white women. They seek to imprison them in the cell of the ideal, consign them to domestic house service, make them bear babies, not because they like children or want to be fathers but to signal their masculinity.[9] Black women writers, though, are the most aggressive on the issue. In *Loving Her* (1974), Ann Allen Shockley represents men as repugnant beasts who tend to equate sexual dominance with Black Power and their own manliness. In this sensual celebration of female love, Shockley speaks aggressively for the lesbian view of the black male's struggle for manliness. Shockley's heroine, Renay, is puzzled by the black heterosexual woman's loyalty to black men: "strangely, they still love their men, work for them, pity them, bear the seed of their spawn, and take the outrage of those who can't be black warriors. I think it is this sympathy, understanding, tolerance and above all, hope that someday their males *will* rightfully become men in our society that helps them to cling to being women. And to the dream of becoming women in the way they would like to be."[10] The pitying tone of this and the subtly expressed assumption that it will be a long time before black males will ever become *men,* let alone warriors, create more havoc with the male heroic image than any straight invective. That is what Michele Wallace gives us in her scornful caricature of the male-generated image of the Black Power hero:

wooly heads, big black fists and stern black faces, gargantuan omnipotent black male organs, big black rifles and foot-long combat boots, tight pants over young muscular asses, dashikis, and broad brown chests; black men looting and rioting in the streets, taking over the country by brute force, arrogant lawlessness and an unquestionable sexual authority.[11]

Wallace expresses the rancor in much of the feminist writing of the last couple of decades: "The picture drawn for us over and over again is of a man who is a child, who is the constant victim of an unholy alliance between his woman and the enemy, the white man." Black women are accused of causing the plight of the black male: "*You* crippled the black man. *You* worked against him. *You* betrayed him. *You* laughed at him. *You* scorned him. *You* and the white man."[12] Shug Avery, in Alice Walker's *The Color Purple* (1982), tells Celie that "Man corrupt everything. . . . He on our box of grits, in your head, and all over the radio. He try to make you think he everywhere. Soon as you think he everywhere, you think he God. But he ain't."[13] More desperately, and only slightly less venomously, Pearl Cleage explains that she writes largely to deal with the brutality of the black man: "I am writing because five women a day are murdered by the men who say they love them. I am writing because rape is. . . . I am writing because I have seen my sisters tortured and tormented by the fathers of their children. I am writing because I almost married a man who beat me regularly and with no remorse."[14]

This new friction, together with the social, political, and economic forces now coming into play, reflects the changes in the perception of what was important to the nation and to African Americans, and the violent Black Power hero and racial violence are eclipsed as urgent topics. Black novelists stop focusing sympathetically with a sense of *contemporary* concern upon such fictional revolutionary guerrilla bands as John O. Killens's Elders in *'Sippi* (1967) or Sam Greenlee's Cobras in *The Spook Who Sat by the Door* (1969). Ernest J. Gaines, who in *The Autobiography of Miss Jane Pittman* (1971) set the standard of that period for the fictional nonviolent militant hero, exemplifies the changes in the novelistic climate of the late seventies and early eighties. *A Gathering of Old Men* (1983), which I discussed in chapter 10 in connection with the new attitudes toward the violent hero, celebrates not black violence against a racist system but rather the success of a group of old men who discover their courage to resist some Cajun

thugs whom even the white sheriff seeks to restrain. Even more indicative
is the experience of Phillip Martin, in Gaines's *In My Father's House* (1978).
In undertaking a quest into his past to try to find an explanation for what
went wrong between himself and his natural son, Martin encounters an all
but anonymous young man named Billy. Billy, a bitter veteran of Vietnam,
has been training some other young blacks in "guerrilla tactics," in order
to confront the corrupt white establishment and, like Sam Greenlee's Dan
Freeman and Blyden Jackson's Aaron Rodgers, bring it down.[15] But the
incident is not part of the Black Power argument. It is an illustration of
Phillip's personal life, an analogy of his flawed relationship with his son, as
well as a more general example of the failed relationships of so many black
men and their sons. It is personal, introspective, and meditative rather than
political. Among women writers, examples of countermovement novelists
abound: Gayle Jones, Rosa Guy, Jamaica Kincaid, Ntozake Shange, Toni
Cade Bambara, Gloria Naylor, and Terry McMillan, who, after Alice
Walker and Toni Morrison, dominate the fiction by African American
women in the 1980s and 1990s. Sherley Anne Williams, one of the few
of this group who deals with racial violence, overlays that theme in her
slave–narrative novel *Dessa Rose* (1986) with an emphasis upon the subtle
and nuanced relationship between Dessa Rose, the runaway slave, and
Rufel, the white woman who harbors her. Dessa proves she is capable of
violence by helping to kill the brutal white men who abuse the slaves in
the coffle they are taking south for sale. But the incident in which both
slaves and white men are killed is much more important to Nehemiah, the
white man who tries to appropriate Dessa's story, than to Williams. He
dwells in morbid fascination upon Dessa's exploit and her "devil's eyes"
and "devil's stare." [16] For Williams, though, the center of the novel's gravity
is the developing mutual respect and cooperation between the two women
rather than dominance through force or vengeance.[17]

SONG OF SOLOMON

In the history of the African American novel of racial violence, Toni
Morrison's *Song of Solomon* (1977) is the most important work since Ralph
Ellison's *Invisible Man* (1952) and James Baldwin's *Go Tell It on the Mountain*
(1953). It is, of all Morrison's novels to date, the one that deals most
pointedly with the topics I have discussed in this book and that most
effectively illustrates the new attitudes toward racial violence. Nor has any
other novel trumped it since. It brings to bear upon the themes of the
Black Power movement and the whole tradition of the debate over racial
violence the concerns and viewpoints of a new sensibility. Morrison writes,

however, as a woman rather than a feminist, and an African American rather than a nationalist. She treats the black male and the violence of his life with a combination of criticism, humor, and affection. The novel is no simplistic feminist put-down of black men. Morrison does not complain, as other feminists did, that men's hints and threats about violence—their outright celebration of it—are part and parcel of their purported historical failure to meet their real obligations as husbands and fathers. She does not ridicule the black man's search for manhood through the Black Power movement or mock it as adolescent arrogance, irresponsibility, or puerile obsession with sex. Because she sees the behavior of her male characters as part of a complex network of historical and mythic forces analogous to that in which the black woman is caught, Morrison's view of men is less adversarial and more sympathetic than that of many of her feminist contemporaries. She has no sexual agenda in the novel, no plan to expose men at their worst and then show them "reforming" along feminist lines. The biblical *Song of Solomon* is the great erotic love poem of the Old Testament. Morrison's novel is a prose song about the special comradeship inherent in the African American male relationship. To be sure, that relationship is fraught with distrust, anger, and competitiveness. But set as it was for so many years in an inescapable circle of white American racial violence, the black male group developed its own code of brotherhood, which redeemed victims and tested heroes. It created ties between its members that may have been painful but that gave the African American man a sense of some identity in a world that made him an alien. No African American novelist renders this world any more convincingly or less sentimentally than Toni Morrison, or with any greater understanding of its weaknesses and conflicts as well as its strengths and harmonies.

It is her deeply sympathetic perception of the psychopolitical dynamic inherent in the black male need to fantasize violent retaliation against white violence and her grasp of the self-destructive implications of that need that make *Song of Solomon* the appropriate novel with which to conclude my discussion of the treatment of racial violence in the African American novel. This comes out specifically in the arguments about violence between Macon ("Milkman") Dead and Guitar Bains, together with the Seven Days Society and its secret charter to retaliate in kind when "a Negro child, Negro woman, or Negro man is killed by whites and nothing is done about it by *their* law and *their* courts."[18] The friendship between Milkman and Guitar, as well as their enmity, illustrates the tensions between black males that arise in the debate over violence and the struggle to decide upon the proper image to emulate. Morrison's story of the clash between Milkman and Guitar shifts attention from the heroic warrior to brotherhood—its pains, contradictions, and supportive power. This shift hints at an awareness of the new violence between young black males that had already begun in the seventies to tear at the fabric of the economically depressed black inner city. It is as if Morrison is saying that brotherhood and selflessness, for all the difficulty in attaining them, are crucial to black identity and survival. The heroic age is past. The time when images must be created to give blacks courage to face white prejudice in the form of violence is past. Blacks must now attend to their own world, make their own choices within their own black world, not ignoring or excluding the real presence of whites but rejecting them as the principal condition of black being. The point is not to affect postures of heroic attacks upon whites but to teach themselves to make the choices for living as full human beings.

Song of Solomon is the story of Milkman Dead, the last surviving member of the Dead family, whose history started with the African slave Shalimar (or Solomon). Like the slaves in the old folktales, Shalimar "flew" back to Africa. He left behind him a town—Shalimar, Virginia—peopled largely by his descendants. When freedom comes Shalimar's youngest son acquires his name, Macon Dead, from a drunken Yankee soldier registering ex-slaves and moves north to Danville, Pennsylvania. Here he becomes such a successful farmer that the local whites kill him for his land and his effrontery. His son, Macon II, and daughter, Pilate, escape the same fate but argue bitterly over a sack of gold they find in the Hunters Cave that hides them. Pilate wants nothing to do with the gold and prevents her brother from taking it as well. Macon's greed severs the family tie and separates him from what is now the truly Dead past. Pilate falls lovingly under the spell of her father's spirit and undertakes an odyssey in search of accommodation with his troubled ghost. Macon, though, believes that she has run off with the gold. From then on he distrusts her, especially when she arrives in the unnamed Great Lakes city where he lives the year before *his* son, Macon III, is born and embarrasses him with her vulgar behavior and indifference to his bourgeois values. Theirs is the polarization of the black community in the years before and after World War I, when a middle class developed and sought to reject the old slave-peasant connections and folk tradition.

By the time Macon III is born in 1931, Macon II has become the wealthiest black man in the Michigan town where he settles. His social rigidity and obsession with owning things reinforce the already well-advanced neurosis of his wife, Ruth, and lead to the severe repression of his two daughters, First Corinthians and Magdalene Called Lena. In a classic instance of a black mother obstructing her son's growth into manhood, Ruth nurses Macon III well into his early childhood as a substitute for the love she has never received from her husband. From this abnormal relationship, Macon III receives the name by which he is thenceforth addressed by nearly everyone. Brought up in the isolation of material plenty and middle-class snobbery by his money-hungry father, Milkman is cut off from his past, kept from the salutary racial and maternal influences of his Aunt Pilate, and rendered powerless to realize the full masculinity of his two ancestral models—his grandfather Macon (Jake) Dead and his great-grandfather Solomon. He complains about undeserved suffering, ignores his sisters as their life potential is sacrificed for him, and exploits his cousin Hagar sexually and then drops her with a polite thank-you (267). By the time he reaches adulthood, he has settled into an enveloping ennui. He "avoided commitment and strong feelings, and shied away from decisions. He wanted to know as little as possible, to feel only enough to get through the day amiably and to be interesting enough to warrant the curiosity of other people" (181). He is filled with "tentativeness, doubt, and inauthenticity" (184). "His life was pointless, aimless, and it was true that he didn't concern himself an awful lot with other people There was nothing he wanted bad enough to risk anything for, inconvenience himself for" (107).

When he is thirty-two years old Milkman finally decides he must leave town and go out on his own. He thinks he finds the financial means for this when his father tells him about the gold Pilate is supposed to have in her possession. Simultaneously, Guitar Bains requires money to carry out an assignment he has just been given by the Seven Days. Their robbery of Pilate gains them only a bag of bones. But Milkman heads for Pennsylvania and Hunters Cave, where he is convinced the gold remains. By this time, though, his search has become an expedition into his past. He finds no gold in Danville, but he does learn a great deal about his grandfather. This only enlarges his ignorance, so he follows the fragile thread of information that leads him to Shalimar. There everything falls into place.[19] He discovers the story of his great-grandfather and deduces that the bones in the bag Pilate has carried since Hunters Cave are those of her father, and that they must be buried on Solomon's Leap. In the meantime, Guitar has decided that Milkman found the gold and tried to steal his share of it. He pursues his old friend to Shalimar and there makes an unsuccessful attempt to kill him.

All these threads come together in the hills above the little town that bears Milkman's great-grandfather's name. As Milkman and Pilate finish burying Jake Dead's bones, Guitar, waiting below, shoots Pilate, apparently intending to hit Milkman. With Pilate dead at his feet, Milkman stands up, knowing that Guitar waits in the night to "try to blow his head off" (341). But his experiences have transformed him. He understands that the significance of his entire life is on the line and that it depends upon how he faces up to his old friend, his "brother man," who wants his life; that it depends upon a readiness he has never had before to put himself at ultimate risk. "You want my life?" he calls down to Guitar. "You need it? Here I am!" He is ready now to give up everything to confirm his being (the hills echo *"am am am"*):

Without wiping away the tears, taking a deep breath, or even bending his knees—he leaped. As fleet and bright as a lodestar he wheeled toward Guitar and it did not matter which one of them would give up his ghost in the killing arms of his brother. For now he knew what Shalimar knew: If you surrendered to the air, you could *ride* it. (341)

This completes the narrative circle begun by Robert Smith, the North Carolina Mutual Life Insurance agent who had sought to "fly" from the Mercy Hospital roof at the beginning of the novel, and the historical one begun by Solomon, when he flew from Solomon's Leap before the novel started. But this is the only way the ending is conclusive—in Milkman's decision to surrender himself to the air and, in doing so, submit to his brotherhood with Guitar. The point of the novel lies in that decisive act. All else is ambiguous. The question of Guitar's mission for the Seven Days drops from consideration. The issue of violence disappears. The motive of Black Power, which turned Guitar into a potential killer of another black man, fades into the motive of brotherhood.

HUEY AND ELDRIDGE

In her first two novels, Morrison had indicated an apparent indifference to the prevailing militant male themes. The female protagonists of *The Bluest Eye* (1970) and *Sula* (1973) are preoccupied with personal relationships and feelings rather than sociopolitical conflicts with whites. The novels contain modest narratives about, respectively, a little black girl who thinks she is ugly and two women whose friendship falls apart to their mutual tragedy. Although they came out during the years of the literary revolutionary hero's greatest popularity, Morrison seems to dismiss the whole affair as so much male posturing. "Those books and political slogans about power," she says, "were addressed to white men. [Black men were] trying to explain or prove something to them. The fight was between men, for king of the hill." [20] Yet, in one of those paradoxes that Morrison herself revels in, these two early novels could be said to be a reinforcement of the Black Power movement, even if we do not consider them to be a consequence of it. In his study of the Black Power era, *a New Day in Babylon* (1992), William L. Van Deburg convincingly argues that Black Power was as much a cultural as a political concept, an argument for the legitimacy of black life in America, of black history, art, folklore, and an attempt to instill in the black masses pride in these cultural forms, tracing its "genesis" back to Henry Highland Garnet, Nat Turner, Marcus Garvey, as well as the writers of the Harlem Renaissance. The dramatists especially sought to render the "richness and internal dynamism" of black life, bringing onstage the language, the dress, the behavior, the music unique to the African American community. For the Black Power militant, the values embodied in these forms worked to unify the people for more effective resistance to racial humiliation.[21] A distinguishing feature of *The Bluest Eye* and *Sula* is the very close attention Morrison gives to these same elements. Morrison does not attribute the motive for such close attention to that special culture to the influence of the Black Power movement. It comes, rather, from her reading of the classic European narratives of the nineteenth century. When she was a girl, *Pride and Prejudice* and *Madame Bovary* stimulated her to want "to capture that same *specificity* about the nature and feeling of the culture I grew up in."[22] Yet the Black Power movement had helped to create an environment receptive to the kind of "specificity" that Morrison sought to convey.

Song of Solomon is very much an artifact of this environment. It appears to be a direct reference to the fight for "king of the hill," as if now that the ground had changed, Morrison wanted to see what black militancy was all about. The Black Power warriors seemed so much in her mind as she wrote *Song of Solomon* that the novel comes across as a deconstruction of the type. The typical hero of the Black Power novel walks "black and tall," as Omar Fletcher puts it.[23] He comes out of the pages like an oversized monument, grimly muscular, humorless. He is the butt of no man's joke; his steely eyes and automatic attack rifle tell us that. Morrison is not interested in this monumental figure. She addresses the issue of violence, to be sure, and the way the Black Power hero might use it, but she views the subject in the context of personal family problems, the structure of the community, and the everyday experience of her Southside citizens. Thus *Song of Solomon* contains arguments about the legitimacy and practicality of retaliatory violence and embodies the two sides of the argument in the characters of Milkman and Guitar. It depicts a lynching-murder, a stabbing, a knife-and-broken-bottle fight, organized retaliation against white brutality, attempted murder by a disappointed lover. The lynching of Emmett Till in 1955 and the bombing of the four little girls in the Sixteenth Street Birmingham church in 1963 are topics of barbershop argument. Morrison's concern, though, is not to pass judgment upon violence or to idealize its user. It is rather to create a black world through the integrity of its own rich particulars—its conflicts, its history, its folklore. The ordinary and the everyday are transfigured by the myth and magic Morrison sees to be so intimate a part of black consciousness. Ghosts return as guides to the living. People fly, or try to, and Pilate lives without a navel. Gothic mystery blends in with black folklore: An apparitional guard protects a hidden treasure, and bones have to be buried. Sexual obsession, greed, jealousy, and hatred pervade the atmosphere; but so do love and mutual concern. Opposites merge into each other. Images and metaphors contain mysterious relationships, so intricate and echoing and shifting that their meaning becomes problematical. This is a uniquely black world, the world Morrison knows and writes about naturally.[24] Violence is one of many elements in this world. Like landscape or climate, class relationships or evil, it is an aspect of the atmosphere the characters must take into consideration in order to live their lives, learn to adapt to, or manipulate. Morrison empties it of its political significance and makes it a matter of self, of personal strength or weakness, acted out by blacks between blacks, in a black world affected by white racism but not determined by it. The novel is not an attack upon or an apology for the values of Black Power. It is an examination of its ramifications in individual lives. As a media event, Black Power had, by 1977, disappeared. But the revolution it started in black thought continues in different form in the novels of a new generation.

What had been a preoccupation in most African American novels of racial violence with the violent hero as a public figure living a life of sociopolitical protest, Morrison turned into an exploration of the African American male and the brotherhood that helps him to form his identity. The Black Power novelists, both the idealizers and the dismantlers of the hero image, acknowledged the importance of brotherhood in the movement but tended to place it, unexamined, in the background of their narratives.[25] Morrison brings it to the front and center of her stage and makes it one of the principal parts of the process by which her protagonist, Milkman Dead, becomes "a complete fully aware human being."[26] The progress that Milkman makes in the novel's action is toward the liberated self-awareness that makes personal commitment possible, not the construction of a new racial arrangement. The human being he becomes is shaped not by his encounter with whites but by his own growth in a black world. And he must do this against the impediments of his upbringing and social environment, not against racism. Morrison is thinking here about a state of mind that only the self can create, a state of complete freedom, characterized by faith and the readiness to risk total commitment to something or someone one values above the self. This does not entail social action or changing the external world. It is a matter of bringing the internal self to that point of confidence where change ceases to be frightening and one's own death becomes "irrelevant." [27] "If you own yourself," says Morrison, "you can make some types of choices, take certain kinds of risks." [28]

Morrison's successful editing career at Random House has a fairly direct influence upon the themes she takes up in *Song of Solomon*. She brings to the novel, indeed to all her novels, the same nonjudgmental neutrality the best editors have toward the books they prepare for the press. This is the neutrality with which she enters the interior of her male as well as her female characters. Morrison says she cherishes all her characters, without insisting they be paragons of virtue. Her editorial work also brought her into contact with Huey Newton and his first autobiography, *To Die for the People* (1972). Newton alludes to her in his acknowledgments as "my editor," one of several people without whom "this book would not have been possible." [29] As the leader of the Black Panther Party, and a man not averse to publicity, Huey Newton was one of the icons of the Black Power movement, receiving much media attention and embodying much of what the public saw of the movement. In meeting with Newton and going through the text of his book, Morrison would have seen a different image from the shallow stereotype of the press, a serious, idealistic young man, not formally well educated, widely but shallowly read, with a quick original mind and a penchant for theorizing. She would also have known him to have a sudden temper and a tendency to become involved in violent scrapes in which people were killed and wounded. He was, in fact, the kind of person that would have interested Morrison, with his steamy, intense public persona superimposed upon an introspective troubled interior, and Morrison's association with him as editor gave her a valuable point from which to observe an archetype of the Black Power movement.

Song of Solomon, of course, is not directly about that movement. Neither Black Power nor the Black Panthers took form until the late sixties. The action of Morrison's novel concludes in 1963, and the Seven Days Society was organized back in the twenties. But the principles upon which the Black Panthers' conception of guerrilla warfare were founded are those with which Morrison's characters are also concerned. For example, Guitar emphasizes the "smallness" of the Days' operation, composed of just seven men, one for each day of the week, which allows them to keep their identity from law enforcement agencies and thus operate more efficiently (159). Huey argues that when the people see the validity of "guerrilla warfare" they will abandon their mass riots and turn to attacking the oppressor in small groups that are more elusive.

When the vanguard group destroys the machinery of the oppressor by dealing with him in small groups of three and four, and then escapes the might of the opprressor, the masses will be impressed and more likely to adhere to this correct strategy. When the masses hear that a gestapo policeman has been executed while sipping coffee at a counter, and the revolutionary executioners fled without being traced, the masses will see the validity of this kind of resistance.[30]

Morrison is not interested in tactics for their own sake, or in Huey's revolutionary theories for their theoretical validity. She seeks the personal implications behind them. Both of Huey's autobiographical books, *To Die for the People* and *Revolutionary Suicide* (1973), suggest a preoccupation with heroic sacrificial death that verges on the messianic. Huey is already using the phrase "revolutionary suicide" in *To Die for the People*. To do nothing, he writes in that first book, is to die the ignominious death of the "reactionary suicide." But to act, to show courage, to believe in the "possibility that we can change the conditions and win"—this may mean death, too, but "If we must die, then we will die the death of a revolutionary suicide . . . of a man rather than the death of a dog."[31] In his argument with Milkman over the validity of the Days' work, Guitar expresses similar sentiments: "If I'm caught," says Guitar, "I'll just die an earlier death than I'm supposed to—not better than I'm supposed to. And how I die or when doesn't interest me. What I die *for* does" (160). These are not unique positions. We find them in argument after argument and novel after novel. It is the commonness of the argument that I emphasize here, and the connectedness between *Song of Solomon* and the ideology of Huey Newton and his attitude toward death. It is precisely this attitude that Milkman acquires when he leaps, indifferent to his own death, from Solomon's Leap toward Guitar. For Morrison, though, this carries "existential," not sociopolitical, importance.[32] This is literally the leap into the abyss so often identified by fifties existentialists as the key to human action in a contingent world. But it is also the metaphor for the personal commitment Milkman learns to make by the end of the novel. For Milkman to be able to achieve "moral resurrection," says Morrison, he must "be able to make that . . . total commitment to some thing, and not really care whether he lives or dies at the end." This means, paradoxically, "that he is alive."[33] Like Carl Jung's modern man searching for his soul, Milkman, on Solomon's Leap, "has come to the very edge of the world, leaving behind him all that has been discarded and outgrown, and acknowledging that he stands before a void out of which all things may grow."[34] His leap, therefore, is not a leap of death but one of life and potential. This is the way Morrison transforms the value of the traditional violent hero—the readiness to die to produce social and political change—into the value of the new sensibility—the ability to make a personal commitment in a black world.

In 1989, of course, Huey is shot on the streets of Oakland in a seedy affair involving drugs, and his killer is sentenced, in 1991, to a long stretch in prison.[35] But Huey's vision of death in the high years of the Black Panthers was anything but seedy. Huey does not limit his perception of death to a theatrical gesture at center stage to elicit the applause of thousands. True, he accepts the role of the "sincere" revolutionary to be sacrificial death.[36] But there is more to "revolutionary suicide" than the trumpets and banners and twenty pallbearers. In a series of discussions with the noted Harvard psychologist Erik H. Erikson, published in 1973 under the title *In Search of Common Ground,* Huey expands the issue to embrace violence and love. Stimulated by Erikson's greater intellectual depth, Huey fastens upon love as the link between the revolutionary and the people for whom he risks his life. In fact, Huey's revolutionary feels a kind of universal love for all humanity, which contradicts the violence embodied in the guns needed for the revolution. When the revolution corrects the imbalance between the oppressor and the oppressed, "we can keep the love and get rid of the gun."[37] That is, he advocates violence not for its own sake but only in order to deal with the exigencies of racial oppression. It is an instrument not of manhood and heroism but of revolution, whose wellspring is love. As the discussion develops, though, Huey finally hits upon the heart of his feelings. His highest love is not for the anonymous "masses" that he and his "vanguard group" must educate in revolutionary methods. It is for his brothers in the Black Panther Party. That is the relationship that most forcefully urges him to action. "If love is gone," he says, "there is no reason to go on—and this is how I feel about the Party. I am willing to make any sacrifice, not because of a suicidal tendency on my part as some psychologists and sociologists have concluded, but because the sacrifice is compensated through the fraternity."[38]

Erikson, speculating from his position as a neo-Freudian, identifies what he sees to be an interesting flaw in the plenitude of brotherhood. In the absence of the father who retains the power and control of the group, brothers attack each other in the universal family struggle to seize the role of the father for themselves. They become antagonists, says Erikson as Huey and Eldridge Cleaver did at the end of the sixties. That argument was over the correct revolutionary strategy for using guns. Huey proposed playing guns down, Eldridge playing them up. In Huey's mind, Cleaver sought violence in the street because it was more heroic and finally "defected from the Party."[39]

Love and brotherhood, violence and death, are precisely what Morrison explores in *Song of Solomon,* showing how they mix antithetically with each other, and in that mixing change shape, modify each other. The brother-hood of the Seven Days is riven by paradox.[40] Tightly united by blood oath and a radical dedication to their mission, its members renounce any normal domestic life or open friendship with other men. They enter a zone of moral contradictoriness that can lead to various kinds of mental breakdown. On the one hand, they join the group because of their intense commitment to and love for their black brothers and sisters. "What I'm doing ain't about hating white people," says Guitar. "It's about loving us. About loving you. My whole life is love" (160). "I loved you all," writes the North Carolina Mutual Life Insurance agent in the notice he tacks on the door of his house before he "flies" from the roof of Mercy Hospital (3). Henry Porter gets drunk, holes up in his room, brandishes a gun at the whores laughing at him down on the street, and cries out, "I love ya! I love ya all. . . . I'd die for ya, kill for ya" (26). On the other hand, the very sentiment that stimu-lated them to join the Seven Days can make them feel unbearably guilty. When this happens, as Guitar explains, their first loyalty is to the other members and the protection of their anonymity. Such loyalty can mean the member's life. Robert Smith, who opens the novel with his suicidal leap in 1931, apparently can no longer face the conflict produced by having to violate his fundamental disbelief in killing in order to do something for his people. Porter's alcoholism is a measure of his pain. What starts as a heroic action in search of desirable social change and racial dignity can result in the opposite. It is a moral oxymoron to kill for love.

Though Morrison had read *In Search of Common Ground,*[41] it would strain credulity to claim any one-to-one connection between it and *Song of Solomon.* Whether she is thinking of the book or not, though, Morrison addresses the phenomenon of broken brotherhood and the contradictori-ness inherent in human motive. Milkman and Guitar do not correspond to Huey and Eldridge. Milkman is totally apolitical and vehemently objects to the principles of the Seven Days. Guitar, on the other hand, contains something of both Newton and Cleaver: Huey's insistence upon love as a driving revolutionary force, for instance; Cleaver's brittle insistence upon the utility of killing, but without his clamor for publicity and his sometimes duplicitous indirectness.[42] But they do act out the antagonism of brothers that interests Morrison, the clash that transcends the racial militancy that drove Huey and Eldridge in those miltant years.[43]

Huey and Eldridge were drawn together by their fervor for the move-ment. They were driven apart by their differing personalities that sought different methods and, ultimately, different goals. Milkman and Guitar are brought together at a much deeper level. As children they complete each other with the innocence of the prelapsarian world. They fought together, dared together, risked together, "rode the wind" together, failed together. They won "dominion" over others by terrifying them, or they rationalized their own defeats with wisecracks (177). Of this union, Guitar is the black brother turned menace, the male-chauvinist black nationalist, the sinister pole of black manhood's fraternity. The "brotherhood" of Guitar and Milkman is the male version of the "sisterhood" between Nel and Sula in *Sula* (1973).[44] Nel and Sula experience a sudden and intense intimacy when they are twelve years old. As teenagers, they have "difficulty distinguishing one's thoughts from the other." Sula brings disruption into Nel's life, but also vitality and spirit. Both friendships break up because of fundamental differences in the characters' personality and upbringing. Guitar is to Milkman what Sula is to Nel, a disruptive but generative force. Nel realizes Sula's importance to her too late and can only seek her at her grave: "We was girls together. . . . O Lord . . . girl, girl, girlgirlgirl," an anguished lament for missed sisterhood.[45] Milkman, who might say to Guitar, "We was boys together," is a kind of male Nel, caught in a middle-class life that enervates him. But Morrison creates a reconciliation between Milkman and Guitar that eludes Nel and Sula.

MILKMAN: LEARNING THE FINAL LESSON

The struggle between Guitar and Milkman that ends on Solomon's Leap embodies the contradictoriness of the world as Morrison sees it. Such close friendships as theirs are like communities. They nurture and they suppress. Of towns like the Lorain, Ohio, in which she grew up, Morrison says, they are "both a support system and a hammer at the same time."[46] Similarly, positive acts and attributes sour; weaknesses transmute into strength. Guitar saves Milkman from alienation as a child, introduces him to his Aunt Pilate, who will become the most positive influence upon him, and pushes him to live his life more intensely (184). But Guitar's love becomes, as Morrison says, "the work of death."[47] His fanaticism makes him paranoid. He insists that Milkman has betrayed him, has stolen the gold that both were to share. He stalks Milkman and kills Pilate. Morrison gives us plenty of reason to believe in this turn in his attitude. He pushes life and compassion, but he also exudes something sinister and menacing. He is, as he tells Milkman, "a natural-born hunter," who "was never afraid to kill. Anything. Rabbit, bird, snakes, squirrels, deer" (85). Indeed, he seems intrigued by death. When Pilate speaks of the death of her father and of the man who fears he is falling off a cliff right in his own kitchen, Guitar is "fascinated, his eyes glittering with lights" (41). And he knows the exact number of blows that Sam Sheppard used to murder his wife (twenty-seven) as well as the fact that the murder weapon was a "hammer," not an axe as another Seven Days member, Henry Porter, thought (100). He has always been intense and political, a scrappy, ebullient defender of the underdog and a fierce resenter of unfairness. The Seven Days does not make him a killer. He joins it *because* he inclines to violence: "Guitar could kill," Milkman realizes, "would kill, and probably had killed. The Seven Days was the consequence of this ability, but not its origin" (211–12). He does not belong to the tradition of the warrior-hero who selflessly leads his people in triumphant revolt against white oppression. He is Morrison's variant of black fiction's avenger—Gofer Gondolier, Josh Green, Perigua, Criddle. Secretive and private, he avoids leadership and messianism but serves his own intense religion like a priest.

There is an evil in Guitar that clearly emerges in the novel's denouement, as he stalks Milkman, irrationally refuses Milkman's reasonable explanation of his behavior, and finally kills the most attractive character in the story. He is the death force that is a permanent part of the male world. The threat he poses is not some temporary obstacle to the triumph of the Good, which the hero will get rid of by virtuous action. It is like the "evil" in *Sula*. "Evil is not an alien force" in that novel, Morrison writes, "it's just a different force." [48] It is the same with the danger Guitar brings to Milkman. It is what Milkman must confront, the test of his mettle that rises periodically out of a world of which it is an inherent part. It is this threat that comes from within the brotherhood that Milkman finally has to confront and resolve in his journey toward his own identity. Guitar first goads Milkman on to go after the gold purportedly held by Pilate in her green bag. Then, in the end, he forces Milkman to decide about commitment. Guitar is brotherhood in all its violent contradictions, its genuine brotherly concerns, its irrationality, its vindictiveness, its peculiarly *male* way of settling scores. Aimless and indifferent for most of his life, Milkman has never engaged the paradox, so he has not developed the psychic muscles to deal with Guitar.

He certainly has not joined the fraternity of black men who gather regularly at the Tommys' barbershop in Southside to thrash out communally the topics that most concern them. From our stereotype of the black male (or any male, for that matter), we would expect these men to concentrate their attention on women. But Morrison makes violence their main topic, not sex. Since they talk of little else, we cannot miss the priority they give to it. They are a community chorus, like the women's sewing circles in her other novels, and pass on the issues touching their sense of manhood most closely. The emotional, illogical, free-wheeling debate they get into over Emmett Till's lynching shows the familiar split in the African American male world about white violence and how black men should respond to it. Some are disgusted that the fourteen-year-old Chicago resident, visiting relatives in Mississippi, should have so imprudently defied the racial customs of the Deep South. He should have known better. Others object that blaming Till amounts to Uncle Tomism, submission to a hateful and oppressive status quo. Through "crisscrossed conversations," the two sides carry on the classic argument. Is it more manly to die standing up to the white man than to realistically knuckle under to white power and control and stay alive? Is cowardice choosing obsequious life over heroic revolt? Is manliness accepting inevitable death? They shout at each other, insult each other, argue incoherently and amateurishly. They are *engaged,* passionate. Above all, they are protective of their own manliness and bridle at the least suggestion by a debating opponent of cowardice.

The point of the scene, however, is not to decide the merit of their arguments but to reveal the dynamics of male relationships. At the height of their argument, Morrison executes an insightful maneuver for just this purpose. She has the men suddenly begin to exchange stories of white "atrocities, first stories they had heard, then those they'd witnessed, and finally the things that had happened to themselves." They all have their tales to tell, and they all recognize the other's story. But while this is "A litany of personal humiliation, outrage, and anger," they turn it back on themselves "as humor," and they start to laugh about their reactions, their fleet escapes, the ruses with which they trick threatening whites. In all this, they deflect "some threat to their manliness, their humanness" (83). While they argue and threaten and show hostility toward each other, the transcendent fact is that they all belong to the same club. The scene dramatizes the tie of common experience by which they are all bound, their membership in the fraternity of Black Men. By telling their stories on themselves among themselves, and laughing at the outrageousness of their experience, they extract some of the sting and demonstrate their fortitude and dignity. Their manliness lies not in their muscular power but in their brotherhood, their competitiveness and hostility combined with their sense of unsentimental closeness.

For all their ability to joke about it, though, their world is full of risk and violence. The worst of this violence originates with whites, which is irrational and difficult to defend against. The Tommys' regulars see the 1930s multiple axe murderer Winnie Ruth Judd as a metaphor for white violence, "crimes planned and executed in a truly lunatic manner against total strangers." Blacks commit more understandable crimes, based upon the male code of behavior toward other black men: "violation of another's turf . . . refusal to observe the laws of hospitality . . . or verbal insults impugning their virility, honesty, humanity, and mental health." Moreover, these crimes (all assuming some kind of assault) are "committed in the heat of passion," not out of madness for their own sake but in order to sustain the just balance of reputation and self-respect. But beneath their joking and their theorizing there is an "unspoken terror" that arises from their common predicament. No matter how innocent they are, they are always vulnerable to police arrest for a crime thought to have been committed by some black man from whom no white law officer bothers to try to distinguish them (100–101). Membership in their black male fraternity may not give them much protection or comfort, but it does provide them company in a dangerous world. In the Tommys' regulars, Morrison shows black men's alienation, their sense of frustration at their powerlessness, their need to take on responsibility, the violence with which they live and to which they turn when their frustration becomes too intense. Milkman, for all his ambivalent shyness and holding back when he comes within their presence, yearns to be one of them, to join their "chorus" "with more than laughter" (184). They may be ineffective, able only to talk and argue about conditions that affect them without the agency to transform the world, but the sheer barbershop *maleness* of the group attracts Milkman the inveterate outsider. Part of the task of his "mythic quest" is to overcome his outsider status.

He does this as an initiate of the hunt on which he is taken by a group of old hands in Shalimar, Virginia, the geographical terminus of what started out to be his search for his Aunt Pilate's "gold-hoard" and ends up as a probe into his family's past. The bobcat hunters of rural, small-town Shalimar occupy a less frenetic, less materialistic setting than that of Michigan. Their "clubhouse" is King Walker's gas station (which no longer dispenses gas), and that is where Omar, Luther Solomon, Calvin Breakstone, and Small Boy meet Milkman for their night trek into the woods. These men are a generation older than Milkman, and they have a lifetime of comradeship between them. They treat each other with the easy jocularity of long-tested affection, strengthened by their mutual passion for the hunting of small game animals like racoon, bobcat and opossum. Guns, dogs, shooting, killing, skinning, eviscerating—these are the things that mark their lives and unite them in fraternity. In the heat of the hunt, they speak to each other across great distances in pre-language, the language of a primitive harmony which these black men know intuitively, not necessarily because they are black but because they are men, with weapons, in their mythic habitat. At the same time, their blackness gives the hunt particular meaning. In the relative isolation of the woods, these black men can be their natural selves, reinvigorated through the old male ritual and insulated briefly from the humiliations of white supremacy. Here they are natural men, untrammeled by the symbols of society or the color that makes them pariahs. They reinforce each other in the medium of a "sympathetic" nature, in which killing is in the marrow of the male experience. It is killing, though, in which the hunters experience a harmony rather than an enmity with their prey. They relish the test and feel the kind of love for the prey that men feel for a respected opponent after the turmoil of struggle, like boys who walk away from their fight with their arms about each other's shoulder. Thus, when the Shalimar hunters tree and then kill the bobcat, they admire its "size," "ferocity," and "stillness" (283), pay homage to an admired antagonist.[49]

These men induct Milkman into a meaningful male group for the first time in his life. The first sign that the initiation will "take" is the test that Milkman is put through alone in the dark woods when he gets separated from the other men, a test in which he must, also for the first time, face himself and his own annihilation without help from anyone. In this moment of deep introspection, he comes to a revelatory insight into his relationship with others. He sees how he had shielded himself from real ties, had avoided both the pain and pleasure of others, raising barriers that insulated him from an uncomfortable world. Now, alone in the dark, he feels that "cocoon" dissolve. In the darkness all the features of his familiar self evanesce, and he becomes what King Lear on the heath calls "unaccommodated man" (3.4.106). "There was nothing here to help him," thinks Milkman, "not his money, his car, his father's reputation, his suit, or his shoes." Here in the mountains "all a man had was what he was born with, or had learned to use. And endurance. Eyes, ears, nose, taste, touch —and some other sense that he knew he did not have: an ability to separate out, of all the things there were to sense, the one that life itself might depend on" (280–81). In this illuminating moment, Milkman finds himself becoming a member of the southern variant of the regulars at the Tommys' barbershop back in Southside. This, though, is a black male world that the Tommys' regulars have no access to: vivid, ancient, instinctive. Here, black men are the hunters, not the hunted, and they have a natural identification with their prey, as they attempt to think like the bobcat in their pursuit of him through the darkness. That is why, when Guitar attempts to throttle Milkman with a wire, he fails. Milkman is assisted by nature—the earth that warns him of Guitar's approach, and his own instincts that lead him to relax and gain the fraction of a second that saves him. In fact, Guitar "had missed" this essence of the South, this camaraderie, this mutual affection, this quasi-mystical connection with nature that reveals what black brother-

hood can be. He had been "maimed . . . scarred" by the ugly and destructive forces of racism; like Saul, who had attacked Milkman with a knife
earlier in the day and whose four front teeth had been knocked out by the
white sheriff in an earlier fracas; like Milkman's own father (who had gone
about imitating *his* father, Jake, in the wrong way). Nevertheless, Milkman's
insight does not separate him from Guitar or Saul or his father. On the
contrary, it reinforces his connection with them. He feels "a sudden rush
of affection for them all" and is certain that "he understood Guitar now"
(282). However these three have responded to their world, Milkman now
recognizes them as black men, part of a circle into which he has just been
taken. And as he walks back through the Virginia woods, for the first time
in his life he feels like a man with a place in the world, "exhilarated by
simply walking the earth. Walking it like he belonged on it; like his legs
were stalks, tree trunks, a part of his body that extended down down down
into the rock and soil, and were comfortable there" (284). As old Jake Dead
had insisted to the other black farmers long ago in Danville, Pennsylvania,
"We got a home in the rock" (237), now Milkman experiences the truth
of the spiritual.

Milkman thinks of Guitar as a kind of integral counterpoint to the main
theme of the hunt itself—the woods, the hunters, the killing. Disruptive
though he may be, he is part of it. His hunter's instinct, even "maimed"
and "scarred," nevertheless identifies him indissolubly with the male world,
an example of the dissonance inherent in that world.[50] The commitment
that Milkman makes as he jumps from Solomon's Leap is an affirmation of
the dissonances as well as the harmonies of brotherhood. The hunt has
prepared him to receive the final lesson for making that affirmation. But
this lesson is to be taught him not by a man but by a woman—his Aunt
Pilate. The inherent defect of the male world is that it lacks a female
sensibility. This is not a moral failure; it is simply part of the real world, like
evil, or the differences in strength or beauty between different people.
Guitar is a male chauvinist and sexist. As a member of the Days, Guitar
"worries" about the collective black woman "Because she's *mine*" (225).
His mother and Pilate are not proud enough, not black enough, not defiant
enough for him. They betray his black nationalist intensity. Does Morrison
give us some reason for doubting that Guitar's shooting of Pilate was a
"mistake" (341)? Milkman, on his side, has rejected the females of his
family—his neurotic mother, his repressed sisters, his spoiled cousin
Hagar.[51] Only Pilate has continued to command his respect, and he sneaked
into her house with Guitar to steal the bag of "gold."

Now, on Solomon's Leap, the bones of her father and Milkman's grandfather safely buried, Pilate becomes a sacrifice to the male brotherhood. It

is a sacrifice, though, she makes without grief or grudging, for only now can her last words have the proper effect upon Milkman. In words so well known that dedicated Morrison readers can mutter them in their sleep, Pilate, dying from the shot fired by Guitar, whispers, "I wish I'd a knowed more people. I would of loved 'em all. If I'd a knowed more, I would a loved more" (340). In sudden understanding, with bleeding Pilate in his arms, Milkman knows "why he loved her so. Without ever leaving the ground, she could fly" (340). All the references to flying in the narrative now disclose their meaning. To fly is to love, and both love and flying call for the "total commitment" that is the prerequisite for Milkman's moral resurrection. Pilate, therefore, herself born out of death, from a mother who died minutes before she pushed herself out of the womb (141), at the moment of her death, has taught Milkman how to "live." What Robert Smith is in the narrow sense, a North Carolina Mutual Life Insurance agent, Milkman becomes in a broader sense, an agent for "mutual life," his own and Guitar's, Pilate's, his great-grandfather's, and perhaps more. He offers this agency in his final act, "which," in Morrison's words, "is echoed in the hills behind him." Milkman's flight into the "killing arms of his brother" thus unites the polar forces at tension in the story, marrying "surrender and domination, acceptance and rule, commitment to a group *through* ultimate isolation." So powerful is this marriage that even Guitar acknowledges it, and as Milkman's "Here I am!" and "You want my life?" echo off the rocky promontories with the words of being— *"Am am am am"* and *"Life life life life"*—Guitar lays down his rifle.[52] The female virtues of sensitivity and love empower Milkman, already trained by the bobcat hunters, to affirm the dangerous, ambiguous, and self-conflicting male circle, bringing the poles of love and death into the peculiar dynamic tension of the black male world.

More importantly for us, he resolves in the single image of his flight from Solomon's Leap the long historical debate over violence. We can see it not only as the commitment that makes him an intensely aware human being, *there* as a conscious person, but as a free and voluntary gesture bringing into a single dichotomous embrace the Black Power revolutionary, the fanatical avenger, the activist—as they reside in their various forms in Guitar—and the nonviolent Christian love as taught to Milkman by Aunt Pilate. Couple the male values of physical conflict with the female values of selfless love and the result is the personal authenticity that Morrison sees to be the true issue in the definition of the black hero. Authenticity, in other words, lies not in Milkman's overpowering the aggressor white but in his totally immersing himself in the blackness of blackness—that which lies in the brotherhood groups, in his relationship with Guitar, and his own family and its past. In the post-Black Power era, Milkman's heroism is purely personal, transcendently courageous and nonviolent, and won as a black among blacks.

RECONCILIATION: THE LAST MOVE

There is a critical argument about the logical consistency of Milkman's final flight as a metaphor for valid achievement. Susan L. Blake suggests that flight, both that of Milkman and that of Solomon, violates "the principle of responsibility to other people"[53] because in both their cases flight means the abandonment of women who had relied on them. Trudier Harris concurs. When Milkman's great-grandfather, the slave Solomon, flies back to Africa, he leaves behind a wife, Ryna, who goes insane, and twenty-one children who are sentenced to a life without a father. What Solomon did, says Harris, is what Milkman has done his whole life, evade his obligations. Thus "the new beginning" for Milkman that seems to occur when he himself jumps off Solomon's Leap is "ambiguous." It is "a selfish celebration of the freedom of an individual judged against the enslavement of twenty-two people."[54] Susan Blake also sees a paradox in the situation: While Milkman's flying brings him closer to the ancestors that make up his past, at the same time it "sets him apart, like the quest hero of myth and fairy tale."[55] Harris puts it this way: In *Song of Solomon* we are confronted with the unanswerable question of where we draw "the line between one person's right and another person's wrong. [Morrison] refuses to allow us to be comfortable in our conclusions because the evidence for such evaluations keeps shifting."[56]

Morrison does insist that flight is inherently contradictory. Flying is not only a metaphor for the ability to make a commitment, she says, it "also has that other meaning in it; the abandonment of other people which is part of flying away, of leaving. . . . If you do leave like that and you do become complete and whole, you do leave other people behind. And that is both a triumph and a risk because you can't do that with a crowd. If you become exceptional and you 'leave,' some of the people you love may be left behind." From Morrison's viewpoint, "irresponsible" may not be an appropriate word for describing the moral nature of Solomon's or Milkman's flight. Leaving people behind is an inescapable result of becoming complete and aware. Pain and loss are unavoidable accompaniments of the victory over oneself that comes with the strength to risk.[57] When Sweet, the woman Milkman sleeps with in Shalimar, asks him whom Solomon left behind, Milkman shouts, "Everybody! He left everybody down on the ground and he sailed on off like a black eagle" (332). This is the same reaction that the storytellers have when they recount the exploits of the flying Africans. Those who are left behind in the story do not see themselves as being badly treated, and those listening to the tales never criticize the flying Africans themselves for not taking others with them. Their main reaction is like Milkman's: pride and amazement. Morrison speaks of hearing the old black men in the town in which she grew up talking longingly about travel. "It's part of black life, a positive majestic thing, but there is a price to pay—the price is the children." But even here emotions are deeply mixed. The children may accuse their fathers of abandonment, but they glory in the older male's exploit. "That is one of the points of 'Song,'" says Morrison: "all the men have left someone, and it is the children who remember it, sing about it, mythologize it, make it a part of their family history." In their flight, the "fathers may soar, they may triumph, they may leave," but in doing so they leave their children with an indelible sense of "who they are."[58] It is Jake Dead, dropped by his father Solomon as an infant and left to be raised by an Indian woman, who has the strength to take his family north and prosper. And it is when he discovers that Solomon, the subject of the children's songs in Shalimar, Virginia, is his great-grandfather that Milkman finally comes into his own. Solomon sets an example, performs a miracle. That the cost is high is the rule of reality. Morrison sees no more validity in trying to decide whether the cost was worth it than she sees in trying to assess the merits of the men's arguments about violence. In both cases, the meaning lies not in a reductive moral or logical conclusion but in the dialectical tension, the dynamic life process, for Morrison's worlds are in constant motion.

An analogous critical argument has gone on concerning the seriousness with which Morrison takes Milkman. Are we to read him as a valid mythic hero or a bumbler wearing clothes too big for himself? In fact, most of the criticism of *Song of Solomon* has focused upon either its association with myth or its use of black folklore, and sometimes both. "Otto Rank's discussion of the birth and childhood of the mythic hero," says A. Leslie Harris, "illustrates the clear connection of Morrison's hero with a mythic heritage."[59] Trudier Harris sees Milkman as a hero, but one deriving from black folklore rather than classical myth, and an ambiguous one at that: "Morrison ultimately intends Milkman as a heroic figure whose heroism can only be defined through dualistic, sometimes ambiguous actions, and whose qualifications for heroism do not depend upon his goodness."[60] Gerry Brenner takes the most extreme stand in opposition. Morrison, he argues, leads the reader unequivocally to mock Milkman's "grandiose illusion" about his ancestors and his being "silly enough to thrill to the notion that the capacity to fly is important." Legitimately discarding Morrison's own interpretation of the role she thought she was giving myth in the novel, but perhaps not so legitimately attributing to her an "unconscious hostility" toward Milkman, he says that Morrison holds him "up to a set of criteria only to ridicule him—albeit subtly." In fact, she "savagely mocks" most of her male characters and hasn't much good to say about her female ones. Her point, suggests Brenner, is to undercut all myths.[61]

Much in the novel makes Brenner's analysis look valid. There is a wide gap in many cases between what we associate with the "hero-work" of the protagonist, whether out of black folklore or classical myth, and the triviality of his and many of the characters' actions. But the ironic position that Brenner claims Morrison "really" assumes toward her characters would make her a Jonathan Swift or Ambrose Bierce, and Morrison does not seem to see herself in those terms. There does indeed appear to be a pervasive understated irony in the manner of Morrison's narrator. If this is irony, though, it is not the satiric irony that scorns and ridicules. It is the irony of the affectionate friend, whose amusement places her at the Archimedean point from which she can lever the inconsistencies and weaknesses into view that the participants cannot see in themselves, but she does so with a feeling of respect won through clear-eyed realism. The ability to do this is in a sense unique to the black woman. Who else has been as close to the black man without being one? Who can understand as well, without the prejudice of vested interest or self-pity, that past of suffering and humiliation, the need for manhood and dignity? It is the combination of what she has *shared* with black men in the American experience as well as the profound differences in that experience, even the woman's sense of being abused and exploited by those who should have protected her, that gives the black woman what Barbara Hill Rigney calls "privileged insights, access to that 'special knowledge' " of the male world.[62] If some black women see their black men through a feminist lens, Morrison does not.

Morrison explains her view of the African American man in her analysis of the first scene of *Song of Solomon*. When insurance agent Robert Smith leaps from the roof of Mercy Hospital, he does not perform a desperate act; he is keeping faith with the people of Southside he has served. Like the crowd that gathers to watch Smith make his leap, says Morrison, the reader should view the act with a mix of tenderness and amusement: amusement from their "unblinking" realization that this is an absurdly impossible act; tenderness from their recognition of Smith's courage and his devotion to them. Over this amusement and tenderness, the reader and the observers experience a "mounting respect" for a man who showed more character than they thought he had. In the same way, the Negroes of Southside pay "their respect" to Dr. Foster, Macon's father-in-law, not because he was a virtuous hero but because he had something in him "that made him *be* a doctor" (333). This is the way we should look at Milkman and his own flight off of Solomon's Leap at the end of the book. It is the way we should look at the male world and its violence.[63] One of Morrison's most interesting traits as a novelist is her readiness to attempt the difficult balance between the heroic and the ridiculous. She is concerned with theme and morality, certainly, but not as a know-it-all woman out to reform benighted and incorrigible men. Her characters are not models of abstract ideas or representatives of moral exempla. She loves them all, she says, but identifies with none of them. That would compromise their fullness, their complex integrity as human beings who are both weak and strong. It is conveying that complexity that she is most interested in, not in taking up a political, moral, or social position and then rewarding or punishing her characters for violating or conforming to those positions. "The point," she says, "is to try to see the world from their eyes. . . . My work is to become those characters in a limited way, to see what they see, not what I see."[64] Morrison does not set herself up as a judge of either Solomon or Milkman; she neither indicts them for being irresponsible nor treats them as unequivocal heroes. Quite the contrary. Equivocalness is the core of their manliness, just as it is the core of Milkman's mythic narrative. And Morrison's *sotto voce* "giggle," as she herself calls it,[65] is a constant catch in the narrator's voice, though not a destructive one. The way to understand Milkman's search is as *both* heroic myth and absurd realism, his flying as *both* legend brought to life in the fulfillment of an ancestral pledge and a farcical representation of the old male irresponsibility. The irony of Morrison's narrative mode is thus closer to the expansive humanity of Ralph Ellison than the naturalistic skepticism of Stephen Crane or the vituperative feminism of Michele Wallace. *Song of Solomon* does take us back to the conclusion of *Invisible Man,* reminding us of Ellison's humane sense of diversity, his pleasure in the human experience, and his refusal to see the world in reductively moralistic terms. "No indeed," says Invisible Man, "the world is just as concrete, ornery, vile and sublimely wonderful as before, only now I understand my relations to it and it to me."[66] Similarly, Milkman's external world is not changed by his discoveries. Only his new understanding has changed. "No reconciliation took place between Pilate and Macon . . . and relations between Ruth and Macon were the same and would always be. Just as the consequences of Milkman's own stupidity would remain, and regret would always outweigh the things he was proud of having done" (338–39).

Morrison makes no attempt to settle the questions at the center of the long debate over racial violence. Instead, she does two things that are hallmarks of the sea change she represents in the African American novel of violence. First, she lays out a new consciousness of the issues, thrusting politics and protest far into the background. Second, as she limits the issues to the black community and gives exclusive prominence to the relationships between its members, she tacitly suggests the disappearance of racial violence from front-stage attention. She replaces the old concern about white violence against blacks and how blacks should respond with a new concern: that the danger of violence now comes more from within than outside the community and is self-destructive rather than socially protective. If Guitar's Black Power retaliation against whites runs the risk of turning in upon the black community, Pilate's love and Milkman's sense of brotherhood offer possibilities of reconciliation. In 1977 Morrison sensed that this reconciliation among blacks, rather than heroic leadership against white violence, was becoming the more urgent issue. Twenty years later, given the statistics on the mayhem in the ghettos, we cannot but admit she was right.[67] This is the need in an era when young black men in the ghettos are killing each other at an unprecedented rate. It is a symptom of something we cannot yet explain, some deep dysfunction that is both personal and social.

With the image of that reconciliatory leap still in our minds, my expedition into the treatment of racial violence and its effects in the African American novel ends. Milkman's ambiguous gesture trails off into the darkness, like Ryna's cries in the night, like a piece of the blues, like a jazz riff. It is an inconclusive image simply because that is the way Morrison sees the world. For her, inconclusiveness is a central characteristic of the black experience she and other artists try to render.

I think about what black writers do as having a quality of hunger and disturbance that never ends. Classical music satisfies and closes. Black music does not do that. Jazz always keeps you on the edge. There is no final chord. There may be a long chord, but no final chord. And it agitates you. Spirituals agitate you, no matter what they are saying about how it is all going to be. There is something underneath them that is incomplete. There is always something else you want from the music. I want my books to be like that—because I want that feeling of something held in reserve and the sense that there is more— that you can't have it all right now.[68]

Morrison thus makes no effort to provide us with a final word on the clash between Milkman and Guitar, the principles and acts of the Seven Days, the tragedies on the bank of the Tallahatchie River or at the church in Birmingham. She provides no solution to the century-and-a-half debate on the violence between blacks and whites. But in a time when militant male stridency was disappearing behind militant feminist stridency, she kept her head and gave specificity to the emotions of the time.

Song of Solomon is a kind of "epilogue" to the century and a half of African American novel making and the novelists' treatment of racial violence. It is also a bridge into a changed stylistic and interpretive atmosphere. The historical and social conditions that in the past have stimulated black novelists' preoccupation with the topic have not disappeared, but they have profoundly changed. Neither lynching nor the race riot, nor the kind of murders practiced in the early days of the civil rights movement, presently exists, except in our historical consciousness. They continue to draw the attention of the African American novelist. Charles Johnson depicts the brutal treatment of captured Africans on an Atlantic slave ship in his philosophically sophisticated *Middle Passage* (1990). Bebe Moore Campbell fictively explores the white, as well as the black, side of the 1955 murder of Emmett Till in *Your Blues Ain't Like Mine* (1992). And Lorene Cary has the escaped-slave heroine of her novel *The Price of a Child* (1995) speak to northern white audiences about the vicious whippings her father received as a bondsman in the South. But the point of these novels is not to raise indignation or establish black identity through the pain of the past. With Toni Morrison, Alice Walker, and Charles Johnson as models, younger black novelists address the issue of racial violence with the intent of giving it and the environment from which it arises the kind of "specificity" that Morrison has spoken of, treating it as an aspect of the black past but no longer charged with a politically racial concern in which whites are the putative audience. In giving their treatment of violence this turn, these novelists have gone a long way toward solving what Stephen Butterfield called, as I quoted him in my Introduction, the "problem" of black autobiography and, by extension, the black novel. It is the problem that "the presence of the white man is the single most pervasive influence in every book." No one would argue that that influence has disappeared altogether from African American fiction in general or the novel of racial violence. But the tone has become less accusatory and more independent. Nor is it only Toni Morrison who illustrates this change. I am thinking in particular of Randall Kenan's *A Visitation of Spirits* (1989), one of the novels of the nostalgic past that so many African American writers find attractive now. Here, old Ezekiel Cross tells a story about when he was fourteen years old, before the changes wrought by the civil rights movement. When a white man in fictional Tims Creek, North Carolina, fails to pay him for his work, he confronts the man with a gun and takes his pay by force. The police put him in jail, but old Judge Flint, while reading him the riot act, delivers him into the hands of his father with orders for a good whipping. There is no white menace in this vignette, no whites overpowering blacks. Instead, Ezekiel's audience is impressed and entertained: "You didn't do that, now did you Cousin Zeke?" The focus is on black lives, not their fear and concern about what whites threaten them with.[69] With the paling[70] of the "influence" of the presence of the white man, racial violence in the African American novel becomes an ingredient of nostalgia as much as indignation, one of the "specifics" of the black past that is more historical than polemical. In such an atmosphere, the issue of victims and heroes and the question of retaliatory violence lose their thematic dynamism, and the old attitudes of the genre mutate into new forms with new preoccupations.

As for more current forms of racial violence, such as widespread brutality in municipal police forces, these have stimulated little novelistic interest. But new conditions have bred new fictive types. Inner-city violence, though hardly the cup of tea of sophisticated middle-class writers like Ntozake Shange, Terry McMillan, and Nelson George, has nevertheless gradually become a more urgent topic as it has gotten increasingly out of control and drawn the attention of an increasingly alarmed public. Besides the work of John Edgar Wideman and Jess Mowry, which I mentioned in the Introduction, back in the late sixties the Los Angeles company Holloway House started publishing its "black experience" line of novels, many of them pop exploitation narratives focusing upon criminal activities in the inner city. Authors like Robert Beck (who writes under the pseudonym of Iceberg Slim), Jame-Howard Readus, Omar Fletcher, and the Donald Goines of the Kenyatta tetralogy,[71] depict Mafia-style assassinations, drug wars, the life of pimps and gamblers, the royalty of the black underworld. Theirs, however, is more intraracial than interracial violence, and that violence calls for its own examination.

Racial violence as a theme in the African American novel has certainly not run out of steam. Like Toni Morrison's notion of jazz and her own novels, though, any study of it must stop rather than conclude, for the beat goes on. The novels I have looked at in my discussion are part of the record of what once was a matter of the most immediate urgency. Now we can experience that urgency only in the pages of those novels. I have tried to put those pages in perspective.

NOTES

INTRODUCTION

1. *Newsweek,* March 25, 1991, p. 38.

2. See Ellen Willis's essay in Paul Berman, ed., *Blacks and Jews: Alliances and Arguments* (New York: Delacorte Press, 1994), p. 184, in which she says that "increasing numbers of black radicals and feminists have rejected nationalism and separatism, challenged many of the conventional assumptions of identity politics and begun to explore race as part of a larger complex of social and cultural formations."

3. Herbert Shapiro, *White Violence and Black Response: From Reconstruction to Montgomery* (Amherst: University of Massachusetts Press, 1988), p. xii. See also Michael True, *An Energy Field More Intense than War: The Nonviolent Tradition and American Literature* (Syracuse, N.Y.: Syracuse University Press, 1995), who tries to make a case for a strong nonviolent tradition in American literature.

4. Stephen Butterfield, *Black Autobiography in America* (Amherst: University of Massachusetts Press, 1974), p. 286.

5. James M. Redfield's foreword to Gregory Nagy, *The Best of the Achaeans: Concepts of the Hero in Archaic Greek Poetry* (Baltimore: Johns Hopkins University Press, 1979), p. ix. I am indebted to my daughter, Melaine Bryant, for bringing this discussion to my attention.

6. John W. Roberts, *From Trickster to Badman: The Black Folk Hero in Slavery and Freedom* (Philadelphia: University of Pennsylvania Press, 1989), p. 1.

7. Frederick Douglass, *The Heroic Slave,* in *Violence in the Black Imagination: Essays and Documents,* ed. Ronald T. Takaki (New York: G. P. Putnam's Sons, 1972), pp. 75, 77.

8. Richard Yarborough, "Race, Violence, and Manhood: The Masculine Ideal in Frederick Douglass's 'The Heroic Slave,' " in *Frederick Douglass: New Literary and Historical Essays,* ed. Eric J. Sundquist (New York: Cambridge University Press, 1990), p. 174.

1. VIOLENCE, VICTIMS, AND HEROES IN THE ANTEBELLUM SLAVE NARRATIVE

1. Theodore Parker, "A Letter on Slavery," dated December 22, 1847, in *The Slave Power,* ed. James K. Hosmer (New York: Arno Press and New York Times, 1969), p. 50.

2. William Craft, *Running a Thousand Miles for Freedome; or, The Escape of William and Ellen Craft from Slavery* (1860), reprinted in *Great Slave Narratives,* ed. Arna Bontemps (Boston: Beacon Press, 1969), p. 331.

3. John Brown, *Slave Life in Georgia: A Narrative of the Life, Sufferings, and Escape of john Brown, a Fugitive Slave, Now in England,* ed. L. A. Camerovzow, Secretary of the British and Foreign Anti-Slavery Society, 2nd ed. (London: W. M. Watts, 1855), p. 66.

4. Charles Ball, *Slavery in the United States: A Narrative of the Life and Adventures of Charles Ball, a Black Man* (1836; rpt. Detroit: Negro History Press, 1970), p. 286.

5. *The History of Mary Prince, a West Indian Slave, Related by Herself* (London, 1831; rpt. New York: Oxford University Press, 1988), p. 7; *The Story of Mattie J. Jackson; Her Parentage—Experience of Eighteen Years in Slavery—Incidents during the War—Her Escape from Slavery; A True Story* (1866; rpt. New York: Oxford University Press, 1988), p. 10.

6. Cf. Marion Wilson Starling, *The Slave Narrative* (Boston: G. K. Hall, 1981), p. 116.

7. Kenneth Stampp, *The Peculiar Institution: Slavery in the Ante-Bellum South* (New York: Random House, 1956), p. 191.

8. Quoted in Eric J. Sundquist, *To Wake the Nations: Race in the Making of American Literature* (Cambridge, Mass.: Harvard University Press, 1993), p. 108, from *Life and Writings of Frederick Douglass,* ed. Philip S. Foner (New York: International Publishers, 1950–75), 1:57–58. "Slavery and Violence: The Slaves' View," chap. 6 Dickson D. Bruce, Jr., *Violence and Culture in the Antebellum South* (Austin: University of Texas Press, 1979), covers some of the same issues as I do in this chapter but from a quite different (an extremely useful) point of view. He fits his discussion of the use of the whip on slaves into his larger study of violence in southern culture as a whole. The slaveowner sees whipping as the instrument of a firm but kind master taking reasonable steps to regulate the behavior of unruly primitives. The slave sees whipping as a caprice of an inconsistent master's wish merely to exert his power, employed erratically and often sadistically. That is, rather than using the literary imagery of the slave narrative, Bruce very ably explains the attitudes toward the racial violence embodied in the whip on the plantation as he finds those attitudes expressed in the slave narrative, ex-slave interviews, diaries, the work of other historians, and folktales of John and Old Marster and animal stories. See also chap. 5 of Bruce's work, "Slavery and Violence: The Masters' View."

9. Brown, *Slave Life in Georgia,* pp. 39, 41.

10. James Olney, ' "I Was Born': Slave Narratives, Their Status as Autobiogra-

phy and Literature," in *The Slave's Narrative*, ed. Charles T. Davis and Henry Louis Gates, Jr. (New York: Oxford University Press, 1985), pp. 152–53, 153, 158.

11. Quoted in Starling, *Slave Narrative*, p. 181.

12. *The Narrative of the Life of Moses Grandy, Late a Slave in the United States of America* (1844); reprinted in *Five Slave Narratives*, ed. William Loren Katz (New York: Arno Press and New York Times, 1968), p. 7.

13. *Twelve Years a Slave; Narrative of Solomon Northup* (1853); reprinted in *Puttin' on Ole Massa; The Slave Narratives of Henry Bibb, William Wells Brown, and Solomon Northrup*, ed. Gilbert Osofsky; Harper and Row, 1969), p. 243.

14. Brown, *Slave Life in Georgia*, p. 67.

15. Quoted in Starling, *Slave Narrative*, p. 113.

16. *History of Mary Prince*, p. 7; *Narrative of Moses Grandy*, p. 18.

17. Henry Louis Gates, Jr., says that the slave narrative has a good deal of the contemporary sentimental novel in it and names the following characteristics: "florid asides, stilted rhetoric, severe piety, melodramatic conversation, destruction of the family unit, violation of womanhood, abuse of innocence, punishment of assertion, and the rags-to-riches success story." See "Binary Oppositions in Chapter One of *Narrative of the Life of Frederick Douglass, an American Slave, Written by Himself*," chap. 3 of Gates's *Figures in Black: Words, Signs, and the "Racial" Self* (New York: Oxford University Press, 1987), p. 83. The essay was originally published in *Afro-American Literature: The Reconstruction of Instruction*, ed. Robert B. Stepto and Dexter Fisher (Modern Language Association, 1978). His further discussion of Douglass's first chapter is not as useful, it seems to me, as his general theory about the slave narrative. His principal goal is to prove that Douglass is a deconstructionist at heart, suggesting in his narrative "overwhelmingly the completely arbitrary relationship between description and meaning, between signifier and signified, between sign and referent" (89). Surely this ascribes far too modern an intent to a strictly nineteenth-century man. See also Philip Fisher's chapter entitled "Making a Thing into a Man: The Sentimental Novel and Slavery," in *Hard Facts: Setting and Form in the American Novel* (New York: Oxford University Press, 1985).

18. Fisher, *Hard Facts*, pp. 105, 98.

19. Ronald G. Walters, *The Antislavery Appeal: American Abolitionism after 1830* (Baltimore: Johns Hopkins University Press, 1976), pp. 76–87, 91, 105.

20. J. M. S. Tompkins, *The Popular Novel in England, 1770–1800* (1932; rpt. Lincoln: University of Nebraska Press, 1961), p. 93.

21. Peter Kolchin, *American Slavery, 1619–1877* (New York: Hill and Wang, 1993), pp. 64–65.

22. Quoted in Tompkins, *Popular Novel in England*, p. 98.

23. William S. McFeely, *Frederick Douglass* (New York: W. W. Norton, 1991), p. 181.

24. William Hill Brown, *The Power of Sympathy* (1789), ed. William S. Kable (rpt. Columbus: Ohio State University Press, 1969), pp. 103, 105, 104. But in his introduction to Charles Brockden Brown's *Ormond* (1799; rpt. New York: Hafner Publishing., 1962), Ernest Marchand distinguishes between the school of sensibility

in which Laurence Sterne can "weep for a dead ass" and the school of benevolence, which would turn sympathy into social action. "The tender sentiment, the melting pity in which early American fiction reveled was less the prelude to benevolent action than an emotional luxury to be delicately savored by the sympathizer. . . . Eighteen-century sentimentalism gradually merged, however, into the humanitarian movement" (xiv, n. 24).

25. Robin Winks, general introduction to *Four Fugitive Slave Narratives* (Reading, Mass.: Addison-Wesley, 1969), p. vi. In *Violence and Culture in the Antebellum South,* Bruce comments on this topic from the viewpoint of the ex-slave: "The association of violence with power and power with sex which has so captured the Western pornographic imagination and which loomed so large in the writings of Anglo-American abolitionists was often advanced by ex-slaves as they attempted to account for the violence of Southern whites. Most commonly, it was said that whites used the threat of violence to have their way with women, or they might offer sex as an alternative to the lash, once having found a pretext for whipping. But a very few people recalled slaveholders who were genuine sadists, for whom the whipping of a stripped woman seemed to provide the greatest pleasure" (140). See also Ronald G. Walters, "The Erotic South: Civilization and Sexuality in American Abolitionism," *American Quarterly,* 25 (1973): 177–201.

26. William L. Andrews, *To Tell a Free Story: The First Century of Afro-American Autobiography,* 1760–1860 (Urbana: University of Illinois Press, 1986), p. 243. This is the indispensable study of the antebellum slave narrative and I will refer to it often. As for the sexual content of the slave narrative and the vulnerability of the slave woman to her white marster's lust, Andrews points to the abolitionist attack on the South as a hotbed of "libidinousness," a southern Sodom, tempting the slave narrators to report "physical torture" in sensational detail and at the same time mask any suggestion of the more taboo subject of sexual abuse (243).

27. Winks, *Four Fugitive Slave Narratives,* p. vi.

28. Robert Darnton, "Sex for Thought," *New York Review of Books,* December 22, 1994, p. 70.

29. Ibid., p. 66.

30. See Frederick Douglass, *My Bondage and My Freedom* (1855), ed. Philip S. Foner New York: Dover Publications, 1969), pp. 87, 79–88; and *The Life and Times of Frederick Douglass* (1881; rpt. Secaucus, N.J.: Citadel Press, 1983), pp. 34–39.

31. *Narrative of the Life of Frederick Douglass* (1845), ed. Houston A. Baker (New York: Penguin, 1982), p. 51. Subsequent page references are to this edition and are indicated in parentheses in the text.

32. Harriet A. Jacobs writes in *Incidents in the Life of a Slave Girl,* (1861), ed. Jean Fagin Yellin (Cambridge, Mass.: Harvard University Press, 1987), "The secrets of slavery are concealed like those of the Inquisition. My master was, to my knowledge, the father of eleven slaves. But did the mothers dare to tell who was the father of their children? Did the other slaves dare to allude to it, except

in whispers among themselves? No, indeed! They knew too well the terrible consequences" (35).

33. Douglass, *My Bondage,* p. 87.

34. Andrews, *To Tell a Free Story,* p. 132.

35. David S. Reynolds, *Beneath the American Renaissance: The Subversive Imagination in the Age of Emerson and Melville* (New York: Alfred A. Knopf, 1988), pp. 59, 61–62. See also Jenny Franchot's treatment of this passage, "The Punishment of Esther: Frederick Douglass and the Construction of the Feminine," in *Frederick Douglass: New Literary and Historical Essays,* ed. Eric J. Sundquist (New York: Cambridge University Press, 1990), pp. 141–65.

36. *The Liberator,* I, 9 (February 26, 1831): 36; I, 11 (March 12, 1831): 43; I, 19 (May 7, 1831): 74.

37. Frances Smith Foster uses this phrase in "Adding Color and Contour to Early American Self-Portraitures: Autobiographical Writings of Afro-American Women," in *Conjuring,* ed. Marjorie Pryse and Hortense J. Spillers (Bloomington: Indiana University Press, 1985), p. 31.

38. See especially de Sade's *Justine* (1791), trans. Richard Seaver and Austryn Wainhouse (New York: Grove Press, 1965), in which the innocent Justine observes from hiding the infamous Dr. Rodin disrobe and then whip, with a sexual pleasure rising to ecstasy, several young boys and girls in his school (536–37).

39. John Weightman, "The Human Comedy of the Divine Marquis," review of Maurice Lever's *Sade: A Biography, in New York Review of Books,* September 23, 1993, p. 8. I was struck also by James R. Kincaid's comments in his review of Peter Gay, *The Bourgeois Experience: Victoria to Freud* (New York: W.W. Norton, 1993), vol. 3. Gay's thesis, says Kincaid, is "that the Victorians were prone to mix cruel aggression and ferocious erotic pleasure." The Victorians "struggle to deal with the joys of aggression. [Gay] argues that our ancestors attempted to work out a set of strategies to 'cultivate' hatred, to both nurture and control it. The 'liberation of aggressive impulses,' he notes, 'was evidently highly pleasurable,' but 'the exacting superego of the bourgeois spoiled much of the pleasure' by resisting what was being whipped onward so vigorously. The Victorian bourgeois culture promoted aggression and also tried eagerly to curb it, employing it for ends both constructive and lethal" (*New York Times Book Review,* September 5, 1993, p. 3). See also Eugene D. Genovese's discussion of the slaveholders' self-serving notion of paternalism in *Roll, Jordan, Roll: The World the Slaves Made* (New York: Pantheon Books, 1974), pp. 87–97; and Andrews's remark in *To Tell a Free Story,* p. 222, that Anthony has been "provoked by an affront to his patriarchal honor and prerogative." Finally, there is the redoubtable Camille Paglia's statement that "intimacy and incest may be psychologically intertwined. Power relations may generate eroticism. Perhaps . . . hierarchy can never be completely desexed." Quoted in Jackie Jones's review of Paglia's *Vamps and Tramps* in the *San Francisco Chronicle Review,* October 23, 1994, p. 3.

40. *Justine,* p. 536.

41. We can appreciate Douglass's literary skill by comparing his account with Maria Monk's of her experience in *Awful Disclosures* (1836; rpt. Hamden, Conn.: Archon Books, 1962), when she is imprisoned in a Catholic monastery, sexually and physically abused by satanic monks and nuns who subject the other young novitiates to sexual *slavery* and punish them when they refuse to submit. Like Douglass, Maria is forced into the role of voyeur, being set to watch the punishment-execution of the youthful Saint Francis. But though, also like Douglass, Maria is too terrified to speak out, the rendering of the scene is awkward, crude, laughable, and without metaphorical resonance; see especially p. 117.

42. Edmund Burke, *A Philosophical Enquiry into the Origin of Our Ideas of the Sublime and Beautiful*, ed. J. T. Boulton (New York: Columbia University Press, 1958), p. 46.

43. Sundquist, *To Wake the Nations*, p. 107.

44. Douglass, *My Bondage*, pp. 246–47.

45. I want it to be clear that I am not picking a fight with Professor Sundquist, whose rich discussion of Douglass's *My Bondage and My Freedom* is the second major revisionist treatment of the work in a decade—William L. Andrews's *To Tell a Free Story* is the other. Sundquist's point about Douglass's second autobiography does not hinge upon the synonymy of these two "languages" or their contradictoriness. His thesis is that the revisions in *My Bondage* make it a more consciously revolutionary work than the *Narrative*, and on that score he is persuasive. As for the question of pity and sentimentality, in her analysis of Hannah Arendt's *On Revolution* (1963), Jean Bethke Elshtain questions the validity of pity as a motive for authentic revolutionary feeling: "Pity *for* is not the same as solidarity *with*," she writes in *Democracy on Trial* (New York: Basic Books, 1995). "Those who pity without limit develop a thirst for power and gain 'a vested interest in the existence of the weak.' Abstract pity invites cheap sentiment and confounds any possibility for genuine political freedom" (122–23).

46. Lawrence W. Levine, *Black Culture and Black Consciousness* (New York: Oxford University Press, 1977), p. 134.

47. Stephen Butterfield, *Black Autobiography in America* (Amherst: University of Massachusetts Press, 1974), p. 20.

48. Jacobs, *Incidents in the Life of a Slave Girl*, p. 165.

49. Genovese, *Roll, Jordan, Roll*, pp. 88, 594, 619.

50. Osofsky, *Puttin' On Ole Massa*, p. 14.

51. Genovese, *Roll, Jordan, Roll*, pp. 598, 594, 620.

52. Andrews, *To Tell a Free Story*, pp. 184–187, 49. Andrews adds that the white man who took down Pomp's testimony disbelieved his claims about the voices.

53. Starling, *Slave Narrative*, p. 114.

54. In Osofsky, *Puttin' on Ole Massa*, p. 349.

55. Ibid., pp. 282, 283–84.

56. William Wells Brown, in ibid., p. 182.

57. *"Uncle Tom's Story of His Life"; An Autobiography of the Rev. Josiah Henson, 1789–1876*, preface by Harriet Beecher Stowe and introductory note by George

Sturge and S. Morley, ed. John Lobb, 2nd ed. with a new introduction by C. Duncan Rice (1858; rpt. London: Frank Cass, 1971), pp. 15–16.

58. Martin R. Delany, *Blake; or, The Huts of America,* ed. Floyd Miller (Boston: Beacon Press), p. 243.

59. Henry Highland Garnet, "Address to the Slaves of the United States of America," in *Black Writers of America,* ed. Richard Barksdale and Keneth Kinnamon (New York: Macmillan, 1972), p. 177.

60. A number of front-rank scholars have in the last decade argued for the superiority of *My Bondage and My Freedom* over the *Narrative.* Where the *Narrative* tends to oversimplify the main characters, says William L. Andrews in *To Tell a Free Story, My Bondage* demonstrates Douglass's acknowledgment of the complexity of the meaning of his slave experience and contains the climactic break with his abolitionist mentor William Lloyd Garrison. Eric J. Sundquist has joined Andrews in attempting to reshape the critical consensus in favor of *My Bondage,* contending that *"My Bondage and My Freedom* tells us far more about Douglass as a slave, and about slave culture generally, than does the *Narrative,* whose main virtue now, as in Douglass's own day, is pedagogical: it is easily absorbed and taught" (*To Wake the Nations,* p. 89). Blyden Jackson, on the other hand, in *The Long Beginning, 1746–1895,* vol. 1 of *A History of Afro-American Literature* (Baton Rouge: Louisiana State University Press, 1989), sees the *Narrative* "as a classic of our national, as well as of Afro-American, literature" (110). Jackson concludes, *"My Bondage and My Freedom* should not be dismissed as a great decline artistically from the *Narrative.* It never, however, is quite as powerful, or as gemlike in its brilliance, as the *Narrative* at its best" (117). David L. Dudley, in *My Father's Shadow; Intergenerational Conflict in African American Men's Autobiography* (Philadelphia: University of Pennsylvania Press, 1991), also finds unequivocally for the superiority of the *Narrative* (35). I, myself, stand firmly in the middle, believing that each of these two quite different books serves its purpose with great flair and effectiveness, the *Narrative* as an abolitionist fable, *My Bondage* as a powerful and complex rendering of Douglass's thinking on his slave experience and its aftermath.

61. Eric Auerbach, *Mimesis: The Representation of Reality in Western Literature,* trans. Willard R. Trask (Princeton, N.J.: Princeton University Press, 1953), p. 19.

62. In *To Tell a Free Story,* Andrews says that Douglass "reaches a dark night of the soul in 1833," when he is broken all but permanently by Edward Covey (125). It is not Andrews's purpose to develop the implications of this analogy, but I am struck by the relevance of the mystical ascent to Douglass's perception of his rise "upward." In this he anticipates Whitman's "Song of Myself," which James E. Miller analyzes as an account of the mystical ascent (*Walt Whitman* [New York: Twayne Publishers, 1962], p. 93). Andrews, though, makes a compelling case for reading the *Narrative* as an American jeremiad, citing Sacvan Bercovitch and seeing Douglass as a hero "of self-reliance," enacting "the national myth of regeneration and progress through revolution" (*To Tell a Free Story,* p. 124).

63. Douglass, *My Bondage and My Freedom,* p. 247.

64. See especially Butterfield, *Black Autobiography in America,* p. 86; and An-

drews, *To Tell A Free Story,* pp. 230–31. Cf. Sundquist, *To Wake the Nations:* "Nat Turner, as Eugene Genovese remarks, was 'a messianic exhorter,' a black slave who nonetheless spoke 'in the accents of the Declaration of Independence and the Rights of Man' " (41); and Eugene D. Genovese, *From Rebellion to Revolution: Afro-American Slave Revolts in the Making of the New World* (New York: Random House, 1979), pp. 116–17.

2. PROTOTYPES IN THE ANTEBELLUM NOVEL

1. I made an arbitrary decision to omit Harriet A. Wilson's *Our "Nig"; or, Sketches from the Life of a Free Black* (1859). This interesting novel, recently turned up by Henry Louis Gates, Jr., and published by Vintage Books in 1983, does contain what might be called racial violence. But it is so fraught with the unique individual meanness of Mrs. Bellmont, the white mistress of the novel's main character, Alfrado, that I concluded it was essentially outside the purview of my topic. The novel is set in an unidentified New England town, and Mrs. Bellmont is a kind of northern female Simon Legree. Yet, she is wicked at heart and is vindictive and mean to everyone. Race is a factor when Mrs. Belmont beats Alfrado, but not the determining one.

2. William Wells Brown, *Clotel* (1853); reprinted in *Three Classic African-American Novels,* ed. Henry Louis Gates, Jr. (New York: Vintage Books, 1990), p. 66. Quotations from the 1853 version of *Clotel* will be taken from this edition, and subsequent page references are indicated in parentheses in the text. When he says that "Brown wrote four distinct versions of *Clotel*" (x), Gates refers to the following: (1) the one he prints here, the earliest edition, which, as he points out, was originally published in London; (2) *Clotelle: A Tale of the Southern States,* which was published in the United States in 1864 and (3) again in 1867; and (4) *Miralda; or, The Beautiful Quadroon: A Romance of American Slavery Founded on Fact* (1860–61). Bernard Bell points out that the latter version "appeared as a serial in the Weekly Anglo-African during the winter of 1860–61." See Bell, *The Afro-American Novel and Its Tradition* (Amherst: University of Massachusetts Press, 1987), p. 354; and J. Noel Heermance, *William Wells Brown and "Clotelle": A Portrait of the Artist in the First Negro Novel* (Hamden, Conn.: Shoestring Press, 1969), who states that the 1864 edition is the version Brown is "pleased enough with . . . that he does not revise it again, and does, in fact, copyright and publish it himself three years later as *Clotelle; or, The Colored Heroine* (133). In *The Coupling Convention: Sex, Text, and Tradition in Black Women's Fiction* (New York: Oxford University Press, 1993), Ann du Cille points out that the 1867 edition contains an additional "four brief chapters (covering only nine pages)" recounting the return of his protagonists, named in this version Jerome and Clotelle, to the United States, Jerome's death in the war, and Clotelle's prosperity and determination "to devote the remainder of her life to the education of the newly freed Negro" (27). The quote from the Natchez *Free Trader* also appears in the appendix to *The Narrative of William Wells Brown: A Fugitive Slave* (1848), reprinted in *Four Fugitive Slave Narra-*

tives (Reading, Mass.: Addison-Wesley, 1969), introduction by Robin Winks and others. The best authority on Brown's life and the confusing status of the *Clotel* texts is William Edward Farrison, *William Wells Brown: Author and Reformer* (Chicago: University of Chicago Press, 1969).

3. Martin R. Delany, *Blake; or, The Huts of America* (1859–62)(ed. Floyd J. Miller pt. Boston: Beacon Press, 1970), pp. 167, 168, 170, 175, 67. Subsequent page references are to this edition and are indicated in parentheses in the text.

4. Wilson Jeremiah Moses, *Black Messiahs and Uncle Toms: Social and Literary Manipulations of a Religious Myth* (University Park and London: Pennsylvania State University Press, 1982); see especially p. 4.

5. Richard Wright, *Native Son* (1940; rpt. New York: Harper and Row, 1966), p. 110.

6. Antonio Bologna describes Ferdinand, the duke of Calabria, as having "A most perverse and turbulent nature" in John Webster's *Duchess of Malfi*, 5.2.101.

7. Quoted from an excerpt in *The Nat Turner Rebellion: The Historical Event and the Modern Controversy*, ed. John B. Duff and Peter M. Mitchell (New York: Harper and Row, 1971), p. 10.

8. Henry Highland Garnet, "Address to the Slaves of the United States of America," in *Black Writers of America*, ed. Richard Barksdale and Keneth Kinnamon (New York: Macmillan, 1972), p. 179. With the bitterness of the Black Power struggle of the late 1960s as background, Julius Lester contends that abolitionists like Garrison, trying to control and determine the fight against slavery, addressed editorials to blacks telling them "violence is wrong." Many blacks agreed, but one group, says Lester, "felt that the only way to get rid of slavery was with a club to the head of the slaveholder." Demands for militant reaction to racial oppression like Garnet's "Address," and Walker's *Appeal* express feelings "that have existed within the black community as long as that community has existed." See Lester, *Look Out, Whitey! Black Power's Gon' Get Your Mama!* (New York: Dial Press, 1968), pp. 40–41, 52.

9. *The Life and Times of Frederick Douglass* (1881; rpt. Secaucus, N.J.: Citadel Press, 1983), p. 282.

10. See my discussion in chapter 3 of Madison Washington, the protagonist of Frederick Douglass's *Heroic Slave,* who advances the same argument as George Green to justify his leadership of the slave mutiny on the brig *Creole.*

11. Kilson quoted in August Meier and Elliott Rudwick, eds., *The Making of Black America,* vol 1 of *The Origins of Black America* (New York: Atheneum, 1969), p. 178.

12. Frederick Douglass, *My Bondage and My Freedom* (1855), ed. Philip S. Foner (New York: Dover Publications, 1969), p. 263.

13. Harriet Beecher Stowe, *Uncle Tom's Cabin; or, Life among the Lowly* (1851–52; rpt. New York: New American Library, 1966), p. 19.

14. Vincent Harding, *There Is a River: The Black Struggle for Freedom in America* (New York: Harcourt Brace Jovanovich, 1981); see especially pp. 68, 102.

15. Martin Delany, *The Condition, Elevation, and Destiny of the Colored People of the United States, Politically Considered* (1852), in Barksdale and Kinnamon, *Black Writers*, p. 201.

16. Addison Gayle, Jr., *The Way of the New World: The Black Novel in America* (1975; rpt. Garden City, N.Y.: Anchor/Doubleday, 1976), pp. 24, 25.

17. Quoted by Victor Ullman in *Martin R. Delany: The Beginnings of Black Nationalism* (Boston: Beacon Press, 1971), pp. 30, 31, 112, 199.

18. Gayle, *Way of the New World*, p. 14. See also Blyden Jackson's typically urbane discussion of the novel in vol. 1 of *A History of Afro-American Literature*, entitled *The Long Beginning, 1746–1895* (Baton Rouge: Louisiana State University Press, 1989), pp. 343–51. After recounting the novel's many weaknesses of stereotype and vulgar fiction, Jackson concludes that, "Even so, Webb is more of a novelist than Brown. Of the two, Webb is easily the one less unable to animate a fiction" (344).

19. Frank J. Webb, *The Garies and Their Friends* (1857), intro. Arthur P. Davis (rpt. New York: Arno Press and New York Times, 1969), p.v. Subsequent page references are to this edition and are indicated in parentheses in the text.

20. Cf. W. E. B. Du Bois, *The Philadelphia Negro: A Social Study* (1899; rpt. New York: Benjamin Blom, 1967), pp. 25–39. Arlene A. Elder also points out the unlikelihood of Walters developing a real estate empire at this time, since virtually no blacks had managed to crack that market; see *The "Hindered Hand": The Cultural Implications of Early African-American Fiction* (Westport, Conn.: Greenwood Press, 1978), p. 11.

21. Cf. Du Bois, *Philadelphia Negro*, p. 37: "in 1837, a quarter of the Negroes were [living] in white families" as domestics.

22. Ibid., p. 32. Du Bois cites a riot in 1849 that began when a mob "set upon" an interracial couple, "a mulatto man who had a white wife."

23. Richard Chase, *The American Novel and Its Tradition* (Garden City, N.Y.: Anchor/Doubleday, 1957), p. 14.

3. SEARCHING FOR THE HERO

1. Eric Foner, *Reconstruction: America's Unfinished Revolution, 1863–1877* (New York: Harper and Row, 1988), p. 6. See also George C. Rable, *But There Was No Peace: The Role of Violence in the Politics of Reconstruction* (Athens: University of Georgia Press, 1984). In chap. 2, Rable nicely explains the psychology of the southern white that led him to treat the freedman like a slave, his expectation of racial relations continuing as they had been in slavery, the assumption that all blacks must continue to show the same deference of slave to master, and his fury when many blacks refused to comply. White employers "continued to flog unruly blacks with cowhide whips and punished infractions by chains, the pillory, and hanging by the thumbs. In the Louisiana interior, black women were still stripped naked and whipped by white men. Planters who used such methods to keep 'their'

Negroes in line became enraged when the freedmen had the temerity to complain to federal provost marshals" (21).

2. Herbert Shapiro, *White Violence and Black Response: From Reconstruction to Montgomery* (Amherst: University of Massachusetts Press, 1988), p. 5.

3. Frances E. W. Harper, *Iola Leroy; or, Shadows Uplifted* (1892) reprinted in *Three Classic African-American Novels,* ed. Henry Louis Gates, Jr. (New York: Vintage Books, 1990), pp. 366, 392.

4. William A. Sinclair, *The Aftermath of Slavery: A Study in the Condition and Environment of the American Negro* (1905; rpt. New York: Arno Press and New York Times, 1969), pp. 4–5.

5. I refer to Lorenzo D. Blackson, *The Rise and Progress of the Kingdom of Light and Darkness* (Philadelphia: J. Nicholas, Printer, 1867); Thomas Detter, *Nellie Brown; or, The Jealous Wife, with Other Sketches* (1871; rpt. Lincoln: University of Nebraska Press, 1996); Mrs. A. E. Johnson, *Clarence and Corinne; or, God's Way* (1890; rpt. New York: Oxford University Press, 1988); and Emma Dunham Kelley, *Megda* (n.p.: James H. Earle, 1892 [copyright 1891]). See also James H. W. Howard's unexceptional fictional slave narrative, *Bond and Free: A True Tale of Slave Times* (1886; rpt. College Park, Md.: McGrath Publishing, 1969). By far the fullest account of these writers, especially Blackson and Howard, is Blyden Jackson's in *A History of Afro-American Literature,* vol. 1, entitled *The Long Beginning, 1746–1895* (Baton Rouge: Louisiana State University Press, 1989).

6. Cf. Thomas Detter's *Nellie Brown; or, The Jealous Wife:* "How often the Negro has been hunted down in the broad sunlight of day, assassinated and murdered, and the assassin permitted to go unpunished, because his victim was as powerless as he was innocent" (157).

7. Richard Slotkin, *Regeneration through Violence: The Mythology of the American Frontier, 1600–1860* (Middletown, Conn.: Wesleyan University Press, 1973), p. 189.

8. William Wells Brown, *The Negro in the American Rebellion* (1867; rpt. New York: Krause Reprint, 1969), p. 13.

9. William J. Simmons, *Men of Mark: Eminent, Progressive, and Rising* (1887; rpt. New York: Arno Press, 1968), pp. 1038–39.

10. Quoted in Emma Lou Thornbrough, *T. Thomas Fortune, Militant Journalist* (Chicago: University of Chicago Press, 1973), pp. 48–49.

11. Quoted in Stephen Ward Angell, *Bishop Henry McNeal Turner and African-American Religion in the South* (Knoxville: University of Tennessee Press, 1992), p. 228.

12. Sutton E. Griggs, *Imperium in Imperio: A Study of the Negro Race Problem* (1899; rpt. New York: Arno Press and New York Times, 1969), p. 244.

13. This is the form of the name John W. Roberts uses in *From Trickster to Badman: The Black Folk Hero in Slavery and Freedom* (Philadelphia: University of Pennsylvania Press, 1989); see especially pp. 207–11.

14. Richard Barksdale and Keneth Kinnamon, eds., *Black Writers of America,* (New York: Macmillan, 1972), p. 460.

15. Simmons, *Men of Mark,* p. 319.

16. Ibid., p. 325.

17. Brown, *The Negro in the American Rebellion,* p. 172.

18. Harper, *Iola Leroy,* p. 23

19. S. P. Fullinwider, *The Mind and Mood of Black America* (Homewood, Ill.: Dorsey Press, 1969); see especially chap. 2.

20. Frederick Douglass, *The Heroic Slave,* in *Violence in the Black Imagination: Essays and Documents,* ed. Ronald T. Takaki (New York: G. P. Putnam's Sons, 1972); pp. 75–77; see also my discussion of William Wells Brown's *Clotel* (1853) in chap. 2. George Green justifies Nat Turner's rebellion with the same argument.

21. William Patrick Calhoun, *The Caucasian and the Negro in the United States* (1902; rpt. New York: Arno Press, 1977), p. 78.

22. Theodore Roosevelt, *The Strenuous Life* (New York: Century, 1900), p. 32.

23. Maurice Thompson, *Alice of Old Vincennes* (Indianapolis: Bowen-Merrill, 1900), pp. 418–19.

24. Garnet, "Address to the Slaves of the United States of America," in *Black Writers of America,* ed. Barksdale and Kinnamon, p. 177.

25. Quoted in Vernon Lewis Parrington, *The Beginnings of Critical Realism in America* (New York: Harcourt Brace and World, 1958), p. 59.

26. Quoted in Werner Berthoff, *The Ferment of Realism* (New York: Free Press, 1965), p. 178.

27. See the Introduction.

28. See Peter Gabriel Filene, *Him/Her/Self: Sex Roles in Modern America* (New York: Harcourt Brace Jovanovich, 1975), especially his discussion through p. 86; E. Anthony Rotundo, *American Manhood: Transformations in Masculinity from the Revolution to the Modern Era* (New York: Basic Books, 1993), especially pp. 279–83. See also Mark C. Carnes and Clyde Griffen, eds., *Meanings for Manhood: Constructions of Masculinity in Victorian America* (Chicago: University of Chicago Press, 1990).

29. Simmons, *Men of Mark,* p. 65.

30. George Washington Williams, *The History of the Negro Race in America* (1883; rpt. New York: Bergman, 1968), 2:85.

31. See Dixon Wecter, *The Hero in America* (New York: Charles Scribner's Sons, 1972), p. 283 et passim. Wecter gives a truer picture of heroic manhood than does Michael Kimmel, who in *Manhood In America: A Cultural History* (New York: Free Press, 1996) tends toward reductivism, seeing only one model of manliness and manhood holding at a given historical time. Wecter points out this isn't so, that the models for manliness were various and contradictory.

32. Brown, *The Negro in the American Rebellion,* p. 86.

33. William T. Alexander, *A History of the Colored Race in America* (1887; rpt. New York: Negro Universities Press, 1968), p. 15.

34. Harper, *Iola Leroy,* p. 272; Sutton E. Griggs, *Unfettered* (1902; rpt. New York: AMS Press, 1971), p. 267.

35. Williams, *History of the Negro Race in America,* 1:111.

36. Ibid., p. 22.

37. The terms "Ethiopianism" and "Afrocentrism" are not synonymous. "Afro-centrism" denotes the theory of the African origins of western civilization, or as the Italian anthropologist Giuseppe Sergi says, "that an ancient dark-skinned race spawned all of the ancient Mediterranean civilizations" (see August Meier, *Negro Thought in America, 1880–1915* [Ann Arbor: University of Michigan Press, 1963], p. 203). See also Molefi Kete Asante, *The Afrocentric Idea* (Philadelphia: Temple University Press, 1987), and Martin Bernal, *Black Athena: The Afroasiatic Roots of Classical Civilization* 2 vols. (New Brunswick, N.J.: Rutgers University Press, 1987–91). The literature on the subject is voluminous, and has now been expanded by the attack upon Afro-centrism, or at least the political correctness and multicultur-alism in which the question has become entangled in the past two decades, by respected classical scholar Mary Lefkowitz in *Not Out of Africa: How Afrocentrism Became an Excuse to Teach Myth as History* (New York: New Republic/Basic Books, 1996) and *Black Athena Revisited,* a collection of essays edited by Lefkowitz and Guy MacLean Rogers (Chapel Hill: University of North Carolina, 1996).

"Ethiopianism" is best defined by George M. Fredrickson in *Black Liberation: A Comparative History of Black Ideologies in the United States and South Africa* (New York: Oxford University Press, 1995). The "narrow and original sense" of Ethiopi-anism, Fredrickson says, was "the redemption of Africa through the exclusive agency of Protestant Christianity." In the nineteenth century this usually referred to African Americans colonizing Africa, carrying back to it the Christianity they learned as slaves in the United States (71). See also J. Mutero Chirenje, *Ethiopianism and Afro-Americans in South Africa, 1883–1916* (Baton Rouge: Louisiana State University Press, 1987), and St. Clair Drake, *The Redemption of Africa and Black Religion* (Chicago: Third World Press, 1970).

38. Alexander, *History of the Colored Race in America,* p. 15. It should be evident that this is not part of the topic concerning the type of education blacks should be given in the South at the turn of the century. Williams and Alexander are examples of a cohort of black writers setting forth the inherent capabilities of black Ameri-cans. Booker T. Washington and W E B. Du Bois, the best-known exponents of the two main views on black education, argue over process and strategy, not genetic or historical status. This early Afrocentric school of thinkers embraces both Du Bois, as the last sentence in the quote from Alexander shows, and Washington, as will become clear in a few sentences.

39. Williams, *History of the Negro Race in America,* 1:109.

40. Ibid., pp. 83, 109. Alexander Crummell makes the same point even earlier in the century: "If a people think that God is a Spirit," Crummell writes, "that idea raises, or will raise them among the first of nations. If, on the other hand, they think that God is a stone, or a carved image or a reptile, they will assuredly be low and rude. A nation that worships stocks, or ugly idols, can never while maintaining such a style of worship become a great nation." Quoted by Wilson Jeremiah Moses in *Alexander Crummell: A Study of Civilization and Discontent* (New York: Oxford University Press, 1989), p. 93.

41. See Slotkin's discussion of the importance of the Indian captivity narrative for the early settlers in *Regeneration through Violence,* pp. 101–2.

42. Eugene Genovese will have none of this. He says in *Roll, Jordan, Roll: The World the Slaves Made* (New York: Pantheon Books, 1974), "Despite a few hints to the contrary, the slaves did not view their predicament as punishment for the collective sin of black people. No amount of white propaganda could bring them to accept such an idea" (245). The post-Emancipation writers I am talking about take up the white argument.

43. Williams, *History of the Negro Race in America,* 1:110.

44. Booker T. Washington, *Up from Slavery* (1901); reprinted in *Three Negro Classics* (New York: Avon Books, 1965), p. 37. This was not a totally new theme, of course. Educated blacks as far back as Phillis Wheatley thought of Africa as "The land of errors, and Egyptian gloom" and thanked God for bringing them "in safety from those dark abodes," as Wheatley writes in "To the University of Cambridge, in New England." But the full myth, from Simon the Cyrenian to the freed slave, takes its complete shape only with Emancipation.

45. See Slotkin, *Regeneration through Violence,* pp. 293–94, 310.

46. Anna Julia Cooper, "One Phase of American Literature," in *A Voice from the South* (1892), Schomburg Library of Nineteenth-Century Black Women Writers (rpt. New York: Oxford University Press, 1988), pp. 195, 197, 198.

47. Simmons, *Men of Mark,* pp. 57–58, 43, 61. This view might also be traced to David Walker and a number of his antebellum contemporaries. In *Alexander Crummell,* Moses points out that Walker "had viewed history as a series of covenants that God had made with consecutive civilizations—first with the biblical Hebrews, then with the Christianized Romans, and finally with Western Europe. Each had violated its covenant, and as a result had been superseded by another race. Americans, the present beneficiaries of a sacred covenant, would likewise fall, unless they ceased to enslave and persecute the Africans in their midst" (138). Moses points out in his footnote to this passage that other expressions of this position can be seen in Dorothy Porter, ed., *Negro Protest Pamphlets* (New York: Arno Press, 1969); Hollis Read, *The Negro Problem Solved; or, Africa as She Was, as She Is, and as She Shall be. Her Curse and Her Cure* (New York: Constantine: 1864); and Frederick Freeman, *Africa's Redemption: The Salvation of Our Country* (New York: Fanshaw, 1852).

48. Simmons, *Men of Mark,* p. 7. This view of manhood as humanness and humanity rather than forcefulness and power is widespread in the African American intellectual community of the age. Alexander Crummell gives voice to it, for example, in his sermon, "The Destined Superiority of the Negro" (1877); see *Destiny and Race: Selected Writings, 1840–1898,* ed. Wilson Jeremiah Moses (Amherst: University of Masschusetts Press, 1992), p. 203 especially. He is most succinct in his address at the founding conference of the American Negro Academy: "To make *men* you need civilization; and what I mean by civilization is the action of exalted forces, both of God and man. For manhood is the most majestic thing in

God's creation; and hence the demand for the very highest art in the shaping and moulding of human souls" (285).

49. Cooper, "One Phase of American Literature," p. 193.

4. THE TRUTH ABOUT LYNCHING

1. Frances E. W. Harper, *Iola Leroy; or Shadows Uplifted* (1892), reprinted in *Three Classic African-American Novels,* ed. Henry Louis Gates, Jr. (New York: Vintage Books, 1990), p. 451. Subsequent page references are to this edition and are indicated in parentheses in the text. I will follow this practice for all the other novels I deal with in this chapter.

2. Joel Williamson, *The Crucible of Race: Black-White Relations in the American South since Emancipation* (New York: Oxford University Press, 1984), p. 185.

3. Robert L. Zangrando, *The NAACP Crusade against Lynching, 1909–1950* (Philadelphia: Temple University Press, 1980), pp. 34, 6–7; James Elbert Cutler, *Lynch-Law: An Investigation into the History of Lynching in the United States* (1905; rpt. Montclair, N.J.: Patterson Smity, 1969), pp. 41, 60, 170. Few students of lynching believe they have discovered the exact number of blacks lynched in the period that starts with 1882, the year that the *Chicago Tribune* began keeping figures. Cutler uses the figures collected by the *Tribune;* Zangrando uses those of the Tuskegee Institute, which also took from the *Tribune.* Though the specific figures differ slightly, both sources show the lynching of blacks peaking in the year 1892, then commencing a downward trend that is never reversed. W Fitzhugh Brundage, in *Lynching in the New South: Georgia and Virginia, 1880–1930* (Urbana and Chicago: University of Illinois Press, 1993), lists by name all the lynching victims he discovers in his study of the practice in Georgia and Virginia. Obviously, this is out of the question for the commentator on all lynching in the United States.

4. Quoted in Zangrando, *NAACP Crusade,* p. 12, cf. Zangrando's chap. 1, "At the Hands of Parties Unknown," for a good summary of the treatment of black reaction to lynching in the years before World War I.

5. See Ida B. Wells, *On Lynchings: Southern Horrors* (1892), *A Red Record* (1894), *Mob Rule in New Orleans* (1900)(rpt. New York: Arno Press and New York Times, 1969), preface by August Meier.

6. Zangrando, *NAACP Crusade,* p. 17. See also Donald L. Grant's remark in his introduction to *The Anti-Lynching Movement, 1883–1932* (San Francisco: R and E Research Associates, 1975), p. vii: "the NAACP was a product of the anti-lynching impulse and . . . it grew strong by opposing lynching."

7. See Grant, *Anti-Lynching Movement:* "As the knowledge grew that lynching was increasingly the greatest obstacle to Black advancement, the reformers moved from [protest during the early stages of lynching] to the creation of protest-oriented organizations" (ix).

8. The bill never became law, of course, because it was prevented by southern

filibuster in the Senate from ever reaching a vote in that body. See John Hope Franklin, *From Slavery to Freedom: A History of Negro Americans,* 3rd ed. (New York: Random House, 1967), pp. 486–87. But this was the first time such a bill had gotten anywhere in the Congress, an illustration of progress on the antilynching front.

9. I list them here in chronological order: Harper, *Iola Leroy* (1892); Walter H. Stowers and William H. Anderson (as SANDA), *Appointed: An American Novel* (1894; rpt. New York: AMS Press, 1977); J. McHenry Jones, *Hearts of Gold* (1896; rpt. College Park, Md.; McGrath Publishing, 1969); Sutton E. Griggs, *Imperium in Imperio: A Study of the Negro Race Problem* (1899; rpt. New York: Arno Press and New York Times, 1969); Pauline E. Hopkins, *Contending Forces* (1900; rpt. Carbondale: Southern Illinois University Press, 1978; and New York: Oxford University Press, 1988); Charles W. Chesnutt, *The Marrow of Tradition* (1901; rpt. Ann Arbor: University of Michigan Press, 1969); Griggs, *Overshadowed* (1901; rpt. New York: AMS Press, 1973); Hopkins, *Winona: A Tale of Negro Life in the South and Southwest* (1902), reprinted in *The Magazine Novels of Pauline Hopkins* (New York: Oxford University Press, 1988); G. Langhorne Pryor, *Neither Bond nor Free: A Plea* (New York: J. S. Ogilvie, 1902); Griggs, *Unfettered* (1902; rpt. New York: AMS Press, 1971); Charles H. Fowler, M.D., *Historical Romance of the American Negro* (Baltimore: Thomas Evans, 1902); E. A. Johnson, *Light Ahead for the Negro* (New York: Grafton Press, 1904); Griggs, *The Hindered Hand; or, The Reign of the Repressionist* (1905; rpt. Miami: Mnemosyne Publishing, 1969); Chesnutt, *The Colonel's Dream* (1905; rpt. Upper Saddle River, N.J.: Gregg Press, 1968); Griggs, *Pointing the Way* (1908; rpt. New York: AMS Press, 1974); J. W. Grant, *Out of the Darkness; or, Diabolism or Destiny* (Nashville: National Baptist Publishing Board, 1909); Robert Lewis Waring, *As We See It* (1910; rpt. College Park, Md.: McGrath Publishing, 1969); W. E. B. Du Bois, *The Quest of the Silver Fleece* (1911; rpt. College Park, Md.: McGrath Publishing, 1969); James Weldon Johnson, *Autobiography of an Ex-Colored Man* (1912), reprinted in *Three Negro Classics* (New York: Avon Books, 1965); Otis M. Shackleford, *Lillian Simmons; or, The Conflict of Sections,* 2nd ed. (Kansas City, Mo.: R. M. Rigby, 1915); Charles Henry Holmes [Clayton Adams], *Ethiopia: The Land of Promise (A Book with a Purpose)* (New York: Cosmopolitan Press, 1917); J. A. Rogers, *From Superman to Man* (1917), 5th ed. (New York: Rogers, 1968); Sarah Lee Brown Fleming, *Hope's Highway* (New York: Neale Publishing, 1918); Herman Dreer, *The Immediate Jewel of His Soul* (1919; rpt. College Park, Md.: McGrath Publishing, 1969).

10. See n. 9 above for the novels they wrote. Du Bois wrote several more novels dealing with violence besides *The Quest of the Silver Fleece,* but they fall outside of the present time period. I will deal with them at the appropriate time.

11. Three of Paul Laurence Dunbar's four novels are about whites: *The Uncalled* (1898; rpt. New York: International Association of Newspaper and Authors, 1901); *The Love of Landry* (1900; rpt. New York: Negro Universities Press, 1969); *The Fanatics* (1901; rpt. New York: Negro Universities Press, 1969). Dunbar's fourth novel, *The Sport of the Gods* (1902; rpt. New York: Macmillan, 1970), about a black

family that moves to New York City from the South and morally deteriorates, does contain violence, but it is intra-rather than interracial; one of the characters murders his mistress. He does make lynching a theme, however, in his two short stories, "The Tragedy at Three Forks" in *The Strength of Gideon and Other Stories* (1900), and "The Lynching of Jube Benson" in *In the Heart of Happy Hollow* (1904). They lie outside my frame of reference.

12. Benjamin Brawley, "The Negro in American Fiction," reprinted in its entirety from *The Dial* (May 11, 1916), in *The Negro in Literature and Art in the United States* (1930; rpt. New York: AMS Press, 1971), p. 186.

13. Sterling Brown, *The Negro in American Fiction* (1937; rpt. Port Washington, N.Y.: Kennikat Press, 1968); Hugh M. Gloster, *Negro Voices in American Fiction* (1948; reissued in 1965 by Russell and Russell by arrangement with the University of North Carolina Press); and Robert A. Bone, *The Negro Novel in America*, rev. ed. (New Haven: Yale University Press, 1965).

14. Addison Gayle, Jr., *The Way of the New World: The Black Novel in America* (1975; rpt. Garden City, N.Y.: Anchor/Doubleday, 1976), p. 31. See also Bernard W. Bell, *The Afro-American Novel and Its Tradition* (Amherst; University of Massachusetts Press, 1987), pp. 58–60.

15. Barbara Christian, *Black Women Novelists: The Development of a Tradition, 1892–1976* (Westport, Conn.: Greenwood Press, 1980), p. 33.

16. Barbara Christian, "The Uses of History: Frances Harper's *Iola Leroy, Shadows Uplifted*," In *Black Feminist Criticism: Perspectives on Black Women Writers* (New York: Pergamon Press, 1985), originally a paper given at the National Women's Studies Association Conference, 1983.

17. Hazel V. Carby, *Reconstructing Womanhood: The Emergence of the Afro-American Woman Novelist* (New York: Oxford University Press, 1987).

18. Dickson D. Bruce, Jr., *Black American Writing from the Nadir: The Evolution of a Literary Tradition, 1877–1915* (Baton Rouge: Louisiana State University Press, 1989).

19. I take the population and mortality rate figures from E. Franklin Frazier, *The Negro in the United States*, rev. ed. (New York: Macmillan, 1975), pp. 175, 180.

20. Edward L. Ayers, *Vengeance and Justice; Crime and Punishment in the 19th-Century American South* (New York: Oxford University Press, 1984), p. 336 n. 16.

21. Brundage, in App. C to *Lynching in the New South,* pp. 293–96, has an interesting and useful discussion of the importance of newspapers in studying lynching. See also Ralph Ginzburg, *100 Years of Lynchings* (1962; rpt. Baltimore: Black Classic Press, 1988), for reprints of representative newspaper articles published between 1880 and 1961. For a summary of white press treatment of lynching, see Rayford W. Logan, *The Betrayal of the Negro, from Rutherford B. Hayes to Woodrow Wilson* (New York: Collier Books, 1965), chap. 12, pp. 223 ff.

22. Trudier Harris, *Exorcising Blackness: Historical and Literary Lynching and Burning Rituals* (Bloomington: Indiana University Press, 1984), pp. 5–7.

23. Ibid., p. 20.

24. Ibid., p. 23. It is It is hard to tell what body of writing Harris refers to in

the passage I am discussing here. The passage is titled "White Men as Performers in the Lynching Ritual" (19–24). In her previous discussion, she has demonstrated the similarity between the treatment of lynching in literary accounts like that in Griggs's *Hindered Hand* (1905) and that in the Vicksburg, Mississippi, *Evening Post* (p2), and the changes in the lynching practice from slavery to post-Reconstruction when the ritual lynching began to take shape. She makes no distinction between newspaper accounts of lynching and literary accounts and refers to writing in slave times as if it were contemporary with writing in the late 1940s. Her discussion of the role of white men in the ritual contains no reference to any titles or dates. Consequently, I am not sure if she means to say in her description of white men using lynching as a sexual release that this is what African American novelists were attempting to show, or whether it is her own psychological analysis of an earlier historical practice from the standpoint of hindsight with the tools of Freudianism.

25. I am thinking of Stowers and Anderson, *Appointed* (1894); Jones, *Hearts of Gold* (1896); Hopkins, *Contending Forces* (1900) and *Winona* (1902)(though this lynching is interrupted by the victim's rescue, it reflects most of the elements of Harris's ritual lynching ceremony); Pryor, *Neither Bond nor Free* (1902); E. A. Johnson, *Light Ahead for the Negro* (1904); Griggs, *The Hindered Hand* (1905); Grant, *Out of the Darkness* (1909); J. W. Johnson, *Autobiography of an Ex-Colored Man* (1912); Holmes, *Ethiopia* (1917); Fleming, *Hope's Highway* (1918); and Dreer, *The Immediate Jewel of His Soul* (1919).

26. "James Baldwin," writes Harris in the course of her analysis of the ritual lynching as a symbolic rape of the black man, "has long argued that the prevailing metaphor for understanding the white man's need to suppress the black man is that attached to sexual prowess" (*Exorcising Blackness*, p. 20).

27. *Winona* was originally published as a serial novel in the *Colored American Magazine* between May and October in 1902.

28. Fiske quoted in Werner Berthoff, *The Ferment of Realism* (New York: Free Press, 1965), p. 178. See my comment on Fiske in the previous chapter.

29. James Harmon Chadbourn points out in *Lynching and the Law* (Chapel Hilli University of North Carolina Press, 1933) that "Only about eight-tenths of one percent of the lynchings in the United States since 1900 have been followed by conviction of the lynchers" (13). That not just white lynchers of blacks but lynchers of any color tended to get away with it without punishment is suggested by Chadbourn's example of a justifiable homicide verdict returned in the trial of some Negroes who "lynched a white youth for the rape of a Negress" (15). Brundage, in *Lynching in the New South,* explains that white lynch mobs tended to escape punishment not only because they had the backing of nearly the entire southern community but because law enforcement throughout the South was too weak to do much about such behavior (33–36). Chadbourn confirms this point but gives it a slightly different spin. He says that some explain lynching not simply as failure to punish law-breaking lynchers but as a response by white mobs to the fear that guilty blacks would be excused by "executive clemency" or freed through "judicial error" (6).

30. Grant, *Anti-Lynching Movement*, p. 36.

31. Ibid.

32. Herbert Shapiro, *White Violence and Black Response: From Reconstruction to Montgomery* (Amherst: University of Massachusetts Press, 1988), pp. 6, 13; Ayers, *Vengeance and Justice,* pp. 157, 231; Eric Foner, *Reconstruction: America's Unfinished Revolution, 1863–1877* (New York: Harper and Row, 1988), p. 121.

33. Grant, *Anti-Lynching Movement*, pp. 108–9.

34. Brundage, *Lynching in the New South,* p. 30.

35. The pun on "Lashum" as the "lasher" of the Overley women turns Buck and his former slave overseer father into the same kind of allegorical figures that Sutton Griggs, in particular, liked. Although the novel contains no other evidence, one wonders about the degree to which Waring is thinking of Dickens in his use of puns that border on caricature. The teachers at Oberlin College, for instance, are Dean Sternly, Professors Smirchum and Narrows.

36. See the quote from James Redfield in the introduction.

37. That this had long been an element in influential black thinking is suggested by Alexander Walters's conclusion to his keynote speech to the December 1898 meeting of the Afro-American Council: "Let us improve our morals, educate ourselves, work, agitate and wait on the Lord." Quoted by August Meier in *Negro Thought in America, 1880–1920* (Ann Arbor: University of Michigan Press, 1963), p. 172.

38. Holmes, *Ethiopia,* preface.

39. Chesnutt, *The Marrow of Tradition,* p. 309; and Griggs, *The Hindered Hand,* pp. 190, 202.

40. Waring, *As We See It,* pp. 110–111; and Du Bois, *The Quest of the Silver Fleece,* pp. 396–97.

41. Christian, "Uses of History," in *Black Feminist Criticism,* p. 165.

42. The question of where Griggs stands as a black writer is one of the many points on which Addison Gayle, Jr., in *The Way of the New World,* picks an argument with Robert Bone in *The Negro Novel in America.* I am not sure, though, that there is so much difference between them. Bone concludes that Griggs has "a blind impulse toward retaliation and revenge" that strives "for mastery with a more moderate, and more realistic approach" (33). Bone seems to regard this as a debilitating conflict in Griggs which the writer cannot control. Gayle, more validly, it seems to me, sees it rather as Griggs's objectivity in presenting "side by side the viewpoints of radical and conservative alike" (73). In the fullest discussion of Griggs to date, Arlene Elder, in *The "Hindered Hand": Cultural Implications of Early African-American Fiction* (Westport, Conn.: Greenwood Press, 1978), concludes that the plethora of events in his five novels stands as a metaphor of the southern world occupied by both races, a "tangled jungle of black and white suffering and guilt that his protagonists will attempt to clear" (73).

43. Jones, *Hearts of Gold,* pp. 90–91.

44. In chap. 7, "The Crusade Justified," of *A Red Record,* Ida B. Wells argues the same point and probably influences later novelists. She insists that her campaign

of agitation is not for revenge but to show white Americans how unfair and cruel they are. Once they have seen the light, they will realize how bad lynching is. She is encouraged by help from other civilized countries and even believes that "there is now an awakened conscience throughout the land, and Lynch Law can not flourish in the future as it has in the past. The close of the year 1894 witnessed an aroused interest, an assertive humane principle which must tend to the extirpation of that crime" (75).

45. S. P. Fullinwider, *The Mind and Mood of Black America* (Homewood, Ill.: Dorsey Press, 1969), p. 28.

46. John Saunders, in Stowers and Anderson's *Appointed,* is the only sympathetic protagonist who is lynched in these novels. Griggs's Bud and Foresta Harper, in *The Hindered Hand,* are not protagonists, but we are given the whole story of their resistance to white violence and their subsequent lynching. Lucius Storms, in Grant's *Out of the Darkness,* is a main actor in the plot but is a villain of sorts who brings his lynching on himself.

47. Wells, *Southern Horrors,* pp. 16, 17, and Preface.

48. See, for example, Cutler, *Lynch-Law;* Chadbourn, *Lynching and the Law;* Walter F. White, *Rope and Faggot* (1929; rpt. New York: Arno Press and New York Times, 1969); Arthur F. Raper, *The Tragedy of Lynching* Chapel Hill: University of North Carolina Press, 1933; David Brion Davis, *Homocide in American Fiction, 1798–1860: A Study in Social Values* (Ithaca, N.Y.: Cornell University Press, 1957); Grant, *Anti-Lynching Movement;* Zangrando, *NAACP Crusade;* Edward L. Ayers, *The Promise of the New South: Life after Reconstruction* (New York: Oxford University Press, 1992); Brundage, *Lynching in the New South.* The most succinct refutation is made by H. C. Brearley in 1935: "Contrary to general belief, an attack upon a white woman is not the principal offense charged against the victims of mobs. In a total of 3,714 lynchings during the period 1889–1930, homicide was the accusation 1,399 times, while actual or attempted rape occurred only 871 times, or 23.5 per cent of the total." Quoted from Brearley's "The Pattern of Violence," in *Culture in the South,* ed. W. T. Couch (Chapel Hill: University of North Carolina Press, 1935), p. 680.

49. Williamson, *Crucible of Race,* pp. 185–88. See also Brundage, *Lynching in the New South,* pp. 58–72. Although his discussion is limited to Georgia and Virginia, he presents one of the more balanced and meticulously researched treatments of the "one crime" as a provocation of lynching, pointing out how impossible it is to generalize for the entire South over a long period of time. Lynchings for rape differed in number and intensity from one section of the country to another, and from the last part of the nineteenth century to the first part of the twentieth. For my purposes, though, it is the impression the novelists have rather than their accuracy that is important.

50. Winfield H. Collins, *The Truth about Lynching and the Negro in the South; In which the Author Pleads That the South Be Made Safe for the White Race* (New York: Neale Publishing, 1918), pp. 52–53.

51. Grant, *Anti-Lynching Movement,* pp. 9–10.

52. Frederick L. Hoffman, *Race Traits and Tendencies of the American Negro* (New York: Macmillan, 1896), pp. 231–32. Adolph Reed, Jr., succinctly calls this "scientific racism, rooted in biologistic defenses of inequality" "The Scholarship of Backlash," *The Nation,* October 30, 1995, p. 506.

53. See especially C. Vann Woodward, *The Strange Career of Jim Crow* (New York: Oxford University Press, 1974), pp. 73–81; Trudier Harris also deals with the argument in *Exorcising Blackness,* pp. 19–24 especially. Michele Wallace strikes a sourer note in *Black Macho and the Myth of the Superwoman* (New York: Dial Press, 1979): "The lynchings, murders, beatings, the miscegenation laws designed to keep the black man and the white woman apart while the white man helped himself to black women, created in him a tremendous sense of personal urgency on this matter [i.e., violence against the black man]. America had not allowed him to be a man. He wanted to be one. What bothered America most? The black man and the white woman. Therefore if he had a white woman, he would be more of a man" (30).

54. Wells, *Southern Horrors,* p. 14; White, *Rope and Faggot,* p. 7; Raper, *Tragedy of Lynching,* p. 260.

55. Grant, *Anti-Lynching Movement,* p. 54. By 1967 and the third edition of his *From Slavery to Freedom,* John Hope Franklin shows just how old and exhausted a debate this was: "Although the impression was widely held that most of the Negroes lynched had been accused of committing rape on the bodies of white women, the records do not sustain this impression. In the first fourteen years of the twentieth century only 315 lynch victims were accused of rape or attempted rape, while more than 500 were accused of homicide and the others were accused of robbery, insulting white persons, and numerous other 'offenses' " (440).

56. Brundage *Lynching in the New South,* discusses the whole issue of rape on pp. 62–72. In *The Promise of the New South,* Ayers says, "Although most lynchings were inflicted in response to alleged murder, most of the rhetoric and justification focused intently on the so-called 'one crime' or 'usual crime': the sexual assault of white women by blacks. That assault sometimes involved rape, while at other times a mere look or word was enough to justify death" (158).

57. See Griggs, *Imperium in Imperio;* Johnson, *Autobiography of an Ex-Colored Man;* Fleming, *Hope's Highway.*

58. Dreer, *The Immediate Jewel of His Soul,* p. 298. This was too ridiculous a charge to pass up, but it must be said that the lynching occurs when, the man accused of rabbit poaching escapes from jail, shooting a couple of officers in the process.

59. Cutler, *Lynch-Law,* p. 172

60. Brown, *Negro in American Fiction,* pp. 100, 105. See also Bone, *Negro Novel in America,* p. 19. There are few issues upon which so many literary critics and historians agree as they do about the role of the African American novelist of the pre-World War I world in disproving the stereotypes of blacks advanced by whites. For example, Barbara Christian writes that the principal importance of *Iola Leroy* is in its clear delineation of "the relationship between the images of black women

held at large in society and the novelist's struggle to refute these images." See her *Black Women Novelists,* p.5.

61. Elder, *The "Hindered Hand,"* p. 9. For other allusions to the propagandistic quality of this fiction, see Gloster, *Negro Voices in American Fiction,* p. 25, passim; Bell, *The Afro-American Novel.* Although Bell does not use the terms "propaganda" and "counterstereotype," he speaks of the African American novel of the early years as an instrument for promoting "some form of deliverance or vision of a new world: moral or political awakening, flight, rebellion, or social reform" (36). Addison Gayle, Jr., in *The Way of the New World,* sees the essence of black fiction between 1901 and 1920 as a "battle for the control of images," how African Americans would be referred to. But he makes no mention of minor novelists like Pauline Hopkins, McHenry Jones, Langhorne Pryor, J. W. Grant, or others. Ann du Cille, on the other hand, referring principally to *Iola Leroy* and *Contending Forces,* writes, "In the midst of a climate that endowed black women (and men) with uncontrollable sexual appetites, these writers created passionless heroines who were pious and pure, if not always submissive and domestic" (*The Coupling Convention: Sex, Text, and Tradition in Black Women's Fiction* [New York: Oxford University Press, 1993]), p. 44.

62. August Meier, preface to Wells, *On Lynchings.*

63. Griggs, "Notes for the Serious," in *The Hindered Hand,* p. 299. The lineage of Griggs's account is interesting. Trudier Harris cites a newspaper story from the Vicksburg, Mississippi, *Evening Post* that "is so comparable in its descriptions of the mutilations and in its phrasing that it is almost certain Griggs had seen the item before writing his novel" (*Exorcising Blackness,* p. 2). In *100 Years of Lynchings* Ralph Ginzburg reprints a portion of the *Evening Post* article, together with an excerpt from a story on the same lynching in the New York *Press* on the same date, February 8, 1904, and Booker T. Washington's letter three weeks later in the New York *Tribune* generalizing from the Holbert lynching upon his opposition to the practice, pp. 62–64. W. E. B. Du Bois, in *The Ordeal of Mansart* (New York: Mainstream Publishers, 1957), has a minister report the same atrocity to a conference in Atlanta, citing the date of 1904 and the place as Doddsville, Mississippi. He uses the actual names of the victims, Luther Holbert and his wife, rather than Bud and Foresta Harper (225–26).

64. Du Bois, "Note to the Reader," in *The Quest of the Silver Fleece.*

65. Raymond A. Cook, *Thomas Dixon* (New York: Twayne Publishers, 1974), p. 70.

66. Elder, *The "Hindered Hand,"* p. 33.

67. Ibid., p. 40. See also Michael Awkward's succinct statement about a perception that persisted "until recently" "that the black artist's primary responsibility was to create protest fiction that explored America's historical mistreatment of blacks, boosting black self-esteem and changing racist white attitudes about Afro-Americans in the process"; "introduction to *New Essays on "Their Eyes Were Watching God,"* ed. Michael Awkward (New York: Cambridge University Press, 1990), p. 3.

68. August Meier writes in *Negro Thought in America* that Hopkins illustrates

the "dualism" that afflicts most of these early novelists: pleading "for a racial literature and racial solidarity, but in her writings [trying] to show how well Negroes had absorbed American middle-class ideals in home life education, and cultural accomplishment"(314).

69. Johnson, *Light Ahead for the Negro,* pp. 17–18.

70. See especially the marriage of Charles Gaston and Sallie Worth in Thomas Dixon, *The Leopard's Spots* (1902; rpt. Ridgewood, N.J.: Gregg Press, 1967), pp. 467–69.

71. Cf. Hazel V. Carby's persuasive point that Frances Harper's lola Leroy marries and answers, in Harper's words, "a clarion call to life of high and holy worth," in *Reconstructing Womanhood,* p. 80.

72. This is, of course, the well-known last line of *Sister Carrie* (1900) and can be found in any edition.

73. The phrase is Eric Auerbach's, from his discussion of the subject in *Mimesis: The Representation of Reality in Western Literature,* trans. Willard R. Trask (Princeton, N.J.: Princeton University Press, 1953), p. 458.

74. William A. Sinclair, *Aftermath of Slavery: A Study in the Condition and Environment of the American Negro* (1905; rpt. New York: Arno Press and New York Times, 1969), p. 115.

5. THE LIMITS OF THE HERO

1. Charles W. Chesnutt, *The Marrow of Tradition,* intro. Robert M. Farnsworth (1901; rpt. Ann Arbor: University of Michigan Press, 1969); James Weldon Johnson, *The Autobiography of an Ex-Colored Man* (1912), reprinted in *Three Negro Classics* (New York: Avon Books, 1965). Page references are to these editions and are hereafter indicated in parentheses in the text.

2. Cf. Hugh M. Gloster, *Negro Voices in American Fiction* (New York: Russel and Russell, 1948): *The Autobiography* is an "adumbration of the Negro renascence of the 1920's" (79). I cite Gloster simply to take note of how far back this universally accepted position goes.

3. Helen M. Chesnutt, *Charles Wadell Chesnutt, Pioneer of the Color Line* (Chapel Hill: University of North Carolina Press, 1952), p. 21.

4. *The Short Fiction of Charles W. Chesnutt,* ed. Sylvia Lyons Render (Washington, D.C.: Howard University Press, 1974), p. 411.

5. This account comes mainly from Helen G. Edmonds, *The Negro and Fusion Politics in North Carolina, 1894–1901* (Chapel Hill: University of North Carolina Press, 1951).

6. Robert A. Lee, "The Desired State of Feeling: Charles W. Chesnutt and the Afro-American Literary Tradition," *Durham University Journal,* n.s. 25, no. 2 (March, 1974): 169.

7. William L. Andrews, *The Literary Career of Charles W. Chesnutt* (Baton Rouge: Louisiana State University Press, 1980), p. 194. As he did with the slave narrative, Andrews has produced here the definitive full-scale work on Chesnutt.

8. Addison Gayle; Jr., *The Way of the New World: The Black Novel in America* (Garden City, N.Y.: Anchor/Doubleday, 1976), p. 65.

9. What Michael True says of the nonviolent activist in *An Energy Field More Intense than War: The Nonviolent Tradition and American Literature* (Syracuse, N.Y.: Syracuse University Press, 1995) applies to Miller and to those figures like Frances Harper's Frank Latimer: "nonviolence is primarily practical and strategic, rather than romantic or utopian" (xxii).

10. Andrews, *Literary Career of Charles W. Chesnutt,* p. 195.

11. Charles W. Chesnutt, *The Colonel's Dream* (1905; rpt. Upper Saddle River, N.J.: The Gregg Press, 1968), p. 294. Subsequent page references are to this edition and are indicated in parentheses in the text.

12. Gloster, *Negro Voices in American Fiction,* p. 43.

13. Cf. Robert E. Fleming, *James Weldon Johnson* (Boston: Twayne Publishers, 1987): Fleming sees *The Autobiography* as an exercise in irony. Thus, though the narrator views himself romantically as a kind of tragic hero tainted by the curse of color from his mother, the reader, says Fleming, "Is more likely to view him as an antiheroic or pathetic character, frequently indulging in self-pity and unable to accept his total identity and assume his position in a race for which he feels little sympathy or admiration" (33) Fleming is ably seconded in his reading of *The Autobiography* by Howard Faulkner, in "James Weldon Johnson's Portrait of the Artist as an Invisible Man," *Black American Literature Forum,* 19, no. 4 (Winter 1985): 147–51. Faulkner also sees the narrator as an antihero, one who, like John Marcher in Henry James's "Beast in the Jungle," experiences an "unlived life" (148).

14. Henry Edward Krehbiel, in *Afro-American Folksongs: A Study in Racial and National Music* (New York: Frederick Ungar, 1913), and John Wesley Work, in *Folk Song of the American Negro* (1915; rpt. New York: Negro Universities Press, 1969), point out that Anton Dvorák was one of the first classical musician-composers to sense that, as Work says, the spiritual in particular "would lend itself to higher development, and that would be a basis for a national music." Dvorák's *New World Symphony* preserves "the characteristics of the Negro music." Work also mentions the transcriptions of "Sometimes I Feel Like a Motherless Child" and "Deep River" by the black composer Samuel Coleridge-Taylor, which "point the way toward the future where lives the dream and hope of the Negro race" *(Folk Song,* p. 99). Johnson's ideas were thus in the wind. See also Eric J. Sundquist's most useful discussion of the issue in *The Hammers of Creation: Folk Culture in Modern African-American Fiction* (Athens: University of Georgia Press, 1992), p. vi especially.

15. James Weldon Johnson, *Along This Way* (1933; rpt. New York: Viking Press, 1968; 3rd printing June 1973), p. 209. Subsequent page references are to this edition and are indicated in parentheses in the text.

16. See, in particular, James Weldon Johnson, ed., *The Book of American Negro Poetry* (1922; rpt. New York: Harcourt Brace and World, 1959), passages from the preface to the 1st ed. pp. 11–17, compared with pp. 447–48 in *The Autobiography.*

17. It is noteworthy to remember that Joe Hamilton kills his black mistress

Hattie Sterling in Paul Laurence Dunbar's *Sport of the Gods* as an example of the final tragic corruption of the Hamilton family by New York City (1902; rpt. New York: Macmillan, 1970), pp. 157–58.

18. Cf. Fleming, *James Weldon Johnson,* p. 23.

19. Cf. ibid., pp. 38–39. My reading of this passage differs diametrically from Fleming's.

20. Frederick Douglass, *My Bondage and My Freedom* (1855), ed. Philip S. Foner (rpt. New York: Dover Publications, 1969), pp. 246–47.

21. Robert A. Bone, *The Negro Novel in America,* rev. ed. (New Haven: Yale University Press, 1965), p. 47; Gayle, *The Way of the New World,* p. 113; Fleming; *James Weldon Johnson,* p. 33.

22. Cf. Carl Van Vechten, Introduction, and Sherman, French, and Company's preface to the original edition of 1912, *The Autobiography of an Ex-Colored Man,* 7th printing (1927; rpt. New York: A. A. Knopf, 1973), pp. vi, xi.

23. As Eric J. Sundquist quite rightly says in his interesting analysis of the folklore aspects of the novel, "Johnson is neither synonymous with his narrator nor entirely separable from him" (*Hammers of Creation,* p. 5).

24. Cf. Richard Wright, "How 'Bigger' was Born," in *Native Son* (New York: Harper and Row, 1966), p. xxi.

6. ART AND LYNCHING

1. Historians differ on precisely when the Renaissance began and when it ended. For my discussion I will use the term "Renaissance" to refer to the period between 1923 and 1933. See especially Cary D. Wintz, *Black Culture and the Harlem Renaissance* (Houston: Rice University Press, 1988). He provides a full and convenient list of historians who have argued the chronological limits of the period, and himself suggests the publication of *Cane* as an appropriate starting point. He provides no specific date for the ending of the movement but points to "the later works of Zora Neale Hurston, Claude McKay, and Langston Hughes," as the signals of the end of the period (2).

2. Alain Locke, ed., *The New Negro* (1925; rpt. New York: Atheneum, 1974), p. 297. Subsequent page references are to this edition and are indicated in parentheses in the text.

3. Robert L. Zangrando, *The NAACP Crusade against Lynching, 1909–1950* (Philadelphia: Temple University Press, 1980), pp. 7–8.

4. The two quotations are from letters dated 1922 and cited by Cynthia Earl Kerman and Richard Eldridge in *The Lives of Jean Toomer: A Hunger for Wholeness* (Baton Rouge: Louisiana State University Press, 1987), pp. 96, 99.

5. Jean Toomer, *Cane* (1923; rpt. New York: Harper and Row, 1969), pp. 66–67. Subsequent page references are to this edition and are indicated in parentheses in the text.

6. James Weldon Johnson, *The Autobiography of an Ex-Colored Man* (1912); reprinted in *Three Negro Classics* (New York: Avon Books, 1965), p. 497.

7. Ralph Ellison, *Shadow and Act,* rev. ed. (New Haven: Yale University Press, 1965), p. 90.

8. W. E. B. Du Bois had pointed out this consequence more than two decades earlier in his study of the second-generation blacks in Farmville, Virginia, demonstrating "the generally corrosive impact of industry upon traditional cultures," as David Levering Lewis puts it in *W. E. B. Du Bois: A Biography, 1868–1919* (New York: Henry Holt, 1993), p. 196.

9. *The Wayward and the Seeking: A Collection of Writings by Jean Toomer,* ed. Darwin T. Turner (Washington, D.C.: Howard University Press, 1982), p. 123.

10. Quoted in Mabel Mayle Dillard, "Behind the Veil: Jean Toomer's Esthetic," in *Studies in Cane,"* ed. Frank Durham (Columbus, Ohio: Charles E. Merrill, 1971), pp. 4–5.

11. Ibid., p. 4.

12. Toomer, *The Wayward and the Seeking,* p. 123.

13. Cf. Charles Scruggs, "All Dressed Up but No Place to Go: The Black Writer and His Audience during the Harlem Renaissance," *American Literature,* 48 (January 1977): 554: "In the context of the scene, the rose symbolizes the grim but magnificent heritage of the Negro past, and in rejecting it, Muriel also rejects the Negro artist who is committed to celebrating that past no matter how ugly it may appear to others. For Toomer, what is positive in the black experience is inextricably welded to the grotesque." Obviously I read this differently. Mr. Barry, the dwarf, is a grotesque, to be sure, but surely must stand not for the Negro artist— Dan is the symbol for that—but for the black folk, distorted and deformed in the city but put to the bathetically sentimentalized uses of the middle class.

14. In *The Harlem Renaissance Remembered,* ed. Arna Bontemps (New York: Dodd, Mead, 1972), p. 39.

15. Cf. Kerman and Eldridge, *The Lives of Jean Toomer,* p. 98.

16. Du Bois said, "I do not care a damn for any art that is not used for propaganda," in "Criteria of Negro Art," *The Crisis,* 32 (October 1926): 296. See also the "Symposium" run by Du Bois in seven 1926 issues of *The Crisis,* entitled "The Negro in Art: How Shall He Be Portrayed?" It appeared in the following volumes and numbers: 31, nos. 5 and 6 (March and April); 32 nos. 1, 2, 4, 5 (May, June, August, September); and 33, no. 1 (November). White writers, critics, and publishers, as well as blacks, contributed to the series. The main gist of the discussions was whether the true racial artist should write propaganda in order to present the race at its best, or write "art" and take as subjects even the race's less savory sides. Langston Hughes's "Negro Artist and the Racial Mountain," which appeared in *The Nation* (June 23, 1926) while Du Bois's Symposium was running, is the best-known example of the debate. It is reprinted in *On Being Black; Writings by Afro-Americans from Frederick Douglass to the Present,* ed. Charles T. Davis and Daniel Walden (Greenwich, Conn.: Fawcett, 1970), pp. 159–63.

17. I pass over several novels that make brief allusions to lynchings that have no effect upon the tone or texture of their narratives or their characters' lives and are not serious attempts to explore the practice. Cf. Claude McKay, *Banjo* (1929; rpt.

New York: Harcourt Brace Jovanovich, 1957), p. 304; Countee Cullen, *One Way to Heaven* (1932; rpt. New York: AMS Press, 1975), p. 168; Nella Larsen, *Passing* (1929; rpt. New York: Arno Press and New York Times, 1969), p. 190.

18. Jessie Fauset, *Plum Bun* (New York: Frederick A. Stokes, 1929), pp. 116, 117.

19. Ibid., p. 291.

20. Langston Hughes, *Not without Laughter* (1930; rpt. New York: Collier Books/Macmillan, 1969), pp. 72–73.

21. Hughes, it might be said, does here what Zora Neale Hurston urged other African American writers of the Harlem Renaissance to do: turn to the folk for authentic style and tale-telling abilities. See her *Jonah's Gourd Vine* (1934; rpt. Philadelphia: Lippincott, 1971); *Mules and Men* (1935; rpt. New York: HarperCollins, 1990); and especially *Their Eyes Were Watcing God* (1937; rpt. New York: Harper and Row, 1990). See also Robert E. Hemenway, *Zora Neale Hurston: A Literary Biography* (Urbana and Chicago: University of Illinois Press, 1977).

22. Nathan Huggins, *The Harlem Renaissance* (New York: Oxford University Press, 1971), p. 231.

23. Wallace Thurman, *Infants of the Spring* (1932; rpt. Carbondale: Southern Illinois University Press, 1979), p. 89. Subsequent page references are to this edition and are indicated in parentheses in the text.

24. Scruggs, "All Dressed Up but No place to Go," pp. 560–61.

25. Cf. Hugh M. Gloster, *Negro Voices in American Fiction* (1948; rpt. New York: Russell and Russell, 1965), p. 172; Robert A. Bone, *The Negro Novel in America,* rev. ed. (New Haven: Yale University Press, 1965), p. 94; Bernard W. Bell, *The Afro-American Novel and Its Tradition* (Amherst: University of Massachusetts Press, 1987), p. 148.

26. George Schuyler, *Black No More; Being an Account of the Strange and Wonderful Workings of Science in the Land of the Free, A.D. 1933–1940* (1931; rpt. New York: Negro Universities Press, 1969), p. 242. Curiously, Trudier Harris does not mention this episode in *Black No More* in her *Exorcising Blackness: Historical and Literary Lynching and Burning Rituals* (Bloomington: Indiana University Press, 1984). It perfectly exemplifies her thesis.

27. Margaret Perry, *Silence to the Drums* (Westport, Conn.: Greenwood Press, 1976), p. 6.

28. Arna Bontemps, *Black Thunder* (1936; rpt. Boston: Beacon Press, 1970), p. 92.

29. W. E. B. Du Bois, *Dark Princess: A Romance,* intro. Herbert Aptheker (1928; rpt. Millwood, N.Y.: Kraus-Thomson, 1974), pp. 60, 53.

30. George Washington Lee, *River George* (New York: Macaulay, 1937), pp. 102–3. Subsequent page references are to this edition and are indicated in parentheses in the text.

31. Du Bois, *Dark Princess,* p. 297.

32. Ibid., p. 22. This image contains considerable pathos, since Du Bois's first child was a son whose hair was "tinted with gold," but he died when he was still

an infant. Why was this so? anguishes Du Bois: "An evil omen was golden hair in my life." With the Maharaja, however, the color line/veil has been lifted, and so he is not an "evil omen," but the promise of a raceless future. See the essay "Of the Passing of the First-Born," in *The Souls of Black Folk* (1903), reprinted in *Three Negro Classics* (New York: Avon Books, 1965), p. 350.

33. Walter F. White, *Rope and Faggot* (1929; rpt. New York: Arno Press and New York Times, 1969).

34. Walter F. White, *The Fire in the Flint* (1924; rpt. Negro Universities Press, 1969) pp. 269, 271.

35. Walter F. White, *A Man Called White: The Autobiography of Walter White* (New York: Viking Press, 1948), p. 68.

36. Gloster, *Negro Voices in American Fiction,* p. 234.

37. For a succinct discussion of the tenant system, see Nicholas Lemann, *The Promised Land: The Great Black Migration and How It Changed America* (New York: Alfred A. Knopf, 1991), pp. 5–21.

38. George Washington Lee, *Beale Street: Where the Blues Began* (New York: Robert O. Ballou, 1934).

39. "Negro Youth Speaks," in Locke, *The New Negro,* p. 47.

40. Compare Thomas Nelson Page, "Spectre in the Cart," in *Bred in the Bone* (New York: Charles Scribner's Sons, 1904): "It was all as silent as the grave. There was no living creature there. Only the great sycamore, from one of its long, pale branches that stretched across the road, hung that dead thing with the toes turned a little in, just out of our reach, turning and swaying a little in the night wind" (96).

41. Waters Edward Turpin, *These Low Grounds* (1937; rpt. College Park, Md.: McGrath Publishing, 1969), p. 328.

42. Ibid., pp. 341, 344.

7. AFTER WORLD WAR II

1. Exceptions to this moratorium are Jenkins Deaderick, who published his own novel, *It Was Not My World,* in Los Angeles in 1942, which contains a Mississippi lynching; and Willard Savoy's *Alien Land* (1949), with which I deal in the latter part of this chapter.

2. Richard Wright dealt with lynching only in his short stories (e.g., "Big Boy Leaves Home") and his poetry before *The Long Dream.*

3. Again, I take my lynching figures from Robert L. Zangrando, *The NAACP Crusade against Lynching, 1909–1950* (Philadelphia: Temple University Press, 1980), p. 8.

4. Cf. Herbert Shapiro, *White Violence and Black Response: From Reconstruction to Montgomery* (Amherst: University of Massachusetts Press, 1988), pp. 341, 369, on the increase in police brutality and legalized lynching.

5. Zangrando, *NAACP Crusade,* p. 174.

6. In Junius Edwards, *If We Must Die* (Garden City, N.Y.: Doubleday, 1963),

lynching is reduced to the blundering of three drunken crackers who cause the death of the black hero not by rope or faggot but by inadvertently severing an artery in his wrist so that he bleeds to death on the way back to town in the wagon of a slow old Negro.

7. Seth Cagin and Philip Dray, *We Are Not Afraid: The Story of Goodwin, Schwerner, and Chaney and the Civil Rights Campaign for Mississippi* (New York: Macmillan, 1988), p. 110.

8. Shapiro quotes this account from Julian Mayfield (in *White Violence and Black Response*, p. 457).

9. William Bradford Huie, "What's Happened to the Emmett Till Killers?" *Look*, January 22, 1957, p. 68.

10. James Forman, *The Making of Black Revolutionaries: A Personal Account* (New York: Macmillan, 1972), pp. 35, 32.

11. Huie, "Emmett Till Killers," p. 68.

12. Cagin and Dray, *We Are Not Afraid*, p. 69.

13. David J. Garrow, *Bearing the Cross: Martin Luther King and the Southern Christian Leadership Conference* (New York: William Morrow, 1986), p. 70; Jack M. Bloom, *Class, Race, and the Civil Rights Movement* (Bloomington: Indiana University Press, 1987), p. 136.

14. Garrow, *Bearing the Cross*, p. 218; Cagin and Dray, *We Are Not Afraid*, p. 120.

15. Martin Luther King, Jr., "The Violence of Desperate Men," in *Talk That Talk: An Anthology of African-American Storytelling*, ed. Linda Goss and Marian E. Barnes (New York: Simon and Schuster, 1989), p. 150.

16. James Baldwin, *Go Tell It on the Mountain* (1953; rpt. New York: Dell, 1985), p. 142. Subsequent page references are to this edition and are indicated in parentheses in the text.

17. James Baldwin, *Notes of a Native Son* (1955; rpt. New York: Bantam Books, 1964), pp. 33, 4, 95.

18. Richard Wright, *The Long Dream*, (1958; rpt. New York: Harper and Row, 1987), p. 78. Subsequent page references are to this edition and are indicated in parentheses in the text.

19. Fishbelly disempowers the establishment by out-thinking Chief Cantley on the matter of some condemnatory canceled checks. Is Wright subliminally influenced by the clever slave tradition of the trickster, or is he consciously but subtly using it with an uncharacteristic ironic playfulness?

20. Cf. Forman, *Making of Black Revolutionaries*, p. 385: "We were a band of sisters and brothers, a circle of trust," he writes, referring to the blacks working in the 1960 Mississippi Summer Project. In the late fifties, North Carolina NAACP activist Robert Williams sees a "new wonderful spirit rising throughout Dixie—this determination to break the chains of bondage and the spirit of valor of a people who just a few years ago were submissive peons in civilization's no-man's-land" in *Negroes with Guns*, ed. Marc Shleiffer, intro. John Henrik Clarke (Chicago: Third World Press, 1973), p. 111. And Bayard Rustin believed that the lesson of the

Montgomery boycott was that "the center of gravity [of civil rights activity] has shifted from the courts to community action," that the people, unified, could now win their freedom. Quoted in Garrow, *Bearing the Cross,* p. 86.

21. August Meier et al., eds., *Negro Protest Thought in the Twentieth Century* (New York: Bobbs-Merrill, 1971), p. 308.

22. I wrote this sentence and used the metaphor of "sites" before I read *History and Memory in African-American Culture* (New York: Oxford University Press, 1994), a collection of essays edited by Genevieve Fabre and Robert G. O'Meally. The seminar that was the occasion of the essays grew from the idea embodied in French historian Pierre Nora's "seven-volume study of France's history and national memory called *Les Lieux de mémoire,*" which is translated as "sites of memory" in this book. The editors' comment on Nora's metaphor reinforces my own approach to this material: "More than ever, we saw novels, poems, slave narratives, autobiographies, and oral testimonies as crucial parts of the historical record. These varied repositories of individual memories, taken together, create a collective communal memory" (9).

23. John Oliver Killens, *Youngblood* (New York: Dial Press, 1954), pp. 472, 475.

24. Robert L. Nadeau, "Black Jesus: A Study of Kelley's *A Different Drummer.*" *Studies in Black Literature* 2, no. 2 (Summer 1971). 13–15.

25. William Melvin Kelley, *A Different Drummer* (1962; rpt. Garden City, N.Y.: Doubleday/Anchor, 1969), p. 133.

26. Ibid., p. 198.

27. Intro. to William J. Simmons, *Men of Mark: Eminent, Progressive, and Rising* (1887; rpt. New York: Arno Press, 1968), p. 43.

28. Ernest J. Gaines, *The Autobiography of Miss Jane Pittman* (New York: Dial Press, 1971), p. 89. Subsequent page references are indicated in parentheses in the text.

29. This is Gaines's adaptation of William Faulkner's perception of Dilsey and her progeny in *The Sound and the Fury,* who "endured."

30. This is the first of a trilogy. It was followed by *Rosiebelle Lee Wildcat Tennessee* (New York: Dial Press, 1980) and *Baby Sweet's* (New York: Dial Press, 1983).

31. Raymond Andrews, *Appalachee Red* (New York: Dial Press, 1978), p. 207. Subsequent page references are to this edition and are indicated in parentheses in the text.

32. Two good guides to this rather overliterary novel are Johanna L. Grimes's article on Forrest in the *Dictionary of Literary Biography* (Detroit: Gale Research, 1984), 33:77–80; and Keith E. Byerman's essay, "Orphans and Circuses: The Literary Experiments of Leon Forrest and Clarence Major," in his *Fingering the Jagged Edge: Tradition and Form in Recent Black Fiction* (Athens: University of Georgia Press, 1985). I gratefully acknowledge my debt to both.

33. Leon Forrest, *There Is a Tree More Ancient than Eden* (New York: Random House, 1973), p. 123. Byerman cogently connects the crucifixion-lynching with the fertility symbolism of the "Osiris-dismemberment" myth. "The murder in 'The Vision' seems designed to bring the divided people back to a state of unity

and purity. But the return to origins must fail because the victim is not a god but a human being, and thus the society's guilt is increased, not assuaged, by his death. His refusal to die marks not the community's renewal, but his own spiritual toughness" ("Orphans and Circuses," p. 248).

34. Bernard Bell says that the Mansart trilogy and *Dark Princess* "are a chronicle of despair in which the only hope for the world is the rise of an independent, industrialized Africa and Asia under the banner of socialism and the leadership of the Talented Tenth of nonwhite nations." See *The Afro-American Novel and Its Tradition* (Amherst: University of Massachusetts Press, 1987), p. 82.

35. W. E. B. Du Bois, *The Ordeal of Mansart* (1957), *Mansart Builds a School* (1959), and *Worlds of Color* (1961), all published in New York by Mainstream Publishers.

36. Du Bois, *Ordeal of Mansart,* p. 70.

37. Du Bois, *Worlds of Color,* p. 348.

38. William Mahoney, *Black Jacob* (New York: Macmillan, 1969), p. 70. Subsequent page references are indicated in parentheses in the text.

39. Sarah E. Wright, *This Child's Gonna Live* (1969; rpt. New York: Dell Publishing, 1970), p. 254.

8. RICHARD WRIGHT AND BIGGER THOMAS

1. Stephen Butterfield, *Black Autobiography in America* (Amherst: University of Massachusetts Press, 1974), p. 286.

2. In *From Trickster to Badman: The Black Folk Hero in Slavery and Freedom* (Philadelphia: University of Pennsylvania Press, 1989), John W. Roberts uses the "double bind" idea to describe the dilemma of the folk badman-hero, who in seeking to preserve "the harmony and integrity of black communal life" employs methods judged moral by his own "philoi" but immoral by the white society against which he struggles. The folk badman, says Roberts, is "an individual who, in breaking the law, ultimately paid for the heroic moment" (214). Roberts's discussion throws much light on the character of Bigger Thomas, and though my own reading of Bigger somewhat resembles Roberts's reading of the badman-hero, I do not see Bigger as a Stackolee, Dupree, or Billy Martin. Nor do I fully concur with Roberts that these black badmen commit their violence "to protect the values of the black community" (214).

3. Richard Wright, *Native Son* (1940; rpt. New York: Harper and Row, 1966), pp. 23, 225. Subsequent page references are to this edition and are indicated in parentheses in the text.

4. Edward Margolies points out that "the full freedom of [Wright's] central characters depends not only on the transgression of society's laws but often on the suppression of other members of society." About these oppositions, says Margolies, Wright is "ambivalent to the end." See "Richard Wright's Opposing Freedoms," *Mississippi Quarterly,* 42, no. 4 (Fall 1989): 413, 414.

5. In *The Emergence of Richard Wright: A Study in Literature and Society* (Urbana:

University of Illinois Press, 1972), p. 137, Keneth Kinnamon speaks of Bigger as a "suffering Christ" whose sacrifice has "redemptive power." It seems to me, though, that Bigger is nearer Satan, whose moral system subverts rather than reinforces the tradition that Christian imagery upholds. It is ironic, not holy, that Bigger redeems. See the rest of my discussion and the following note.

6. Compare Christopher Lasch's definition of "the republican tradition" of America as including "the fullest use of one's powers," in *The Revolt of the Elites and the Betrayal of Democracy* (New York: W. W. Norton, 1995), p. 155.

7. Houston A. Baker, Jr., Introduction, *Twentieth Century Interpretations of "Native Son"* (Englewood Cliffs, N.J.: Prentice-Hall, 1972), p. 11. There is also James Baldwin's reference in his essay "Many Thousands Gone," which says quite a different thing. Bigger, says Baldwin, scorns all appeals to his humanity in the end of the novel, actually *wanting* to die "because he glories in his hatred and prefers, like Lucifer, rather to rule in hell than serve in heaven" (in *Notes of A Native Son* [1955; rpt. Boston: Bantam Books, 1964], pp. 34–35. This seems to me quite wrongheaded, serving Baldwin's total attack on the novel rather than a judicious reading.

8. Richard Wright, *Black Boy: A Record of Childhood and Youth* (New York: Harper and Brothers, 1945), p. 65. Subsequent page references are to this edition and are indicated in parentheses in the text.

9. I should point out that little seems to have changed since Wright wrote these words in 1945. Gayle Pemberton writes in her 1992 book *The Hottest Water in Chicago* (Boston: Faber and Faber) that in the United States the "necessity of concentrating on surviving in black skins saps the energies; not only does it keep real political and social power in the hands of whites, but it makes the self no more than a sociological fact, dancing, marionette-style, to a degrading tune." Quoted by Nancy Mairs in her review of the book, " 'Minority' Is for Statisticians,' " *New York Times Book Review,* August 2, 1992, p. 17.

10. Richard Wright, "The Ethics of Living Jim Crow," in *Uncle Tom's Children* (New York: Harper and Row, 1965), p. 5; and *Black Boy,* p. 6.

11. Among many other critics, Russell Carl Brignano cites this same passage and says of it, "This restlessness of youth is emphasized throughout the work. The street operates as a symbolic barrier dividing different worlds. It additionally functions as a symbolic path of flight. . . . As the youthful Wright continually tries to push aside the alluring white curtains, a lesson is eventually gained: the Southern whites have established severe penalties for a black man's venturing beyond the curtains" (*Richard Wright: An Introduction to the Man and His Work* [Pittsburgh: University of Pittsburgh Press, 1970], p. 8). Brignano makes no allusion to the fact that the oppressor here is the rigidly Seventh Day Adventist black household.

12. See also Albert Stone's interesting discussion of this first episode, in which he concludes that "fire is the comprehensive metaphor of self which unites and explains Wright's identity" (*Autobiographical Occasions and Original Acts: Versions of American Identity from Henry Adams to Nate Shaw* [Philadelphia: University of Pennsylvania Press, 1982], p. 129).

13. Others have also failed to resist the compulsion. Cf. Katherine Fishburn, *Richard Wright's Hero: The Faces of a Rebel-Victim* (Metuchen, N.J.: Scarecrow Press, 1977), p. 87: Bigger Thomas, she says, has "a dual heritage, exhibiting traits of both the eternal rebel, Prometheus, and the eternal victim, Sisyphus." Eugene E. Miller, in *Voice of a Native Son: The Poetics of Richard Wright* (Jackson: University Press of Mississippi, 1990), pp. 122–23, points out that Wright mentions "the motif of Prometheus" in an unpublished manuscript entitled "Memories of My Grandmother" and "seems to connect [it] with a theme of revolt." Miller suggests that Fred Daniels in "The Man Who Lived Underground" carries the Promethean fire but fails. Keneth Kinnamon declares that Wright sees Bigger as "a revolutionary potentiality" (*Emergence of Richard Wright*, pp. 125–26).

14. Among others, Keneth Kinnamon has noted Wright's repeated use of fire as metaphor and image. He cites Henry F. Winslow in his review of *The Long Dream*, "Nightmare Experiences," *The Crisis*, February 1959, as the first critic to observe this pattern. Cf. Kinnamon's Introduction to his *New Essays on "Native Son"* (New York: Cambridge University Press, 1990), p. 10.

15. Aeschylus, *Prometheus Bound*, trans. Michael Townsend (San Francisco: Chandler Publishing, 1966), lines 409–412.

16. Michel Fabre, *The Unfinished Quest of Richard Wright* (New York: William Morrow, 1973), p. 10.

17. Addison Gayle, Jr., in *Richard Wright: The Ordeal of a Native Son* (Garden City, N.Y.: Anchor/Doubleday, 1980): "The temptations to draw conclusions in line with those who believe that the FBI and the CIA were directly involved in Wright's sudden death are great. To do so, however, based upon the facts of the documents, would be wrong. . . . What I found was a pattern of harassment by agencies of the United States Government, resembling at times a personal vendetta more so than an intelligence-gathering investigation" (xv).

18. Richard Wright, *The Outsider* (1953; rpt. New York: Harper and Row, 1965), p. 440.

19. If, as Robert Hemenway says, "the train motif is well known" in African American folk and literary tradition, Wright's locomotive image is certainly not that of the spiritual "Get on Board, Little Children" but rather of the "damnation train" that John Pearson, of Zora Neale Hurston's *Jonah's Gourd Vine* (1934), employs in his last powerful sermon. Hemenway quotes Pearson's "vision" of the train in its entirety and points out that Hurston had copied it verbatim during her trips to the South to collect folklore:

> I heard de whistle of de damnation train
> Dat pulled out from Garden of Eden loaded wid cargo goin' to hell
> Ran at break-neck speed all de way thru de law
> All de way thru de prophetic age
> All de way thru de reign of kings and judges—
> Plowed her way thru de Jurdan
> And on her way to Calvary, when she blew for de switch

Jesus stood out on her track like a rough-backed mountain
And she threw her cow-catcher in His side and His blood ditched de train
He died for our sins.
Wounded in the house of His friends.

If Wright knew either the conventional imagery or the Hurston passage in particular—and it is impossible to tell if either is the case—he certainly adapted it to his own use. I have never been convinced Wright felt much folk tradition in his own bones, and though there is an uncanny closeness of meaning between his and the sermon's imagery, his wording comes nearer to modern existential myth (see Friedrich Durrenmatt's short story "The Tunnel," for example) than to an appropriation of folklore such as Hurston makes in *Jonah's Gourd Vine*—this in spite of his comment in "Blueprint for Negro Literature" that "Negro folklore remains the Negro writer's most powerful weapon." Hemenway also says something more interesting regarding black folklore relevant to Richard Wright: "In the notes to *Mules and Men,*" he writes, "Zora observed that the devil in black folklore is not the terror he is in European folklore. Rather, he is a powerful trickster who often competes successfully with God." The idea is that blacks tend to side with the enemy of whites and to call into doubt the purported goodness of a white God who endorses oppression and slavery. Sonia Sanchez's *We a BaddDDD People* demonstrates how they can reverse the moral vocabulary in an act of celebration and defiance. See Robert E. Hemenway, *Zora Neale Hurston: A Literary Biography* (Urbana and Chicago: University of Illinois Press, 1977), pp. 197, 223–24. I personally see none of the trickster or the ironic signifying that characterizes so much of the folk tradition in Wright's passage. He is grim and self-celebrating here rather than ironic.

20. In his 1849 review, "Narratives of Fugitive Slaves," Ephraim Peabody links the slave narratives with epics like the *Iliad* and the *Odyssey* and the stories of romance popular in the Middle Ages and the Renaissance. See *The Slave's Narratives,* ed. Charles T. Davis and Henry Louis Gates, Jr. (New York: Oxford University Press, 1985). See also William L. Andrews, *To Tell a Free Story: The First Century of Afro-American Autobiography, 1760–1860* (Urbana: University of Illinois Press, 1986), pp. 230–31: Andrews claims that references to Frederick Douglass as "devil" in *My Bondage and My Freedom* (1855) make him a kind of Prometheus, a "serpent who tempted [his fellow slaves] to rebel," who both attracts and repels whites. This, says Andrews, connects him with the English poets of the romantic movement, Shelley and Byron.

21. Albert Camus's *The Rebel* was published in French in 1951, as *L'homme révolté* (Librairie Gallimard), the English translation in 1956 (Alfred A. Knopf). See also my article "The Violence of *Native Son,*" *Southern Review,* 17, no. 2 (April 1981): 303–20; reprinted in *Richard Wright: A Collection of Critical Essays,* ed. Arnold Rampersad, New Century Views (Englewood Cliffs, N.J.: Prentice-Hall, 1994), pp. 12–25.

9. THE REBEL STIRS

1. Stephen B. Bennett and William W. Nichols, in "Violence in Afro-American Fiction: An Hypothesis," *Modern Fiction Studies,* 17, no. 2 (Summer 1971): 228, use the term "apocalyptic rage" for the violence used in African American novels as a means for gaining self-knowledge, dignity, and sense of identity. It is a phrase, as Bennett and Nichols point out, most "commonly associated" with the black militants appearing in the novels of the years in which they write. I would not apply it to any but one or two of the novels I have discussed up to now, and to none of the novels I discuss in this chapter.

2. Ann Petry's Lutie Johnson thinks bitterly that the streets she is forced to live on "were the North's lynch mobs": *The Street* (1946; rpt. Boston: Beacon Press, 1985), p. 323. In *12 Million Black Voices* (1941; rpt. New York: Thunder's Mouth Press, 1988), Richard Wright calls the "kitchenette" "our prison, our death sentence without a trial, the new form of mob violence that assaults not only the lone individual, but all of us, in its ceaseless attacks" (106).

3. Richard Wright, introduction to St. Clair Drake and Horace Cayton, *Black Metropolis: A Study of Negro Life in a Northern City* (New York: Harcourt Brace, 1945), pp. xviii, xxviii, xxvii.

4. William Attaway, *Blood on the Forge* (Garden City, N.Y.: Doubleday and Doran, 1941), p. 173. Subsequent page references are indicated in parentheses in the text.

5. George Groh, *The Black Migration: The Journey to Urban America* (New York: Weybright and Talley, 1972), pp. 47, 49; Nicholas Lemann, *The Promised Land: The Great Black Migration and How It Changed America* (New York: Alfred A. Knopf, 1991), p. 6.

6. Gilbert Osofsky, *Harlem: The Making of a Ghetto* (New York: Harper and Row, 1964), p. 111.

7. Ibid., p. 187.

8. Sterling Brown, *The Negro in American Fiction* (1937; rpt. Port Washington, N.Y.: Kennikat Press, 1968), p. 149.

9. Carl Offord, *The White Face* (New York: Robert McBride, 1943), p. 313.

10. Curtis Lucas, *Third Ward Newark* (Chicago: Ziff Davis, 1946), p. 197.

11. Philip Kaye, *Taffy* (New York: Crown Publishing, 1950), pp. 229, 232.

12. Petry, *The Street,* pp. 429, 434.

13. Chester Himes, *The Primitive* (1955; rpt. New York: New American Library, n.d.), p. 157. Subsequent page references are to this edition and are indicated in parentheses in the text.

14. Chester Himes, *My Life of Absurdity: The Autobiography of Chester Himes* (Garden City, N.Y.: Doubleday, 1974), p. 1.

15. Nathan C. Heard, *A Cold Fire Burning* (New York: Simon and Schuster, 1974), p. 85.

16. *Invisible Man* receives lengthy treatment in the three major literary histories

of the African American novel: Robert A. Bones, *The Negro Novel in America,* rev. ed. (New Haven: Yale University Press, 1965); Addison Gayle, Jr.), *The Way of the New World: The Black Novel in America* (Garden City, N.Y.: Anchor/Doubleday, 1976); and Bernard W. Bell, *The Afro-American Novel and Its Tradition* (Amherst: University of Massachusetts Press, 1987). Several book-length studies treat Ellison and his work: Robert G. O'Meally, *The Craft of Ralph Ellison* (Cambridge, Mass.: Harvard University Press, 1980); Robert List, *Dedalus in Harlem: The Joyce-Ellison Connection* (Washington, D.C.: University Press of America, 1982); and Mark Busby, *Ralph Ellison* (Boston: Twayne Publishers, 1991). The most recent bibliography of Ellison's work and the criticism of it appears in Busby. He lists all the critical essay collections published to date, along with special journal issues devoted to Ellison and parts of books and separate articles.

17. Bennett and Nichols, "Violence in Afro-American Fiction," pp. 224–25.

18. Ralph Ellison, *Invisible Man* (1952; rpt. New York: Vintage Books, 1972), p. 4; hereafter cited as *IM.* Subsequent page references are to this edition and are indicated in parentheses in the text.

19. Valerie Smith points out that Bledsoe also practices "duplicity" (*IM,* 151) in "The Meaning of Narration in *Invisible Man,*" in Robert O'Meally, ed., *New Essays on "Invisible Man"* (New York: Cambridge University Press, 1988), p. 28.

20. Cf. James M. Redfield's foreword to Gregory Nagy, *The Best of the Achaeans: Concepts of the Hero in Archaic Greek Poetry* (Baltimore: Johns Hopkins University Press, 1979), p. ix, which I quote in the introduction and elsewhere.

21. "On Initiation Rites and Power: Ralph Ellison Speaks at West Point," in *Going to the Territory* (New York: Random House, 1986), pp. 44–45. The Invisible Man is not a copy of Lord Raglan's figure; to the contrary, he is a kind of parody of Lord Raglan's Robin Hood, Achilles, Ulysses, Hengist and Horsa, Cuchulainn. See especially John S. Wright, "The Conscious Hero and the Rites of Man: Ellison's War," in O'Meally, *New Essays on "Invisible Man,"* p. 158: Lord Raglan's "myth of heroic biography" guides "the ritual understructure" of the novel, with the IM as the "mock-mythical hero" patterned on Raglan's biographies. "Barbee," says Wright, "has mastered the myth of heroic biography," using it in his eulogy of the Founder. But for Ellison it is a "parody of leadership," according to Larry Neal ("Ellison's Zoot Suit," in *Ralph Ellison: A Collection of Critical Essays,* ed. John Hersey [Englewood Cliffs, N.J.: Prentice-Hall, 1974]) pp. 164–65), and in the same essay collection William J. Schafer ("Ralph Ellison and the Birth of the Anti-Hero") also sees the mythic hero as a factor in the novel.

22. Larry Neal ("Ellison's Zoot Suit," in Hersey's *Ralph Ellison*) alludes to Cruse's account of the New School writer's conference of 1965 in which H. Aptheker, John Henrik Clarke, and John Killens all attack Ellison for his abandonment of social realism (63). The Cruse discussion occurs in Harold Cruse, *The Crisis of the Negro Intellectual from Its Origins to the Present* (1967; rpt. New York: William Morrow, Apollo edition, 1968), pp. 506–11. James E. Walton, In "The Student and Teacher as Readers of *Invisible Man,*" in *Approaches to Teaching Ellison's "Invisible Man,"* ed. Susan Resneck Parr and Pancho Savery (New York: Modern

Language Association, 1989), talks about how his black students always prefer Richard Wright, Langston Hughes, Malcolm X, "and others" (26–27). In *The Craft of Ralph Ellison,* O'Meally speaks of the suspicion in which Ellison was held in the sixties by the radicals of the Black Arts movement (4).

10. THE RISE OF THE BLACK REVOLUTIONARY

1. See Noel Schraufnagel's discussion of many of the novels I discuss in this chapter and in Chapter 9. He finds a movement from "Apologetic protest" and "individual rebellions" in such works as early pieces by Ernest J. Gaines and John A. Williams, Baldwin's *Another Country* (1962), William Gardner Smith's *The Stone Face* (1963), Sarah Wright's *This Child's Gonna Live* (1969), and Junius Edwards's *If We Must Die* (1963), to "coordinated insurrections" in "militant protest" novels like Ronald Fair's *Many Thousand Gone,* (1965), John O. Killen's *And Then We Heard the Thunder* (1962), John A. Williams's *The Man Who Cried I Am* (1967), and Sam Greenlee's *The Spook Who Sat by the Door* (1969). Schraufnagel, *From Apology to Protest: The Black American Novel* (De Land, Fla.: Everett/Edwards, 1973), p. 171.

2. Quoted in Robert Weisbrot, *Freedom Bound: A History of America's Civil Rights Movement* (New York: W. W. Norton, 1990), p. 188.

3. Ibid., p. 186.

4. Joseph Boskin, *Urban Racial Violence in the Twentieth Century* (Beverly Hills, Calif.: Glencoe Publishing, 1976), p. 77.

5. Benjamin Muse, *The American Negro Revolution: From Nonviolence to Black Power* (Bloomington: Indiana University Press, 1968), p. 248.

6. Nicholas Lemann, *The Promised Land: The Great Black Migration and How It Changed America* (New York: Alfred A. Knopf, 1991), p. 160.

7. *Malcolm X Speaks: Selected Speeches and Statements,* ed. George Breitman (New York: Grove Press, 1966), pp. 9, 21.

8. Cf. William McCord et al., *Life Styles in the Black Ghetto* (New York: W. W. Norton, 1969), p. 267.

9. During the "James Meredith March against Fear" through Mississippi. See, for example, Weisbrot, *Freedom Bound,* pp. 197–99; Cleveland Sellers, *The River of No Return: The Autobiography of a Black Militant and the Life and Death of SNCC* (New York: New American Library, 1973), pp. 34–36; and William L. Van Deburg, *New Day in Babylon: The Black Power Movement and American Culture, 1965–1975* (Chicago: University of Chicago Press, 1992), p. 32.

10. Jack M. Bloom, *Class, Race, and the Civil Rights Movement* (Bloomington: Indiana University Press, 1987), p. 209.

11. Quoted from Robert L. Scott and Wayne Brockried, eds., *The Rhetoric of Black Power* (New York: Harper and Row, 1969), pp. 94–95.

12. Quoted in Weisbrot, *Freedom Bound,* p. 264.

13. Muse, *American Negro Revolution,* p. 245.

14. *Malcolm X Speaks,* p. 198.

15. See, for instance, Huey Newton's *To Die for the People: The Writings of*

Huey P. Newton, intro. Franz Schumann (New York: Random House, 1972), and *Revolutionary Suicide,* with the assistance of J. Herman Blake (New York: Harcourt Brace Jovanovich, 1973); and Reginald Major, *A Panther Is a Black Cat* (New York: William Morrow, 1971).

16. Scott and Brockried, *Rhetoric of Black Power,* p. 86.

17. *In Search of Common Ground: Conversations with Erik H. Erikson and Huey P. Newton* (New York: W. W. Norton, 1973), p. 68.

18. See Hugh Pearson's account of Brown's development from a shy young follower in SNCC into its firebrand leader in *The Shadow of the Panther: Huey Newton and the Price of Black Power in America* (Menlo Park, Calif.: Addison-Wesley, 1994), pp. 138–40. Pearson also composes a very clear and useful account of the transition from nonviolence to violence in the rhetoric of the civil rights movement; see especially chaps. 5 and 6.

19. Cf. Weisbrot, *Freedom Bound,* p. 285.

20. Nick Aaron Ford, "The Negro Novel as a Vehicle of Propaganda," *Quarterly Review of Education among Negroes,* 9 (July 1941): 135–39.

21. Addison Gayle, Jr., *The Way of the New World: The Black Novel in America* (Garden City, N.Y.: Anchor/Doubleday, 1976), pp. xviii-xix.

22. Addison Gayle, Jr., ed., *The Black Aesthetic* (Garden City, N.Y.: Anchor/Doubleday, 1972), p. xxii.

23. Ibid., p. xxi.

24. Gayle, *The Way of the New World,* pp. 325, 335.

25. Ron Karenga, "Black Cultural Nationalism," in Gayle, *The Black Aesthetic,* pp. 36, 32.

26. Cf. James H. Cone, *Black Theology and Black Power* (New York: Seabury Press, 1969). Cone interprets the Bible as a supporter of the concept of Black Power. But he is no more given to advocating violence explicitly than are the Black Power spokespersons he backs. Instead, he hints at it with words that could be taken as incitement to violence, or not. His main point is that the Gospel endorses violence. "Through Christ the poor man is offered freedom now to rebel against that which makes him other than human." Thus "the message of Black Power is the message of Christ himself" (36–37). Our "ultimate allegiance" is to God and his creation. Therefore, any violation by the state of that creation justifies any reaction in its defense. "Through disobedience to the state, [the Christian black man] affirms his allegiance to God as Creator and his willingness to behave as if he believes it. Civil disobedience is a duty in a racist society" (137).

27. John Edgar Wideman, *Brothers and Keepers* (New York: Penguin Books, 1984), p. 114.

28. The Black Aesthetic is not a precursor of deconstructionism. The Black Aesthetic critics are themselves propagandizers, not just analysts. They have a political program to push, are deeply conventional, and have the traditional view of language and literary metaphysics. The deconstructionists are skeptical about language, and they identify the overt or implicit political programs authors stand on rather than identify *with* them.

29. Julian Moreau [J. Denis Jackson], *The Black Commandos* (Atlanta: Cultural Institute Press, 1967), p. 21. Subsequent page references are indicated in parentheses in the text.

30. John O. Killens, *'Sippi* (New York: Trident, 1967), p. 431.

31. Sam Greenlee, *The Spook Who Sat by the Door* (1969; rpt. New York: Bantam Books, 1970), p. 248.

32. In Weisbrot, *Freedom Bound,* p. 206.

33. Frantz Fanon, *The Wretched of the Earth,* trans. Constance Farrington (New York: Grove Press, 1968), p. 37.

34. Blyden Jackson, *Operation Burning Candle* (New York: Third Press, 1973), pp. 209, 176, 174, 219. In this edition, Aaron's last name is spelled both "Rogers" (95) and "Rodgers" (159).

35. Nivi-Kofi A. Easley, *The Militants* (New York: Carlton Press, 1974), p. 53. Subsequent page references are indicated in parentheses in the text.

36. Gayle, *The Way of the New World,* p. xix.

37. John A. Williams, *This Is My Country Too* (New York: New American Library, 1965), p. 3.

38. John A. Williams, *The Man Who Cried I Am* (1967; rpt. New York and Chicago: Thunder's Mouth Press, 1985), p. 371. Subsequent page references are to this edition and are indicated in parentheses in the text.

39. Williams, *This Is My Country Too,* p. 37.

40. *Violence in America: Historical and Comparative Perspectives,* prepared under the direction and authorship of Hugh Davis Graham and Ted Robert Gurr (New York: NAL, 1969), p. 408.

41. John A. Williams, *The Junior Bachelor Society* (Garden City, N.Y.: Doubleday, 1976), p. 247.

42. Alice Walker, *Meridian* (1976; rpt. New York: Pocket Books, 1986), pp. 219, 220. Subsequent page references are to this edition and are indicated in parentheses in the text.

43. Alice Walker, "Recording the Seasons," in *In Search of Our Mothers' Gardens* (New York: Harcourt Brace Jovanovich, 1983), p. 225.

44. Cf. "The Black Writer and the Southern Experience," in Walker, *In Search of Our Mothers' Gardens.*

45. Joseph Nazel, *Black Uprising* (Los Angeles: Holloway House, 1976), p. 220.

46. Ernest J. Gaines, *A Gathering of Old Men* (1983; rpt. New York: Vintage Books, 1984), p. 208.

11. THE FALL OF THE REVOLUTIONARY

1. Martin Luther King, Jr., *Where Do We Go from Here?* (New York: Harper and Row, 1967), p. 59.

2. Ibid., p. 37.

3. Harold Cruse, *The Crisis of the Negro Intellectual from Its Origins to the Present* (1967; rpt. New York: William Morrow, Apollo edition, 1968), p. 354.

4. Donald Goines, *Kenyatta's Last Hit* (Los Angeles: Holloway House, 1975), p. 10. All four of Goines's novels are published by Holloway House, which calls Goines and three writers I refer to later in the chapter—Omar Fletcher, Jerome Dyson Wright, and Roosevelt Mallory—"black experience" writers.

5. *Inner City Hoodlum* (1975). For the details of Goines's death, see Eddie Stone, *Donald Writes No More* (Los Angeles: Holloway House, 1974), pp. 222–23.

6. Arnold Kemp, *Eat of Me, I Am the Savior* (New York: William Morrow, 1972), pp. 45, 243.

7. Bill Webster, *One by One* (Garden City, N.Y.: Doubleday, 1972), p. 257. Curiously, the *New York Times* reports that a "black teen-ager" in Fort Worth, Texas, claimed mitigation of his shooting two other black men by reason of "urban survival syndrome," which is the fear that other blacks will kill him before he can kill them (April 21, 1994, p. A9, National Edition).

8. Roosevelt Mallory, *Harlem Hit* (Los Angeles: Holloway House, 1973), p. 127.

9. Omar Fletcher, *Walking Black and Tall* (Los Angeles: Holloway House, 1977), p. 159.

10. Alison Mills, *Francisco* (Berkeley, Calif.: Yardbird Publishing, 1974), p. 33.

11. Barry Beckham, *Runner Mack* (New York: William Morrow, 1972), pp. 161, 211.

12. Sanford Pinsker, "About *Runner Mack:* An Interview with Barry Beckham," *Black Images,* 3 (Autumn, 1974): 39.

13. Ishmael Reed, *The Free-Lance Pallbearers* (1967; rpt. New York: Bantam Books, 1969), pp. 110, 111. Subsequent page references are to this edition and are indicated in parentheses in the text.

14. Cf. John O'Brien, ed., *Interviews with Black Writers* (New York: Liveright, 1973), p. 217.

15. John Edgar Wideman, *The Lynchers* (New York: Harcourt Brace Jovanovich, 1973), p. 113. Subsequent page references are indicated in parentheses in the text.

16. O'Brien, *Interviews with Black Writers,* p. 218.

17. John Edgar Wideman, *Reuben* (1987; rpt. New York: Penguin Books, 1988), p. 118.

18. Ibid., p. 44.

12. IT ENDS IN BROTHERHOOD

1. See the dates set by William L. Van Deburg in the title of *New Day in Babylon: The Black Power Movement and American Culture, 1965–1975* (Chicago: University of Chicago Press, 1992).

2. See Van Deburg, *New Day in Babylon,* pp. 302–3.

3. Cf. Nicholas Lemann, *The Promised Land: The Great Black Migration and How It Changed America* (New York: Alfred A. Knopf, 1991), pp. 214–15.

4. Nikki Giovanni, "The True Import of Present Dialogue: Black vs. Negro" in *Black Feeling, Black Thought* (1968; rpt. Detroit: Broadside Press, 1970); I quoted from *The Black Poets,* ed. Dudley Randall (New York: Bantam Books, 1971), p.

318; Elaine Brown, *A Taste of Power: A Black Woman's Story* (New York: Pantheon Books, 1992), chap. 12, "Becoming Huey's Queen." Brown says that when she and Huey moved about New York during a political visit, she was proud when he "made it known that I was his" (246). She also quotes a member of Ron Karenga's Los Angeles-based US organization on the protocol of conversation between the brothers and sisters and the organization of mealtime: "Sisters, he explained, did not challenge Brothers. Sisters, he said, stood behind their black men, supported their men, and respected them. In essence, he advised us that it was not only 'unsisterly' of us to want to eat with our Brothers, it was a sacrilege for which blood could be shed"(109). The sisters served their brothers at the table.

5. This academic doctor of philosophy married George Jackson, who lacked even a high school diploma; cf. Huey P. Newton, *Revolutionary Suicide* (New York: Harcourt Brace Jovanovich, 1973), p. 307.

6. See Calvin Hernton, "The Significance of Ann Petry," in *The Sexual Mountain and Black Women Writers* (New York: Anchor/Doubleday, 1987).

7. See Morrison's interview with Rosemarie Lester, in Nellie Y. McKay, ed., *Critical Essays on Toni Morrison* (Boston: G. K. Hall, 1988), p. 49, an edited transcript of a radio broadcast over the Hessian Radio Network, Frankfurt, West Germany, 1983, first published here. Also see Robert Staples, *Black Masculinity: The Black-Male's Role in American Society* (San Francisco: Black Scholar Press, 1982), p. 10; and Nellie Y. McKay, "An Interview with Toni Morrison," *Contemporary Literature*, 24, 4 (December 1983): "There was a comradeship between men and women in the marriages of my grandparents, and of my mother and my father. The business of story-telling was a shared activity between them, and people of both genders participated in it" (415).

8. Alice Walker, *In Search of Our Mothers' Gardens* (New York: Harcourt Brace Jovanovich, 1983), p. 251.

9. Calvin Hernton, *Scarecrow* (Garden City, N.Y.: Doubleday, 1974), pp. 284–85.

10. Ann Allen Shockley, *Loving Her* (Indianapolis: Bobbs-Merrill, 1974), pp. 44, 111.

11. Michele Wallace, *Black Macho and the Myth of the Superwoman* (New York: Dial Press, 1979), p. 36.

12. Ibid., pp. 18, 16.

13. Alice Walker, *The Color Purple* (1982; rpt. New York: Washington Square Press, 1983), p. 179.

14. Pearl Cleage, *Deals with the Devil and Other Reasons to Riot* (New York: Ballantine Books, 1993), p. 7.

15. Ernest J. Gaines, *In My Father's House* (New York: A. A. Knopf, 1978), p. 161. See James William Gibson, *Warrior Dreams: Paramilitary Culture in Post-Vietnam America* (New York: Hill and Wang, 1994), chap. 10, "Have Gun Will Travel: Hit Men, Mercenaries, and Racist Groups Join the New War," pp. 195–230. Gibson discusses the several guerrilla training camps created by various individuals with far-right political and social orientations who were fighting a "New War" against

all minorities and immigrants, who were, by definition, Communists. For example, Arizonan Robert Matthews "formed a paramilitary group called the Sons of Liberty that trained in the Arizona desert. He said to a reporter at the time: 'The way this country is headed, there must be changes or people will die. Can't they see? The people of Arizona, of the whole country, are woefully unprepared for this chaos. We must return to the constitutional law of the land' " (216).

16. Sherley Anne Williams, *Dessa Rose* (1986; rpt. New York: Berkley Books, 1987), p. 13.

17. Andrée-Anne Kekeh reads the novel quite differently: "in the struggle against the authoritative 'historical' discourse that Adam Nehemiah represents, Dessa Rose's memories give her the ability to tell a tale of resistance disrupting the written text of Adam Nehemiah and how, in her further encounter with Mrs. [*sic*] Rufel, 'Mammy' serves as a potent repository . . . enabling Dessa Rose to achieve full voice and undermine Mrs. Rufel's paternalistic discourse." Quoted from "Sherley Anne Williams's *Dessa Rose:* History and the Disruptive Power of Memory," in Geneviève Fabre and Robert G. O'Meally, eds.. *History and Memory in African-American Culture* (New York: Oxford University Press, 1994), p. 219. Rufel is the wife of Bertie Sutton, hence not "Mrs. Rufel," and later comes to be called Ruth. Kekeh's reading is a bit too reductive and mechanical in my view, omitting especially the warm relationship the two women have by the end of the story, helping each other, outwitting the white men they encounter, and accumulating a sizable amount of money through a slave-selling scam in which they cooperate.

18. Toni Morrison, *Song of Solomon* (1997; rpt. New York: New American Library, 1978), p. 155. Subsequent page references are to this edition and are indicated in parentheses in the text.

19. Milkman's experience in Danville and Shalimar is echoed in Julius Lester's autobiography, *All Is Well* (New York: William Morrow, 1976), in which he visits the birthplace of his father in northern Mississippi in 1966. He seats himself among the old black men near the railroad station of Batesville and asks one of the men if he has heard of Square Lester. " 'Sho!' he exclaimed. 'Square Lester! He been dead a long time.' 'I'm his great grand-boy,' I said, softly, 'Lawd today!' the old one exclaimed. 'This here is Square Lester's great grand-boy!' After the general noises of exclamation had died, he continued, 'Square Lester was famous around here' " (131).

20. Jean Strouse, "Toni Morrison's Black Magic," *Newsweek,* March 30, 1981, p. 55.

21. Van Deburg, *New Day in Babylon,* pp. 31, 40, 51, 278. For his notion of the black "experience" drama, Van Deburg cites Geneviève Fabre, *Drumbeats, Masks, and Metaphor: Contemporary Afro-American Theatre* (Cambridge, Mass.: Harvard University Press, 1983), pp. 106–215.

22. Strouse, "Toni Morrison's Black Magic," p. 54.

23. Omar Fletcher, *Walking Black and Tall* (Los Angeles: Holloway House, 1977). The story is about Malcolm Lumumba's killing spree of vengeance against

white police he thought were responsible for the death of his family. The paperback book blurb reads: "Violence was the only thing that made him feel alive . . . feel like a man again!"

24. In *The Voices of Toni Morrison* (Columbus: Ohio State University Press, 1991), Barbara Hill Rigney suggests that Morrison's writing is uniquely feminine, that her narratives are all "dreamscape," often "surreal . . . largely because of [her typically feminine] refusal to mark dreams as distinct or separate from 'reality' . . . diffused, fluid, always erotic" (27). Morrison, though, thinks of herself simply as a black person who writes about blacks because that is what she knows. "When I view the world, perceive it and write about it, it's the world of black people. . . . It's not deliberate or calculated or self-consciously black, because I recognize and despise the artificial black writing some writers do." See *Black Women Writers at Work*, ed. Claudia Tate (Harpenden, Herts., England: Oldcastle Books, 1985), p. 118.

25. As is the case in so many other generalizations one might make about the Black Power novel, John A. Williams is an exception to this one, too. His exploration of the relationship between Max Reddick and Harry Ames in *The Man Who Cried I Am* (1967) is in a sense the main focus of the novel. The friendships between Aaron Rodgers and his Vietnam buddy Frank in Blyden Jackson's *Operation Burning Candle* and Dan Freeman and Pete Dawson in Sam Greenlee's *Spook Who Sat by the Door* (1969) have the quality of afterthoughts and take up little of the author's attention.

26. Ntozake Shange, "Interview With Toni Morrison," *American Rag*, November 1978, p. 48. See also Susan L. Blake, "Folklore and Community in *Song of Solomon*," *MELUS*, 7, 3 (Fall 1980): 77–82. In one of the most probing and most quoted articles on the novel, Blake suggests that "the end of Milkman's quest is not the discovery of community, but a solitary leap into the void" (79). Milkman's discovery in the end is, she says, personal and existential rather than communal. I do not challenge her on the point, I am simply interested in a slightly different emphasis: that it is the black context rather than the black-white one that conditions Milkman's experience and that the leap is confirmation of his brotherhood with Guitar.

27. Shange, "Interview with Toni Morrison," p. 48. During a reading and discussion by Morrison that was broadcast on the San Francisco Schools Network on December 12, 1992, she says that at the end of the novel Milkman "has that combination of risk and commitment and love and self-knowledge and . . . he's willing to risk something for somebody whom he loves more than himself."

28. Tate, *Black Women Writers at Work*, p. 125.

29. Huey P. Newton, *To Die for the People* (New York: Random House, 1972), p. ix. Huey could probably thank Morrison for editing out much awkward and wordy phrasing. For example, in *The Black Panther* newspaper, from which several of the book's sections are taken, Huey writes, "the masses will see the validity of this type of approach to resistance." In the version edited by Morrison, the same

passage reads: "the masses will see the validity of this kind of resistance." See G. Louis Heath, ed., *The Black Panther Leaders Speak* (Metuchen, N.J.: Scarecrow Press, 1976), p. 15.

30. Newton, *To Die for the People,* pp. 14–15.

31. Ibid., p. 22.

32. Cf. the comment by Susan L. Blake, referred to in n. 26 above, that Milkman's jump from Solomon's Leap at the end of the book "is not communal but existential" ("Folklore and Community," 79). More specifically and broadly, Wilfred D. Samuels and Cleonora Hudson-Weems draw the parallel between Milkman's leap and the existentialism of the fifties, using words like "authentic," "bad faith," "inauthentic existence," and "existential responsibility," in *Toni Morrison* (Boston: Twayne Publishers, 1990), pp. 53–54.

33. Shange "Interview," p. 48.

34. Carl Jung, *Modern Man in Search of a Soul,* trans. W. S. Dell and Cary F. Baynes (New York: Harcourt Brace, n.d.), p. 197.

35. Cf. the *San Francisco Chronicle,* August 23, 1989, p. 1; the *New York Times,* August 23, 1989, p. 6a; *Jet,* "Huey Newton Killer Gets Thirty-two Years to Life in Prison," December 23, 1991, p. 28; and Hugh Pearson, *The Shadow of the Panther: Huey Newton and the Price of Black Power in America* (Menlo Park, Calif.: Addison-Wesley, 1994), chaps. 1, 14.

36. Newton, *Revolutionary Suicide,* pp. 5, 17.

37. *In Search of Common Ground: Conversations with Erik H. Erikson and Huey P. Newton,* intro. Kai T. Erikson (New York: W. W. Norton, 1973), p. 110. Huey quotes Mao Zedong: "We are advocates of the abolition of war, we do not want war; but war can only be abolished through war, and in order to get rid of the gun, it is necessary to take up the gun" (49).

38. Ibid., p. 138.

39. Newton, *To Die for the People,* p. 52. Pearson, in *Shadow of the Panther,* has quite a different explanation of the clash between Huey and Eldridge. Cleaver left the party during the power struggle that ensued when Huey was released from jail in August 1970 and disagreements arose over the leadership of David Hilliard. When Huey refused to criticize Hilliard after complaints by members nationwide, the dissidents went over to Cleaver, in exile in Algeria. In a San Francisco talk show, with Cleaver on a phone hookup, Huey became angered when Cleaver attacked his position on Hilliard and other issues and subsequently "expelled" him. Cleaver, in turn, "expelled" Huey, and the party split deeply (see especially pp. 222–34).

40. Pearson in *Shadow of the Panther,* calls Huey "a whirlwind of contradictions" (257).

41. I am indebted for this information to Ms. Morrison's kind answer to my query through her assistant, René Shepperd, in a letter dated May 31, 1994.

42. There are few cleverer Black Power manifestos than Cleaver's "Allegory of the Black Eunuchs," in *Soul on Ice* (1968; rpt. New York: Dell Publishing, 1969), in which three young black men criticize a cowardly Uncle Tom for not having

given his life to the liberation of his people in the decades before the civil rights movement. The three celebrate the guerrilla fighter and the shedding of white blood. But we get the feeling that Cleaver does not want himself to take responsibility for these ideas. Unlike Huey, who addresses himself simply, literally, and straightforwardly to the expression of his revolutionary purpose and methods, Cleaver waffles through metaphor and adroitly guileful phrasing. Guitar, like Huey, is at least direct and self-responsible.

43. Dorothy H. Lee cites "the mutual love" between Guitar and Milkman, which makes them "antagonists and brothers," in *"Song of Solomon:* To Ride the Air," *Black American Literature Forum,* 16 (Summer 1982): 69.

44. Cf. Rigney, *Voices of Toni Morrison,* p. 51: "Guitar represents . . . the repressed and wild part of Milkman's self, just as Sula fulfills the role for Nel." See also Samuels and Hudson-Weems, in *Toni Morrison,* p. 71: The intricate relationship between Milkman and Guitar is "akin to that which developed between Nel and Sula, in that there seems to be reciprocity until, through misunderstanding, one experiences betrayal."

45. Toni Morrison, *Sula* (1973; rpt. New York: Bantam Books, 1975), pp. 45, 72, 149.

46. Quoted in Amanda Smith, "Toni Morrison," *Publisher's Weekly,* 232 (August 21, 1987): 50.

47. Shange, "Interview," p. 48.

48. Tate, *Black Women Writers at Work,* pp. 125–26, 129. See also Rigney, *Voices of Toni Morrison,* p. 51.

49. Dorothy H. Lee's comments on the hunt are the fullest of those who have written on it. The hunters, says Lee, clearly "love the beast they dissect" and participate in "the ancient tribal rites in which hunters symbolically internalize the courage and other attributes of the prey by consuming it" (*"Song of Solomon:* To Ride the Air," p. 69). For further mythic implications of the passage, see Richard Slotkin, *Regeneration through Violence: The Mythology of the American Frontier, 1600–1860* Middletown, Conn.: Wesleyan University Press, 1973), p. 156: Tracing the development of the hunter figure in colonial American writing, Slotkin speaks of "the mysterious sense of identification between hunter and hunted that so many writers have remarked." Slotkin also refers suggestively to Timothy Flint's discussion of Daniel Boone's participation in the frontier "fire hunt," which is a kind of "local manhood ritual, testing the youth's ability to successfully deal with the powers of nature and the powers of society," as they hunt the panther and the bear at night lighted only by lanterns—just as the Shalimar hunters light their way (424).

50. Ralph Story, in "An Excursion into the Black World: The 'Seven Days' in Toni Morrison's *Song of Solomon,*" *Black American Literature Forum,* 23, 1 (Spring 1989), sees the Days expressing "a dissonance which has always characterized the Afro-American world" (157).

51. Hagar, says Morrison, "is a spoiled child." See McKay, "Interview with Toni Morrison," p. 419.

52. This is the explanation of the passage given by Morrison in "Unspeakable Things Unspoken: The Afro-American Presence in American Literature," which first appeared in the *Michigan Quarterly Review*, 28, 1 (Winter 1989): 9–34. Harold Bloom reprinted it in his *Modern Critical Views: Toni Morrison* (New York: Chelsea House, 1990), pp. 201–30. My reference is to the Bloom text, p. 225.

53. Blake, "Folklore and Community," p. 80.

54. Trudier Harris, *Fiction and Folklore: The Novels of Toni Morrison* (Knoxville: University of Tennessee Press, 1991), p. 106.

55. "Folklore and Community," p. 80.

56. Harris, *Fiction and Folklore,* p. 88.

57. Shange, "Interview," p. 48. See also Samuels and Hudson-Weems, *Toni Morrison,* pp. 69–70, who discuss Blake's comment on abandonment and Morrison's explanation.

58. Mel Watkins, "Talk with Toni Morrison," *New York Times Book Review,* September 11, 1977, p. 50; also quoted in Karla F. C. Holloway and Stephanie A. Demetrakopoulos, *New Dimensions of Spirituality: A Biracial and Bicultural Reading of the Novels of Toni Morrison* (Westport, Conn.: Greenwood Press, 1987), p. 87. Morrison writes the sentiment into the text of *Song of Solomon:* "Shalimar left his [children], but it was the children who sang about it and kept the story of his leaving alive" (336).

59. A. Leslie Harris, "Myth as Structure in Toni Morrison's *Song of Solomon,*" *MELUS,* 7, 3 (Fall 1980): 71.

60. T. Harris, *Fiction and Folklore,* pp. 87–88.

61. Gerry Brenner, *"Song of Solomon:* Morrison's Rejection of Rank's Monomyth and Feminism," *Studies in American Fiction,* 15, 1 (Spring 1987): 17, 23, 24, 18. Brenner seems to see Morrison's treatment of Milkman as James B. Colvert saw Stephen Crane's technique of authorial irony, in which the characters judge themselves and their world from their "narrowing and deluding point of view," whereas the narrator sees them from a broader and "ruthlessly revealing point of view," in "Structure and Theme in Stephen Crane's Fiction," *Modern Fiction Studies,* 5 (Autumn 1959): 200.

62. Rigney, *Voices of Toni Morrison,* p. 2. Rigney concludes that Morrison's treatment of Milkman may be "partially ironic" or "parodic," but at the same time her approach is " gentle, meant to heal rather than to wound, to correct rather than to punish." I never get the feeling that Morrison feels a responsibility—or the ability—to "correct" any of her characters, only to explore.

63. Bloom, *Modern Critical Views,* pp. 224–25.

64. McKay, "Interview with Toni Morrison," pp. 423–24.

65. Speaking of the mythic structure of Milkman's quest and her own ambivalent attitude toward it, Morrison says that "Sotto (but not completely) is my own giggle (in Afro-American terms) of the proto-myth of the journey to manhood. Whenever characters are cloaked in Western fable, they are in deep trouble; but the African myth is also contaminated" ("Unspeakable Things Unspoken," p. 226).

66. Ralph Ellison, *Invisible Man* (1952; rpt. New York: Vintage Books, 1972), p. 563.

67. The cry of alarm in an article in *Newsweek,* November 29, 1993, p. 66, is only one of many that fill today's media: that 159 of every 1,000 black males under the age of twenty-four die as victims of homicide (compared with 17 out of 1,000 white males).

68. McKay, "Interview with Toni Morrison," p. 429. Curiously, Dorothy Scarborough, a well-known folk song collector of the 1920s, though talking of the blues rather than jazz, makes something of the same point in her book *On the Trail of Negro Folk-Songs* (1925; rpt. Hatboro, Penn.: Folklore Associates, 1963), foreword by Roger D. Abrahams: The blues, she says, have a "jerky tempo," and their stanzas end "abruptly, leaving the listener expectant for more." The African American's "free music" "ends with a high note that has the effect of incompleteness" (264).

69. Randall Kenan, *A Visitation of Spirits* (New York: Grove Press, 1989), p. 157.

70. I use this word in full knowledge of Dr. Johnson's contempt for the pun as the lowest form of humor.

71. See chapter 11, herein.

INDEX

813.0093 Bryant, Jerry H.
BRY

Victims and heroes.

42510

$18.95

DATE			